Aaron Goodrich

A History of the Character and Achievements of the Socalled Christopher Columbus

Aaron Goodrich

A History of the Character and Achievements of the Socalled Christopher Columbus

ISBN/EAN: 9783744748599

Printed in Europe, USA, Canada, Australia, Japan

Cover: Foto ©ninafisch / pixelio.de

More available books at **www.hansebooks.com**

A HISTORY

OF THE

CHARACTER AND ACHIEVEMENTS

OF THE SO-CALLED

CHRISTOPHER COLUMBUS.

BY

AARON GOODRICH.

"As the most obscure soldier of an army may sometimes by a fiery arrow destroy the strongest fortress of the enemy, so may the weakest man, when he makes himself the courageous champion of truth, overcome the most solid ramparts of superstition and error." MANOU.

WITH NUMEROUS ILLUSTRATIONS, AND AN APPENDIX.

NEW YORK:
D. APPLETON AND COMPANY,
549 & 551 BROADWAY.
1874.

TO THE MEMORY

OF THE

PATRIOT, SCHOLAR, JURIST, STATESMAN, AND FRIEND,

WILLIAM HENRY SEWARD,

WHO,

DURING A LONG AND EVENTFUL LIFE,

SUFFERED PATIENTLY, AND LABORED EARNESTLY AND WISELY,

FOR THE ADVANCEMENT OF HIS RACE,

THIS WORK

IS AFFECTIONATELY DEDICATED

BY AARON GOODRICH.

A few months before his lamented death, while this work was yet in progress, Hon. WILLIAM H. SEWARD *had kindly permitted its dedication to himself, but, in the interval which elapsed before its completion, the nation was called to mourn the loss of one of her greatest sons, and the author that of a revered and beloved friend. It is, therefore, as a tribute to his memory, that this volume is inscribed.*

"Gold is the most precious of all commodities; gold constitutes treasure, and he who possesses it has all he needs in this world, *as also the means of rescuing souls from purgatory, and restoring them to the enjoyment of paradise.*"—(COLUMBUS's letter to the sovereigns, July 7, 1503.)

"When Simon saw that through laying on of the apostle's hands the Holy Ghost was given, he offered them money, saying, 'Give me also this power, that, on whomsoever I lay hands, he may receive the Holy Ghost.' But Peter said unto him, 'Thy money perish with thee, because thou hast thought that the gift of God may be purchased with money.'"—(Acts viii. 18–20.)

PREFACE.

In giving the present work to the public, in sending it forth a single champion against a host of opponents, many of whom are the flower of literary chivalry, the author is aware that its reception will not be altogether a friendly one; he has, however, devoted several years of thought and study to the subject which is now imperfectly treated, and the deeper he has dived into the secrets of unpublished or forgotten history, the more firm have become his convictions that some proclamation of the truth should be made, some protest entered against the further propagation of a falsehood under the name of history.

If, in his attempt to do this, he should appear too solely to attach himself to one side of the case, too severely to censure, and to dwell too particularly on the errors and crimes of his hero, on the partiality and inaccuracy of historians, let it be remembered that for three centuries only one side of the case has been presented, the one laudatory of Columbus; that during all that time nothing has been left unwritten which could excite the enthusiasm and admiration of the reader in his behalf: histories have hitherto been written solely to praise him; the writer appears, therefore, as the self-constituted counsel for the opposite side, the vindicator, however inadequate, of the truth of history; he would show the injustice which has been done to worthy men who lived when Columbus lived, whom the latter and his advocates ruthlessly assail, and would prove that what has hitherto been termed the history of a great man is but a gilded lie, a whited sepulchre, fair without, but within full of rottenness and dead men's bones.

In this attempt he departs widely from the plan of any former history of the discovery of America; he treats some subjects which at the first blush appear irrelevant, or at any rate far-fetched, in their association with the inscription on the title-page; yet he feels assured that upon reflection the reader will find no subject broached which has not a direct bearing on the statements contained in the life of Columbus, the facts revealed, or the theory which is inevitably deduced from these facts.

Works of genius, human greatness, cannot, it would seem, be too largely or too enthusiastically extolled; the historian should, however, bear in mind that justice more than enthusiasm is his mission: however small a portion of the history of humanity his work may embrace, however ardently he may be enamored of his subject, he should see to it that he does not commit injustice toward any individual, land, race, or age; that he sacrifices no truth, immolates no worthy name to the shrine which he would honor.

This conception of the higher moral duties of the historian is too rarely entertained; the learning of antiquity is ignored that the pride of modern times may be inflated, great names of all ages are unjustly thrust into oblivion or condemned to ignominy, that some one or more of their contemporaries may be made to embody all the greatness and virtue which belonged to a generation. Examples of this will rise innumerable to the mind of the scholar and thinker.

In many lands, in many races, humanity has risen to the acme of intelligence, then sunk again into the insignificance of ignorance and superstition. As centuries have succeeded centuries in the great calendar of time, races and nations in regular rotation have had their childhood, their manhood, their old age: their childhood, simple and credulous; their manhood, vigorous, and, as far as things of this world can be, perfect; their old age, which sinks them into the puerility of childhood without its hope and promise; with some, old age has terminated in moral or actual death and extinction, but as each falls into this sad and inevitable dotage, another race, youthful and vigorous, springs up, which must tread the same path, attain substantially the same perfection, and decline into the same insignificance. Not without thought did the wise man of the Hebrews declare, when his race was at the height of its strength and glory, that there is no new thing under the sun; the hopes, aspirations, emotions, plans, and projects, which to the youth appear a part of himself and his generation, individualizing it and him especially, have all been experienced and projected before him, by his sire, grand- and great-grandsires; even so, the science, learning, and civilization which appear to pretentious modern times especially to distinguish them, and to prove the law of progression, had been discovered, achieved, attained by the remote nations of antiquity, in what are termed dark and prehistoric ages.

The injustice done is not altogether willful; the present is surrounded as with an atmosphere by its great thoughts and achievements, while in the past these are only represented by isolated results or obscure traditions: what wonder, then, that the men of the present should regard the times in which they live, the age in which their race attains its perfect manhood, as teeming with more thought and brain, throwing greater light, and nearer grasping perfection, than those gone by, each of which in its turn looked with like self-gratulation on its own attainments, and with like misconception and injustice on those of its predecessors?

It is with a conviction of this great fact, with a belief that there is no new thing under the sun, that races and nations rise inevitably in turn, and in turn as inevitably fall, that the writer, while endeavoring to sink the so-called Christopher Columbus to his just level in the estimation of posterity, and raise to theirs those of his contemporaries whose fame was sacrificed to create the fictitious glory with which he has been endowed, also endeavors to rehabilitate the memory of past generations whose achievements have been ignored or denied for the especial aggrandizement of modern times. Hence the chapters on the Ancients and the Northmen.

The writer may therefore ascribe a twofold object to his work:

1. To place in its true light the character of a man the importance of whose connection with the history of America has been magnified; in whom have been incorporated, at the sacrifice of justice and truth, the thoughts, deeds, and glory which belong in far greater measure to his contemporaries.

2. To enter a protest, however feeble, against the spirit of the age, which would incorporate in modern times all the greatness of past ages, and arrogates to itself the honor of inventing or discovering sciences and arts which had been carried to as great perfection as human intelligence will permit, before the so-called history of the world began.

With this twofold object in view, seeking ever the guidance of justice and truth, the author has written the present work. Its success or failure cannot alter his convictions that the cause he has espoused is a righteous one, and that it is worthy a far abler pen than his, not only to rehabilitate those who have been unjustly contemned, but also to cast down idols which have become the objects of base and ignoble, because blind and unthinking, worship.

AARON GOODRICH.

ST. PAUL, MINNESOTA, *July* 6, 1873.

LIFE OF COLUMBUS.

CHAPTER I.

ARCHITECTURAL ACHIEVEMENTS OF THE ANCIENTS.

It has been too much the custom of modern writers to disparage the achievements of the ancients, that they may thereby magnify the deeds and exploits of those in whose interests they write; hence we are taught that, in ancient times, the facilities

BAALBEC.

for promulgating knowledge were small, the ideas entertained of astronomy and the form and size of our planet primitive to a ridiculous extent; the ships rude in construction and unable to leave the coast; while many of the phenomena of Nature, which are now in daily use, were totally unknown. How unjust are these teachings we will endeavor briefly to expose.

It is universally admitted that one branch of knowledge leads almost inevitably to another; that the whole vast array of sciences and arts move in a circle, linked hand-in-hand, as it were, one with another; when, therefore, we find a nation or people incontestably preëminent in one or more of these, we may, should their learning and achievements have fallen into oblivion, naturally infer that in other branches they equally excelled.

As the modern traveler visits the fallen cities of Asia, and pauses amid the ruins of Babylon, Nineveh, Tadmor in the Desert, grand even in their decay, he can scarce imagine an ignorant people inhabiting such noble structures, still less planning and erecting them; these fallen stones and prostrate columns, in their colossal size and beauty, put to shame the fairest of our modern architectural monuments. We allow that here the people of the past were preëminent, we concede them perfection in the extraordinary, yet deny them the knowledge of even the ordinary attainments of less civilized nations. Let us, however, rapidly review their achievements, not only in architecture, of which living proof exists, but in geography, astronomy, navigation; let us study somewhat the facts which have been handed down to us, obscured by superstitious constructions, metaphorical or poetical language, and that inevitable and too often impenetrable veil which the mighty hand of Time casts over all things; then, following the laws of cause and effect, let us arrive, if possible, at a more just appreciation of the mighty nations that have preceded us.

The earliest architectural monument of which we find any mention is that of the Tower of Babel; though, indeed, Josephus, speaking of the learning and achievements of the sons of Seth, writes: "They studiously turned their attention to the knowledge of the heavenly bodies and their configurations. And, lest their science should at any time be lost among men, and what they had previously acquired should perish, ... they erected two columns, the one of brick and the other of stone, and engraved upon each of them their discoveries, so that in case the brick pillar should be dissolved by the waters, the stone one might survive to teach men the things engraved upon it, and at the same time inform them that a brick one had formerly been also erected by them. It remains even to the present day in the land of Siriad."[1]

This interesting account of the antediluvian Siriadic columns excepted, the Tower of Babel remains first in the list of the architectural efforts of the ancients. The Hebrew tradition has most probably given us but an erroneous idea of the reasons inductive to the undertaking; we contend that it is too much the rule among modern writers upon antiquity, to take for granted the superstition, and, we may almost so express it, infantile ignorance, of what they term the primitive races. Scientific research has proved the world to be far older than biblical history would lead us to suppose; the so-called primitive races must, then, have had an earlier origin, and have attained a more advanced stage of civilization, than is generally accorded them. tradition tells us that Babel was intended to become a temple for the worship of Baal, which worship was that of the sun, moon, stars, light, heat. Astronomy was long a study in the East; we have read how, even in an antediluvian period, the sons of Seth had made and recorded their discoveries, and we know that the Hindoos were at an early age far advanced in this science. The flat plains and clear skies of Babylon are admirably adapted for observatories, and the learned men inhabiting them, passing their lives in the contemplation of the heavenly bodies, might easily be supposed to worship these by the unenlightened masses, who, in their ignorance, might adopt the apparent religion. We know that to this day the enlightened Persian, the so-called worshiper of the sun, when accused of such an act, will reply, not without some contempt for the ignorance of the Christian, that in paying respect to the Deity he turns toward the sun, the greatest of his works, but no more thinks of worshiping that orb than does the Christian devotee the emblems which decorate his churches.

If the Tower of Babel was, as we believe, intended for an astronomical observatory, or gnomen, the confusion which resulted in the abandonment of the enterprise is not difficult to account for; the most learned men of the land and of the countries round about must have been assembled to superintend

[1] It has been said that Josephus here confounds Seth with the Egyptian Pharaoh Sesostris.

its erection,² and what more probable than that these same learned men, each eager for the adoption of his own peculiar views, should desire them carried out at the expense of those of others? Hence disagreement, contests, division, and the final abandonment of the work; the diverse languages spoken by the learned of different countries, which were unintelligible jargon to the ignorant, might easily have been believed by the masses to have caused the dispersal, and would account for the traditional confusion of tongues. The vast pile amid the ruins of Babylon, called Birs Nimroud, is supposed by many curious antiquarians to be the remains of this once famous tower; Nimrod, desiring to embellish the metropolis of his vast empire, is said to have completed it, raising it to the height of seven hundred feet.

The great city of Babylon, the oldest and largest of which we have any account, is itself now but a vast and chaotic heap of ruins. Herodotus has, however, left us a detailed and vivid description of its splendors as well as of the greatness of its sovereigns. Fifty miles square, surrounded by a wall eighty-seven feet through at the base, and, though three hundred and fifty feet high, so broad at the summit that four chariots could drive abreast, one hundred gates of massy brass giving entrance to it, the first aspect of this city must have been imposing indeed. "Yet," writes the Father of History, "its internal magnificence exceeds whatever has come within my knowledge." May we not echo the sentiment, even at the present stage of *advanced civilization?* Where shall we now find such a palace as that of Nebuchadnezzar, six miles in circumference, entered by gates of wrought brass and adorned with statues of gold and silver? Here were the hanging-gardens, styled even by the Greeks, that most refined and artistic nation, one of the wonders of the world; an artificial mountain four hundred feet high, terraced on all sides; the tallest trees of the forest grew upon these terraces, fountains and flowers adorned them; the massive stone pillars and arches supporting them were protected from the action of moisture from the soil by sheetings of lead and zinc, the soil was irri-

---

² In the "Paschal Chronicle," written in the fourth century, we find the following: "About the time of the construction of the tower, a certain Indian of the race of Arphaxad made his appearance, a wise man, and an astronomer, whose name was Andubarius; and it was he that first instructed the Indians in the science of astronomy."

gated by means of hydraulic machinery which drew up water from the Euphrates. The magnificent Temple of Belus, the Jupiter Belus of the Greeks, was one of the chief among the superb buildings of Babylon, and indeed the beauties of that city alone would occupy more space than our brief chapter will allow; these have all disappeared. *"Babylon is fallen. The beauty of the Chaldees' excellency is laid low;"* a few ruined mounds point the place where once she stood; the stones of her mighty walls and superb temples have builded cities which in the days of her glory were not known; those uncouth mounds have indeed served somewhat to demonstrate how far more advanced were knowl-

TADMOR.

edge and civilization two thousand years ago than the pride of modern ages would care to have known. Here were found glass of exquisite transparency, ornaments of fine earthen-ware, alabaster, and marble, and, still greater the discovery, the magnifying-lens, which is called a modern invention.

How many other great ruins might we not name, that silently testify to the greatness of the past! Baalbec, with its airy columns, so light and graceful against the eastern sky, that the beholder cannot realize that they are formed of stones similar to the huge masses fallen around; glorious old Thebes, where the silent

Sphinx has sat for more than four thousand years, and whose beautiful monuments were conveyed by the greatest of modern conquerors to adorn the greatest of modern cities; Tadmor in the Desert, the far-famed Palmyra of the Greeks and Romans, built or adorned by the wise man of Israel—the beautiful words of Volney as he contemplated its ruins may well apply to the many fallen cities of the East : " Here once flourished an opulent city; here was the seat of a powerful empire. A busy crowd once circulated in these streets now so solitary. Within these walls, where a mournful silence now reigns, the noise of the arts, the shouts of joy and festivity, incessantly resounded; these piles of marble were regular palaces; these prostrate pillars adorned the majesty of temples; these ruined galleries surrounded public places. Here a numerous people assembled for the sacred duties of religion, or the anxious cares of subsistence; here Industry, parent of Enjoyment, collected the riches of all climes; here the purple of Tyre was exchanged for the precious thread of Serica; the soft tissues of Cashmere for the sumptuous tapestry of Lydia; the amber of the Baltic for the pearls and perfumes of Arabia; the gold of Ophir for the tin of Thule.

"Now naught remains of its vast domination but a doubtful and empty remembrance! To the tumultuous throng which circulated under these porticoes, has succeeded the solitude of death. The opulence of a commercial city is changed to hideous poverty. The palaces of kings are become a den of wild beasts; flocks fold on the area of the temple, and unclean reptiles and creeping things inhabit the sanctuary of the Most High."

Thus it is with the glorious cities of the past, thus must it also be with those of the present; even so shall the traveler yet meditate in solitude where now are London, Paris, and become amazed at the vast pile of ruins which was once the great Cathedral of Cologne—Time must annihilate all. With what admiration mingled with awe do we not, then, gaze at the gigantic structure overlooking the plains of Jizeh (Gish)! Here Time has been powerless, during four thousand years, to destroy, and the Great Pyramid has been preserved through all these ages, perhaps to teach us the great moral lesson of our own insignificance, and that what we term progress may sometimes be retrogression.

For centuries it was believed that the Great Pyramid, like

many of the other more modern pyramidal structures which are found in the valley of the Nile, was destined as a place of sepulture for Egyptian kings, but the curious researches of many learned men in this century have opened a wider and far more interesting field for the antiquarian, and have demonstrated that this vast monument was raised to be an eternal standard for weights and measures, also for an astronomical observatory; so perfectly are the statements made, in support of this theory, in accordance with the measurement of the pyramid, that it is impossible to regard as accidental such wonderful concurrence.

That the Great Pyramid was not intended for a receptacle of the dead is evident from various facts, the foremost of which is that no hieroglyphics or inscriptions are found within or without. It is well known that the Egyptians never entombed their dead without some such inscription being placed on the monument.

When the Great Pyramid was in its original state, that is to say, when each of the angular sides, rising from a perfect rectangular base, and joining in a perfect point at the summit, was covered with polished beveled casing-stones, it presented a perfect geometrical figure, its height being to twice its base as the diameter of a circle to its circumference. This assertion, first made by Mr. John Taylor in his remarkable work on the pyramid, has since been confirmed by the learned research of Prof. Piazzi Smyth, Royal Astronomer of Scotland; it was contradicted by many professed antiquarians and Egyptologists, who, in their measurement of the base of the pyramid, had failed to make allowance for the heap of rubbish which has accumulated on the rocky platform upon which it is built, as also to ascertain with any certainty how far the marble casing which once covered the pyramid extended beyond its present limits; these difficulties were finally removed by the finding of the sockets cut in the solid rock base, wherein the corner-stones of the pyramid were set, and the important discovery, by Colonel Howard Vyse, of two of the white marble casing-stones, *in situ*, a discovery which, besides enabling the pyramid to be measured correctly, also permits us to form some idea of its external appearance in its pristine perfection—smooth, polished marble "shining resplendent afar" in a sloping plane, the workmanship as exquisite as that of an optician, the joints so fine as to be almost imperceptible to the close observer, and this with stones nearly five feet high, eight feet broad, and twelve feet long; the cement joining these two stones is as firm and solid as it was four thousand years ago. Portions of other casing-stones have been found, efforts to sunder which at the joints have resulted in the breaking of the marble itself, without accomplishing the object.

Since the above discoveries, every attempt to measure the pyramid has served to bring a nearer result, to prove the perfection of the plan; and, if there are yet some fractional differences, learned geometricians avow that the more perfect their means of measurements, the more perfect the result shows the form of the pyramid to be.[a] The self-conceit of the modern man of science must receive a slight shock when he is forced to admit that the facilities for making perfect measurements were greater four thousand years ago than at the present day. When the French academicians visited Egypt in 1799, they found, much to their astonishment and admiration, that the orientation of the pyramid (the correspondence of its four corners with the four cardinal points) was exact within a fraction, and nearer approaching exactness than any modern orientation; and it has since been found that the fractional difference they noted diminishes as greater perfection of calculation is employed, and would perhaps totally disappear should modern science be able to discover the means employed by the builders of the pyramid to fix

---

[a] Prof. Smyth, perhaps the most learned of modern writers on the subject, says: "Modern theoretical science no doubt both can compute and actually has computed the proportion to a far greater degree of closeness, to three hundred places of decimals, for instance; but modern science is unfortunately very unequal. Some theoretical points are pursued to an excessive extent, past all visible use, while the application of others to Nature and art is left in a sadly crude condition; and with regard to realizing the proportion now spoken of in a building, the moderns have never reached any thing at all equal to the accuracy of the Great Pyramid. . . . In their measurement of the pyramid, the moderns have had an advantage over the primeval builders of it; and how have they come off in the trial? Why, it has been shown that the exactness of the pyramid has improved under every advance of exactness in the measures applied to it; and whether the differences of modern measures, in their first stage of coarseness, differed from each other by several degrees or subsequently by several minutes, and latterly by a few seconds only, the pyramid itself was ever found in the mean position among them, like the bull's eye in the centre of a target, though the bullet-holes of bad shooters might be found more frequently at all points of its circumference; and whose marks, therefore, seen by themselves, would give subsequent visitors exceeding trouble in concluding precisely what the marksmen had been firing at."—(Prof. SMYTH, "Our Inheritance in the Great Pyramid," chap. ii., p. 25.)

orientation. The fractional inexactness which occurs in measurements may also be the result of the different standards of measure employed at the present day from those of the Egyptians four thousand years ago, which appear to have been much more minute. Prof. Smyth, after a succession of ingenious calculations, declares that the standard measure employed at the building of the Great Pyramid was an inch, this pyramidal inch being $\frac{1}{500,000,000}$ part of the earth's axis of rotation, and within one-thousandth part the same as the present English inch. Should this wonderful assertion be correct, and to us there appears no reason to doubt its exactness, what a perfect standard of measurement is here handed down to us, and with what advantage might it not be adopted! It is superior even to the French metre, which is declared to be $\frac{1}{10,000,000}$ of the quadrant of the earth's meridian, science having shown that much variation may exist in the shape of that meridian, but fixing the unit measure by the earth's axis at once gives us a perfect and invariable standard.

The Great Pyramid, then, considered in its external phase, after its completion, presented an exact geometrical solid figure, (about seven hundred and sixty feet broad at the base, and in vertical height about five hundred feet), perfect in orientation, perfect in workmanship, polished and smooth as glass; thus it stood for three thousand years, a sealed and wondrous mystery to the beholder, exciting in the ardent imagination of the East visions of unheard-of wealth, secrets, spells long forgotten, concealed within its walls; yet its silent majesty was long respected, perhaps because a subterranean entrance or descending passage which existed in this as in other pyramids, was considered in early ages as the only entrance, and prevented curiosity from sooner beginning the work of destruction, which has, alas! in modern times advanced only too rapidly.

In 820 A. D. the Caliph Al-Mamoun, his cupidity excited by the legends aforesaid of hidden treasures, determined to enter the pyramid; the subterranean entrance was now totally concealed by sand; the workmen of the caliph therefore began ruthlessly to quarry into the polished marble surface of the north side. Long and laborious was the task; at last, aided by the sound of a falling stone, they reached a narrow passage, the primitive subterranean one through which the Romans and others had penetrated downward into the building; but the stone which had fallen, once a part of the polished ceiling of this passage, revealed by its fall another, ascending instead of descending; a portcullis of stone, which, though evidently intended to be raised, was too heavy for the present workers to move, obstructed their advance; round it they therefore quarried an entrance into the passage; thus unexpectedly revealed, this led them to what is now termed the Grand Gallery, which ascends at an angle of 26°, and is one hundred and fifty feet long, twenty-eight feet high, built of hard, polished cyclopean stone; from this gallery the eager seekers for treasure, believing they had now reached the goal, emerged into the final chamber, which was thirty-four feet long, seventeen broad, and nineteen high, built of polished granite so exquisitely finished and cemented that the joints could hardly be perceived on the closest inspection; yet the blocks thus finished were so large that eight roofed the apartment, eight floored it, eight flagged the ends, and sixteen the sides; but beauty and symmetry were alike lost upon the eager horde that first broke the solitude and silence which for thousands of years had reigned in this mystic recess: they had hoped to find treasures untold within its walls, and it contained nothing save an empty stone coffer without a lid! They abandoned the chamber in disgust.

The work of destruction on the outside of the pyramid commenced two hundred years later; the exquisite marble casing-stones and much of the solid masonry were carried away, and served to build many edifices in the city of Cairo. The vast pyramid, though desecrated and shorn of all its pristine beauty, still remains a mystery, reminding the traveler that "Time sadly overcometh all things and is now dominant, and sitteth on a Sphinx, and looketh into Memphis and old Thebes, while her sister Oblivion reclineth semi-somnorous on a pyramid, gloriously triumphing, making puzzles of Titanian erections, and turning old glories into dreams. History sinketh beneath her cloud. The traveler, as he passeth amazedly through these deserts, asketh of her who hath builded them, and she mumbleth something, but what it is he heareth not."[4]

In latter days those who visited the Great Pyramid, the King's or Porphyry Chamber, the empty coffer, began to con-

---

[4] "Remarks on Mummies," Sir Thomas Browne: Wilkins's edition.

sider more deeply into the matter. True it had long been accepted as a fact that the pyramid was built to receive the carefully-embalmed body of some great Egyptian king; but if so, why was the coffer (the only object in the chamber) empty, without inscription? Why was the chamber ventilated by admirably-constructed air-holes, which demonstrated the intention of the builders that it should be visited with impunity? These questions, indeed, remained unanswered. The riddle was unsolved till, within the last twenty years, a school of men arose,

PLAINS OF GISH.

represented indeed but by the smallest numbers, who assert that the Great Pyramid was built for the noble purpose of preserving an unalterable standard for weights and measures. Very curious have been the results of the investigations which ensued; we can, however, but briefly mention a few.

It was found that the English measure for wheat, called a quarter, was exactly one-fourth of the cubic contents of the coffer. The chamber is exquisitely constructed to further physical experiments; protected on all sides from heat and cold by one hundred and eighty feet of solid masonry, the temperature would be invariably 68° Fahr., or 20° Centigrade, being one-fifth of the distance between the freezing and boiling points of water. The temperature of the country, we know, has not changed, the vegetation being the same as that described by Herodotus. The porphyry coffer is hewn out of one solid rock, so that when struck it gives forth a bell-like sound. Here, then, the standard measure of capacity may become a standard measure of weight; the filtered water of the Nile, drawn up from a reservoir in this cool, invariable temperature, would serve the purpose, as does distilled water at the present day; the standard measure of capacity would therefore be the interior of the coffer, and the standard measure of weight the weight of its contents in water at a temperature of 20°, the coffer at the same time typifying the earth's mean density with great exactness. We have already spoken of the measure of length, the inch, as if to confirm our belief that this was the standard. Over the last door that leads to the king's chamber are five lines, drawn parallel; these present the pyramidal cubit, each cubit fifty inches, each inch $\frac{1}{500,000,000}$ of the earth's axis of rotation.

Nor is the measurement of time forgotten. The three years of three hundred and sixty-five days, and our leap-year of three hundred and sixty-six, the twelve months of the year, the seven days of the week, are all typified, not in figures or hieroglyphics, but by the simple overlapping or grooving of the polished stones in the gallery, antechamber, and king's chamber. If all this be accidental coincidence, then verily is accident more wonderful than forethought! Further proofs are not wanting in support of this theory. The ancient Saxon chaldron, a measure for wheat, whence the English are said to derive their *quarter* (which represents one-fourth of the contents of the chaldron) bears strong resemblance in dimensions to the pyramidal coffer, and may very possibly have been transmitted from that source. The tradition that the coffer was destined for some such purpose as the one we ascribe to it, is evidently prevalent in the East. Hekekyan Bey, of Constantinople, writes of this chest: "Deposited by the Aryans in the sanctuary of the first pyramid, as a record of their standard metric system."

The vast functions of the pyramid were evidently still more numerous. The sun's rays, obstructed by its sides and apex, cast shadows on the sandy plain, which, as they wax and wane, indicate the hours of the day. The plain of Gish formed one great dial, superior to the small metallic one proportionately to its size; here the heavenly bodies record their own history, and lay down their own charts. Astronomy, indeed, played no small part in the building of the pyramid; through the long inclined passage the north-star was seen in 1817 at the period of its culmination, a fact which excited great interest, and led to the inference that the polar star occupied the same position when the pyramid was built: calculations were made, and it was found that, though the present polar star could not have been visible, owing to the precession of equinoxes, the star *a Draconis*, which must have been the polar star four thousand years ago, would have occupied the same position. The builders of the pyramid appear, therefore, not only to have fixed its orientation from this observation of the star, but to have intended the passage itself to be an observatory whence accurate astronomical calculations could be made; we need not add that they must have been learned in astronomy to base such practical operations upon that science.

Here, then, we have the standard measurement of weight, capacity, length, time, the practical uses of astronomy, and wonderful facilities for making observations and correct calculations in that science, all preserved in one building four thousand years ago, by a people who, to arrive at such wonderful accuracy of result, must have long been versed and preëminent in all scientific knowledge (for we cannot bring ourselves to believe in the sudden divine revelation of this knowledge which reason tells us can only be acquired by, and was only intended by the Omnipotent to reward, the thought, wisdom, and patient industry of generations). "Wise in all the learning of the Egyptians," was an expression in the days of Moses and of Solomon; we to-day find that we are *not* wise in all the learning of the Egyptians, that our knowledge is often infinitely inferior to theirs, that we are unable even justly to measure and calculate their work. Can we believe that the scientific results and coincidences we have recorded are accidental? Or, admitting they were planned, that a polished people like the Egyptians would have expended such vast labor, research, and learning, to fashion a tomb or sarcophagus for some real or unborn person? We answer: No! the Great Pyramid was never intended for such a purpose; an ignorant people was incapable of planning it, and a learned people superior to the task of rearing it for any other than national objects.

Could the builders of this proud monument of a nation's glory have looked with prophetic eye, down the dark vista of time, to that fearful day that witnessed the destruction of the Alexandrian Library—beheld the genius of unnumbered ages consigned to the flames—above all, had they foreseen that an ignorant people should arise and fill the earth, who in affected wisdom, pointing to this august structure of other days, should attribute to its founders objects or motives incompatible with true greatness, their efforts might have ceased, their arms have been paralyzed.

Long might we linger, did space permit, among the architectural monuments of Egypt, her temples, obelisks, sphinxes, and colossal statues—volumes could not exhaust the subject; but we must leave this land of mystery, and leaving it we arrive naturally at its offspring, Greece. Cadmus and Moses left Egypt nearly simultaneously,* the one migrating to Greece, the other to Judea; the former introduced into his new country much of the learning and many of the customs of the father-land.

The three orders of architecture, Doric, Ionic, and Corinthian, are generally declared of Grecian birth; the first two must, however, be excepted, for the Doric column bears strong evidences of Egyptian extraction, and an Ionic column was found amid the ruins of Nineveh, others on the banks of the Tigris; so that this order is proved to be of Asiatic origin. Another style, said to be invented by the Greeks to perpetuate the humiliation

---

* Diodorus Siculus *who wrote in the first century* B. C., *gives the following account of and reasons for the Exodus of Cadmus and Moses:* "There having arisen in former days a pestiferous disease in Egypt, the multitude attributed the cause of the evil to the Deity; for a very great concourse of foreigners of every nation then dwelt in Egypt, who were addicted to strange rites in their worship and sacrifices: whence the natives of the land inferred that, unless they removed them, there would never be an end to their distresses. They immediately, therefore, expelled these foreigners; the most illustrious and able of whom passed over in a body (as some say) into Greece and other places, under the conduct of celebrated leaders, of whom the most renowned were Danaus and Cadmus. But a large body of the people went forth into the country which is now called Judea, situated not far distant from Egypt, being altogether desert in those times. The leader of this colony was Moses, a man very remarkable for his great wisdom and valor. When he had taken possession of the land, among other cities he founded that which is called Jerusalem, which is now the most celebrated."—(Diod., lib. xl.)

of some of their captives, the caryatid, or supporting figure, taking the place of a column, is also found in several Egyptian temples; the only order, therefore, of pure Greek extraction is the Corinthian.

The Pandroseum, with its caryatids; the ancient Temple of Corinth; the Sysipheum, which Strabo speaks of as in ruins; the magnificent Temple of Minerva at Athens, the oldest Grecian edifice, perhaps, whose remains permit us to form an adequate idea of the grandeur and beauty of the perfect whole—these and many others, amid the picturesque mountains and valleys of Greece, recall to us the days of her glory, when Phidias, Scopas, and Praxiteles, wrought their exquisite handiwork, when all that was noble, learned, and beautiful, was found within her shores. Few will be the readers who are not familiar with the names, at least, of her monuments, and, thanks to her exquisite works of art, which are yet unrivaled, as also to the rich inheritance of literature and science she has handed down to us, the civilization of this country is not often questioned.

Greece in turn bequeathed civilization to Rome, which is also rich in monuments, better known and more modern than those of the former; what need to dwell on the grandeur of the Coliseum, the Pantheon, the glorious Column of Trajan, the Arches of Titus and Constantine, or to describe the remnants of palaces and temples, the ruins of the Forum, the Capitol, amid which Gibbon resolved to write his "Decline and Fall of the Roman Empire?" These are so often depicted with pen and pencil as to be familiar to nearly all.

These two lands, Greece and Italy, contain the greater part of ancient architecture to be found in Europe. Other countries, indeed, possess scattered and isolated fragments, but to find an accumulation of ruins which denote the existence of a civilized people ages ago, we must traverse the ocean; to find remnants of cities that were old when Greece was in its infancy, we must come to the NEW WORLD! The reader will here imagine, no doubt, that allusion is made to the Aztec civilization of Mexico, which Prescott depicts in such glowing colors; but, while admiring the research and perseverance displayed by that eloquent writer, we regret that the "authorities" which he quotes, and which would be beyond refutation had the stories of the Spanish Conquest deserved the name of history, were in reality but one mass of fiction, owing to the despotic empire exercised by the Church and its desire to make all redound to its glory, as also to the self-glorification of the chief actors in the scene, who were their own historians, and not unwilling to play the part of conquerors of a civilized and warlike nation. The Spaniards, at the time of the Mexican Conquest, had but just emerged from their wars with the Moors or Arabs, a people who had inherited from the East art, wealth, and learning, as well as a poetic and fiery imagination, and a taste for gorgeous display; who had enriched Spain beyond measure, built the Alhambra and embellished Granada, and who in most arts and sciences were superior to their conquerors. The adventurers

RUINS IN CENTRAL AMERICA.

who reached Mexico were not willing to assume a secondary position to the heroes of the Moorish wars, they therefore depicted the primitive Indian of the forest in colors of Oriental splendor, and magnified their own exploits to the greatness of those of the Cid.

No blame attaches to Mr. Prescott, who, resting in good faith upon a "weight of authority" which is in reality but a fiction, the work of fraud, bigotry, and vain ambition, transmits to us those splendid fables. That they are fables there can be little doubt; no vestiges of past grandeur appear in those places where the splendid towns described by Cortez and his contemporaries

ANCIENT AMERICAN RUINS.

are said to have been situated, and where towns of the same name still stand; no remains of stately palaces, basins carved in solid rock, gardens, and strong walls, are to be found on the site of the fabulous city of Tezcuco; had these wonders existed there must surely have remained some traces; even had the stones been taken to build the present town, they would still be recognizable, but this is built of *adobe* or dried mud-bricks, and there are no signs of its ever having been otherwise; so with Mexico, so with Tacuba. Furthermore, the Indian of the present day does not recognize or appear to have any knowledge of the ancient ruins in Central America; it is well known that the traditional history of the Indian is handed down with almost as much accuracy as

RUINS IN CENTRAL AMERICA.

our own written records, and descends unvaried from father to son; if, therefore, their race had ever reached any thing like the civilization attributed to the Aztecs, some remembrance of its past glories would still be preserved among its descendants.

The fine carving of the ruins in Yucatan and elsewhere in Central America appears to have been executed in the same manner as in Egypt; the tools used in the latter country were, we know, of bronze or copper, hardened by some process unknown to our time; the arrow-heads and hatchets of the Indians were of sharpened stone or flint. Is it likely that their race could once have possessed the art of forging and hardening metals to such perfection as the workmanship on the ruins in question denotes, and then become totally ignorant of that art? These ruins appear, indeed, throughout, of Egyptian, Phœnician, or perhaps Asiatic origin, and show signs of great wealth having been expended upon them. Some of the cities are declared to be as large as Thebes. We find among them the Egyptian square column with its carved hieroglyphics. All the ornaments, images, and vessels which have been found, bear the unmistakable Egyptian type, notably the statue found at Palenque, which is inscribed in hieroglyphics at the base, and holds in its hand an indented ornament, supposed by some to be the mural crown of the Phœnician Hercules. The statues and carvings are all colored. Fine specimens of painting are found, showing this unknown people to have been further advanced in this art than in that of sculpture. The flesh-tints are of that peculiar red-brown which the Egyptians always used. Another notable Egyptian feature is the pyramidal form of building. True, the Mexican pyramids are truncated, bearing on their summits palaces or temples, nevertheless, this peculiar style of architecture is common to Egypt and Central America. The pyramid at Copan is almost equal in size at the base to the Great Pyramid, though less perfect in proportion and workmanship; that on which stands the palace at Palenque even bears traces of having been covered with polished stones similar to the casing-stones of the Great Pyramid. The pyramidal gate-ways of Egypt also appear to have existed in America. Specimens are found at Copan. The serpent, which is carved on the tomb of Pharaoh Necho, and which is one of the chief emblems of the Egyptians, forms one of the principal features of adornment in the Nuns' Hall at Uxmal. A copper coin found at Palenque was impressed with the same emblem.

The Spaniards, finding a square stone or altar, on which were beautifully-carved figures of warriors leading captives by the hair, immediately declared this to be a representation of human sacrifice, and termed the altar "the sacrificial stone," as having been consecrated to this loathsome rite. We believe, however, that the Spaniards, themselves under the power of priestcraft, were too ready to give every emblem, statue, or hieroglyphic, a religious meaning, and were too apt to interpret that meaning to the detriment of the unfortunate Aztecs. The latter were probably as innocent of the crime of human sacrifice as they were of having erected the stone in question, which is a remnant of the long-extinguished race that first peopled America, raised by them, no doubt, to commemorate their victories. Kenrick describes a similar stone as existing in one of the temples of the Upper Nile, on which appears a king "holding a number of captives by the hair, who stretch their hands out toward him in an attitude of supplication, while he threatens to strike them with a hatchet."[6]

We might multiply, *ad infinitum*, the points of resemblance between the ancient ruins of America and those of Egypt, a resemblance which can scarcely be considered accidental, as it comprises the history of the habits, customs, and worship of a people. This resemblance we can record as an incontestable fact, but discoveries have hitherto been too limited to admit of any thing but surmise in accounting for it. The ruins in America are in a more advanced state of decay than those of Egypt—shall we therefore believe that here was the parent race, the birthplace of Egyptian art? that the Asiatic nation which gave civilization to Egypt had previously spread itself eastward to this continent?[7] or shall we rather believe that the Phœnicians, when they flourished at Tartessus or Tarshish (the present Cadiz), trading with, perhaps colonizing, the British Islands, extended their voyages as far as America, and colonized the latter, whose ancient monuments mark the decadence of Egyptian art?

Be this as it may, the Spaniards in 1492, the Northmen five hundred years previously, were not the first to establish a connecting link between the Eastern and Western Hemispheres; thousands of years before their time, a people had risen, in what is now termed the New World, to a civilization similar if not equal to that of Egypt. This civilization flourished evidently during many hundred years, as the many inland cities of which remains are visible testify. These must have taken centuries to arrive at such dimensions, and prove that inland home commerce existed, sufficient for the support of millions. This, then, was no sea-coast colony of rapid growth and extinction, but a nation that

---

[6] Kenrick, vol. i., p. 8.
[7] In our own day Japanese junks have drifted uncontrolled from the shores of that island to those of Alaska and California. Some such accident may have revealed to the Asiatics the so-called *New* World, thousands of years ago.

slowly and steadily increased in numbers and wealth, how many thousand years ago we know not; but this we know, that trees more than a thousand years old have been found growing on the ruins in Central America, which could only have commenced growth many years after the buildings had fallen into decay.

How this people became extinct is yet a mystery. Was it some internal war? some fell disease or black death? or, more

TOMB OF SESOSTRIS.

likely, did savage tribes overcome and destroy them, as barbarism seems ever to destroy civilization? These are questions yet unanswered. Future discoveries, perhaps, of other ruins, in a better state of preservation, may throw greater light on the subject. All we are able now to do is, to travel amazedly through these ruins. Here, indeed, History, to our eager query, "Who hath builded them?" mumbleth something, but what it is we hear not.

CHAPTER II.

ASTRONOMY, GEOGRAPHY, NAVIGATION, LEARNING, AMONG THE ANCIENTS.

As well might we attempt to determine the antiquity of intellectual man as to fix the age of astronomy. That it is almost coeval with humanity we may, however, reasonably infer, for it is not curiosity, or even a love of science, but the dictates of necessity which impel us to its study: by it the seasons are determined, the proper dates fixed for civil and religious affairs, the favorable periods for voyages on the vast ocean ascertained. Without it there would be no possibility of fixed rules and regulations; thus is astronomy indispensable to agriculture, politics, and religion. In tracing back its history, the most we can do is, to observe the ancient landmarks, and note the early fragments which have come down to us bearing upon the subject. These are sufficient to show that at a very early age mankind had reached such proficiency in that science as to render it probable that their knowledge was as complete as that of the present day.

The Hebrew historian claims for his people the honor of having first studied the heavens; but the Hindoos, according to their own record, are the most ancient astronomers of whom we have knowledge. They computed eclipses 3102 years B. C., and, as their calculations at this early period represent the state of the heavens with astonishing accuracy, and appear upon examination to be even more correct than those they subsequently made, it is evident they were the result of actual observation. It was the Hindoos who for greater facility of calculation invented the ten numeral figures which the Arabs introduced into Spain, and which have now superseded the old Roman method of computing by means of the letters of the alphabet.

India, then, as far as we can trace back, appears to have been the cradle of astronomy. She spread her knowledge eastward to China and Japan, westward to Chaldea and Egypt, who in turn bequeathed it to Phœnicia and Greece. Learned men of these lands appear to have determined the motion and volume of the stars, the constellations were named in writings both sacred and profane, the signs of the zodiac fixed many centuries anterior to our era. One of the learned men of our day, who for forty years labored to decipher the hieroglyphics of the ancients, found upon a coffin or Egyptian mummy-case (now in the British Museum) a delineation of the signs of the zodiac and the position of the planets; the date to which they pointed was the autumnal equinox of the year 1722 B. C. Prof. Mitchell, to whom the fact was communicated, employed his assistants to ascertain the exact position of the heavenly bodies belonging to our solar system on the equinox of that year. This was done, and a diagram furnished by parties ignorant of his object, which showed that on the 7th of October, 1722 B. C., the moon and planets occupied the exact points in the heavens marked upon the coffin in the British Museum.

The Egyptians had, we have already shown, a most perfect knowledge of astronomy, and applied that science to such practical uses that a knowledge of it must have been common to all. Mathematics and geometry are said to have had their birth with them. Diodorus writes:

"They pay great attention to geometry and arithmetic. For the river, changing the appearance of the country very materially every year, causes many and various discussions among neighboring proprietors, about the extent of their property; and it would be difficult for any person to decide upon their claims without geometrical proof founded on actual observation: of arithmetic they have also frequent use, both in their domestic economy and in the application of geometrical theorems, besides its utility in the cultivation of astronomical studies; for the orders and motions of the stars are observed at least as industriously by the Egyptians as by any other people whatever; and they keep a record of the motions of each for an incredible number of years, the study of this science having been, from the remotest times, an object of national ambition with them.

"They have also most punctually observed the motions,

periods, and actions of the planets . . . . and not uncommonly predict the failure of crops, or an abundance, and the occurrence of epidemic diseases among men and beasts; foreseeing also earthquakes and floods, the appearance of comets, and a variety of other things which appear impossible to the multitude."

The most ancient astronomer of Greece, Thales, acquired much of his great learning in Egypt. Six hundred years before Christ he computed the diameter of the sun, and is said to have predicted that memorable eclipse which on the 30th of September, 610 B. C., stayed the effusion of blood and caused an armistice between the Medes and Libyans. Pythagoras, one of his disciples, taught the principles of our solar system, also that the moon reflected the sun's rays, and described accurately the nature of comets. He is said to have been the first to observe that Venus is alternately the evening and the morning star. Eratosthenes measured the diameter of the earth, 200 B. C., by an arc of the meridian, which is the means now employed. Epicurus speaks incidentally as a matter of course, of "the world turning as it does round the axis of the heavens, and that too with surprising rapidity." But the work of the ancients which may be called the most complete that has come down to us is that of Claudius Ptolemy, well named the Prince of Astronomers. In the second century of our era he wrote at Alexandria his admirable works. He determined the latitude and longitude of more than four thousand places, and gives the history of ancient astronomy, with an elaborate list of the stars as known to him and older astronomers. The term "colossal," given by the great Humboldt to the work of Ptolemy on geography, applies as well to his astronomical labors. Beroseus[8] repeats the following Babylonian tradition, which, whatever may be thought of it as a theory, shows what study and calculation were expended by the ancients on these matters: he maintains that all terrestrial things will be consumed when the planets which now are traversing their different courses shall all coincide in the sign of Cancer, and be so placed that a straight line could pass directly through all their orbs; but the inundation will take place when the same conjunction shall occur in Capricorn. In the first is

---

[8] Beroseus, or Berosus, lived in the fourth century B. C., and was the contemporary of Alexander the Great. His works are quoted by Josephus, by Alexander Polyhistor, who wrote in the second century B. C., by Eusebius, and others.

the summer, in the last the winter of the year. The great year of Aristotle is that in which the planets, in completing their course, return to the sign from which they originally started together when God set them in motion; in the winter of this year comes the deluge, its summer brings the conflagration of the world. This periodical revolution or conjunction is fixed by Orpheus at one hundred and twenty thousand years, and by Copandras at one hundred and thirty-six thousand. Other writers contend that the heavenly bodies shall no more coincide in their original positions.

No science seems to have been held by the ancients in such veneration as the noble one which lifts men above the petty strife and turmoil of the world, causing them to contemplate the immense expanse of the heavens and numberless stars. Among all the splendors of the Persian Chosroes, the most magnificent was perhaps a dome supported by a forest of forty thousand columns, which was adorned with one thousand globes of gold, imitating the motions of the planets and constellations of the zodiac:

> " 'Twas thus he taught the fabric of the spheres,
> The changeful moon, the circuit of the stars,
> The golden zones of heaven."

Many of the proudest achievements of the ancients, both in art and letters, have been lost, mutilated, or so falsified that it is difficult to form a just idea of the original. Notwithstanding these disadvantages under which they must labor, enough remains to prove that they had arrived at many just conclusions touching astronomy, and the form and size of our planet, so that, from the days of Nimrod to our own, the ignorant only can have believed the earth to be other than spherical, the ridiculous story touching Columbus and the sages of Salamanca to the contrary notwithstanding. If this knowledge was attained without the aids of which we boast, their achievements should be regarded as more wonderful than ours. It may, however, be as well to conclude that, as in all ages human nature has under the same circumstances been about the same, an equal amount of learning, thought, and similar instruments, have ever been employed; in short, that there is no new thing under the sun, and that "wisdom shall not die with us." *

* It is generally believed that Galileo was persecuted by the Church, and tortured by the Inquisition, on account of discoveries made by him in astronomy. In this be-

The attainments of the ancients in astronomy are less often contested than their knowledge of geography, in which they are represented as decidedly deficient; nevertheless, with the aid of those fragments of their writings which have come down to us, we are able in great measure to refute the charge. Certainly interest and enterprise were as nearly connected and as great as at the present day. The huge ships propelled by sails, with hundreds of oarsmen to take the place of the latter during calms or adverse winds, guided by the magnetic needle (their knowledge of which we shall presently prove), afforded even greater advantages than modern sailing-ships. Pharaoh Necho sent out a formidable exploring expedition, about 600 B. C., manned by Phœnicians, which, descending the Red Sea and circumnavigating Africa, reached the Pillars of Hercules in the third year and returned to Egypt by the Mediterranean, thus performing at that early period the voyage, in an inverse direction, for which Vasco de Gama, two thousand years later, became so renowned, with the additional navigation of the Mediterranean and Red Seas. Herodotus is disposed to discredit the accounts of this voyage, for the best reason that could well be given to establish their veracity: that is, he writes that the Phœnicians asserted that during a portion of their voyage the sun was in the north.

A gentleman of our day, who, after seven years' study, travel, and observation, finds the sources of the Nile to be the several lakes mentioned by Ptolemy, and corresponding in number, form, size, and location, with the description of the latter, is thought worthy of knighthood, and hailed with triumph by his learned brethren. If these honors are to be paid to one who has sufficiently informed himself to enable him to indorse the correctness of

lief we do not fully concur. Books much older than Galileo were then preserved at Rome and Pisa, containing those very theories for which it is alleged this Pisan was persecuted; these records have come down to our time. It is more just and reasonable to suppose that he and his books were condemned by the Inquisition on account of an attack made upon that body in the preface of a book for the publication of which he had obtained a license from the holy office, as is alleged, by deception or falsehood. Would the Church destroy his book for affirming that the earth revolved round the sun in little more than three hundred and sixty-five days, while carefully preserving the writings of the ancients in which they proclaim the same doctrines? We would not here defend the Inquisition, or justify the tyranny of the Church; yet, let it be remembered that Pope Urban VIII. granted an annual pension of one hundred crowns for the support of Galileo in the evening of his days, and one of sixty crowns to his son.

Ptolemy, what honors should we not pay to the memory of the great geographer of seventeen hundred years ago?

The question, however, touching the geographical knowledge of the ancients which most interests us in the present work is: Were they or were they not ignorant of the existence of the Western Hemisphere? Without reverting to what we have said in the preceding chapter touching the resemblance between the ruins of Central America and of Egypt, in accounting for which we can only have recourse to hypothesis, we may rest upon a sure foundation our belief that they were not. Although most writers on the discovery of America, and extravagant eulogists of Columbus, affect either utterly to ignore, or to regard as fables, the allusions in ancient writings to a land which can be no other than that which we now call the New World, those who assisted Columbus in his undertaking and instructed him in the course he was to pursue, were actuated and inspired mainly by these allusions. Columbus himself, seeking to give a learned air to his enterprise, and to draw attention from the real source whence he derived his knowledge, dwells largely upon these ancient fragments, as does also his son.[10]

We will not multiply quotations, but will content ourselves with the following from Plato, which so accurately describes the situation of America that the reader must indeed be obstinate who will not believe that he described a country which had been known, and did not marvelously imagine one which should coincide so well with the situation of the real continent:

"That sea" (the Atlantic) "was then navigable, and had an island fronting that mouth which you in your tongue call the Pillars of Hercules .... *and there was a passage hence to the rest of the islands, as well as from these islands to the whole opposite continent that surrounds that real sea* .... the Atlantic Island itself was plunged beneath the sea, and entirely disappeared; whence even now that sea is neither navigable nor to be traced out, being blocked up by the great depth of mud which the subsiding island produced."[11]

We cannot conceive, when we observe the character of the writings of Plato, that he could have any object in deceiving or misleading his readers. A disciple of the sublime Socrates, his aim

---

[10] *See* Fernando Columbus's "History of the Admiral," chapters vi., vii., viii., ix., x.
[11] Plato, "The Timæus," Davis's translation.

was to elevate and instruct mankind. With regard to the "great island" of which he speaks, we see no reason to term it the "*fabled* island of Atlantis," as do most authors. Wonderful submersions and convulsions have in our own day changed the aspect of coasts. The groups of islands east of the West Indies may be remains of one vast island; their broken nature renders this hypothesis probable. Why should we not, observing the correctness of the greater part of the above description, accept the whole as truthful, instead of rejecting the whole as a fable because one part records an event which, though wonderful, is by no means impossible? If this great island were submerged it must have taken years before the sea became navigable; by that time men had ceased to consider it as such, and, drawn toward other interests and pursuits, had abandoned or forgotten the "islands and the whole opposite continent which surrounds that real sea," which could have been none other than the West Indies and the Continent of America. It is not probable that the learned, or even ordinarily educated, ever became totally ignorant or oblivious of the existence of this continent, while a convulsion so terrible as must have been the one recorded by Plato would have deeply impressed the masses, whose vague and traditional accounts of the event may have given rise to those legends respecting the horrors pervading "*the shadowy*" or "*gloomy* ocean" which are said to have been prevalent in the time of Columbus.

Why should we wonder that the allusions to the Western Hemisphere are so vague, or be so assured that Atlantis was a fable? were not Herculaneum and Pompeii lost for more than a thousand years, their existence forgotten, and those authors mentioning them accused of inventing fables to mislead the ignorant? Yet after all those years an accident revealed to astonished modern times the "fabulous cities of Herculaneum and Pompeii," and with them the habits and customs in their minutest details of a people who had been thus buried in the midst of the affairs of daily life, by the flood of molten lava and fiery shower of ashes, and who are proved to have rivaled, if not excelled, us in all the refinements of civilization. The hardened lava can be hewn asunder, the ashes swept away, but none can roll back the mighty ocean, nor disclose what its waves conceal; this must remain till the day when the sea shall give up its dead.

Nothing more fully proves the advanced stage of civilization in the earliest ages, than the extensive commerce which was carried on. In the infancy of nations and peoples, the desire for the acquisition of property is indeed implanted in the breast of man, but this desire cannot develop into commerce till the nation is wealthy and populous. In the days of the Hebrew patriarchs, he who first sat down at a spring, or reposed in the grateful shade of a tree, acquired a right to possess the same, which was respected by subsequent visitors. Abraham exclaims to Lot, when their flocks have become so numerous as to render a separation necessary :

"Is not the whole land before thee? separate thyself, I pray thee, from me: if thou wilt take the left hand, then I will go to the right; or if thou depart to the right hand, then I will go to the left. And Lot lifted up his eyes, and beheld all the plain of Jordan, that it was well watered everywhere . . . . even as the garden of the Lord . . . . Lot chose him all the plain of Jordan ; . . . . and Abraham dwelled in the land of Canaan."

We are not, however, to suppose that all nations were thus primitive in the days of the Patriarch. As well might it be maintained that the world is at present sparsely populated because there are vast regions in America where a citizen may acquire an ample homestead simply by a residence of a few years on the spot of his choice. Trade and commerce were already well systematized. Gold and silver, in exchange for wares, had taken the place of barter, at the time of which we speak. Abraham paid four hundred shekels of silver, such as were current with the merchant, for the cave of Machpelah; and Joseph was sold to the Ishmaelitish merchants, who were on their way to Egypt with spices and perfumes, for twenty pieces of silver.

An extensive commerce was carried on by the Phœnicians, the earliest merchants of antiquity of whom we have knowledge. To their great mart, Tyre, the merchants of every nation brought their choicest goods. The beauteous slaves of Greece, soft linen, purple dyes and silks of Syria, embroideries of Egypt, perfumes of Arabia, horses and horsemen, mules, wheat, honey, balm, iron, gold, silver, precious stones, even tin from Cornwall, all found ready sale in the vast markets of "the crowned city whose merchants were princes."[19]

---

[19] No more glowing description of the commercial greatness of a city can be imagined than that in which Ezekiel (chapter xxvii.) enumerates the many peoples who traded with Tyre.

Carthage and Alexandria rivaled and succeeded Tyre as the great commercial marts of the world. Arabia Felix, when that country was the medium through which passed the commerce between Egypt and India, seemed to concentrate the wealth of the world within its borders. The doors of the dwellings were of ivory studded with rich jewels; the pillars glistened with gold and silver; aromatic woods were burned to cook food; and so cloyed with rich perfumes were the inhabitants of this happy land that we are told they burned pitch and goat's-hair under their noses to stimulate their sense of smell. Among the many castes into which the people of India were from the earliest ages divided, merchants are distinctly mentioned, so that we may conclude that trade was established in that country from the remotest periods.

The staple articles of commerce with the ancients do not seem to have greatly varied from those of the present day, they consisted of rich silks, precious stones, and metals, linens, slaves, ivory, ebony, purple dyes, spices, wines, horses, mules, sugar, wheat, honey, fans from China, carved images, flint-glass, etc. This vast commerce can scarcely have existed without carrying the science of navigation to a very advanced state. The Phœnicians, there is no doubt, navigated all the known seas and very probably crossed the Atlantic.[18] The voyage of the Carthaginian Hanno, about six hundred years before Christ, a curious record of which was found suspended in the Temple of Saturn at Carthage, and the expedition of Pharaoh Necho before mentioned, are the earliest great enterprises in navigation which have come down to us.

The "Periplus" of Hanno is apparently an official document recording a voyage of discovery which the Carthaginians decreed should be made with a view to establishing Liby-phœnician colonies. Modern writers have not been wanting who, seeking to cast doubt upon the authenticity of the "Periplus," would detract from the knowledge and enterprise of antiquity. Falconer has, however, ably refuted these aspersions; and, as the descriptions given by Hanno correspond to the aspect of the shores which he

---

[18] In the tomb of Rameses the Great is a representation of a naval combat between the Egyptians and some other people, supposed to be the Phœnicians, whose huge ships are propelled by sails. In these, guided by their stone of Hercules, or mariner's compass, they were enabled boldly to leave the coast.

declares to have coasted, we may regard the fact as established that, six hundred years before our era, a voyage of discovery was made, which was worthier in its objects than that of Columbus.

It is not possible that the art of ship-building should have reached such perfection as it undoubtedly did in early times, had not navigation been extensive enough to demand such perfection. The dimensions of the most ancient vessel on record, the ark of Noah, three hundred cubits long, fifty broad and thirty high, are almost precisely the same as those of the fastest vessels of the present day, which are three hundred and twenty-two feet long, fifty broad, and twenty-eight and a half in height. The ships of the Egyptians were often upon a most magnificent scale. The fleet with which Sesostris conquered all the countries adjacent to the Red Sea is described in ancient Egyptian chronicles to have been composed of four hundred large vessels.[14] That which Alexander ordered to be constructed on the banks of the Hydaspes, one thousand miles inland, was of one thousand ships; with these he descended the Indus, and, on reaching the ocean, sailed to the Persian Gulf. The Indians seem to have had large fleets.[15] Archimedes superintended the building of a ship for Hiero of Syracuse which surpassed in magnificence any thing of which we read. The wood which would have built fifty ordinary galleys was expended in its construction. It contained galleries, gardens, stables, fish-ponds, mills, baths, an engine to throw stones three hundred pounds in weight, and arrows twelve yards long. Its floors were inlaid with scenes from Homer's "Iliad." A temple of Venus was also among the wonders it contained.

The famous voyage of St. Paul to Rome was effected in three vessels. In the first, no doubt a small coasting one, he went from Cesarea to Myra, where he went on board an Alexandrian corn-ship, which was wrecked off the cost of Malta; this ship contained a cargo of wheat, and two hundred and seventy persons, all of which were carried by another Alexandrian corn-ship, besides its own crew and cargo, by Syracuse and Rhegium, to Puteoli. Now, as it is usual to allow a ton and a half per man in

---

[14] Diodorus Siculus, "Canon of the Kings of Egypt."
[15] Diodorus Siculus relates that four thousand ships opposed the invasion of Semiramis into India.

transport-ships, it will be safe to conclude that the average ancient merchant-ships ranged from five hundred to a thousand tons burden. The vessel in which the great obelisk of the Vatican was transported to Rome carried eleven hundred tons of pulse as ballast, besides the obelisk, which weighed fifteen hundred tons.

Nor did the ships of the ancients lack many so-called modern improvements. The chain-cable, which we have seen patented in our own day, was well known to the Venitii, whose galleys are thus described by Julius Cæsar:

"Their bottoms were somewhat flatter than ours, the better to adapt themselves to the shallows, and sustain without danger the regress of the tides. Their prows were very high and erect, as likewise their sterns, to bear the hugeness of the billows and the violence of tempests. The body of the vessel was entirely of oak, to stand the shocks and assaults of that tempestuous ocean. The benches of the rowers were made of strong beams of about a foot in breadth, and fastened with iron nails an inch thick. *Instead of cables, they secured their anchors with chains of iron.*"

A Roman vessel of the time of Trajan had been sunk in the Lake Ricciola; it was raised after more than thirteen hundred years, and found to be in a good state of preservation; the planks were of cypress and pine, calked with linen rags, and covered with Greek pitch; the outside was covered with sheets of lead fastened with small copper nails. So the idea of metal sheeting is no more modern than that of the chain-cable.

All this, it will be argued, were useless to sail across a vast expanse of water, without a knowledge of the magnet, the magnetized needle, or mariner's compass.

The invention of the compass is commonly attributed to a pilot of Amalfi.[16] His name, and the date of so memorable an event, are alike misty and uncertain. In our time he is known

---

[16] The Amalfitans boasted their descent from Roman citizens sent to Byzantium by Constantine the Great, and who, after shipwreck on the way, established themselves at Melfi, the name of which they transferred to their new city built on the shores of the Gulf of Salerno, on the spot where Pæstum formerly flourished. In the ninth century, the republic of Amalfi was already the mistress of the commerce of the Levant, and her maritime code was adopted throughout the Mediterranean and Ionian Seas, as was formerly that of Rhodes. Sicilians, Arabs, Africans, Indians éven, frequented her mart to exchange their respective products. Her *tari* were the most approved circulation throughout the Levant until the Venetian *ducat* prevailed.

as Flavio Gioia, but writers nearer to his own day call him Giri and Gira, and give him the Christian name Giovane. In like manner, the year 1302 has been selected for the discovery, out of a number of dates to which it is assigned in the older authors. The particulars of the man's history are unknown, nor is there a scrap of historical evidence that he either discovered or even improved the mariner's compass. On tracing to its origin a story so generally received, reiterated as it is in most books of reference, and accepted in Italy as an article of the national creed, we find the authority for it lost in tradition and guess-work. The celebrated Antony Panormita, one of the great poets of the fifteenth century and secretary of Alphonso, King of Naples, has embalmed in verse the tradition of the discovery at Amalfi:

"First Amalfi gave to seamen the use of the magnet."

And elsewhere:

"Of the magnet, Amalfi
Boasts the noble discovery."

In more recent times this story has been received by local writers, who, indulging a lively fancy, have appeared to see in the arms of Amalfi the heraldic symbol of the mariner's compass, and have thereupon alleged that the city did in fact take the compass for its arms, to perpetuate the memory of its invention by the citizen Giovane Gira or Giri, or Flavio Gioia. It is not improbable that the sign of the compass which still remains over the door of a certain dwelling in that renowned seaport originally suggested the tradition, and may have served to commemorate a famous nautical instrument-maker who had made some improvement in the indications of the points of the compass and in the suspension of the magnetic needle.

Notwithstanding this absence of all historic testimony, our students' guides and Italian patriotism[17] cleave to a story which will not bear serious examination. For there is a cloud of witnesses that long before the era of Gioia the compass was in familiar use in Europe, and that in the East the knowledge of the

---

[17] In the naval action off Lissa, in July, 1866, the first hostile encounter of iron-clad fleets in the world's history, the Flavio Gioia and Christoforo Colombo figured as dispatch-boats on the Italian side.

polarity of the magnet, and its application to traveling by sea and land, were of immemorial antiquity.

The first notice of the compass in European literature appears in the accounts of the voyages of the Northmen. "The Landnamabok" has this passage in the second chapter of the first volume:

"Floke Vilgedarson set out about the year 868 from Rogaland in Norway to rediscover Iceland. He took with him three ravens to act as guides. It was the custom of our ancestors when looking out for land to let fly these birds. If they returned to the ship, it was presumed they were still far from land, but if they flew away they were watched, and the direction they had taken followed as a sure guide to land. To consecrate the ravens to this use, Floke offered a great sacrifice at Smörsund, where his vessel was at anchor. For at that time the navigators of Scandinavia did not make use of the loadstone."

This was written about the year 1075, and, though the last clause is not absolutely correct, as we shall presently see, it yet proves that the polarity of the magnet and its use in navigation were by that time, at any rate, perfectly familiar to the Northmen.

A century later, in the year 1190, the use of the magnet at sea is used as a simile in a French satirical poem—a proof that it could not even at that date have been recently invented, but was notorious and familiar to all. The title of the poem is "La Bible," the author was Guyot de Provins. The writer, after having declaimed against every state, proceeds to attack the court of Rome. The pope, according to him, should be what the polar star is to the mariner, the one conspicuous, fixed, unchanging, infallible guide. In natural connection with this, he goes on to speak of the magnet, the loving-stone which reveals the place of the Tresmontaigne when clouds and mist obscure it. But we will, as nearly as we can render it in English, give the entire passage:

> "Would that our Holy Father the pope
> Resembled th' immovable star.
> Very clearly they see it—
> The mariners, they trust to its ray:
> By that star they go out and home,
> They hold on their way with all calm.

It is known as the Tresmontaigne,
It is fixed, central, and certain.
While others shoot, wander, revolve,
This star is the centre of all.
The seaman knows an art that can't deceive:
The compass[18] is his sacred oracle.
The potent charm of the magnet
(A stone dark and ugly in look,
Yet to it iron fondly adheres),
Gives its impulse to the needle
Which then, cased, and freely suspended,
Set in movement unhindered,
True and certain points to that star.
The sky with sea in mist confused,
No moon or constellation to be seen,
The needle's lighted up without delay:
The sailor has no fear of going astray,
To th' invisible star points the faithful iron,
And on the trackless deep his way is sure.
Unchanging, central, bright, that star,
Such surely should our Holy Father be."

Another notice of the compass is found in the "History of the East and West" by the Cardinal Jacques de Vitry, Bishop of Tusculum and Ptolemais, a legate of the pope in the fourth Crusade and in the army of Montfort against the Albigenses, A. D. 1204–1210. He calls the magnet *adamas* (English adamant), a name very much in vogue in the middle ages, in lieu of *magnes* (magnet). The passage in question is this:

"The magnet (*adamas*) is found in India. It attracts iron, by some hidden quality. The iron needle, after it has touched the magnet, always turns toward the north-star, which does not move, as if it were the centre of the firmament, the other stars revolving around it. Wherefore the magnet is very necessary to navigators at sea." [19]

It is evident that it is not a new discovery that is here described a century before Gioia's reputed discovery, but an established usage, and an instrument necessary to mariners, the use of which was notorious.

Another conspicuous authority on the same point, in the thirteenth century, is Brunetto Latini, poet, philosopher, astrolo-

---

[18] *L'Amanière.*   [19] "Historia Hierosolimitanæ," cap. 89.

ger, of Florence. He had the honor of instructing "the divine Dante," and foretold the glory of his pupil's genius. Having been banished from Florence with his party, the Guelphs—as was subsequently Dante himself, who was also sentenced to be burnt alive, and never dared return to his beloved home—Brunetto settled in France, where he wrote his "Trésor de Sapience," a sort of encyclopædia, in the Romance language. In this work, he makes mention of the loadstone and the magnetized needle, and, though the description is not altogether accurate, it admits of no doubt about the use of the needle in the navigation of the period:

"Take a magnet, that is calamite. You will find it has two faces, one lies toward the north pole, the other toward the south pole. Each of the faces draws the needle toward that pole to which that face is turned; and thereby mariners may be deceived if they are not on their guard."

Brunetto had before this paid a visit to England, and spent some time at Oxford with the illustrious monk, the greatest of mathematicians from Archimedes down, the chemist whose wonderful discoveries secured him ten years' incarceration as a magician, the marvel of his age—Roger Bacon. Brunetto, in a letter to his friend Guido Cavalcanti, also a celebrated poet of Florence, gives the following account of his visit to Oxford. We trust it will be found sufficiently interesting to justify our giving a translation of the whole letter:

"The Parliament being summoned to assemble at Oxford, I had an opportunity of visiting that famous school, of which you have heard so much—happily somewhat sooner than, from the nature of my avocations, I might have otherwise done.

"The English word *parliament* is said, by some learned men here, to be derived *quasi parium lamentum*, because the English barons (peers) at these meetings complain of the enormities of their country. But I am of opinion it is borrowed from our word *parleure* (speech), and *parleor* (an orator), as indeed there are a great many speakers, and often much virulent speech delivered in these assemblies.

"Our journey from London to Oxford was made in two days, not without difficulty and danger; for the roads are bad, and we had to climb hills of hazardous ascent, which to descend are equally perilous. We passed through many woods considered here as dangerous places, as they are infested with robbers; which indeed is the case with most roads in England. This is connived at by the neighboring barons, for the consideration of sharing the booty, and the robbers serving their protectors on all occasions, personally, and with the whole strength of their band. However, as our company was numerous, we had not much cause to tremble.

"Accordingly, the first night we arrived safely at Sherburn Castle, in the neighborhood of Watlington, under the chain of hills over which we passed at Stocquinchurque.

"This castle was built by the Earl of Tanquerville, one of the followers of the fortunes of William the Bastard of Normandy, who invaded England, and slew King Harold in a battle which decided the fate of this kingdom. As the barons are frequently embroiled in disputes and quarrels with the sovereign and with each other, they take the precaution of building strong castles with lofty towers and deep moats, with drawbridges, posterns, and portcullises. They also make a provision of victuals in case they happen to be besieged, so as to hold out for a considerable time. They have also a large collection of all arms and machines for defense.

"The country around Oxford is beautiful. The city is watered by the Cherwell and the Isis, or Ouse, which rivers wander over the land in many a wild meander. As I stood viewing these scenes from the surrounding hills, this thought occurred to me: 'Medicine and the useful arts are commendable pursuits. But a petty trade is considered ignoble; if it be large, and very productive, it benefits a large number without vanity, and is not to be lightly esteemed. No pursuit, however, is better than agriculture, more satisfactory or more worthy of a gentleman (*franc home*).' Then I remembered the words of Horace:

> 'Happy is he quitting all trades, who,
> As did they of the olden time,
> Cultivates his land and rears his beasts,
> Unknown to usurers, and unjust to none.'

The number of scholars in this high-school is about three thousand: indeed, their number is too great, inasmuch as the revenues of their houses are insufficient for their support, so that they are constrained to ask relief at the butteries of the great barons and the cabins of their vassals. This is true chiefly of those educated to be priests and to display the religion and the faith of Jesus Christ, with the rewards of the good, and the sufferings of the wicked. The others, who are to practise law and physic, or other learned profession, live with their respective societies, without wrong and without scandal.

"You may be assured I did not fail to see Friar Bacon as soon as possible. He is the only one I could hear of that is skilled in Hebrew and Greek. Even the Latin they use is not that of Tully, and, as the doctors know nothing of the Romance tongue, my communication with them was very slight. But I had ample amends in the frequent conversations I had with this mirror of good learning.

"For, unlike one described by Horace—

'He seeks not smoke from flame,
But light from smoke to give.'

"As the friar studied long in Paris, he makes himself well understood in the Romance language, according to the *patois* of France."[20] Friar Roger Bacon is a Cordelier of the order of Saint Francis; he is a D. D., a good physician, and the greatest chemist, mathematician, and astrologer, of the present age. He is, moreover, a profound philosopher, and has made a number of discoveries which have brought upon him the imputation of sorcery and magic. This absurd idea rises above the common people and even the scholars, and makes his own community and

---

[20] The Romance language was a popular Latin, in use over the greater part of Europe, modified in different countries to adapt it to the idiom of the respective races. From the twelfth to the fourteenth centuries the University of Paris was the means of diffusing "the *patois* of France" far and wide. Of England, Germany, and Italy, it used to be said:

"Filii nobilium dum sunt juniores
Mittuntur in Franciam fieri doctores."

Thus the *French*, the dialect of the provinces north of the Loire only, prevailed over the *Provençal*, the southern dialect of the Romance, that of the Troubadours. Roger Bacon and Chaucer used it; Frederick II., the German emperor, wrote his poems, and Marco Polo his adventures, in the idiom of Paris; and we find Brunetto corresponding in it with his fellow-townsmen of Florence. Dante and Petrarch had not yet formed the Italian.

Europe has at present seven literary modifications of the Romance language. Of these, three preserve the name; the *Rouman*, of the Danubian Principalities; the *Roumansch*, or *Romanese*, of the Grisons of Switzerland; and the *Lower Romanese*, called also the *Latinique*, of the Engadine, on the borders of the Tyrol The languages of Italy, Spain, Portugal, and France, are the other members of the family.

the doctors fear and shun him. This makes him cautious about his experiments; but he assures me he has placed on record his several discoveries, and that they will be found after his death among his papers, for they do not suit the times we live in, when all learning is a vain study of abstruse speculations producing nothing useful. I told him the story which you and I have both frequently heard, of the Brazen Head—how that he and his brother in religion, Friar Thomas Bungey, had labored seven years to complete it, in order to know whether it would not be possible to inclose England within a wall and rampart, and that they failed after all to receive the answer, because not expecting it so soon, they were both out of the way, and did not hear the reply which the oracle had made. It is very certain that the friar has invented many wonderful machines, in particular, a head of brass which utters certain sounds. This is undoubtedly the Brazen Head which gave rise to the story of the oracle. He showed me curious mirrors of his invention. One sort sets fire to any combustible, when under the sun's rays; another, in which figures are made to appear and disappear at pleasure; a third, which enables a person to discover objects at a great distance, not discernible by the naked eye."[21] In the pursuit of these discoveries he has spent a great deal of money. He has now succeeded to a large property; and his family, being wealthy, had liberally supplied him with means. He told me that he knew a method of combining saltpetre with charcoal in certain proportions, so as to produce wonderful effects on being touched with the least possible spark of fire."[22] I had no oppor-

[21] The discovery of an instrument of long sight by the arrangement of convex and concave glasses in a tube, is generally attributed to a Dutch spectacle-maker of Middlebourg, about the year 1600; its application in the telescope, to Galileo, who began with a magnifying power of four, then of seven, finally of thirty, with which he made out the satellites of Jupiter and the lunar mountains. We see that, nearly four centuries before, Bacon had anticipated them. The Chinese had such instruments in use long ages before the Christian era.

[22] The discovery and use of gunpowder are of much older date than is generally allowed. The German monk, Berthold Schwarz, is commonly credited with the invention. But it is noticed in the works of two churchmen who lived a century before Schwarz—Albertus Magnus, the Dominican monk, who gave up an archbishopric, to be free to pursue his scientific researches; and our present acquaintance, Friar Bacon.

Gunpowder was employed in Europe certainly as early as 1257, if not before, at the siege of Niebla, in Spain; and there is no doubt of its having been in use by the Arabs much earlier. In an Arab treatise on engines of war, in the early part of the

tunity of witnessing the experiment, but some persons in whose presence he had performed it assured me that it had the closest resemblance to thunder and lightning. It is, I suppose, on account of the great noise, that the good friar is so cautious of making any trial of it except in retired places, laboring as he does under the suspicion of being a necromancer. He further showed me a black, ugly stone, the magnet, to which iron readily adheres. If a needle be rubbed upon it, and then left free to float on the surface of water by means of a reed, the point of the needle turns, and remains steadily pointing to the polar star. So that, be the night ever so obscure, and neither star nor moon be visible, the mariner by the help of the needle holds on his right course. This discovery, which appears so useful to all who voyage by sea, encounters great prejudice, even on the part of seamen, so that pilots use it with caution for fear of falling under the suspicion of magic, as every thing which is not understood is commonly attributed to some infernal agency. The time will come, no doubt, when these prejudices, which are so great a hinderance to research into the secrets of Nature, will die out, and mankind will then reap the benefit of the labors of Friar Bacon, and do justice to the genius and industry which now meet with mistrust and obloquy."

We next come upon works of very great value: an elaborate "Review of Ancient Astronomy," by John-Baptist Riccioli, the great astronomer of Ferrara, also a churchman; and, by the same author, a treatise in twelve books on geography and hydrography. In chapter xviii. of the tenth book of this latter work, a chapter on the compass, we are informed that—

"Under the reign of Saint-Louis (1226–'70), French navigators used the magnetized needle, which they kept swimming in a little vase of water, supported by two tubes so as not to sink."

Riccioli claims for the Northmen from a remote antiquity the use of the magnet in their navigation. He says:

thirteenth century it is described under the name by which it is at present known. The Arabs may have imported it from China; but the so-called Greek fire, which was introduced into Greece from China by Callinichus, architect of Heliopolis, in the year 673, was nothing else than gunpowder, which was thrown in the form of fusees and explosive shells. The Roman fireworks, which began to be used in theatrical representations about the end of the third century, were also of Chinese origin. Records of that wonderful people carry back the use of gunpowder to a very high antiquity.

"In the seventh century, the navigators of the Baltic and of the German Ocean, instead of a needle, used a triangular piece of iron wire, which swam in a small vessel of water, and the use of this instrument was considered among them to be of great antiquity (*valde antiquus*)."

It is remarkable that the compass which Vasco de Gama found in use among the pilots of the Indian Ocean was similar to this of the Northmen, only, instead of being of iron wire, it was a simple iron plate magnetized, supported on the surface of a vase of water in the same way. This we learn from the Cicero of Portugal, Bishop Osorio, who, about the middle of the sixteenth century, wrote a great work, "De rebus Emmanuelis virtute et auspicio gestis" ("The Golden Age in Portugal").

After the learned authorities, it is pleasant to turn to a professor of the gay science, and to find the minstrel as good a witness as the mathematician. Gauthier d'Espinois commences one of his ballads with this simile:

> "As ever the magnet inclines
> The needle, when the charm's once wrought:
> So who my lady's beauty divines,
> He too's irretrievably caught."

Gauthier was a friend of Thibaut IV., King of Navarre (1205–'53), who, besides being a renowned warrior and Crusader, also cultivated literature and poetry, and left at his death a number of ballads, more than sixty of which are still preserved.

The poem of Gauthier's reminds us of a more ancient idyl, from the pen of Claudian, the last of the line of classical poets, in whom appeared once more, before its final extinction amid the decay and ruins of the Latin Empire, the genius of Horace and Virgil. Claudian had the misfortune to be court-poet to a *roi fainéant*, Honorius; a reign made memorable by the sack and pillage of Rome by the Goth Alaric in the year 409. The poem which we borrow from Claudian, offers an ingenious allusion to the loves of Mars and Venus, founded on

THE MAGNET.

> "O thou, with anxious mind worming out the secrets of Nature,
> Seeking to unravel her mysteries:
> How the moon wanes and increases, what power eclipses the sun:
> Who wouldst search out the cavern of the winds,

And what convulses the bowels of the earth:
Thou wouldst know—who sends the cloud with the lightning-flash,
And speaks in the solemn responding peal,
And what light determines the colors of Iris.
If thy understanding grasp the truth, inform me also,
For I long to resolve these problems.
A stone there is by the name of Magnet,
Colorless, unattractive, despised;
Its lot is not to adorn the hair of the Cæsars,
Or the alabaster throat of the virgin,
Nor does it set off as a clasp the warrior's tunic:
Yet the powers of this dark stone are prized above the fairest gems,
And whatever the Indian fisherman may produce
Of Oriental pearls, it will surpass.
That stone—it lives! but to iron it owes its life,
And by the unbending bar it is fed:
Iron is its nourishment, its stimulus, its banquet;
It renews through iron its exhausted strength;
This rude aliment animates its members
And long preserves a latent vigor.
The iron absent, the magnet languishes,
Sadly numbed with hunger it succumbs,
And thirst dries up its opened veins.

"Mars, with blood-stained lance chastising cities—
Venus, who resolves the miseries of mortals by her tender gifts,
Have in common the sanctuary of a golden temple.
The divinities have not the same image:
Mars appears in the glistening iron,
The *loving-stone* represents the Cyprian goddess.
The priest with the accustomed rites celebrates their union
The torches light the dance, myrtle crowns the temple-gate,
The nuptial purple veils the lovers' couch;
Then appears a prodigy unheard of:
Venus of her own force ravishes her spouse.
Recalling the bonds of which the gods were witnesses,
Her voluptuous breathing attracts the limbs of Mars:
Around the helmet of the God her arms are clasped,
And with live chains she holds him captive.
She sustains his weight—while he,
Excited by the amatory impulse of her breath,
Allows himself to be ensnared with bands invisible.
At the Hymen, Nature herself presides.
A tenacious breath is the marriage-bond;
Their stolen bliss with joy the gods renew.
What secret heat constrains the sympathetic metals?
What inspires the mutual penchant under their rude exterior?

> The loving-stone glows and betrays a conscious trouble
> In the presence of the friendly steel;
> Which, in turn, learns the lesson of a placid love.
> Thus, with a look does Venus soften and arrest her bosom's lord,
> When, heated with blood and brandishing naked steel,
> He urges his fierce coursers and whets their rage.
> Alone, she encounters them: she stills his raging heart,
> She tempers its fury with a milder flame.
> Peace is restored to his soul. Murderous fights
> He forgets. The blood-red crest is seen to stoop—for a kiss!
> O Love, thou cruel boy! What sway is not allowed thee?
> Thou art indifferent to the thunder-bolt of Jove.
> The Thunderer himself, attacked by thee, is fain to quit
> Olympus, and amid the waves bellows as a bull.
> Thy arrows pierce the frozen crag, and forms inanimate:
> Rocks feel thy darts. A secret ardor consumes the loadstone
> Whose blandishments the hardened steel cannot resist.
> Thy flames prevail against the heart of marble."

This notion of the attraction of Love has given its name to the magnet in many languages. Chin-Tsang-ki, the author of a Chinese Natural History, under the title of "Pent-tzou-chi-hy," written twelve hundred years ago, says of the loadstone:

> "It attracts iron as a tender mother attracts her
> Children by love. Hence its name Tsu-chy (loving-stone)."

This name has also been adopted by the Japanese from the Chinese.

In the ancient language of the Hindoos, the Sanscrit, which has been a dead language now some twenty-two hundred years, the magnet was called *thoumbaka*, the *kisser*, also *ayaskàntaman'i*, *the precious stone beloved of iron*. These names remain in the modern Indian tongues, Hindoostani, Bengali, etc., and in Singhalese, the *loving-stone*.

In some of the European languages also the sentiment is found. The French call it the *aimant*, the loving one. In Spanish and Portuguese it is *iman*, equivalent to *amante*, the lover. The intimate connection for eight hundred years with Asia accounts for the prevalence of Oriental ideas and of Oriental names in the Peninsula.

In colder latitudes and among more roving populations, utility and hardy activity displace the tender and soft. In Dutch and Swedish it is known as the sailing-stone (*zeilsteen*, and *segel sten*).

In the British Islands, it is the leading, directing, drawing stone. This last is the sense of the Irish *tarrangart, the drawer,* and of the Welsh *tywysfwn, the conductor:* while the English *loadstone* corresponds with the notion of the *loadstar* that leads or guides in the heavens. In Icelandic, the identical sense, the conducting or leader stone (*leider-stein*). But we have seen Brunetto Latini give it in his Romance language, the name of calamite, by which it is at present best known in Italy and the Levant (It. *calamita,* Gr. καλαμίτα). This name is supposed to refer to the primitive way of suspending the needle on reeds so as to float on the surface in a vase of water. *Kalamis,* in Greek, signifies a reed, and *kalamites* a dweller among reeds, and this was the name of a very green little frog whose name and address were thus contained in one word. The word calamite in the Romance language preserved the sense of *green frog,* and was applied to the magnetized needle from its supposed resemblance to the frog floating on reeds. Hugo Bertius, who lived in the reign of Saint-Louis, King of France, gives a graphic account of this frog-like apparatus. The Hebrew term *kalamitah* for this stone may, however, have the priority of age. It is not found in the Bible, but its near congener, *chalamish,* is found Deut. viii. 15, and xxxii. 13, and Psalm cxiv. 8. In the last-cited text it seems to have the sense of a *cut or sharpened stone.* The Talmud calls it *the Stone of Attraction.* The ancient Hebrew prayers contain allusions to the magnet under the name of *Kalamitah,* and also of *Magnis.* The latter appellation (as *magnis, magnes, magnetes, maghnathis, magnet, magneet,* or other terminations to suit the idiom of the people) appears to be almost universal, even where, as in English, it is popularly known by another name. It has no such other name in German, Russian, and Magyar. In Arabic, Turkish, Persian, and kindred languages, every object has a number of names,[23] scientific, popular, and figurative: *al-maghnathis* is the usual designation in them all of this stone; one of its other names is the *Stone of Devils,* and another, the *Stone of Attraction.* There is no doubt that magnet is a Greek word, probably from its having been found in great abundance in the province of Magnesia, in Lydia. The ancient name of the capital of Magnesia was Heraclea, or city of Hercules; hence the magnet was often called

---

[23] As many as a thousand, five hundred, and, commonly, hundreds.

Λίθος ἡρακλεία, rendered in English the stone of Hercules, also Μαγνήσιος λίθος and Λυδικὴ λίθος, the Magnesian, and the Lydian Stone. According to Nicander, a physician who wrote medicine in verse, about two hundred years before Christ, it was the shepherd Magnes who introduced the stone to the knowledge of mankind, and who gave it his own name. He is said to have made the discovery when, at the head of his flock, he suddenly found himself fastened to the soil by the nails of his sandals and the iron point of his staff.

There can be little doubt that the Phœnicians made use of the compass in their voyages. Ancient Phœnician coins bear the impress of a vessel, at the prow of which stands a woman (their goddess Astarte) holding in one hand a cross and with the other pointing the way : the cross symbolized the mariner's compass or cross of the ancients, which is thus described by an Arabian writer of the thirteenth century (1242), Boulak Kibdjalick : " They take a cup of water, which they shelter from the wind ; they then take a needle, which they fix in a peg of wood or straw, *so as to form a cross;* they then take the magnes and turn round for some time above the cup, moving from left to right, the needle following ; they then withdraw the magnes, after which the needle stands still and points north and south."

The cross, then, was a fit emblem or coat-of-arms for a great commercial and maritime people, like the Phœnicians. The compass was their guide ; they symbolized it by the goddess Astarte, who, with her magnetic cross, indicated to them a path across the pathless waves.

Hercules was the patron divinity of the Phœnicians. This was also natural ; the magnes, or *stone of Hercules*, was indispensable to the mariner, as it was the chief agent in making the compass which was his guide.

The name given to the magnet by the ancient Egyptians shows that they were acquainted with its two opposite properties of attraction and repulsion. The loadstone was called the bone of Haroeri, and the iron the bone of Typhon. Haroeri was the son of Osiris[24] and of Isis, who conceived him while in the womb of her own mother Rhea, so that he was born at the same

---

[24] In Egypt brother and sister often became man and wife. While in Egypt, Abraham and Isaac gave out that Sarah and Rebecca were not wives, but might at any moment be taken in marriage by their pretended brothers if not *otherwise engaged*.

moment with both his parents. Isis was the emblem of the generative and fructifying powers of Nature—Haroeri that of the Universal Cause: while Typhon, also a son of Rhea, having destroyed Osiris, the Egyptian Messiah, the benefactor of humanity, became the emblem of Destruction, the ideal of the powers of Nature inimical to man, as among the winds the dread *Typhoon*. The crocodile and the scorpion are sacred to Typhon. Considering Nature, in the state of union and decomposition, under the symbol of Haroeri and Typhon, the Egyptian priests seem to have seen an image of these conditions in the action of the loadstone on the iron, according as the stone attracted or repelled the metal.

Indeed, ample evidence exists that the characteristics of magnetism, and, to some extent, the closely-related phenomena of electricity, were known both to Egyptian priests and to Greek naturalists. Diogenes Laërtius, in his "Lives of the Philosophers," gives a list of Aristotle's works, among which is a volume on the loadstone, entitled Περὶ τῆς Λίθου—a precious contribution to science which has not survived the lamentable destruction of the great Greek libraries. But we have preserved fragments of a work of that truly encyclopedic master, on stones in general—their extraction, the mines and the countries that supplied them, their properties, varieties, colors, and their application in the arts and in medicine. In this work, Περὶ τῶν Λίθων, Aristotle described no less than *seven hundred* different kinds of stones, minerals, and metals, the greater part of which were unknown even by name to the non-artistic majority of men. We cite the following passage from this work as a condensed exposition of all that can be said even to this day upon the magnetic forces in the loadstone, upon magnetism by influence or artificial magnets, and especially on the polarity of the magnet:

"The occult force by which this stone attracts iron, acts even through interposed *solid* bodies as well as through the air. It has not only an attractive force, but also that of repulsion; by the one angle it flies from the iron, while with the other face it attracts it. The one face, of itself regards the north, the opposite one the south. Now, the magnet has the property of infus-

Cleopatra was the wife of her two brothers successively, Ptolemy XII. and XIII., as well as the mistress of Cæsar and of Marc Antony.

ing these forces into an iron bar—which on being applied to the loadstone immediately exercises both attraction and repulsion, and assumes precisely the same direction—the one angle regarding the north, the other the south. If to this iron you apply another bar, the former will produce the same effects upon the latter as the loadstone itself."

In the work on the Soul, Περὶ Ψυχῆς, of the same great genius, he reverts to this topic, speaking of the loadstone as ἡ λίθη, *the stone, par excellence:*

"*"Εοικε δὲ καὶ Θαλῆς ἐξ ὧν ἀπομνημονεύουσι, κινητικόν τι τὴν ψυχὴν ὑπολαβεῖν, εἴπερ τὸν λίθον ἔφη ψυχὴν ἔχειν, ὅτι τὸν σίδηρον κινεῖ.*"

" Now, even Thales seems, according to what has been handed down concerning him, to have held that whatever communicates movement possesses a soul; 'thus, the stone,' he said, 'has a soul because it sets iron in motion.'"

Ancient Chinese topographical works also contain allusions to the minerals of their own and neighboring countries, and describe situations where they abound. The "Nan Chouan i wey chi," or "Memoirs on the Phenomena of the Southern Territories," relate that—

" On the capes and headlands of the Chang-haï (the southern sea on the coasts of Tonquin and Cochin-china) shallows abound, and a vast amount of magnetic stone, so that the large foreign ships which are fastened with iron plates are attracted as they approach the coast and drawn inshore by the great accumulation of loadstones, and they cannot get past such spots, which are very numerous in the south."

It is a remarkable coincidence that the greatest of ancient astronomers, Claudius Ptolemy, was aware of this phenomenon in the China seas. In the very detailed enumeration and description of the coasts and islands of those waters, contained in the second chapter of the seventh book of his "Geography," he says:

" Σατύρων νῆσοι, ὧν τὸ μεταξὺ μοῖραι ῥοά [25] . . . . Ταύτας οἱ κατέχοντες οὐρὰς ἔχειν λέγονται, ὁποίας διαγράφουσι τὰς τῶν σατύρων. φέρονται δὲ καὶ ἄλλαι συνεχεῖς δέκα· ἐν αἷς φάσι τὰ

---

[25] Ptolemy's zero of longitude was on the meridian of the Fortunate Islands (Canaries), the westernmost land known to him. His localities are identified by data more reliable than his figures, which are often wide of the truth.

σιδήρους ἔχοντα ἥλους πλοῖα κατέχεσθαι, μήποτε τῆς ἡρακλείας λίθου περί αὐτὰς γεννωμένης. διὰ τοῦτο ἐπιούροις ναυπηγεῖσθαι· κατέχειν γε καὶ αὐτὰς ἀνθρωποφάγους καλουμένους Μαννιόλας."

"The islands of the satyrs, the centre one of which is 171° .... Those who inhabit these isles are fabled to have tails, such as are drawn for satyrs. There are said to be other islands to the number of ten, lying near these, at which ships having iron fastenings are arrested by the stone of Hercules there existing, wherefore ships are put together with treenails. The islands are said to be in the possession of man-eaters called Manioles."

Centuries earlier, one greater than Ptolemy had made allusion to this phenomenon. Aristotle, who, accompanying his pupil Alexander the Great in his Asiatic expedition, accumulated vast stores of facts in natural history in the many countries overrun, affirms in the above-mentioned work, Περὶ τῶν Λίθων, that—

" On the coasts of the Indian Ocean are masses of magnetic rock. If vessels approach, they lose their nails and iron fastenings, which are attracted away from the vessels so that the force of cohesion of the wood cannot retain them. On account of these dangers, ships that navigate those seas are not fastened with iron nails, but with nails of soft wood that swell in the water."

Galen, the great Greek physician, also writing a work on stones, declares:

" On the coasts of the Indian Ocean the magnet is found in great abundance, so that seamen dare not take their ships in close to the shore if fastened with iron nails, nor must they have any sort of iron-work; for, on approaching those magnetic cliffs, all the nails and whatever of iron they possess are attracted away by the magnetic force."

The mention of Galen reminds us of a word upon our theme from another physician, who was also busy with stones, Marcellus Empiricus, physician of Theodosius the Great, the last sovereign of an undivided Roman Empire. He says:

"The loadstone, called *Antiphyson*, attracts and repels iron."

These words show a familiarity, as early as the fourth century, with the inverse action of the poles of the magnet or the existence of two magnetic fluids. The term *Antiphyson* admirably expresses this *natural incompatibility*.

St. Ambrose (in the sixth century) gives a narrative of a Theban's voyages in the Indian Ocean. Speaking of the island Taprobana (Ceylon), he says:

"There are about a thousand other islands called Mannioles, which are subject to the chief of the four kings of Taprobana. In them is found in great abundance the stone called *magnes*, which attracts the nature of iron by its force: so that, if a ship approach that has iron nails, she is retained there and cannot get farther, by I know not what hinderance, the source of which is in that stone. For this reason wooden nails are exclusively used to fasten ships in that trade."

The abundance of magnetic rocks and sands in the Eastern seas is noticed in a later age by the Arab geographers. Cherif-Edrisi, who wrote a number of geographical treatises, and constructed a terrestrial globe in silver for King Roger of Sicily about the middle of the twelfth century, relates of El-Mandeb, at the Red Sea straits called Bab-el-Mandeb (the Mandeb *Gate*):

"It is a mountain surrounded on all sides by the sea, and highest on the southern side. Its direction is northwest, and its length twelve miles. Where it approaches the Abyssinian coast it is broken into islets and reefs of considerable extent, so that that part of the sea is not navigable. In the midst of these reefs and isles, there is a range called Moorookein, not very much elevated above the level of the sea. It is a continuous mass of magnetic rocks, and no vessel fastened with iron nails may venture to pass near it, without risk of being drawn inshore and retained there."

In his geographical works this author mentions repeatedly the use of the magnet in navigation. A similar account of masses of oxide of iron on the coasts of Arabia and India, is given by Baïlak, a native of Kipchak, near Cairo, who wrote also an elaborate and most curious treatise on stones, called "Thesaurus of Merchants for the Knowledge of Stones." He devotes a considerable space to a description of the loadstone, its properties and uses in navigation, and it is evident that he is not writing of an art newly invented or received, but of an apparatus generally known and used in the Levant. What he says of the use of the magnetic fish, in the Indian seas, goes, with other authorities cited, to show that this was the primitive form of sea-compass all the world over:

"I was an eye-witness, during a voyage from Tripoli in Syria to Alexandria, in the year 640, of the practice of the Syrian pilots in making use of the loadstone.

"The night was so obscure that no star could be perceived so as to enable the seamen to make out the four cardinal points. But there was a vase filled with water placed in the interior of the ship, on the surface of which floated a needle fixed in a wooden or reedy float in the form of a cross, the needle having first been rubbed with a loadstone just large enough to fill the palm of the hand, or smaller. The needle thus magnetized, by its two points looks north and south. Navigators in the Indian Ocean, instead of the needle and its reed or wooden float, as with us, make use of a magnetic iron fish, hollow, and so constructed that when it is thrown into the water it swims, and it indicates by its head and tail the two points south and north. The explanation of the fish floating, though of iron, is this: that all metallic bodies, even the hardest and heaviest, when made into hollow vessels, displace a larger quantity of water than their weight, and not only swim on the surface, but can carry a weight as a counterpoise to the water displaced."[26]

Baïlak reminds us of a very common school experiment in physics. After having exhibited the needle fixed on a pivot, the operator places it on a disk of cork floating in a vase of water. The disk is observed to turn slowly round and stop exactly when the needle acquires the identical direction it had when on the pivot. In this experiment it is an important point that the disk *turns only*, in one sense or the other; it does not *advance* either toward the north or the south, whence the conclusion is that the force acting on the needle is in reality not attractive but simply directing.

The iron fish recalls the notion of the old Provençal and Levant sailors before mentioned, of a *green frog*, in their name of the instrument, calamite, a notion beyond all doubt of Oriental origin: the creature is known to the Burmese navigators as *the lizard*.

The names by which the case or instrument containing the needle is known, generally express the simple notion of a box or inclosure. In the northern languages—English, Dutch, Ger-

[26] It is a pity Baïlak did not let us know whether this principle, so clearly enunciated, had been utilized in the construction of iron ships, in his day.

man, Russian, and the Scandinavian dialects—there is but one word, *compass*, or *kompass*, signifying the encompassing or inclosing thing. The *box* is more distinctly expressed by the Italian name *bussola*, equivalent to the modern word *bossolo*, a box, whence, in Portuguese and Polish, *bussola*, and in French *boussole*, and modern Greek *mpousoulas*. There is also in Arabic a word applied to the compass—one of its numerous names in that language—very much resembling in sound the Italian name; it is *moossaleh*, and in Arabic the initial *m* has frequently a cold in the head, and is pronounced *b*."⁷ This Arabic word signifies a *dart* or *point*, which seems artistic and characteristic of the instrument, while the notion of a *box* would represent the rude appreciation of a person ignorant of the essential contents. It is possible that *bussola* is derived from the Arabic word, and may not have been suggested by the low Latin *buxis* or any other word signifying box.

It is also possible that the word originated in the Arabic name for the ocean. Edrisi (El Edressi), an Arabian writer on geography, of the twelfth century, says:

"The outer ocean, that in which the compass was necessary, is called El Bahar el Bossul, the violent (boussale is the present name for the compass), as distinguished from El Bahar El Muit."

The Italians or Amalfitans in their trade with the Saracens must have become in a measure acquainted with the language of the Arabs, hence perhaps the word *bussola* was first applied, in Italian, to the compass.

The popular name of the compass in the Turkish marine is *pousola*. But its most accepted designation in Arabic and in the kindred dialects, the Turkish and Persian, is *kibléh námeh*, signifying *mirror of the south*, and *kibleh numá, indicator of the south*. Most likely this denomination came from the Chinese, who hold that the magnetic needle points to the south, and call it *chi nan, indicator of the south*. The south is most in honor throughout Asia. In China the throne is always turned toward the south, as is the principal façade of all public buildings. The south is considered *the front*, the north *the back*, of the world. The piety of the Mussulman supports this opinion. He turns his face, in saying his prayers, toward the temple of Mecca, which is, in general, situated southward from Mohammedan countries.

---

⁷ E. g., *Mahomet*, often pronounced *Bophomet*.

The Arab word *kibléh*, therefore, signifying that which should be *in front, or facing* us, is applied to the southern part of the heavens, means *south*, and to the *southward*. Perfectly synonymous with it, is the Chinese word *thsian*, which is used in both acceptations.

We have seen that, in the days of Roger Bacon, the use of the compass was one of the arts supposed to have some connection with an infernal agency. We have not, however, found in the languages of Europe, which we have mentioned,[28] this idea of necromancy expressed in the popular name of the instrument. The Spanish alone has this merit. In that language, the name by which the compass is known, is not allied with, or derived from, its name in any other tongue: it conveys distinctly the notion of sorcery or divination. *Brujo* means a man in pact with the Evil One, a sorcerer. The verb *brujulear* is, to practise divination. *Brujula* is the compass. Those who gave it this name evidently considered it, in some degree, of preternatural and magical origin; hence we find the Spanish pilots avoid the general term compass, *brujula*, preferring the more specific and technical needle, *la aguja*. On the other hand, among the followers of the Prophet, the compass is an essential part of the material of devotion. The pious Mussulman in prayer, as we have said, turns his face toward the temple of Mecca, and carries the compass about him habitually with this purpose.

In the writings of the Arabs, and of the Chinese from a very early date, traces abound of their acquaintance with the variation of the compass, though the discovery is one of the *reputed* glories of Columbus, founded on an entry in the journal of his first voyage under date of September 17, 1492. But, if he understood the phenomenon, he has not done himself justice, since the journal records his conviction that the *star* had shifted, not the needles. Fournier, on the other hand, in his "Hydrography" (chapter x., of book xi.), attributes the earliest record of the needle's declination to Sebastian Cabot. We feel no doubt, however, that the pilots both of England and the Peninsula had made the observation before the days of Columbus and

---

[28] Guyot de Provins calls it *Amanière* in the poem already cited. This was probably a modification of *Aimant*. It was afterward known as *la Marinière*, no doubt on account of the services it renders mariners.

Cabot. The publication of his journal has given Columbus the preëminence in the European roll of fame.

But Kow-tsung-chy, author of a work of great erudition, a medico-natural history, given to the world about the year 1110 of our era, gives the following notice of the loadstone, and of the polarity and the declination of the magnetic needle:

"It is covered with small slightly-reddish spots, and its surface is studded with rough points. It attracts iron and adheres to it, and on that account is called *The stone that sniffs the iron.* When rubbed with the loadstone, an iron-pointed instrument acquires the property of pointing to the south—not, however, absolutely due south, declining always toward the east. This needle, on being passed through a reed so as to float on the surface of water, turns to the south, but always with a declination toward the point Ping," (that is, east 5° 6′ south) "which is the great central fire."

The Chinese, who regard the south as the principal pole, speak of the declination of the magnetic needle at Peking as pretty constantly 2° to 2° 30′ *east*, while European observers, reckoning from the opposite pole of the needle, would call it *west* declination. Nevertheless, the Chinese have not always taken into account in their public works this variation of the compass. Thus, the east and west walls of Peking, constructed under the second emperor of the dynasty of Ming, are not due north and south, but decline 2° 30′ from south to east. Hence it is evident that the walls were oriented by the compass without allowing for declination of the magnetic needle.

Nothing is more curious than the accidental vestiges, like so many fossil traces, of the practical arts which are supposed to be of modern and European invention, among the oldest records of Central Asia—often in the midst of poetic fictions and the extravagances of Eastern mythologies. In the earliest chapters of Chinese annals, the magnet, its attractive force, its polarity, its application, are thus revealed as the property of the various Tartar tribes in wandering over the trackless steppe. At the head of the caravan went a car, on the box of which stood the figure of a presiding genius, whose right arm, outstretched, contained a magnet. However the car turned and returned, the hand of the genius pointed ever to the south. Modern Chinese history attributes the invention of this magnetic car to the great Emperor Wang-ti, who reigned about 2,700 years before Christ. But the passage in the Waï-ki, the most ancient chronicle, cited as the record of the invention by Wang-ti, has nothing to show that it was then first invented, or that it had not previously been a well-known resource of travelers. The chronicle sets forth simply that Wang-ti, in a campaign against a formidable pretender to the throne, at a time when the fogs were so dense as to throw his troops into disorder, had such cars made in order that his army might distinguish the four quarters, or cardinal points, so that each division might occupy its proper position. This inter-

CHINESE MAGNETIC CAR.

esting passage of the Waï-ki is cited in the "Tung-Kian-Kang-Mou," or "Grand Annals of China," which also borrows from another ancient chronicle an account of a diplomatic mission from the Yue-chang-Chi, a nation occupying a part of the peninsula of Malacca, to the Emperor Ching-Wang, 1,110 years before Christ.

"The Yue-Chang-Chi, who are to the south of Kiao-Chi" (Anam), "sent three envoys, separately, with presents to the emperor, of white pheasants. They sent word, at the same time that as the distance was very great, and the country intersected with lofty mountains and deep rivers, a single envoy might not reach the court, and that they judged it best to send three.

"Chiou-Kung (uncle and prime-minister of the emperor) received the envoys and said: 'If the benefits of our prince's virtue had not been widely diffused, he would not have received this homage; if his mode of government and his laws were not known and approved everywhere, our prince would not have counted these nations among his vassals.' The envoys declared the motive of their mission: 'The senate and the white-haired old men of our country have come to the conclusion that, as during three years, Heaven had sent neither furious winds nor protracted rains; that, as there had been no convulsions inland or inroads of the sea, a holy person must have appeared in the Central Kingdom (China). Hence they send us, to present the homage of our people.'

"Chiou-Kung then conducted them to the temple of the ancestors of the imperial family, and offered a solemn sacrifice before the images of the ancient kings. The embassy, on returning to their own country, missed their way, whereupon Chiou-Kung presented them with five traveling-cars, constructed to show the south. The envoys of the Yue-Chang-Chi, traveling by these cars, reached safely the sea-coast, which they followed as far as the kingdoms of Fou-nan and Lin-y" (Gulf of Bengal), "and reached home the year following. The cars which showed the south were always driven in advance to show the way to the company behind, and to let them know the position of the four cardinal points."

We also read that, when the emperor went out in state, the procession was always headed by the magnetic car, which was driven by the emperor's master of the horse. To familiarize the people with the four cardinal points was considered one of the most important ends of state progress; and magnetic cars were officially distributed to governors of provinces and the great nobles.

But the magnetic car for long journeys was provided with another ingenious contrivance—destined to measure and report the distance traversed. By a sort of clock-work set in motion by the wheels of the car, at the end of every league a figure of a man in wood, with a wooden mallet, was made to start out and give a smart tap on a drum, and a wheel made one revolution.

At the tenth revolution, another wooden manikin overhead rang a bell.

Unhappily, in the year 223 before Christ, the Emperor Chi-Wang-ti ordered all the historical monuments of legislation and of the government and progress of the country to be collected and burnt, with the view, not only of abolishing the ancient laws and constitution, but of extinguishing the very memory of the past. The application of this decree seems to have extended beyond the writings—to their authors and students—for we find that no less than five hundred men of letters who had concealed themselves in the mountains were hunted out, and condemned, together with their libraries and papers, to the flames.

The mischief was to a certain degree retrieved by this barbarian's successor, who had all the books that had escaped the flames carefully sought out, and surviving traditions committed to writing. The works of Confucius (Kung-tze), and other reputed sacred books, were recovered; but alas! the destruction of records of art and science had been but too successful. Especially scanty are the records of navigation. There are, however, preserved allusions to voyages to the mouths of the Indus, in which the vessels are said to have been directed by the magnetic needle pointing to the south. The "You Kio Kou zu Kiounglin," or, "The Garden of Red Jasper for Youth to rejoice in the Treasures of Antiquity," a sort of cyclopædia, attributes to Choo-Kung, who lived 1,100 years before our era, the construction of both magnetic cars and compasses. And the "Grand Annals of China," entitled "Tung Kian Kang-mou," in relating the wars of the great Emperor Wang-ti, already mentioned, cite ancient authorities with which we are unacquainted, to the effect that during his reign the compass, of which the needle pointed to the south and the north, was in use, and that by means of its indications of the quarters of the heavens, buildings were oriented, and merchants and travelers performed their journeys. These are the sole passages in which the use of the compass as such is expressly mentioned as in use at that remote period, though it could not be doubted that, once the polarity of the magnet known, as has been shown by the example of the magnetic car, so ingenious a people would not fail in mechanical appliances suited to the special circumstances and requirements of each class of the community. Indeed, the magnetic rod in the arm of a wooden figure was in all probability an elaboration of an original mechanism, which must have been simpler and on a smaller scale, as in the form of a magnetized needle made to float on water or to move freely on a pivot. There is, then, every reason to believe that the use of the compass in China is of an antiquity more remote than the reign of Wang-ti, which, as we have said, was about 2,700 years before the Christian era.

The instrument chiefly in use at that early period appears to have been the water-compass, which we have already seen in use by the Northmen and the Arabs. In a vase filled with water the needle was made to float, supported by two reeds.

The following passage, from a curious and voluminous collection of facts and observations, of manners and usages, in North and East Tartary, by Nicolaes Witsen, the celebrated Burgomaster of Amsterdam, published about the middle of the last century, shows that, down to a comparatively recent period, the compass of this primitive type universal was still in use in the Chinese waters. This extract, which has other statements fitted to arrest attention, forms part of a chapter on the peninsula of the Corea, the land forming the east coast of the great inland water called the Yellow Sea, on the northwestern part of which is the Gulf of Pe-che-li and the mouth of the Pei-ho, on whose banks stands Peking:

"Het Buskruit, zoo wel als den Druk, is van voor duizend jaer by hen, zoo zy zeggen, bekent geweest; gelijk als mede het compas, hoewel van andere gadaente als hier te lande, want zy bedienen zich slechts van een klein houtje voor scherp en achter stomp, 't geen in een tobbe waters werd geworpen, en dus met de scherpe punt Zuyden wyst; na allen schyn zal daer binnen de Magnetische kracht verborgen zyn. Acht strecken winds weten zy te onderscheiden. De compassen zyn ook van twee houtjes, kruiswys over malkander gelegt, daervan een der cinden 't geen Zuyden wyst wat vooruit stecht."

"Gunpowder and printing have been known to them, so they say, above a thousand years: the same of the compass, though of a somewhat different form to ours. They use only a small bit of wood, sharp in front and blunt behind; this is placed in a tub of water, and the sharp point points to the south, in all probability from the magnetic force concealed therein. They distinguish eight points or rhumbs of winds. They have also compasses composed of two pieces of wood laid over each other crosswise, of which one of the ends which shows the south projects."

But the compass without water, in which the magnetic needle rest on a pivot, is also very ancient in China. The needle rarely exceeds an inch in length and not a line in thickness. It is suspended with extreme delicacy and is singularly sensitive, that is, it appears to move with the slightest movement of the box to east or west, although in fact the magnet and the perfection of the mechanism which contains it, consist in this, that the needle is deprived of all movement, and remains constantly directed to the same point of the heavens, whatever be the rapidity with which the box of the compass may be turned, or the other objects which surround it. This regularity of their compass is the result of a Chinese invention. A band of thin copper is placed about the centre of the needle and fixed by the edges on the outside of a small hemispheric cup, reversed, of the same metal. This cup admits a pivot of steel, which comes from a cavity made in a circular bit of cork or very light wood, which forms the box of the compass. The surface of the cup and that of the pivot are perfectly polished, so as to avoid any sort of friction. The edges of the cup are proportionably large, adding to its weight, and act so that the cup tends to preserve the centre of gravity in any and every situation of the compass. The cavity in which the needle is thus suspended has a circular form, and is only just sufficient to take the needle with the cup and pivot. Over the cavity there is a thin piece of transparent talc, which prevents the needle being affected by the outer air, while permitting the observation of its slightest movement.

The small needle of the Chinese compass has a great advantage over those which are used in Europe, with respect to the inclination toward the horizon, which in the European compasses requires that one end should be heavier than the other to counterbalance the magnetic attraction. But this inclination differing in different parts of the world, the needle can be absolutely correct only in the place where the instrument was constructed. In the short and light needles suspended in the fashion of the Chinese, the weight which is below the point of suspension is more than sufficient to overcome the magnetic force of the inclination in every part of the globe. Thus these needles never have any deviation in their horizontal position.

The Chinese compass is, apart from the magnetic needle, quite a work of art, representing a highly-elaborated system of physics and astrology. In this sketch we can do no more than give a rough notion of it; to enter into detailed explanation would unduly tax the interest of our readers in Chinese habits of thought and their antique learning, which however, at present remote, will soon become one of the most interesting inquiries, especially in America, whither the magnetic charm of political equality and personal freedom, together with the bounteous gifts of Nature, attract an exodus from every clime, of the stamina and the hope of the nations.

The surface of the compass, outside the space in which the needle performs its function, is divided into a great number of concentric divisions, which are intersected by an infinity of lines in a direction from the centre to the circumference. The inner circle contains the characters of the eight principal points, represented by animals, as in the signs of the zodiac. The second has four-and-twenty compartments, representing the four-and-twenty winds. In the third and fourth circles, the same number of compartments, with inscriptions having a moral and mystical import. The fifth contains seventy-two compartments, twelve of which remaining blank, the other sixty are filled with combinations of the two cycles of twelve and of six. As a specimen of the whole, we will give one of the series of cyclical signs:

Ou,		the Horse	= South.
	Wei,	" Sheep	= S. $\frac{1}{8}$ W.
	Chin,	" Ape	= S. $\frac{2}{8}$ W.
Yeou,		" Hen	= West.
	Siu,	" Dog	= W. $\frac{1}{8}$ N.
	Haï,	" Pig	= W. $\frac{2}{8}$ N.
Tsu,		" Rat	= North.
	Tcheou,	" Ox	= N. $\frac{1}{8}$ E.
	In,	" Tiger	= N. $\frac{2}{8}$ E.
Mao,		" Hare	= East.
	Chin,	" Dragon	= E. $\frac{1}{8}$ S.
	Szu,	" Serpent	= E. $\frac{2}{8}$ S.

The sixth circle contains one hundred and twenty compartments. The seventh, again, only twenty-four. The eighth contains the sixty combinations before mentioned, with some slight variation. The ninth, tenth, and eleventh, are modified repetitions of the preceding. The twelfth circle contains, in sixty combinations, the names twelve times repeated of the five Chinese elements, combined with the five divisions of the year, the five regions of the world, and the five principal colors. Thus:

Moo,	Wood,	Spring,	East,	Green.
Ho,	Fire,	Summer,	South,	Red.
Too,	Earth,	Mid-year,	Midst,	Yellow.
Kin,	Metal,	Autumn,	West,	White.
Chooi,	Water,	Winter,	North,	Black.

The thirtieth circle contains the three hundred and sixty degrees of the twenty-eight celestial palaces (or the zodiac), contained in the fifteenth circle.

The fourteenth contains the symbols of the foregoing.

The fifteenth circle contains the twenty-eight palaces of the Chinese ecliptic, which are:

In the South:

1. *Tsing*, the Well, containing less than 30 degrees.
2. *Kouei*, " Evil Genius, containing 2½ "
3. *Lieo*, " Willow " 13½ "
4. *Sing*, " Star, containing more than 6 "
5. *Chang*, " Bended Bow, " 17 "
6. *Y*, " Light, containing less than 20 "
7. *Thin*, " Motion, " more " 18 "

In the West:

8. *Khouei*, the Seat [corporeal], containing 18 degrees.
9. *Leoo*, " Vacuum, more than 12 "
10. *Wei*, " Stomach, containing 15 "
11. *Mao*, " Pleïades, " 11 "
12. *Py*, " End, " 16½ "
13. *Tse*, " Beak, " 3½ "
14. *Tzan*, " Addition, " 9½ "

In the North:

15. *Teoo*, the Bushel, containing more than 22 degrees.
16. *Neoo*, " Ox, " 7 "
17. *Neu*, " Woman, " 11 "

18. *Heu,* " Vanity, containing less than 9 "
19. *Ouei,* " Danger, " 16 "
20. *Chy,* " Edifice, " less than 18 "
21. *Py,* " Wall, " more than 9 "

In the East:

22. *Kio,* the Horn, containing more than 12 degrees.
23. *Kang,* " Neck, " " 9 "
24. *Ti,* " Origin, " less than 16 "
25. *Fang,* " House, " more than 5 "
26. *Sin,* " Heart, " 6 "
27. *Wei,* " Tail, " 18 "
28. *Ki,* " Sieve, " 9½ "

Such, then, was the knowledge possessed in the earliest ages of what is generally termed a comparatively modern invention; such were the facilities possessed by the ancients for making long voyages, for crossing the wide ocean. We see no reason to doubt, therefore, that they were as eminent in navigation as history allows them to have been in other arts. The astrolabe, somewhat similar in construction to the armillary sphere, but more simple, found favor with the astrologers of the East in their observations of the stars; as early as 150 B. C. we find it used by the Egyptian astronomer Hipparchus.

Thus far we have shown a few of the many "great modern inventions" which were undoubtedly known to the ancients,[29] and may we not justly infer that others were equally well known which are not mentioned in the writings which have reached us, or mention of which has been misconstrued. Does not the wise and ancient author of the book of Job accurately describe the art of printing in the exclamation: "O that mine adversary had written a book! . . . O that my words were now written! O that they were printed in a book! That they were graven with an iron pen and lead in the rock forever!"

Here are allusions to the arts of writing, printing, lithography, stereotyping, and book-making, of which Bildad the

---

[29] Diodorus especially admires, among the many arts and inventions of the Egyptians, their mode of rearing poultry by artificial heat; his minute description of the process would enable any ordinary mechanic to proceed on the same principle; yet the "invention of rearing poultry by artificial means" has been patented in our day, and extolled as one of the great proofs of progress in human intelligence.

Shuhite asks no explanation; we may therefore infer that Job was speaking of matters well understood."

Addison tells us that Strada," " in one of his prolusions, gives an account of a chimerical correspondence between two friends by the help of a certain loadstone which had such virtue in it that, if it touched two several needles, when one of the needles so touched began to move, the other, though at never so great a distance, moved at the same time, and in the same manner.

" He tells us that the two friends, being each of them possessed of one of these needles, made a kind of dial-plate, inscribing it with the four-and-twenty letters, in the same manner as the hours of the day are marked upon the ordinary dial-plate. They then fixed one of the needles on each of these plates in such a manner that it could move round without impediment, so as to touch any of the four-and-twenty letters. Upon their separating from one another into different countries, they agreed to withdraw themselves punctually into their closets at a certain hour of the day, and to converse with one another by means of their invention.

" Accordingly, when they were some hundred miles asunder, each of them shut himself up in his closet at the time appointed, and immediately cast his eye upon the dial-plate. If he had a mind to write any thing to his friend, he directed his needle to every letter that formed the words which he had occasion for, making a little pause at the end of every word or sentence, to avoid confusion. The friend, in the mean while, saw his own sympathic needle moving of itself to every letter which that of his correspondent pointed at. By this means they talked together across the whole continent, and conveyed their thoughts to one another in an instant, over cities or mountains, seas or deserts."

Allowing for slight incongruities and possible exaggerations of one who, ignorant of the real nature of electricity, confounded the properties of this phenomenon with those of the loadstone, this anecdote embodies the whole system of telegraphing with a dial-plate as it is now practised in some European countries. It is far from improbable that friends in very early times may

---

[30] Job seems, moreover, to have a realizing sense of the awful advantages possessed by a reviewer over the unfortunate enemy who should have written a book.

[31] A writer of the sixteenth century.

have used electricity (the existence of which was known in the time of Thales) as a means of correspondence, and that electric telegraphing was known, if not universally, at least to the learned. Yet, to this century is generally unhesitatingly ascribed the honor of discovering it.

We might multiply conjectures, and enumerate many intimations we possess—some vague and shadowy, others amounting almost to certainty—that the discoveries in science which we boast of as modern, are only rediscoveries or revivals of *quasi* forgotten knowledge of the ancients; though, owing to the destruction which time and the vandalism of man have effected, proofs may never be sufficient to place this question beyond doubt.

But, however hotly the scientific knowledge of the ancients may be contested, there is one field of learning in which they are avowedly unsurpassed, nay, unequaled—this is the wide field of literature.

No modern lyric is more rich in metaphor or passionate in language than the Song of Solomon; no poet has been more inspired by the majesty of the Supreme Being, the beauties of the earth, and the grandeur of the heavens; none has more pathetically described grief, or more nobly the duties of the righteous man in prosperity or adversity, than he who wrote the wonderful book of Job. The Proverbs and Ecclesiastes, in their adaptation to the wants of our own age, prove that, in the weakness and wisdom of human nature, at least, there is no new thing under the sun.

The poems of Homer, even translated into a less musical and perfect language, thrill the heart to hear, and fire the soul of many a school-boy with his first admiration for great and noble deeds. Less is known of this author than of many an inferior genius; of his birthplace and parentage we are alike ignorant; only, as we read those glorious pages, the dim vision of a blind old man with flowing beard and majestic mien rises before us, refuting the modern theory that they are not the inspiration of one great genius, but the effusions of a dozen or more minstrels. The "Iliad" and "Odyssey," written more than two thousand years ago, are said to have been the first epic poems; if so, epic poetry was perfect at its birth, so perfect that all subsequent epics, taking these two as their models, fall far short of them in excellence. "In great things," says Quintilian, "what sublimity of expression; and, in little, what a justness and propriety—diffusive and concise, pleasant and grave, admirable both for his copiousness and brevity!"

The wisdom of Moses, the jurist and historian, is apparent, whether he composed or selected his admirable laws; that which often appears trivial to the thoughtless shows wonderful knowledge of what is injurious or beneficial to individuals and nations.[32]

The more we study the literature and theology of that ancient people, the Hindoos, the more we are impressed by the profound thought and wisdom displayed, the purity of the doctrines enunciated, the high moral standard of excellence maintained, as also the poetic language and imagery of their writings.[33]

[32] Take, for instance, the prohibition to eat swine's flesh, which so often causes a smile. There is a note in the Talmud stating that the use of this meat is forbidden on account of the small insect which infests it. Late events, the fearful ravages of the trichinæ in Germany, and even in some parts of the United States, have shown the wisdom of this law, particularly as enacted for the inhabitants of a warm climate.

[33] The general idea entertained of the religious belief and customs of the Hindoos is but an erroneous one, thanks to the misinterpretations, perhaps not wholly unintentional, of the earliest modern writers on the subject; they, as a rule, record only the forms of superstitions which were erected upon the original pure foundation by a corrupt and ambitious priestcraft, and which mark the decadence of the Hindoo religion and people.

Later writers, the researches of such men as Schlegel, Colebrook, William Jones, Strange, and the remarkable work of M. Jacolliot, "La Bible dans l'Inde," give us a more just conception of this race, probably the parent of our own.

The original pure Hindoo religion recognized but one God (as did the sages of Greece, in spite of its mythology). In the Vedas, the ancient sacred writings of the Hindoos, which the learned declare to have been written more than three thousand years before Christ, we find the Deity thus defined: "He who exists by Himself, who is in all, because all is in Him." And, again, with surpassing majesty of thought; "The Ganges flows—it is God; the ocean roars—it is God; the wind blows—it is He; the cloud that thunders, the lightning that flashes—it is He. As from all eternity the universe existed in the spirit of Brahma, so to-day is all that exists his image." Can we boast of any grandeur or more beautiful definition of Divine eternity and omnipresence?

To those who imagine the Brahminical religion as instigating its votaries to put faith in empty and absurd forms, rather than in worthy actions, let us quote a few maxims from the teachings of Manou, the Hindoo philosopher and legislator, who cannot have written less than four thousand years ago:

"Of all things pure, purity in the acquisition of riches is the best. He who preserves purity in becoming rich, is really pure, and not he who is purified with earth and water." (Will not the just and thoughtful applaud this maxim in the present age of corruption?)—" As the body is purified by water, so is the spirit by truth."—" Sound

Five hundred and fifty years before our era, in a land of which Columbus possessed but a mythical knowledge, and regarded as a realm of barbarous idolatry and wealth, Confucius led men to admire and practise virtue for the sake of virtue only, and laid the foundation for the high and enlightened moral civilization which still distinguishes his disciples.[84]

doctrines and good works purify the soul. The intelligence is purified by knowledge."—" Science is useless to a man without judgment, as a mirror to a blind man."—" The man who only appreciates the means, according as they conduce to his success, soon loses his perception of the just, and of sound doctrines."

Nor were the psychological ideas of the Hindoos less elevated than their morality was pure. Chrishna taught: "The soul is the principle of life, which sovereign wisdom employed to animate bodies; matter is inert and perishable, the soul thinks and acts, and is immortal." The profound philosophy of Greece, the theology of to-day, has given us no better or more concise definition.—The elevation of woman, indispensable to true civilization, was enjoined, her status and mission chivalrously defined, in the Vedas: "He who despises woman, despises his mother."—" There is no crime more odious than to persecute women, and take advantage of their weakness to despoil them of their patrimony. When women are honored the divinities are content, but where they are not honored all undertakings fail." "Women should be shielded with fostering solicitude by their fathers, their brothers, their husbands, and the brothers of their husbands, if they hope for prosperity."

[84] That morality and a wise conception of the same belong especially to no sect, time, or people, is evidenced by the fact that the Golden Rule of Christianity, beautiful and comprehensive, was thus laid down by Confucius five hundred years before the birth of Christ: "What you do not like when done to yourself, do not do to others." "In the way of the superior man there are four things, to none of which have I as yet attained: To serve my father as I would require my son to serve me; to serve my elder brother as I would require my younger brother to serve me; to serve my prince as I would require my minister to serve me; to set example in behaving to a friend as I would require him to behave to me."—("Doctrine of the Just Mean," chapter xiii.) The whole of this chapter is replete with wisdom, and is dictated by a calm, elevated philosophy, teaching men that virtue consists in doing their duty conscientiously in whatever situation they may be placed. "The superior man," we read, "can find himself in no situation in which he is not himself. He does not murmur against Heaven, nor grumble against men. Thus it is that the superior man is quiet and calm, waiting for the appointments of Heaven, while the mean man walks in dangerous paths, looking for lucky occurrences." Resignation to Divine will and philosophic moderation are here forcibly enjoined. It is to be regretted that the translation of Confucius (of which we here make use) by the Rev. James Legge, is made with the avowed object of lessening the fame of the great philosopher, and the credit of his followers, by placing in an unfavorable light the moral doctrines of this most enlightened Chinese school; and it is to be feared that sectarian partiality may have allowed itself, here and there, to misinterpret sentiments, particularly as these are expressed in a language every word of which is susceptible of several interpretations. Nevertheless, it has been impossible for the translator to conceal the wisdom and sublimity, blended with sound practical sense, of the teachings inculcated on the Chinese by their beloved master. The following, selected at random from the *Analects*, may serve as an

Philosophy, the pure teachings of morality, have never since flourished as in the days when Socrates taught the doctrine of the immortality of the soul, which his disciple Plato developed to a still higher spiritualism. The teachings of these and the whole school of great philosophers who flourished long ago, contain all the requisites for making men good and nations prosperous.

History was well understood by the ancients. Herodotus is styled the father of that useful branch of literature, not, we may reasonably suppose, because he was the first historian, but because his writings are the first treating on that subject only which have come down to us complete; as also, no doubt, on account of the inimitable style he employed in his narratives, simple, picturesque, and vivid in description, which, as he recited them beneath the blue skies of Greece during the excitement of the Olympic games, brought the far-off countries through which he had traveled, and their inhabitants, before the minds of his enthusiastic listeners. If we reflect upon the fact that most of the ancient historians found time, amid the toils and occupations

example of the system: "The superior man in *every thing* considers righteousness to be essential. He performs it according to the rules of propriety. He brings it forth in humility. He completes it in sincerity. This is indeed a superior man."—"The master said, 'Alas! there is no one that knows me!' Tsze-Kung said: 'What do you mean by thus saying that no one knows you?' The master replied: 'I do not murmur against Heaven, I do not grumble against men. My studies lie low, my penetration rises high. But there is Heaven—that knows me.'"—"I will not be concerned at men's not knowing me, I will be concerned at my own want of ability."—"The wise man is correctly firm, not firm merely."—"He who exercises government by means of his virtue may be compared to the north polar star, which keeps its place, and all the stars turn toward it."—"Learning without thought is labor lost, thought without learning is perilous."—"The master said: 'Yew, shall I teach you what knowledge is? When you know a thing, to hold that you know it, and when you do not know a thing, to allow that you do not know it. This is knowledge.'"—"They who know the truth are not equal to those who love it, and they who love it, are not equal to those who find delight in it."—"Now the man of perfect virtue, wishing to be established himself, seeks also to establish others; wishing to be enlarged himself, he seeks also to enlarge others. To be able to judge of others by what is nigh in ourselves, this may be called the art of virtue."—"Let the will be set on the path of duty, let perfect virtue be accorded with, let relaxation and enjoyment be found in the polite arts."—"In language it is simply required that it convey its meaning."—"Fine words and an insinuating appearance are seldom associated with virtue."

What exalted doctrines are these! What wisdom and observation of human nature are displayed, and withal what modesty! "To this I have not attained," says the sage of his golden rule; and, again, "A transmitter and not a maker, believing in and loving the ancients, I may compare myself to our old P'ang."

of the soldier or of the statesman, to leave such valuable records to posterity; that Xenophon, the Hebrew Josephus, Julius Cæsar, etc., were distinguished warriors as well as eminent writers, it may be conceded that human intellect has not much advanced since those times.—" The treasury of remedies for the soul" was inscribed over the entrance of the library of Osymandias at Thebes three thousand years ago, and who to day will invent a more apt and beautiful definition? We pride ourselves on our common-school system, yet find it recorded of Charondas, lawgiver of Catania, who lived five hundred years before our era: "He made another law, better than these, and neglected by the older legislators—for he enacted that all the sons of the citizens should be instructed in letters, the city paying the salaries of the teachers. For he held that the poor, not being able to pay their teachers from their own property, would be deprived of the most valuable discipline."

The learning of the East was transferred to Europe, especially to Spain, by the Arabs. The Caliph Almanzor, early in the ninth century of our era, turned his attention from religious learning and warlike exploits, to profane science. He cultivated astronomy with ardor. His successor, Al-Mamoun, by means of agents in Constantinople, Syria, and Egypt, caused many of the great scientific works of Greece to be collected. These were translated by his order, and his subjects enjoined to study them with the assurance that the elect of God are they who best improve their mental faculties, and that teachers of wisdom are the light of the world. A subordinate officer donated two hundred thousand pieces of gold to found a school in Bagdad, and endowed the same with an annual revenue of fifteen thousand dinars. The learning of the Greeks and Arabs overspread the East. The Ommiades of Spain caught the ardor; Bagdad and Cordova became names synonymous with that of Athens in the days of her glory; great libraries were collected, both public and private. We read of a doctor who declined an invitation to reside at the court of Bokhara because the transportation of his library alone would require four hundred camels. That of the Fatimites numbered one hundred thousand manuscripts elegantly translated and beautifully bound. Free access to these was given to the students of Cairo, while in Spain the Ommiades possessed a library of six hundred thousand volumes, forty-four of which were employed in the catalogue alone. Cordova, Malaga, Almeria, and Murcia, boasted of more than three hundred writers, and nearly one hundred public libraries were open in Andalusia. The writings of the Grecian sages appeared in the Arabic, in which language only, many have been preserved to us. The Caliph Al-Mamoun supplied costly instruments for astronomical observation. Twice his mathematicians correctly measured a degree of the earth's circle, and determined that our globe was twenty-four thousand miles in circumference.

Such was the learning of the Arabs, a people who enlightened Spain for hundreds of years, and were only driven from that country immediately before Columbus sailed on his first voyage. They cannot have failed during all those years to impart some of their knowledge to the Spaniards, yet we are informed by historians who have the air of believing their assertion, however improbable it may appear when tested by reason, that the learned men of Salamanca, convoked to hear Columbus propound his "startling theory," treated with ridicule the idea of the earth's being spherical.

What are the proofs we possess that the knowledge of the ancients was incomplete? Imperfect globes, defective maps, errors in the statements found in ancient MSS., as they have reached us—these are cited as evidence of the ignorance of the past. It should be remembered that a desire to impress the young with an idea of our own importance, has induced many to select the *defects* of a particular age or country as proofs of its real status; the vainglorious author, finding among the ancients two works, one containing correct views touching the form of our earth, the other declaring it to be flat, would too often content himself with holding up the latter as evidence of ancient ignorance and modern progress. In what light may we not be placed centuries hence? It will only be necessary for some curious antiquary to deposit in one of the museums a few flint arrow-heads collected from the fields, or one of the Pembina carts [15] which for the last thirty years have annually borne the merchants and merchandise of Prince Rupert's Land to the city of St. Paul, for coming generations to declare that Americans in the nineteenth century were ignorant of the use of metals!

[15] These carts, caravans of which often number as many as a hundred and fifty, are manufactured entirely of wood and green hide; not a particle of metal enters their composition; even the linchpin is of wood.

Is it not time that a more just, generous, and reasonable spirit pervade the civilization of our age? that, while we glory and delight in the great deeds of our race and age, we do not consider that great deeds belong to them alone? that, while eagerly seeking after knowledge and enacting laws to impart it, we do not imagine, and thereby prove gross ignorance, that knowledge is our special inheritance, and that the people of the past were less favored by their Creator than are we?

The Hindoo philosopher Narada, reputed to have lived before the Deluge, reasons thus: "Never resort to the argument, 'I do not know this, therefore it is false.' We must study to know, know to comprehend, and comprehend to judge."

This is the proper spirit; heroes and scholars are not less heroic or learned because others as great as they have preceded them, nor will it dim the lustre of the present to be just to the memory of the past.

CHAPTER III.

THE NORTHMEN IN AMERICA.

WHILE the greater part of Europe was plunged in the intellectual darkness which pervaded the middle ages, while the monk in his cloister toiled laboriously during a lifetime to perpetuate some one work of saintly or classic lore, and the masses were ignorant, superstitious, the slaves of feudal lords and barons scarcely less ignorant than themselves, a people flourished in the

LANDING OF THE NORTHMEN.

extreme north, with whom enterprise and freedom were neither dead nor stagnant, who possessed scientific knowledge and applied the same to practical purposes; a people simple, fearless, and energetic, republicans in practice if not in name, with whom chieftains were the fathers and protectors of their followers, sharing their perils and respecting their rights; a pagan people indeed, worshipers of Odin and Thor, believers in the joys of Walhalla, yet doers of deeds so noble as to be worthy the most enlightened Christian: such were the Northmen; such their simple records, which bear every impress of truth, prove them to have been. Issuing from an Asiatic hive, they early overran Norway and Sweden; their language, the old Danish or *Dönsk tunga*, is now only preserved in Iceland, which they colonized in the year 875; in 985 they rediscovered and colonized Greenland; the same year the American Continent proper was discovered by them, and, during the first years of the eleventh century, they made thither frequent voyages, residing, for periods of several years, at different times, in what is now called New England. To this they were actuated by motives far different from those of Columbus: they did not come in search of gold or slaves, but to gather by industry the natural products of the land, carrying on therewith a flourishing trade between the continent, Greenland, Iceland, and Norway. No absurd visions of untold wealth, no dreams of Ophir, haunted their brain; nor did they seek by false representations to inveigle others into bearing all the burdens, while they should reap all the profits, of their expeditions; they were the worthy pioneers of European settlement on our shores; a hardy race, counting on their own labor to develop the natural resources of the lands they discovered.

The voyages made by the Northmen to America are recorded in the Sagas or ancient Icelandic records, manuscripts of undoubted authenticity, and of a date far anterior to Columbus.

The settlement of Greenland by them undoubtedly took place; allusions to it and the colonies formed there are constantly occurring in Norse or Icelandic records. Letters and learning flourished in Iceland when the rest of Europe was intellectually stagnant; histories and annals are therefore copious. The last bishop was appointed to Greenland in 1406, when the colony consisted of two hundred and eighty settlements, all of which evidently became extinct; at what time after communication with the parent-country ceased, or from what causes, is not known, yet few acquainted with history will doubt their having existed. Once in Greenland, this continent was nearer the settlers than their fatherland: it would have been difficult for them *not* to discover it. Indeed, throughout Icelandic chronicles and history, there are constant allusions to this discovery. In a geographical treatise called "Description of the Whole Earth," written toward the end of the thirteenth century, we read: "England and Scotland are one island; but each is a separate kingdom. Ireland is a great island. Iceland is also a great island north of Ireland. All these countries are situated in that part of the world called Europe. Next to Denmark is lesser Sweden; then is Œland, then Gottland, then Helsingeland, then Vermeland, and the two Kvendlands, which lie north of Biarmeland. From Biarmeland stretches desert land toward the north, until Greenland begins. *South of Greenland is Helluland; next is Markland, from thence it is not far to Vinland the good, which some think goes out to Africa.*" We thus see that the geographical knowledge of the Scandinavians, not only with regard to Europe, but also touching the position of the new continent, was correct. As to their supposition that Vinland extended to Africa, it is an avowed hypothesis, and, at any rate, but a small error, compared to Columbus's persistent declaration that the island of Cuba was Asia.

Thanks to the eminent labors of Prof. Rafn, the Icelandic histories of pre-Columbian discoveries in America have become well known to the curious; while, through the more accessible works of Toulmin Smith, Beamish, and last, but not least, De Costa, the general reader has been convinced of the fact, which is now no longer disputed, that the Northmen were the first modern discoverers of this continent. This fact is now so generally conceded, and stands upon so sure a foundation of almost contemporaneous documents, that argument is happily not needed to establish the justness of the Northmen's claims; it will only be necessary for us to give a brief synopsis of these early histories, and note here and there the contrast existing between the spirit which animated the semi-pagan people on the one hand, and the bigoted devotee Columbus on the other, to prosecute their discoveries; this contrast redounds by no means to the credit of the latter.

We shall not here dwell upon the intellectual and commercial activity which early characterized the Northmen, save to observe that they were sufficient to render the discovery of America by them a natural consequence of their ever-extending voyages and explorations. Between Norway and Iceland, Iceland

and Ireland, there were communication and traffic; the people of the latter island were further advanced in civilization than their neighbors the Britons. Tacitus tells us of Ireland that "the approaches and harbors are better known" (than those of Britain), "by reason of commerce and the merchants." The Northmen, we have seen, possessed the magnetic compass; they were particularly remarkable as a seafaring people. When they had reached Iceland, the distance to Greenland was comparatively trifling; a passage thence to America, a natural sequence of their westward course. In recording their voyages, we shall not attempt laboriously to explain the identity of each place described by the Northmen—this has already been done by Rafn; we shall only quote the result of his labors. Slight possible flaws in his identification have been pointed out by De Costa, but the main fact, that the lands discovered were those portions of America extending from Labrador to Florida, is admitted by all who have studied the records, who agree that they describe with wonderful accuracy the aspect and products of that region, and that such accuracy, it is scarcely needful to say, cannot be the result of chance, nor the descriptions have been written for other lands. Circumstantial evidence, scientific proof, of this are exhausted by Rafn in his "Antiquitates Americanæ," to which comprehensive work we refer the reader, should he still be disposed to doubt that the following narratives are proofs of pre-Columbian exploration and settlement in America.

Eric the Red had, in the spring of 986 A. D., emigrated to Greenland from Iceland, and there formed a settlement. One of his followers was Heriulf, whose son Biarne was absent on a voyage to Norway at the time of his departure. Biarne had always made a point of spending the winter with his father; on his return to Iceland, he determined that this winter should form no exception to his rule, and that he would follow Heriulf to the land whither he had traveled, a somewhat arduous undertaking, as he possessed no chart or directions save that the new settlement lay to the westward. "He was," we read, "a promising young man. In his earliest youth he had a desire to go abroad, and he soon gathered property and reputation, and was by turns a year abroad and a year with his father. Biarne was soon in possession of a merchant-ship of his own." When Biarne returned with his ship from his Norway expedition, he would not unload, but said to his crew, "I will steer for Greenland if ye will go with me." They one and all agreed to go with him. Biarne said, "Our voyage will be thought foolish, as none of us have been on the Greenland sea before."

They set sail and encountered continuous northerly winds which drove them southward; the fog became so dense as to conceal the surrounding ocean. When the weather at length cleared they found themselves in sight of a land plentifully wooded and gently undulated; this, however, Biarne concluded could not be Greenland, as it varied greatly from the descriptions of that country which had been given him. He therefore left it to the larboard, and, sailing two days, saw another land, flat and woody; the wind was now southwest; they passed a third land, mountainous and covered with glaciers; this they coasted sufficiently to find that it was an island, but did not go ashore. They now stood out to sea, a strong southwest wind still prevailing, which brought them, after four days' swift sailing, to Greenland, and to the very cape where Heriulf had settled. This was the first discovery of America by the Northmen. Like the discovery of the West Indies by the pilot Sanchez, it was the result of chance, but the chance was itself the result of hardy enterprise. Biarne started from Iceland in search of Greenland, of which he only knew by hearsay; driven south, he discovered instead America. The narrative which records his voyage describes accurately the points upon which he touched, which, it has been agreed, were: first, Cape Cod; second, Nova Scotia; third, Newfoundland. Biarne's impatience to rejoin his father before the winter set in, caused him to neglect any exploration of the lands he thus accidentally visited. For this he was censured by his countrymen; they could hardly understand his refraining from becoming acquainted with the new country and its products. The spirit of discovery was then rife with the Northmen.

Leif, son of Eric the Red, bought Biarne's ship, equipped and manned it with a crew of thirty men; one of these was Tyrker, "a man from the south," probably a German, who had long been a retainer of Eric, and was much attached to Leif from his boyhood. When all was ready, the latter besought his father to become the commander of the expedition. Eric at first declared himself to be too old for the undertaking, but yielded finally to the solicitations of his son. As he rode down to the ship his horse stumbled and threw him, disabling his foot. "It is destined," said he, "that I should never discover more lands than this Greenland on which we live." He remained therefore at home, and Leif commanded the ship. The above incident, simply related, and Biarne's devotion and eagerness to rejoin his father, give us a pleasant knowledge of the love and respect which existed among the Northmen between father and son, even when the latter had attained to manhood. Leif purchasing his ship from Biarne (the avowed though accidental discoverer of the lands), organizing, and defraying the expenses of the expedition, then modestly desiring that his father, not himself, should be its chief, contrasts strongly with Columbus, who entirely concealed the source whence he derived his information, resorted to fraud and false promises to obtain his equipment, and finally insisted, as only the little-minded can insist, upon being vested with sounding titles and surrounded by puerile obsequiousness.

Leif set sail in the year 1000 A. D. to revisit the lands seen by Biarne; he first reached the island which the latter had coasted. He said: "It shall not be said of us, as it was of Biarne, that we did not come upon the land; for I will give the country a name, and call it Helluland" (*hella*, a stone). They went on board again, and put to sea, and reached another land. Sailing toward it, they put out a boat, and landed. "This country was flat and woody, surrounded by cliffs, and a low shore of white sand; they called it Markland (*Woodland*)." Thence they sailed two days, with a northeast wind, and came to an island which lay eastward of the main-land, and entered a channel, which separated the island from the main-land promontory. Sailing westward, they came to a river, which flowed from a lake into the sea; they entered the river, and thence the lake, in which they cast anchor. This was evidently Mount-Hope Bay, which they reached by Pocasset River and Seaconnet Passage. On the shores they constructed huts, or booths, for temporary shelter, but, upon determining to spend the winter there, they enlarged their quarters and built houses. The place was called Leifsbüder (*Leif's Booths*).

"The country appeared to them of so good a kind that it would not be necessary to gather fodder for the cattle for winter. There was no frost in winter, and the grass was not much withered. Day and night were more equal than in Greenland and Iceland; for, on the shortest day, the sun was in the sky between Eyktarstadr and the Dagmalstadr." [36]

When the houses were completed, Leif divided his men into two companies, one of which kept watch at the settlement while the other explored the surrounding country. He shared alike with his men, accompanying them in their explorations one day, and the next remaining at home. He enjoined them not to separate, nor to extend their travels too far. He is described in the narrative as "a stout, strong man, and of manly appearance; and was besides a prudent and sagacious man in all respects."

One day the exploring party returned, and it was found that Tyrker, the German, was missing; Leif, much concerned, immediately started with twelve men in search of him, but had not proceeded far when they met him. "Leif soon perceived that his foster-father was quite merry. Tyrker had a high forehead, sharp eyes, with a small face, and was little in size, and ugly; but was very dexterous in all feats. Leif said to him: 'Why art thou so late, my foster-father; and why didst thou leave thy comrades?' He spoke at first long in German, rolled his eyes and knit his brows; but they could not make out what he was saying. After a while, and some delay, he said in Norse: 'I did not go much farther than they, and yet I have something altogether new to relate, for I have found vines and grapes.' 'Is that true, my foster-father?' said Leif. "Yes, true it is,' answered he, 'for I was born where there was no scarcity of grapes.'" Tyrker, far away from his fatherland, which he had probably not seen since childhood, was evidently moved to strange

---

[36] Rafn thus explains this passage: "In Vineland the sun rose, on the shortest day, at the beginning of *Dagmal*, and set at the close of *Eykt*. As the ancient Northmen divided the horizon into eight grand compartments, called *āttir*, so they also made a corresponding octuple division of the solar day into aliquot parts, called *eyktir*, each of which was consequently equal to three hours. *Stadr* signifies limit, or boundary, and, when used in reference to the rising and setting of the sun, it denotes, in the morning, the commencement, and, in the evening, the close of the Eykt. *Dagmalstadr* is, therefore, half-past seven o'clock A. M., and *Eyktarstadr* half-past four P. M. The sun therefore rose at half-past seven o'clock and set at half-past four on the shortest day, which was consequently nine hours long. This circumstance gives for the latitude of the place 41° 24' 10". The latitude of Seaconnet Point and of the south point of Conannicut Island is 41° 26', and of Point Judith 41° 23', which three headlands bound the entrances to what is now called Mount-Hope Bay, and which was doubtless called *Hopsvatn* by the ancient Northmen."

emotion at the sight of vines such as grew around the home of his earliest recollections. This episode and the simplicity with which it is narrated, is, as Mr. De Costa justly claims, "a stroke of genuine nature, something that a writer, framing the account of a fictitious voyage, would not dream of." It is well known that grapes formerly grew wild in great abundance in the vicinity of Mount-Hope Bay, hence the names *Martha's Vineyard* and Vineyard Sound.

Henceforth, the occupation of Leif and his companions was twofold—felling and hewing timber, and gathering grapes. Leif called the land Vineland. In the spring they sailed with a fair

GRAPES DISCOVERED BY THE NORTHMEN.

wind for Greenland. When, in sight of land, Leif steered to the windward, his men inquired the reason; he replied, "I mind my helm, and tend to other things too. Do you see any thing?" They said they saw nothing remarkable. Leif replied that he saw something which was either a ship or a rock; on examination, the crew pronounced it a rock. "But he saw so much better than they, that he discovered men upon the rock. 'Now I will,' said Leif, ' that we hold to the wind, that we may come up to them if they should need help; and, if they should not be friendly inclined, it is in our power to do as we please, and not theirs.' Now they sailed under the rock, lowered their sails, cast anchor, and put out another small boat which they had with them. Then Tyrker asked who their leader was. He said his name was Thorer, and that he was a Northman. 'But what is your name?' said he. Leif told his name. 'Are you the son of Eric the Red of Brattahlid?' he asked. Leif said that was so. 'Now I will,' said Leif, 'take ye and all on board my ship, and as much of the goods as the ship will store.' They took up this offer, and sailed away to Ericfiord with the cargo, and thence to Brattahlid, where they unloaded the ship. Leif offered Thorer and his wife Gudrid, and three others, lodging with himself, and offered lodging elsewhere for the rest of the people, both of Thorer's crew and his own. Leif took fifteen men from the rock, and thereafter was called Leif the Fortunate. After that time, Leif advanced greatly in wealth and consideration. That winter sickness came among Thorer's people, and he himself and a great part of his crew died."

Though Leif had explored a portion of the country, and could not, therefore, share the reproach which Biarne had incurred, there was an evident opinion among his countrymen that further exploration should be made.

Leif had been baptized in Norway at the suggestion and solicitation of King Olaf, about the year 999. In the following year he first introduced Christianity into Greenland. Old Eric the Red does not, however, seem to have taken kindly to the new creed, for we find it recorded of him that, when the people called his son Leif the Fortunate, he said; "These two things went against one another; that Leif had saved the crew of the ship, and delivered them from death, and that he had brought that bad man into Greenland; that is what he called the priest." We read, however, that the old man was, after much urging, baptized. He died soon after Leif's return from Vinland (1001); the latter, therefore, assumed his father's place at the head of the Brattahlid settlement, and it was his brother Thorwald who, in the spring of 1002, sailed to prosecute his discoveries. For this purpose he lent Thorwald his vessel and gave him ample instructions. It is likely that the Northmen made observations and charts during their voyages, which were sure guides to those who followed them; their knowledge of the compass would enable them to do this, and facts go far to prove that they availed themselves of the ability. Leif first reached Newfoundland, the most northerly and last point seen by Biarne. He does not touch upon other lands, as he most likely would have done had his instructions been vague (as Biarne himself did when sailing for Greenland with nothing but description to guide him). He next visited *Markland* (Nova Scotia), which was the second seen by Biarne, and lastly Vinland, which was in the vicinity of the first point of land Biarne's expedition had sighted. These were evidently the points he made for, and he found them without difficulty. Now Thorwald, sailing by Leif's chart, makes immediately for Leifsbüdir, touching at no intervening points (at least no mention is made of his having done so) till he reached the bay. Here he staid two winters, making Leifsbüdir headquarters, and sending thence exploring parties. One of these went south in the ship's boat, how far we are not able to determine, as the details of Thorwald's expedition are more meagre than those of the other narratives, owing no doubt to the death of the chief before returning to Greenland. In the year 1004 Thorwald set out in his large ship to explore northward, encountering bad weather when opposite a cape (evidently the extreme point of Cape Cod); and, the keel of his ship being damaged, he said to his companions, "We will stick up the keel here upon the *ness*," and call the place Kialarness" (Keel Promontory), "which they did." The ship being repaired, they sailed east to a point of land covered with trees, said to be Point Alderton, below Boston. When they had landed, Thorwald said: "Here it is beautiful; and I would willingly set up my abode here."

Soon after they were attacked by hostile Skrællings (*natives*). "Then," said Thorwald, "we shall put up our war-screens along the gunwales, and defend ourselves as well as we can, but not use our weapons much against them."

"They did so accordingly. The Skrællings shot at them for a while, and then fled away as fast as they could. Then Thorwald asked if any one was wounded, and they said nobody was hurt. He said: 'I have a wound under the arm. An arrow flew between the gunwale and the shield, under my arm; here is the arrow, and it will be my death-wound. Now I advise you to make ready with all speed to return; but ye shall carry me to the point which I thought would be so convenient for a dwelling.

---

*⁷¹ The Northmen called all points of land, or promontories, *ness*.*

It may be that it was true what I said, that here would I dwell for a while. Ye shall bury me there, and place a cross at my head and one at my feet, and call the place Crossness.'"

Having obeyed these last instructions, his companions returned to Leifsbüdir, spent the winter in loading their ships, and returned in the spring, "bringing heavy tidings to Leif."

Thorstein Ericson hearing the fate of his brother Thorwald, determined to bring his body from Vinland to Greenland. He equipped the same vessel and set sail, accompanied by his wife Gudrid, but his expedition was unfortunate, and he returned to Greenland without reaching any of the lands his brothers had visited. He died that winter.

During the next summer (1006) two ships came from Iceland, one of which was commanded by Thorfinn Karlsefne, a man of wealth and illustrious birth, his ancestors being noble Danes, Norwegians, Swedes, Irish, and Scotch, some of them kings or of royal descent; the other was commanded by Biarne Grimolfson and Thorhall Gamlason. Each ship had a crew of forty men.

"Leif and other people rode down to the ships, and friendly exchanges were made. The captains requested Leif to take whatever he desired of their goods. Leif, in return, entertained them well, and invited the principal men of both ships to spend the winter with him at Brattahlid. The merchants accepted his invitation with thanks. Afterward their goods were moved to Brattahlid, where they had every entertainment they could desire; therefore their winter-quarters pleased them much. When the Yule-feast began, Leif was silent and more depressed than usual. Then Karlsefne said to Leif: 'Are you sick, friend Leif? you do not seem to be in your usual spirits. You have entertained us liberally, for which we desire to render you all the service in our power. Tell me what it is that ails you.' 'You have received what I have been able to offer you' said Leif, 'in the kindest manner, and there is no idea in my mind that you have been wanting in courtesy; but I am afraid lest, when you go away, it may be said that you never saw a Yule-feast so meanly celebrated as that which draws near, at which you will be entertained by Leif of Brattahlid.' 'That shall never be the case, friend,' said Karlsefne; 'we have ample stores in the ships; take of these what you wish, and make a feast as splendid as you please.' Leif accepted the offer, and the Yule began; and so well were Leif's plans made, that all were surprised that such a rich feast could be prepared in so poor a country. After the Yule-feast, Karlsefne began to treat with Leif as to the marriage of Gudrid . . . . and in the end it turned out that Karlsefne married Gudrid (widow of Thorstein Ericson), and their wedding was held at Brattahlid, this same winter.

"The conversation often turned, at Brattahlid, on the discovery of Vinland the Good, and they said that a voyage there had great hope of gain. And, after this, Karlsefne and Snorre made ready for going on a voyage there the following spring. Biarne and Thorhall Gamlason, before mentioned, joined him with a ship" (1007).

The first land this joint expedition reached after the isle of Disco, which they called Biarney, or *Bear Island*, was evidently some part of Labrador. They found on it great stones and many foxes; they named it Helluland it Mikla, or Stony-land the Great, to distinguish it from Newfoundland, which Leif had first named Helluland, and which they now called Helluland it Litla (the Little). The description in the ancient narrative is said to answer perfectly to the aspect of that region. Sailing southward a day and a night, they came to a land covered with woods, in which were many wild animals. This was Nova Scotia, which in 1501 will be called Tierra Verde, or *Greenland*, on account of these same forests, by Don Gaspar de Corte Real, and which Leif had already appropriately named Markland (Woodland). They then came to an island supposed to be Sable Island, where they killed a bear. Thence they reached Kialarness (Cape Cod), and saw the keel which Thorwald had there set up. The shores of this cape, long and barren wastes of sand, stretching along the coast to an apparently endless extent, they named Furdusstrandir (Wonderful Shores), "because they seemed so long passing by." The coast then became indented with coves, and they ran the ship into a bay, whither they directed their course. "King Olaf had given Leif two Scots, a man named Haki, and a woman named Hekia; they were swifter of foot than wild animals. These were in Karlsefne's ship. And when they had passed beyond Wonder-strand, they put these Scots ashore, and told them to run over the land to the southwest, three days, and discover the nature of the land, and then return. They had a kind of garment that they called *kiafal*, that was so made that a hat was on top, and it was open at the sides, and no arms; fastened between the legs with a button and strap, otherwise they were naked. When they returned, one had in his hand a bunch of grapes, and the other an ear of corn. They went on board, and afterward the course was obstructed by another bay. Beyond this bay was an island, on each side of which was a rapid current, that they called the *Isle of Currents* (Straumey)."

This island was probably Nantucket, which was evidently at one time united with Martha's Vineyard. The name they gave it shows that they possessed knowledge of the Gulf Stream. On this island, we read: "There was so great a number of cider-ducks there, that they could hardly step without treading on their eggs. They called this place 'Stream Bay.' This was Buzzard's Bay; the eggs were probably those of the gull which still frequents that part in great numbers. Here we are told they brought their ship to anchor, and prepared to stay. They had with them all kinds of cattle. The situation of the place. was pleasant, but they did not care for any thing except to explore the land. Here they wintered, without sufficient food. The next summer (1008), failing to catch fish, they began to want food. Then Thorhall the hunter disappeared. . . .

"They found Thorhall, whom they sought three days, on the top of a rock, where he lay breathing, blowing through his nose and mouth, and muttering. They asked why he had gone there. He replied that this was nothing that concerned them. They said that he should go home with them, which he did. Afterward a whale was cast ashore in that place, and they assembled and cut it up, not knowing what kind of a whale it was, they boiled it with water, and devoured it, and were taken sick; then Thorhall said: 'Now you see that Thor is more prompt to give aid than your Christ. This was cast ashore as a reward for the hymn which I composed to my patron Thor, who rarely forsakes me.' When they knew this, they cast all the remains of the whale into the sea, and commended their affairs to God. After which the air became milder, and opportunities were given for fishing, and from that time there was an abundance of food, and there were beasts on the land, eggs in the island, and fish in the sea."

It is somewhat amusing to find these newly-converted and evidently sincere Christians, still believing in the efficacy of prayer to their ancient gods; with them it seems to have been a matter of supremacy of one god over the other. Thorhall was evidently a most disagreeable personage, not altogether undeserving of his fate. We read next: "They say that Thorhall desired to go northward around 'Wonder-strand,' to explore Vinland, but Karlsefne wished to go along the south shore.

"Then Thorhall prepared himself at the island, but did not have more than nine men in his whole company, and all the others went in the company of Karlsefne. When Thorhall was carrying water to his ship, he sang this verse:

'People said when hither I
Came, that I the best
Drink would have, but the land
It justly becomes me to blame—
I, a warrior, am now obliged
To bear the pail;
Wine touches not my lips,
But I bow down to the spring.'

"And when they had made ready and were about to sail, Thorhall sang:

'Let us return
Thither where our countrymen rejoice,
Let the ship try
The smooth ways of the sea;
While the strong heroes
Live on Wonder-strand,
And there boil whales,
Which is an honor to the land.'

"Afterward he sailed north, to go round Wonder-strand and Kialarness, but, when he wished to sail westward, they were met by a storm from the west and driven to Ireland, where they were beaten, and made slaves.

"And, as merchants reported, there Thorhall died."

We see, by this incidental allusion to merchants and their bringing news from Ireland, that the trade between the latter and Iceland was then flourishing.

Karlsefne, with Biarne, Snorre, and the rest, sailed south till they reached the same river, flowing from a lake into the sea, which Leif had entered, and erected his booths.

They evidently passed to the west of these, toward Mount Hope. They named the place *Hóp* (to form a bay, to recede).

MOUNT HOPE.

It is curious that the present name of the bay and hill is Mount Hope, derived from the Indian word *Haup*. May not the latter have been a vestige, remaining with the natives, of the language of the Northmen? There is certainly no doubt that the descriptions in the narratives, both of Leif and Karlsefne, of the lake and approaches to it accurately correspond to Mount-Hope Bay; indeed, this is a point no longer disputed.

In this region they found corn growing on the low land, vines on the higher; the rivers were full of fish. They put their cattle out to pasture, and rested.

"When spring came (1009) they saw, one morning early, that

FIRST EUROPEANS TRADING WITH INDIANS.

a number of canoes rowed from the south round the *ness;* so many as if the sea were sown with coal; poles were also swung on each boat. Karlsefne and his people then raised up the shield, and when they came together they began to trade, and those people would rather have red cloth; for this they offered skins and real furs. They would also buy swords and spears, but this Karlsefne and Snorre forbade. For a whole fur-skin, the Skrællings took a piece of red cloth a span long, and bound it round their heads. Thus their traffic went on for a time; then the cloth began to be scarce with Karlsefne and his people, and they cut it into small pieces which were not wider than a finger's breadth, and yet the Skrællings gave as much as before, and more."

A bull, belonging to Karlsefne, happening to roar, disturbed this peaceful trading with the Indians, who, frightened at the sound, fled in dismay; they soon returned making hostile demonstrations; hard pressed by superior numbers, the Northmen fled to the rocks, where they could make a stand. Freydis, a daughter of Eric, who with her husband accompanied the expedition, indignant at the flight of her countrymen, defied the Indians, so that, awe-struck at her conduct, and moreover routed by the Northmen in the rocks, they fled to the woods. "Karlsefne and his people now thought that they saw, although the land had many good qualities, that they still would always be exposed there to the fear of attacks from the original dwellers. They decided, therefore, to go away, and return to their own land."

They therefore sailed to the Straumey, whence Karlsefne, with one of the ships, sailed in quest of the malcontent Thorhall, the other ship and crew remaining behind. Rounding Kialarness, Karlsefne proceeded northwest; the land lay to his left; this was covered with thick forests, and mountains which were supposed by them to form one range with those of Hôp.

Karlsefne returned to Straumfiord after a fruitless search, and there spent the winter of 1010. In the spring of that year they all sailed for Greenland. At Markland they saw five natives. They captured two boys whom they instructed in the Norse tongue, and the Christian religion. Karlsefne reached Greenland safely with a rich cargo of timber, grapes, and furs.

Biarne Grimolfson, however, was driven out into the ocean, and his ship was attacked by worms, which riddled it completely. The heroic magnanimity of Biarne in this emergency, as well as the fortitude displayed (with one exception) by the unfortunates doomed to inevitable death, are best related in the simple language of the Saga:

"Biarne Grimolfson was driven with his ship into the Irish Ocean, and they came into a worm sea, and soon the ship began to sink under them. They had a boat which was smeared with sea-oil—for the worms do not attack that. They went into the boat, and then saw that it could not hold them all; then said Biarne: 'As the boat will not hold more than half of our men, it is my counsel that lots should be drawn for those to go in the boat, for it shall not be according to rank.' This they all thought so generous an offer that no one would oppose it. They then did so, that lots were drawn; and it fell to Biarne to go in the boat, and half of the men with him, for the boat had not room for more. But when they had gotten into the boat, an Icelandic man that was in the ship, and had come with Biarne from Iceland, said, 'Dost thou mean, Biarne, to leave me here?' Biarne said, 'So it seems.' Then said the other, 'Very different was the promise to my father, when I went with thee from Iceland, than thus to leave me, for thou saidst that we should both share the same fate.' Biarne said: 'It shall not be thus; go down into the boat, and I will go up into the ship, since I see that thou art so

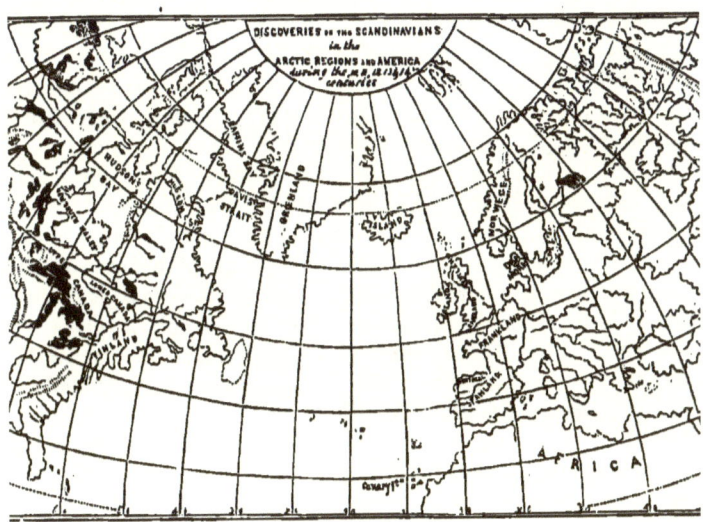

anxious to live.' Then Biarne went up into the ship, and this man down into the boat, and after that they went on their voyage until they came to Dublin, in Ireland, and there told these things; but it is most people's belief that Biarne and his companions were lost in the worm sea, for nothing was heard of them after that time."

Other voyages were made, and it is evident that communication was kept up with Vinland till intercourse between Greenland and Europe ceased, and the rigor of the climate or other causes had destroyed the vigorous Norse colony in the former. As late as the year 1347 it is recorded in the "Annals of Iceland," a sort of contemporaneous chronicle, that among the wrecks of the year was "a Greenland ship which had been on a voyage to Markland." We might also enlarge upon the tradition, which very possibly has truth for its foundation, that the Irish, as early as the Northmen, visited and colonized the southern portion of North America, and had there formed an extensive settlement. The land south of Vinland was called by the Northmen, Huitramannaland (White-man's Land), or Great Ireland. The Irish, to whose maritime and commercial activity we have already alluded, may very possibly have extended their voyages so far; but this cannot yet be stated as a fact, and still remains a mere tradition. Not so the voyages of the Northmen to our continent; these have become a certainty. They also made extensive explorations in the arctic regions, but of these we shall not here speak, contenting ourselves with having recorded their more important explorations along the coast of North America.

And, having read the narratives of these Norse voyagers, how can we sufficiently admire their conduct and motives, especially when contrasted with those of the much-lauded Columbus? Thorwald asks "whether any one is hurt," before even alluding to his own mortal wound; and when he does so it is with manly fortitude and resignation. Biarne Grimolfson gives his life for a cowardly follower, and accepts certain death, that he may be true to a promise given. Can one such act be found in the far more recent life of Columbus, whose continual I becomes monotonous, who ignores all save himself, whines and whimpers at the slightest danger, real or apparent? Leif Ericson himself starts in search of a missing follower, and, finding him, greets him kindly. When two of Columbus's luckless crew lose themselves, they are by his orders cast in irons and put on short rations, to expiate their heinous offense. Attacked by hostile Indians, Thorwald says, "We shall defend ourselves as well as we can, but not use our weapons much against them." Greeted by peaceable Indians, Columbus orders the ship's gun fired in their midst, in order "to abate their pride and make them not contemn the Christians." [36]

All the Norse leaders, Biarne Heriulfson, Leif and Thorwald

---

[36] Fernando, "Historia del Amirante," chapter xciii.

Ericson, Karlsefne, Biarne Grimolfson, worked for the common good, and were as much loved and respected by their followers as Columbus was hated and despised by his.

We have here given but a short sketch of the Northmen and their achievements in America, because the field has already been thoroughly explored. The evidence, climatic, geographical, and astronomical, that the Sagas describe the Eastern coast of North America, has been unanswerably set forth by Rafn, and the matter placed beyond cavil. Historians of Columbus, however, either utterly ignore, or slightingly allude to, the achievements of these predecessors of their hero, on whom they have determined to heap all the honors belonging to various men and various ages. To this the candid and impartial will scarcely consent. If the discovery by Columbus in 1492 of the islands of San Salvador and San Domingo was the discovery of the Continent of America, then the discovery and permanent colonization of Iceland and Greenland, six hundred years before by the Scandinavians, was also the discovery of that continent; the portion of main-land coasted by Columbus was avowedly but small, and he professed to be in Asia. The Northmen, on the contrary, visited all the eastern coast of America, from the extreme North to Florida, formed settlements, and for centuries carried on commerce with the products of what are now the most civilized, populous, and enlightened portions of America; and the American might well feel relief and pride at the knowledge that the first of his race to touch upon his native shores were the heroic Norsemen:

"Kings of the main, their leaders brave,
Their barks the dragons of the wave."

CHAPTER IV.

PRINCE MADOC AND THE ZENI BROTHERS.

IN treating of pre-Columbian visits to America, it would be unjust wholly to omit mentioning the voyages said to have been made to that continent by Prince Madoc, in the twelfth and the Zeni brothers in the fourteenth century. Insufficiency of evidence prevents these expeditions from taking a prominent place in the domain of history, yet the traditionary accounts of them, ignored by too partial historians of Columbus, go far to prove that the voyage of the latter was no such startling undertaking as has been represented; that the realms which lay beyond the Atlantic were not shrouded in all the mystery of the unknown; nor the ocean itself regarded with that superstitious terror recorded by his eulogists, in order to enhance his courage and superiority over his contemporaries.

Cambrian chroniclers speak confidently of a voyage made by Prince Madoc in the year 1170, to a Western continent. This land is said to have been fertile, and peopled by a race differing in features and complexion from those of Europe. Subsequent writers contend that this new land was no other than the Continent of America.[19]

What may be the amount of credit justly due to these statements is not now easy to determine; yet it is evident that the earlier of these accounts were not written for the purpose of defrauding Columbus. Hakluyt, Humboldt, and others, have given this subject more or less consideration. While it is still shrouded in mystery, there can be little doubt that Madoc made a voyage to distant lands. His name and family were not so obscure as to admit of his disappearing from the scenes of turmoil

[19] The similarity between the name of Madoc and that of the Modoc tribe of Indians has been commented upon by some, who ascribe a Welsh descent to the latter.

and blood with which Wales was afflicted after the death of his father, without attracting the notice of historians of his time, nor is it probable that he remained concealed in his native land, or that he fixed his abode in any portion of the earth with which the isle of Britain had intercourse.

Prince Madoc is the hero of one of Southey's ablest poems. He prefaces it with the following history, which contains all that is known at the present day of the Welsh navigator:

"The historical facts on which this poem is founded may be related in a few words. On the death of Owen Gwyneth, King of North Wales, A. D. 1169, his children disputed the succession. Yorworth, the elder, was set aside without a struggle, as being incapacitated by a blemish in his face. Hoel, though illegitimate, and born of an Irish mother, obtained possession of the throne for a while, till he was defeated and slain by David, the eldest son of the late king by a second wife. The conqueror, who then succeeded without opposition, slew Yorworth, imprisoned Rodri, and hunted others of his brethren into exile. But Madoc, meantime, abandoned his barbarous country, and sailed away to the west, in search of some better resting-place. The land which he discovered pleased him; he left there part of his people, and went back to Wales for a fresh supply of adventurers, with whom he again set sail, and was heard of no more. Strong evidence has been adduced that he reached America."

The poem of Madoc, Mr. Southey informs us, drew upon him the indignation of an American pamphleteer, who denounced him, as having "meditated a most serious injury against the reputation of the New World, by attributing its discovery and colonization to a little vagabond Welsh prince—this being a most insidious attempt against the honor of America and the reputation of Columbus."

To such lengths of blind partiality will men be carried, who care less for the truth of history than for the fame of its creatures. Early historians were not thus scornful of Madoc and his voyages; witness Purchas, who writes: "I will not say but that in these times of old, some ships might come some time by casualty into these parts, but rather forced by weather than directed by skill; and thus it is likely that some parts of America have been peopled . . . . The most probable history (account) in this kind is (in my mind), that of Madoc ap Owen Gwyneth, who, by reason of civil contentions, left his country of Wales, seeking adventures by sea; and, leaving the coast of Ireland north, came to a land unknown, where he saw many strange things." [40]

NICOLO and ANTONIO ZENO flourished in Venice, during the latter part of the fourteenth century (1380). They were active members of a family of warriors, navigators, statesmen, diplomats, and historians; few families have a prouder record than the Zeni; Nicolo and Antonio added to its fame by the adventurous character of their voyages, especially by that in which it is averred that the latter visited the Continent of America.

Purchas, in speaking of discoveries made in the northern parts of the New World, Greenland, New France, etc., says: "The first knowledge that hath come to us of those parts was by Nicholas and Antonio Zeno. . . . Master Nicholo Zeno, being wealthy, and of a haughty spirit, desiring to see the fashions of the world, built and furnished a ship at his own charge, passing the Straits of Gibraltar, held on his course northward, with intent to see England and Flanders, but, a violent tempest assailing him, he was carried he knew not whither." [41] He finally reached Friesland, according to the same old author, and was there with his companions saved from death at the hands of the natives, by Zichmui, who was a chief or ruler in that province. This chief, appreciating the nautical skill of Nicolo, placed him in command of his navy, and subjugated sundry islands. "After divers notable exploits," Nicolo armed three vessels in which he visited *Engroneland* (probably Iceland). Here he found a monastery, and a church dedicated to St. Thomas; this was "hard by a hill, that cast out fire, like *Vesuvius* and *Etna;* there is a fountain of hot water with which they heat the church of the monastery, and the friars' chambers; it cometh also into the kitchen so boiling hot that they use no other fire to dress their meat."

Nicolo returned to Friesland in 1395, and died there; his brother Antonio succeeded to his fortune and honors, and was employed by Zichmui in an expedition to Estotiland. This country we are told lay "to the west of Friesland; the people there possess some gold, sow corn, and make beer;" farther south,

---

[40] "Pilgrimage," pp. 725, 726. The story of Madoc has been carefully examined by John Williams, LL. D. (London, 1791), to which the curious are referred.
[41] "Pilgrimage," p. 735.

they go naked. In one region they visited, the ground was covered with the eggs of wild-fowl. The country was very extensive, and was regarded as a new world. After this voyage Antonio returned to Venice, where he died soon after, in 1405.

Such are the meagre data which have come down to us. Scanty as are the details, they go far to corroborate the assertion that Zeno touched upon the American Continent. Purchas says of the regions above named (New France, etc.), "The best geographers are beholden to these brothers for that little knowledge they have of these parts."

CHAPTER V.

INTRODUCTION TO THE HISTORY OF COLUMBUS.

THERE is an ancient Indian fable which reads: "This beautiful world we inhabit rests on the back of a mighty elephant; the elephant stands on the back of a monster turtle; the turtle rests upon a serpent; the serpent on nothing." It well typifies the many splendid histories of Columbus, eloquent in the praise of their hero, proceeding often from the most eminent authors, and resting upon a stupendous "weight of authority" which is in itself nothing, or, worse than nothing, falsehood; yet, so deeply rooted are these falsehoods in the minds of the multitude, and so difficult are first impressions to erase, that many years will elapse before the question, "Who discovered America?" will not be answered unhesitatingly with the name of Christopher Columbus. Where one author, regarding truth as of more importance than the reputation of any real or pretended hero, labors to show matters pertaining to this discovery in their true light, ten, nay, a hundred, will unreflectingly repeat the universally accepted theory, and stamp it indelibly on the minds of another generation. Great writers have immortalized, poets idealized, and priests would canonize Columbus. In the vindication of truth, the work is truly great, the laborers few, and the attempt to prove that this saintly demi-god was neither great, noble, heroic, nor even honest, appears but a thankless task.

"There is a certain meddlesome spirit," writes Washington Irving, in his "Life of Columbus," "which, in the garb of learned research, goes prying about the traces of history, casting down its monuments, and marring and mutilating its fairest trophies. Care should be taken to vindicate great names from such pernicious erudition. It defeats one of the most salutary purposes of history, that of furnishing examples of what human genius and laudable enterprise may accomplish."[43]

We, too, believe that one of the most laudable purposes of history is to furnish examples of what human genius and enterprise can accomplish, and far be it from us to pry with meddlesome spirit; but, we would ask, Were genius and enterprise concentrated in Columbus only? If others were the authors of a scheme which he imperfectly carried out, should not *their* names be vindicated, *their* genius extolled? If the monuments existing are false, should they not be overthrown, and the real ones raised triumphantly to the pedestals from which they have been so long and unjustly dethroned? Above all, is not truth the greatest and most worthy object of history?

These questions, we believe, answer themselves. Before attempting to mar one of the fairest trophies of history, let us discover by whom this trophy was raised; in a word, let us examine what constituted history, and especially Spanish-American history, at the time of Columbus. Let us not be deterred from rejecting a statement which is evidently untrue, because of the "weight of authority" upon which it rests; nor let us blindly accept a false assertion because sanctioned by an Inquisitor; neither will we denounce in general terms the authorities so often quoted, but endeavor to show their defects and errors, that the reader may himself judge how much is to be accepted as truth, and how much as the result of priestly tyranny, personal vanity, and interested deceit.

"The writing of history, so far as regards the New World," Lord Kingsborough remarks, "was by the law of Spain restricted to men in priestly orders."

To a small work on Mexico, by Boturini, are appended—

1. The declaration of his faith.
2. The license of an Inquisitor.
3. The license of the judge of the Supreme Council of the Indies.
4. The license of the Jesuit father.
5. The license of the Royal Council of the Indies.
6. The approbation of the qualificator of the Inquisition.
7. The license of the Royal Council of Castile.

[43] Irving, "Life of Columbus," book i., chapter v.

Beyond all this, the person must be of sufficient influence to obtain the favorable notice of the bodies thus represented.

Nor was this the end of the difficulty: the license of any one of these officials could be revoked at pleasure; and, when republished, the work had to be reëxamined.

The penalty attached to the possession of a book not thus licensed was death."

In 1524 Venetian merchants were arrested, by the Holy Office, for selling Bibles with commentaries, by a writer of the twelfth century, Rabbi Solomon Raschi; and their release could not be obtained by the Venetian ambassador, because it was alleged that they were arrested for selling books against the Faith.

Such was the tyranny which weighed upon historical writers; and it is not difficult to perceive how all these censors would deal partially with Columbus. By representing himself as the chosen of God, the champion of the Christian religion, carrying the light of the Gospel to heathen nations, by performing the smallest acts with affectation of religious ceremony, by inserting scriptural and religious sentences in his most trivial letters, by recounting miracles and interviews with God, by giving, in fact, a religious coloring to all his acts, he became the *protégé* of the Church, which has continued through all after-centuries to regard him as one of her most zealous votaries, and is now strenuously urged to place him among her saints.

Pope Alexander VI. (Roderigo Borgia) deeded the Continent of America to Spain, solely on the statement of Columbus." To attack the latter was, therefore, to attack the justice of the pope's bull, and an indirect imputation on papal infallibility. "The learned and excellent divine Guistiniani," who published, we believe, the first polyglot edition of the Psalms, was bitterly assailed, and his book condemned to be burned," because, in a note appended to the nineteenth Psalm, containing a sketch of

---

[43] Wilson, "New History of the Conquest of Mexico," chapter, ii., p. 81; Lord Kingsborough," vol. vii., p. 269.

[44] Count Roselly de Lorgues, in his "Life of Columbus" (vol. i., chapter xi., p. 400), speaking of this matter, says: "The pope has faith in Columbus. He yields full credence to him and justifies his calculations. *It is solely on Columbus that he depends; it is relying on Columbus that he engages in the vast partition of the unexplored world, between the crowns of Spain and Portugal. Every thing the messenger of the cross proposes is granted in full, as a thing that is indicated by Providence.*"

[45] Fernando, "Historia del Amirante," chapter ii.

the life of Columbus (suggested by the words "*In omnem terram exivit sonus eorum, et in finis mundi verba eorum*"), there are some statements which are not considered sufficiently flattering to that individual. An examination of this note will prove to the reader how trivial an offense was sufficient to cause the destruction of a valuable work. One of the chief enormities it contains is the allegation that in his early life Columbus was a mechanic; this, his son and historian regards as an unspeakable insult.

Laical censors, owing their authority to the same royal favor which protected Columbus, would naturally regard any history, detrimental to the latter, as militating against the Queen of Castile. Thus it was that in Spain it became necessary for all who would write a history of the New World, to extol Columbus and the Church.

To ecclesiastical tyranny and popular prejudice may be added the exaggerations and falsehoods of the chief actor of the scene, whose statements are accepted as gospel truth, even when at war with reason, common-sense, or known facts, and we shall perceive how difficult it will be to wade through errors, partiality, and injustice, and arrive at the truth regarding the character and deeds of this Columbus and his contemporaries. We have seen how history was compiled in his time. Subsequent Spanish historians, finding, even in the facts recorded, much which would militate against the honor of their country, as well as of the individuals concerned, have endeavored to soften the cruelties and enormities perpetrated; while the modern American writer identifies the glory of his country with that of Columbus, and considers that to record any thing which is not highly in praise of the latter, is to insult America. How far this spirit is carried we may judge from the following passage in Washington Irving:

"Herrera has been accused also of flattering his nation, exalting the deeds of his countrymen, and softening and concealing their excesses.

"There is nothing very serious in this accusation. To illustrate the glory of his nation is one of the noblest offices of the historian; and it is difficult to speak too highly of the extraordinary enterprises and splendid actions of the Spaniards in those days. In softening their excesses he fell into an amiable and pardonable error, if indeed it be an error for a Spaniard to endeavor to sink them in oblivion."

When we read such sentiments from the pen of one of America's ablest writers, we confess that we lose some confidence in his statements. If history were to become the medium through which writers exaggerate the good and conceal the bad in their respective countries and favorite heroes, how vainly should we search for truth in the history of the same events, written in nations variously interested!

The historian has a nobler mission. The good and great he should indeed extol, that after-generations may be impelled to like actions; but that which is disgraceful, cruel, or dishonorable, he should fearlessly condemn; he thus becomes the faithful mirror in which good and bad are alike reflected, exerting a salutary influence in his own country, believed and respected in others.

Illustration of tortures inflicted upon obnoxious or heretical authors of the time of Columbus. The instruments below the burning psalter represent the "Morning Star," or "Holy-water Sprinkler" (so called derisively), with which the blood of heretics was drawn. (*See* Meyrick's "Description of Ancient Arms and Armor at Goodrich Court," vol. ii., plates 92, 93.)

CHAPTER VI.

CONTEMPORARIES OF COLUMBUS.—FERDINAND AND ISABELLA.

IF it is necessary to demonstrate the spirit in which his history has hitherto been written, before attempting a truthful biography of Columbus, it is not less necessary, in order to form a just estimate of his character, to become acquainted with those of his contemporaries with whom he had more or less relation, and who have been favored or injured, according as they were favorable to him; or as their character and achievements, superior to his, would, unless willfully belittled, diminish greatly the meed of praise which has been accorded to him.

The most prominent of these were Ferdinand of Aragon and Isabella of Castile, who are so intricately connected with the history of Columbus that it becomes necessary to elucidate their character, that the reader may judge of their conduct with regard to the latter. It has been too customary to lay the blame of all the calamities which Columbus entailed upon himself, by his deception and inhumanity, upon the "cold and calculating Ferdinand,"[46] " who is represented as having persistently endeavored to frustrate his lofty designs. These charges become void when we consider the marriage articles between Ferdinand and Isabella, signed and sworn to January 7, 1469, in which Ferdinand promised faithfully to respect the laws of Castile; to fix his residence in that kingdom, and not to quit it without the consent of Isabella; to alienate no property belonging to the crown; to prefer no foreigners to municipal offices (his subjects were foreigners in Castile); to make no appointments, civil or military, without her consent or approbation; to resign to her, exclusively, the right of nomination to ecclesiastical benefices, etc., etc."[47]

They lived together, not like man and wife, whose estates

[46] Irving, "Life of Columbus," book xviii., chapter iii.
[47] Prescott, "Ferdinand and Isabella," chapter iii.

were blended, and subject to the direction of the husband, but like allied monarchs, with separate and independent claims to sovereignty, each having their envoys, ministers, counselors, secretaries, and treasurers, and were often removed from each other while superintending their respective interests."⁸ The subjects of Ferdinand were not allowed even to visit the western

FERDINAND OF ARAGON.—(From an Old Engraving in the Burgundian Library.)

⁴⁸ Irving, " Life of Columbus," book ii., chapter ii. Voltaire, " Essai sur les Mœurs." Ferdinand complains thus of his consort: " The reason why you do not write, is not because there is no paper to be had, or that you do not know how to write, but because you do not love me, and because you are proud. You are living at Toledo, I am living in small villages. . . . The affairs of the princess " (their daughter) "must not be forgotten. For God's sake, remember her, as also her father, who kisses your hands, and is your servant." We shall see how the unhappy daughter he alludes to was remembered.

islands when discovered. He was subject to the Queen of Castile, and perfectly unanswerable for any of her proceedings. Astute and suspicious as he no doubt was, he may have mistrusted the adventurer Christopher Columbus, but he was too jealously prevented from having any voice in the affairs of state for his suspicions to have any effect.

Isabella, the patroness of Columbus, has been handed down to posterity as of *"glorious memory,"* the *"sweet queen."* Prescott tells us "her honest soul abhorred any thing like artifice." She is represented as the type of womanly gentleness, virtue, and truth, coupled with masculine courage and intelligence; but, alas! as we peruse her history, and see her character reflected in the numerous dispatches she wrote, we perceive that the priesthood, which raised her to the throne of Castile, has done much toward embellishing her character, and endowing her with fictitious qualities. Transferred, at the early age of sixteen, to a court which Prescott terms "a brothel, private morals too loose to seek even the veil of hypocrisy;" frequently betrothed to men who, if not yielding to the wishes of those who treated for their marriage with the future Queen of Castile, died in a manner as mysterious as sudden; owing her throne itself to a scandalous imputation against her brother's wife, and the brand of illegitimacy affixed to her niece, her early life too soon made her familiar with the immorality and unscrupulous intrigue of the court of Spain at that period.

The fearful fires of the Inquisition filled Spain with a ghastly glare, and it was Isabella who applied the torch. She petitioned for the establishment of Torquemada as grand-inquisitor. Whole towns and villages were depopulated, and their wealth poured into the royal coffers. Living and dead were alike persecuted; bodies were exhumed and burned, while the crown confiscated the wealth of the heirs. Isabella herself says: "I have caused great calamities, and depopulated towns, lands, provinces, and kingdoms;" but this was all done, she protested, from love of Christ and his Holy Mother! Those were liars and calumniators who said she had done so from love of money, for she had never touched a maravedi proceeding from the confiscated goods, but had employed the money in educating and giving marriage-portions to the children of the condemned. It would seem discourteous, if not unjust, to doubt so solemn a declaration; but, as we peruse the state papers, we find orders emanating from the queen which differ widely from the spirit of the above profession. For instance, one Pecho of Xerez was condemned for heresy; his property, amounting to two hundred thousand maravedis, was confiscated. The widow, whose portion was twenty thousand maravedis, was reduced with her children to the utmost destitution. As a special favor, Isabella granted them thirty thousand maravedis, while the remaining hundred and seventy thousand she appropriated to herself. Such cases abound; and while so-called bounties, such as the above, are always recorded, silence is preserved touching the many instances in which she appropriated the whole of the confiscated property. So terrible did her persecutions become, that the pope resolved to send a legate to Spain to investigate the proceedings of the Inquisition. Isabella strove to prevent this.

"She used corruption on a large scale, larger even, as she declared, than was agreeable to herself. The final result was, that the courts of Spain and Rome came to an understanding respecting the person who was to be sent as legate. He received rich donations in Spain, and his inquiry was reduced to a mere form. It is characteristic of the queen, that the only condition she made was that his Holiness should absolve her from simony."[49]

The Inquisition was thus firmly established. Victims multiplied; two thousand men and women were burned, a greater number condemned to living death in the dungeons of that terrible institution, homesteads were abandoned, and thousands fled to neighboring countries. "The queen was implored to relent, but she answered that it was better for the service of God and herself to have the country depopulated, than to have it polluted by heresy."

The *archivero* of Barcelona of that time has recorded a long list of *autos-da-fe*, the victims were of all classes—clergymen, officers in the army, tailors, and cobblers, but there is a disproportionately large number of widows of merchants. Mr. Bergenroth, recording this fact, shrewdly inquires, "Were they really more inclined to heresy, or were they only rich, and comparatively defenseless?"[50]

[49] G. A. Bergenroth, "Introduction to Spanish State Papers," vol. i., 1485–1509.
[50] Idem

Such was the beneficent rule of this virtuous queen over her own subjects. Her relations with foreign powers are equally to her discredit. Her correspondence teems with the grossest insincerity and heartlessness. Her cruel neglect of her daughter shows her to have been sadly deficient in that domestic virtue and affection for which she has been so much praised; a notable example of her deceptive policy and grasping avarice is found in the negotiations which took place for the marriage of her daughter. She established a marriage brokerage in England, where she carried on the disgraceful business for many years, driving bargains, or seeking to do so, upon the persons of her daughters, conducting these negotiations more with an eye to filling her coffers, than to her own honor or her daughters' integrity. Her confidential agent at the court of England was Doctor de Puebla, selected, it is said, "because he was so uncommonly honest," but who, indeed, was a consummate knave, as is abundantly proved, not only by his making himself the medium of the abominable falsehoods he was instructed to utter by the queen, but by the following chapter of his history, contained in the Spanish archives under date of the 18th of July, 1488:

"*The Spanish Merchants residing in London to Sanchez de Londoño and the Sub-prior of Santa Cruz.*

"De Puebla had asked Henry to give a bishopric to him and other good livings to his sons and relatives. On account of the king having refused to do so, he had delayed the conclusion of the treaty of marriage. When Henry was in his greatest difficulties with Scotland and Perkin" (Warbeck), "De Puebla had repeated his demands. Henry had answered that he was unfit to become a bishop, because he was a cripple. De Puebla then proposed that the bishopric should be given to a certain procurator of Henry in Rome, from whom he had got one thousand gold crowns, for his promise to procure letters for him from the King and Queen of Spain to the pope, recommending him for a cardinal's hat. Henry was in such great difficulties then, that he had acceded to the proposals of De Puebla, and promised fifteen thousand crowns a year, besides, to one of his sons. As soon as De Puebla had obtained what he wanted, he concluded the marriage, which was so advantageous to Henry, that, in consequence of it, peace with Scotland was concluded, Perkin turned out of Scotland, and the rebels punished. Some merchants from Genoa had subjected themselves to a penalty in England; they gave five hundred crowns, and cloth, and silk, for the marriage, to De Puebla, who settled their affair with Henry.

"De Puebla had sold two licenses of the king for importing wine and woad, in Spanish vessels, to Spanish merchants, for two hundred crowns.

"Francisco de Arvieto, of Orduña, had paid De Puebla one hundred gold crowns for a pardon for perjury.

"Similar things are done almost daily by De Puebla. When he took part in the negotiations with Flanders, he persuaded the archduke to impose a duty of one gold florin on every piece of English cloth, the consequences of which have been to cause prolonged debates and great disasters.

"There is not a Spanish captain, or even a single sailor, who is not obliged to pay more or less to De Puebla if he has any thing to do in England. De Puebla often takes money from both parties if he has to decide a lawsuit. He is a spy and secret informer in all kinds of contraventions committed by subjects of any nation, only for the purpose of making money by his information. He and his servants sell testimonials of all kinds.

"De Puebla constantly complains that he is badly paid, and he begs money from the king and the gentlemen of the court. He lives meanly. He has been three years in a house of a mason, who keeps dishonest women. He eats with them and with all the apprentices at the same table, for twopence a day. His landlord robs men who come to his house, and the ambassador protects him, in his dishonest trade, against the police.

"The consequence of all this is that the Spaniards are less esteemed and worse treated in England than any other foreigners."

Elsewhere we read, "In a word, De Puebla was a liar, flatterer, calumniator, beggar, spy, secret informer, enemy of truth, full of lies."

The above are a few of the leading traits of character which seem to have so endeared De Puebla to Isabella that she retained him in office after those who had been sent to England to investigate his character and conduct had reported that "all the paper in England would not suffice to describe the character of that man."

Her letters of instruction to him contain statements not only false but disgusting, and, though avarice and deceit are palpable throughout her multifarious and protracted negotiations to marry her daughter, now to this prince, now to that, and now to some other, she affects to be making great sacrifices "for the love of Christ and his Holy Mother." In 1490 she writes to De Puebla, calling him her "virtuous and intimate friend," urging him to persuade the King of England to declare war on France; similar efforts were made to induce the King of Scots to join the coalition against France, and Isabella offered him her daughter, Princess Katherine, as an inducement—the said princess was then betrothed to Arthur, Prince of Wales; but Isabella kept that betrothal secret, that she might impose upon other parties.

Henry of England obtaining an inkling of the above transaction, and not being quite satisfied, he was reassured by Isabella, who informed him that the King of Scots was to be the only dupe, and that it was to prevent the latter from aiding Warbeck, the so-called Duke of York. The huckstering with regard to the marriage of Isabella's children fills the reader of her dispatches with disgust—the manner in which the matter was discussed being worse, if possible, than the object intended.[51]

---

[51] Honest De Puebla writes his affectionate mistress that he has examined the person of her intended son-in-law, first clothed, then naked, and lastly when sleeping, and declares him possessed of admirable parts.

Isabella was not to be outdone, even by the despicable De Puebla, for we find her subsequently seeking to drive a bargain upon the real or pretended *virginity of her widowed daughter*, and for proof referring to Doña Elvira, "the first lady of the bedchamber." Fearing that the latter may not be believed, she would establish the fact by a cloud of witnesses.

On the 16th of June, 1502, she writes the Duke of Estrada: "Be careful also to get at the truth as regards the fact whether the Prince and Princess of Wales consummated the marriage, since nobody has told us about it. You must, moreover, use all the flattering persuasion you can to prevent them from concealing it from you." On the 12th of July of the same year, she continues to instruct the duke in this delicate mission as follows:

"But now you must see of how great importance it is that there should be no delay in making the agreement for the contract of marriage of the Princess of Wales, our daughter, with the Prince of Wales who now is . . . . Therefore, since it is '*already known for a certainty that the said Princess of Wales*,' our daughter, '*remains as she was*

De Puebla writes to Ferdinand and Isabella, July 18, 1488, as follows:

"When speaking of the marriage, the king" (Henry VII.) "broke out into a *Te Deum laudamus*."

"The English declared, with regard to the alliance, there was not much to confer about, and began directly to speak of the marriage. They were exceedingly civil, and said a great many things in praise of Ferdinand and Isabella; that being done, they asked the Spaniards to name the sum for the marriage-portion.

"The *Spanish ambassador* replied that it would be more becoming for the *English* to name the marriage-portion, because they had first solicited the marriage, and their party is a son. The *English commissioners* asked five times as much as they had asked in Spain.

"The Spanish ambassador proposed to refer this amount to Ferdinand and Isabella, who would act liberally in proportion to the confidence shown them.

"The English commissioners said that such a proceeding would be inconvenient for both parties, and that Ferdinand and Isabella would not agree to it.

"The Spanish ambassador complained that the English were unreasonable in their demands. Bearing in mind what happens every day to the Kings of England, it is surprising that Ferdinand and Isabella should dare to give their daughter at all. This was said with great courtesy, in order that they might not feel displeasure or be enraged.

"The English commissioners abated one-third.

"The Spaniards proposed that, as there was sufficient time for it, two or four persons should be selected as umpires.

here' (*for so Doña Elvira has written to us*), endeavor to have the said contract agreed to immediately, without consulting us; for any delay that might take place would be dangerous. See also that the articles be made and signed, and sworn to at once, and, if nothing more advantageous can be procured, let it be settled as was proposed. In that case let it be declared that the King of England has already received from us one hundred thousand scudos in gold, in part payment of the dowry, and let that be made an obligatory article of the contract, with a view to restitution, in accordance with the former directions given you. Let it be likewise stipulated that we shall pay the rest of the dowry when the marriage is consummated, so please God; that is, if you should not be able to obtain more time. But, take heed, on no account to agree for us to pay what still remains of the dowry until the marriage shall have been consummated. . . . Be very vigilant about this, and endeavor to have the contract made, without delay, and without consulting us. Do not, however, let them see you have any suspicion of hinderance, or show so much eagerness that it may cause them to cool."

The English commissioners declined it, and gave their reasons.

"The Spaniards desired the English to name their lowest price.

"The English abated one-half.

"The Spaniards said that this marriage would be so advantageous to the King of England that he ought to content himself with what is generally given with princesses of Spain.

"The English desired to have every thing defined, in order to avoid disputes after the conclusion of the marriage. They asked twice as much as they had asked in Spain.

"The Spanish ambassador offered one-fourth.

"The English asked why, as the money was not to come out of the strong boxes of the king and queen, but out of the pockets of their subjects, they should not be more liberal. They referred to old treaties with France, Burgundy, and Scotland, proving by them that even higher marriage-portions were given."

When the marriage is at length concluded, there is a large amount of negotiation as to who shall pay the passage of the Princess Katherine to England, and who shall clothe her. We read in one dispatch:

"Ferdinand and Isabella are to send the princess in a decent manner, and at their own expense, to London.

"They are to dress their daughter suitably to her rank" (*honorifice*), "and to give her as many jewels, etc., for her personal use as becomes her position."

In answer to which, Isabella writes De Puebla:

"King Henry asks them to bind themselves to give their daughter ornaments and apparel, without deducting the amount from the marriage-portion. Such a proceeding is against custom. Husbands provide the dresses of their wives. They are willing to buy as many dresses and ornaments for the Princess Katherine as the English wish, provided the cost be deducted from the marriage-portion, and, if not, they will give what *they* think proper. . . . He is to inform himself what the dowry of the queen would be in such a case, and to secure to the Princess Katherine a somewhat larger dowry than other Queens of England have enjoyed."

Again Isabella insists that " one-half, or one-third, or at any rate the fourth part" (of the marriage-portion), "must be accepted in ornaments and apparel for the person and household of the infanta."

This daughter became a widow on the 2d of April, 1502. The news does not seem to have reached Isabella until more than a month after the death of the English prince. She loses no time, but on the 10th of May, 1502, commissions the Duke of Estrada to endeavor to conclude a marriage between her widowed daughter and the Prince of Wales, surviving brother of her late husband, with instructions as to dower, etc., etc.

This done, it is not till two days later that she writes, for the eye of King Henry, the following letter of condolence to her minister at London: "Have read with profound sorrow the news of the death of Prince Arthur. The affliction caused by all their former losses has been revived by it. But the will of God must be obeyed."

Richard III. excited disgust by courting a widow beside the bier of her late husband. Had Isabella chanced to be in England at the death of this son-in-law, it seems probable that negotiations for a second husband for her bereaved daughter would have preceded the funeral of the first.

Again, her deceit is manifested by the following instruction to Estrada, who is negotiating for this second marriage: "In case that you hear any thing of the King of France, appear as if you did not know it, until after the treaty of marriage is concluded." (The King of France had just declared war on Spain.) "Afterward you must show to the King of England the relation which we send you of the matters between us and the King of France."

All this bargaining for a daughter's marriage, and the duplicity with which it is carried on, certainly evince that avarice, meanness, and deceit, were attributes of Isabella's character. But, should further proof seem necessary, it may be found in the following extracts from a document in which Isabella commissions Estrada to raise an army in England:

"*Queen Isabella of Spain to Ferdinand, Duke of Estrada, October* 3, 1503.

" If the King of England should not be inclined to afford us further assistance, he must, at any rate, be pleased to give us the assistance which is obligatory upon him; and, upon our forwarding the money, send us troops. *Tell him that you have the money,* and that we pray and require him to be willing, immediately, to send two thousand English infantry, picked men and well armed .... this being done, you shall endeavor to make them embark instantly .... try your utmost to have the troops you shall thus send, the best chosen, and the best armed, that it is possible to obtain; and get them to come as soon as ever they can. ... As regards the pay that will have to be made to the said troops, endeavor to let it be as little as possible .... (three ducats per month are suggested). ... *Borrow the money that will be required for the aforesaid pay,* agreeing for us to repay it in England, on the terms stipulated by you .... But, should you not have ships at present, in which the said infantry can come as above said, you must not give them any pay. Endeavor, however, to find out how many troops are to come .... spread abroad a report in England that there are many more troops going to Spain; because, as you will see, such tidings and rumors will inspire France with fear, and will produce a favorable impression in Italy.

"If you should see that it will not annoy the King of England our brother, and the chief men of his kingdom, and that it can do no harm, make use of the Princess of Wales, our daughter; that is to say, should you not be able to obtain the money necessary for the dispatch of the said troops; .... in that case, you shall say to her, by virtue of my letter of credence which I will send, that you pray her to raise, upon her jewels and plate, the money which may be necessary for the dispatch of the two thousand infantry."

This dispatch concerning the army might naturally be supposed to pertain to Ferdinand, but the reader will perceive that it bears the name of Isabella alone; it contains as much falsehood and duplicity as could well be inclosed in so small a space. First, her agent is instructed to tell the king he has the money; secondly, to borrow the money on the credit of Isabella; thirdly, to obtain it by pawning the jewels and plate of Princess Katherine. Nor can the meanness be overlooked with which she stipulates for the best troops, best equipped, poorest paid, and most hastily concentrated; and then, if she should not be ready to transport them, they are to receive no pay. Furthermore, her agent is charged to circulate a false report with regard to the number of troops. Finally, let us consider the financial condition of the Princess Katherine (who is to raise the necessary funds), from her own account. She had always been kept in straitened circumstances till, in 1502, she writes to her father thus :

"No woman, of whatever station in life, can have suffered more than she has. None of the promises made to her on the occasion of her marriage, have been kept. Repeats once more that which has formed the principal part of all her letters, namely, the necessity of sending a suitable ambassador with sufficient means of subsistence. The circumstance that the former ambassadors were not properly provided for, has been the cause of all her sufferings .... Has never told him the whole extent of her misery. Has been treated worse in England than any other woman. ... Has not more than five women in her service. They have not received the smallest sum of money since they were in England, and have spent all that they possessed. Cannot think of them without pangs of conscience. No money could pay their services and sacrifices, which have continued during six years. Has been unable to pay a single penny to the courier who takes this letter."

Alonzo de Escobal, of the household of Princess Katherine, writes to Almazan (September 6, 1507): "He would not mention his great necessity if there were any other means to remedy it; begs him to remind the king in what poverty the servants of the Princess of Wales live. Thinks he has a right to ask at least his salary, is obliged to sell his clothes. Has seen the Princess of Wales only three times since Doña Elvira has left her. Doña went away in a horrible hour; but such things are better suited for conversation than for letters."

Again the Princess of Wales writes :

"That her necessities have risen to such a height, that she knows not how she shall be able to sustain herself, now that even her household goods have been sold."

Few will deny, after perusing the extracts we have given, that Isabella is proved, by her own words and acts, to have been an unloving wife, an unnatural mother, a cruel and despotic sovereign, a deceitful and treacherous ally, an avaricious and unscrupulous woman. It is easy to perceive how in spite of all this so much partiality has been shown her, often to the detriment of her husband. Besides the favor of the Church, for which she professed so much zeal, the chivalry of the Spaniards has always made them remember she was a lady, and they have dealt courteously with her. Moreover, her marriage did not smother the old rivalry and strife between the *Corona* and *Coronilla*. Isabella represented the *corona*, or great crown of Castile, while Ferdinand merely represented the *coronilla*, or small crown of Aragon. Castile never regarded him with favor, considering him an intruder, who had much to gain and little to lose by his alliance, and the opinion of Castile, as the leading and larger portion of the kingdom, has been received as that of all Spain. It is difficult for the most impartial historian not to be influenced by such a judgment, unless he refer to the original papers and letters of the time, and with their assistance form an opinion of his own.

That we may not appear wantonly to have inveighed against a sovereign who has so long been considered a shining light, we will not rest solely upon the views we may have derived from our own investigation, but will quote the conclusions at which Mr. Bergenroth, who spent many years in arduous study amid the archives of Simancas, has at length arrived. His familiarity with the state papers renders him abundantly competent to give an opinion:

"Neither Ferdinand nor Isabella scrupled to tell direct untruths, and make false promises, whenever they thought it expedient to their policy. But if any distinction is to be made, certainly Queen Isabella excelled her husband in disregard to veracity. It even seems to have been a matter of understanding between them that, whenever any very flagrant falsehood was to be uttered, she should be the one to do it. . . . Ferdinand had not the reputation, among princes of his time, of being a very untruthful man. . . . The queen often spoke of her dress. She dwelt much upon her simplicity, and laid great stress on the circumstance that she had been obliged to receive the French ambassadors twice in the same costume, while she spent large sums to the glory of God, and the good of the world. This kind of letters have often been published, and have not a little contributed to exalt her as a pious character. But such persons as had opportunities of seeing her, and of judging by their own observations, could not find words expressive enough to describe the splendor of her attire. . . . Machada assured the King of England that a single toilet of Queen Isabella amounted in value to two hundred thousand scudi, and that he never saw her twice, even on the same day, whether it were at an audience, a bull-fight, or a ball, in the same costume; we may, therefore, con-

ISABELLA OF CASTILE.—(From an Authentic Engraving in the Burgundian Library.)

jecture that she carried on her person the greater portion of the contents of the royal exchequer. . . . Neither Ferdinand nor Isabella were scholars. They spoke and wrote Spanish well, but seemed to have been unable to understand any other language. With regard to their moral character, the queen has been extolled as simple-hearted and pious, while a large amount of opprobrium has been cast upon the king. But it is very difficult, where two persons are so intimately united as Ferdinand and Isabella, to decide what measure of praise or blame attaches to the one or the other. They quarreled sometimes about their private concerns. It could scarcely be otherwise, when we remember that Ferdinand had four illegitimate children by different mothers. But in their aggressive foreign policy, and in their measures of oppression at home, they were always agreed. . . . She (Isabella) appears to have been very liable to mistake her own interests for those of God, whose name she constantly had on her lips, or to substitute self-gratification for real love of the people. For instance, in her letter to Henry VII., dated September 15, 1496, she enlarged in the most touching terms on the blessings of peace, and concluded by saying that, if it were possible to avoid thereby the calamities of war, she would not only send one and more than one embassy to the King of France, but that she would go to him in her own person, and ask him to make peace, not sparing herself any trouble or pains whatever. No words can be more becoming a great and pious queen. It is to be regretted that, in the same letter, she urged the King of England to declare war on France, and thereby to render the bloodshed and slaughter more general even than it was. . . . Queen Isabella left behind her, or, more accurately speaking, acquired after her death, the reputation of having been almost a saint. But, unhappily, the sanctity of Isabella was only of a spurious kind. Her subjects, who had suffered from her iron rule, had formed a widely different idea of her. When, on Tuesday, the 17th of November, 1504, she died at Medina del Campo, crowds assembled under the windows of her palace, but not to bless her memory. From curious criminal proceedings instituted some years later against Sarmiento, *corregidor* or mayor of Medina, we learn that he did not hesitate to declare that her soul had gone direct to hell, for her cruel oppression of her subjects, and that King Ferdinand was a thief and a robber. Nor was Sarmiento the only person who thought thus, as the witnesses deposed that all the people around Medina and Valladolid, that is to say, where the queen was best known, had formed the same judgment of her."

We will conclude with the following opinion, at which Mr. Bergenroth arrives, and which appears pertinent and correct·

"We are not reduced to depend upon public opinion, knowing enough of her to judge for ourselves; and, to any one acquainted with the lawless times of her youthful years, it must be obvious that, had she really been so pious, so meek, and self-sacrificing a princess as her admirers would fain have us believe, she would have been trodden under foot, instead of usurping, as she did, the crown of her niece."

This brief investigation of the character of Isabella has appeared to us necessary. She has hitherto been regarded as of an almost saintly nature; the mere fact of such a woman having tendered her gracious protection and friendship to Columbus, would of itself speak highly in his favor. But, when we become acquainted with the true character of Isabella, it is easy to understand how she cajoled him as long as his splendid falsehoods promised to gratify her cupidity, and abandoned him when his untruthfulness was discovered.

Ferdinand, who has been made the scape-goat, was, as we have already shown, wholly unanswerable for the proceeding of Isabella in this as in all matters pertaining to Castile. In spite of this unanswerable evidence, Mr. Irving does not hesitate to say: "Let the ingratitude of Ferdinand stand recorded in its full extent, and endure throughout all time. The dark shadow which it casts upon his brilliant renown will be a lesson to all rulers, teaching them what is important to their own fame in their treatment of illustrious men."

CHAPTER VII.

CONTEMPORARIES OF COLUMBUS—(CONTINUED)

AMERIGO VESPUCCI.

The leading incidents in the life of Vespucci are better known than his character is rightly judged; we will therefore give but a rapid sketch of the former, and, in speaking of the lat-

ter, dwell somewhat upon certain facts which, it appears to us, go far toward rehabilitating the memory of this great man, who has been so unjustly censured and condemned.

AMERIGO was the son of Nastagio Vespucci and Lisbetta Mini his wife. The family was an old and honored one in the fifteenth century; before the time of Amerigo they had left the little village of Peretola, whence they originated, and came to Florence, where they resided in the stately mansion which was afterward a hospital for the sick under the care of the Brothers of St. John of God. In this house Amerigo was born, on the 9th of March, 1451. Over the entrance is an inscription commemorating the fact, also the achievements of the great man; it reads thus:

"AMERIGO VESPUCCIO PATRICIO FLORENTINO
OB REPERTAM AMERICAM
SUI ET PATRIAE NOMINIS ILLUSTRATORI
AMPLIFICATORI. ORBIS. TERRARUM.
IN HAC OLIM VESPUCCIA DOMO
A TANTO VIRO HABITATA
PATRES SANCTI IOANNIS DE DEO CULTORES
GRATAE MEMORIAE CAUSSA." [66]

Amerigo passed his youth in study, under Giorgi Antonio Vespucci, his uncle (a Dominican friar who instructed many of the youth of Florence), and on reaching manhood he entered the commercial career in the famous house of the Medici. As confidential agent of this house, he was in 1492 sent to Spain to superintend business transactions in that country. The trust reposed in him by such eminent men as the Medici and Berardi is a sufficient encomium upon the capacity and honesty of Vespucci; and not the least proof of his integrity is the fact that the suspicious King Ferdinand of Aragon (who regarded Columbus as an impostor, or at best an unworthy adventurer) reposed such confidence in him that he appointed him to assist in the discoveries he desired to be made in the West. The antecedents of Vespucci seem far better to have qualified him for a serious under-

[66] "To Americus Vespucius, a noble Florentine,
Who, by the discovery of America,
Rendered his own and his country's name illustrious,
The amplifier of the world,
Upon this ancient mansion of the Vespucci,
Inhabited by so great a man,
The Holy Fathers of St. John of God
Have erected this tablet, sacred to his memory.

taking than those of Columbus. During his well-spent youth he had made geography, cosmography, and astronomy, objects of special study, while the nautical experience of the latter had been gained during a long career of piracy.

The first voyage of Vespucci was at the instance of King Ferdinand, in 1497, as is stated in his letter relating the events which took place therein.[a] His detractors seek to cast odium upon him, by declaring this letter an invention, and the voyage a fiction. This charge may be refuted by reference to the letter itself. From the description contained in it of the bay of Venezuela, that province received its name. He writes:

"We landed in a port where we found a village built over the water, like Venice. There were about forty-four houses, shaped like bells, built upon very large piles, having entrances by means of drawbridges, so that, by laying the bridges from house to house, the inhabitants could pass through the whole. When the people saw us they appeared to be afraid of us, and, to protect themselves, suddenly raised all their bridges, and shut themselves up in their houses. While we stood looking at them and wondering at this proceeding, we saw coming toward us by sea about two-and-twenty canoes, which are the boats they make use of, and are carved out of a single tree. They came directly toward our boats, appearing to be astonished at our figures and dress, and keeping at a little distance from us. This being the case, we made signals of friendship, to induce them to come nearer us, endeavoring to reassure them by every token of kindness; but, seeing that they did not come, we went toward them. They would not wait for us, however, but fled to the land, making signs for us to wait, and giving us to understand that they would soon return. They fled directly to a mountain, but did not tarry there long, and, when they returned, brought with them sixteen of their young girls, and, entering their canoes, came to our boats and put four of them into each boat, at which we were very much astonished, as your excellency may well imagine. Then they mingled with their canoes among our boats, and we considered their coming to speak to us in this manner to be a token of friendship. Taking this for granted, we saw a great crowd of people swimming toward us from the houses, without any suspicion. At this juncture, some old women showed them-

---

[a] F. A. de Vanhagen, "Analyse Critique de la Vie de Vespuce."

selves at the doors of their houses, wailing and tearing their hair, as if in great distress. From this we began to be suspicious, and had immediate recourse to our weapons, when suddenly the girls, who were in our boats, threw themselves into the sea, and the canoes moved away, the people in them assailing us with their bows and arrows.

VESPUCCI IN VENEZUELA.—(Reduced from Herrera's "History of the West Indies.")

At the time Vespucci's letter was published, no description of the countries in question existed; yet his minute accounts of the appearance, religion, and customs of the inhabitants, as well as of the vegetation, formation of the coast, etc., were corroborated by subsequent visitors to that part of America between Honduras and Chesapeake, which we are led to infer was the scene of his first voyage. He must, therefore, have either visited the country, or possessed the gift of divination."

Other writers, equally virulent against the Florentine discoverer, declare that he sailed in a subordinate capacity under Vincent Yanez Pinzon, and Juan Solis. This is an ungenerous attempt to belittle a great man. Isabella had, at the urgent instigation of Columbus, passed a decree forbidding any voyages to the islands recently discovered, except under the command of the latter. This decree was revoked in 1494, in favor of all subjects of Castile, who were thenceforward authorized to prepare expeditions at their own expense, or at that of the crown, for the purpose of discovering Western lands for Castile. They were obliged to depart from Cadiz, having presented themselves before the officers of the crown to obtain a license. Amerigo being an alien, employed by the King of Aragon, could not, therefore, openly command an expedition, and it was probably nominally conducted by Vincent Yanez and Juan Solis. These men were skillful pilots. Vespucci was, however, their equal if not superior in cosmographical knowledge; and, although his letters, contrasting in this point strongly with those of Columbus, are singularly devoid of all personal allusion to himself of a laudatory character, they evidently emanate from a man of intellect and science, carefully noting the appearance and habits of a new country and people, for the purpose of reporting the particulars. It is believed, therefore, that the expedition, by whomsoever nominally conducted for the purpose of evading the national edict, was really directed by Amerigo.

The second voyage of Vespucci was in 1499, and we have reason to believe he was accompanied by Alonzo de Ojeda, from whom, however, he became separated during the voyage, Ojeda's return to Spain being previous to that of Vespucci. In this voyage he touched upon the most easterly point of Brazil, and coasted northwestward as far as the island of Curaçao and the gulf of Paria, where he writes he bought pearls of the natives for a mere nothing. He then sailed for Hispaniola, where he was to take on provisions and repair his ships. His crew were maltreated by those who were in the island with Columbus, "from envy I believe," he writes, but refrains from entering into particulars. He returned to Spain on the 8th of September,

[14] Varnhagen, " Analyse critique," p. 94.

1500. He was received, we are told, with great joy by all, particularly by the king and queen. He brought fine pearls and precious stones of great value, which were placed in the royal gallery. His fame spread far and wide, and in his native city, Florence, there was great exultation over his success—so great that public places were, by order of the signiory, illuminated three nights, which was considered a great honor, accorded by vote, with much solemnity, to the worthiest and greatest citizens only."

While he was in Seville, reposing from the fatigues of these two voyages, the King of Portugal sent thither agents who were to persuade him to prosecute for that monarch the discovery of Brazil, which Cabral had accidentally made in 1500. Vespucci consented, and it was in the service of Portugal that he undertook his third voyage. He explored the coast of Brazil southward, and some authors state that, in adopting a southeastern course, he discovered an island which was no other than Giorgio; this, however, is merely hypothetical. The details of this, as of the other voyages, are to be found in the authentic letters of Amerigo, which were published during his lifetime. On his return to Lisbon, in September, 1502, so great was the satisfaction of the King of Portugal at the manner in which he had conducted the enterprise, that in May, 1503, six caravels were placed at his disposal, wherewith to search for a southwestern passage to the Indies. In this he was not successful, and, after being separated from the other ships (one of which he afterward rejoined), he again touched on Brazil, followed its coast southward till he reached Cape Frio, where he took on a large quantity of Brazil-wood; he also built a fortress and founded a small factory, and returned to Lisbon on the 18th of June, 1504. Ferdinand of Spain was now eager to regain his services. His rare knowledge and experience rendered him equally valuable to each of the rival monarchs. Ferdinand prevailed, and in 1505 Vespucci returned to Spain. About this time he married a lady of Seville, Maria Cerezo, by whom, however, he left no children. Amerigo now occupied himself in fitting out ships for an expedition which was to go in search of the spice-lands of Asia. These preparations, though commenced in 1505, were not completed

---

[55] Bandini, "Vita di Amerigo Vespucci," cap. iii., p. 45.

till 1507, from the fact, perhaps, of its having been stipulated that the ships were to be new ones.

There is a possibility of Vespucci having made a fifth voyage during this interval, which some writers believe was the cause of the peculiar favors accorded him by the Spanish crown; it is as probable, however, if not more so, that the king, recognizing his merit and learning, desired to profit by them. However this may be, the office of Pilot-Major of Spain was created for him in 1508, and he was charged to examine and instruct all pilots in the use of the astrolabe, to ascertain whether their practical knowledge equaled their theoretical; also to revise maps, and to compose one of the new lands, to be regarded as standard."

⁵⁶ The royal order, appointing Vespucci to this office, which was read and published in all the cities, villages, and hamlets of the kingdom, reads thus: . . . "We command that all pilots of our kingdom and lordships, who now are, shall henceforward be, or desire to be, pilots on the said route to the said islands and *terra firma* which we hold in the Indies, and other parts of the ocean seas, shall be instructed and possess all necessary knowledge of the use of the quadrant and astrolabe; and in order that they may unite practice with theory, and profit thereby in the said voyages which they may make to the said lands, they shall not be able to embark as pilots in the said vessels, nor receive wages for pilotage, nor shall merchants be able to negotiate with them as such, nor captains receive them on board their ships, *without their having been first examined by you, Amerigo Despuchi, our pilot-major, and receiving from you a certificate of examination and approbation,* certifying that they are possessed each one of the knowledge aforesaid; holding which certificate, we command that they be held and received as expert pilots, wherever they shall show themselves. for it is our will and pleasure that you should be examiner of the said pilots. And, that those who do not possess the required knowledge, shall the more easily acquire it, we command that you shall instruct, at your residence in Seville, all such as shall be desirous of learning and remunerating you for your trouble.

" And as it might well happen that at first there should be a scarcity of examined pilots, and that thereby vessels might be detained, and damage and loss ensue to the people of the said islands and the merchants and others who trade therewith, we command you, the said Amerigo, and give you license to choose from among the pilots and mariners who have voyaged thither, the most able, that for one voyage or two, or for a certain space of time they may supply the demand, while others are acquiring the necessary knowledge, and on their return you shall assign to them a period in which they may learn whatever they may be deficient in. And as it has been told us that there are many different charts, by different captains, of the lands and islands of the Indies belonging to us, and by our orders recently discovered, the which charts differ greatly from each other, both in the route indicated and in the position of the lands, which causes much inconvenience—therefore, that there may be order in all things, it is our will and pleasure that a standard chart shall be made; and, that it may be the more correct, we command the officer of our Board of Trade in Seville to call an assembly of our most able pilots, that shall at that time be in the country, and, in presence of you, the said Amerigo Despuchi, our pilot-major, there shall be planned

He led this comparatively tranquil life for four years, and died the 22d of February, 1512. He left no wealth, having seemingly lost sight of pecuniary interest in his desire to prosecute voyages of discovery; his papers he left to his nephew, Juan Vespucci. A pension was granted his widow, which after her death was made reversible to her sister.

In none of his writings does Vespucci claim for himself advancement, honor, or emolument, nor does he seek to delude his patrons with visions of untold wealth. His letters are the easy effusions of a great mind filled with admiration at the fertile regions, balmy climate, and primitive races of the New World. Ever modest, he merges himself in the greatness of his undertaking; and, if the civilized world with one accord gave his name to the regions he was the first in modern times to visit, it was a tribute which it deemed just, and paid unasked. Why, then, should we be taught to consider this judgment unjust? When the Church, with its Inquisition, before whose severe censorship all works of history (and more especially those relating to the new lands) had to pass, was laboring with unremitting zeal for the aggrandizement of Columbus, and the ignoring of all his contemporaries, no opposition was raised in Spain to the naming of the con-

---

and drawn a chart of all the lands and islands of the Indies, which have hitherto been discovered belonging to our kingdom; and upon this consultation, subject to the approval of you, our pilot-major, a standard chart shall be drawn, which shall be called the *Royal Chart*, by the which all pilots must direct and govern themselves. This shall remain in the possession of our said officers, and of you, our said pilot-major; and no pilot shall *use any other chart, without incurring a penalty of fifty doubloons*, to be paid to the Board of Trade of the Indies in the city of Seville. We also command all pilots of our kingdoms and lordships that henceforward shall go to the said lands of the Indies, discovered or to be discovered, that should they find new lands, islands, bays, or ports, or any other thing worthy of note, they shall mark it upon the said Royal Chart, and, returning to Castile, shall go and give an account thereof to you, our said pilot-major, and to the officers of the Board of Trade in Seville, that all may be put down in its place in the said Royal Chart, to the end that navigators may be the more apt and learned in navigation. Moreover, we command that none of our pilots, who shall henceforward navigate the ocean seas, shall be without their quadrant and astrolabe, and the appurtenances thereof, under penalty of being disqualified for service for as long a time as it shall be our pleasure, and shall not be able to resume their position without our special license, and without paying a fine of ten thousand maravedis to the said Board of Trade of Seville. And it is our will and pleasure that in virtue of the above, you, the said Amerigo Despuchi, shall use and exercise the said functions of our pilot-major, and shall be able to do, and shall do, all things pertaining to that office, contained in this our letter," etc.—NAVARETTE, " Coleccion de los viajes y Descubrimientos," etc., etc., vol. iii., p. 299.

tinent after its first explorer. Moreover, we read that the name was given by a royal mandate emanating from the crown of Castile. Apiano,"⁷ who wrote almost contemporaneous with Columbus and Vespucci, makes no mention of the former in his chapter on America, but merely states that this " fourth part of the world received its name from Amerigo Vespucci, discoverer of the same, . . . in 1497, by order of the King of Spain." Viscount Santarem, in a life of Vespucci, which evinces extreme hostility to the latter, and unbounded partiality to the cause of Columbus, seeks to account for the naming of the continent from the fact that a "*host of eminent geographers and historians who wrote during the lifetime or immediately after the death of Columbus, ascribe the discovery of the New World to Amerigo, and name it after him* in their histories, geographies, and maps." He adds, "Which name Apian, Vadiamus, and Camers, have since widely spread through Strasbourg, Friburg, and Vienna, while the prodigious celebrity of the little book of Apian has propagated the evil by innumerable editions published in Holland and elsewhere." He might have said in Spain,⁶⁸ in the language of which country the work was published, having passed the severe censorship of the Church, Crown, and Inquisition, to which, as we have already stated, all works relating to the new lands were subjected. If, therefore, we find in a book, bearing the impress of the Inquisition, a statement militating against the claims of Columbus, which we know the Inquisition sought to further to the utmost, we may very reasonably infer that statement to have been regarded as incontestable. *We know* that Columbus lived upon friendly terms with Vespucci for more than seven years after the latter had publicly laid claim to the discovery of the continent.⁶⁹ Las Casas, moreover, writes : "I cannot but wonder that Hernando Colon, a clear-sighted man, who, *as I certainly know, had in his hand* Amerigo's account of his travels, should not have remarked in them any deceit or injustice toward the admiral." We presume that Fernando, as well as his father, was more competent to judge of the causes of their silence upon

---

⁵⁷ An eminent geographer and astronomer.

⁵⁸ The Spanish copy of Apiano, from which our extract is taken, was published only fifteen years after the death of Columbus.

⁵⁹ Herrera, relating events which happened in 1501, tells us, as of an old story, that "Americus Vespuccius was, with Ojeda, *still persisting* in arrogating to himself the honor of having discovered the continent." Columbus died in 1506.

this subject than Las Casas, or any other of their extravagant admirers; and had there been the least pretext for refuting the statements of Vespucci, or denying his achievements, it is not likely they would have failed to do so; yet in after-years the votaries of Columbus raised the hue-and-cry of imposition against Vespucci; they tampered with his letters, changing dates,[60] suppressing or perverting facts, that there might be apparent inconsistency in his narrative. The man thus assailed is proved to have led a noble and useful life, earning and retaining the respect of all with whom he had relations, not excepting Columbus, whom he is accused of having wronged, and who seems to have quarreled with every man connected with him or the Western lands, saving Amerigo Vespucci only. The following letter is sufficient proof of the light in which Columbus regarded Amerigo:

"To my very Dear Son Diego Columbus:

"My dear son, Diego Mendez departed from this place on Monday, the 3d of this month. After his departure I conversed with Amerigo Vespucci, the bearer of this, who has been summoned to court upon matters of navigation. He has always been desirous of pleasing me, and is a very worthy man. Fortune has been unpropitious to him, as to many others, and his labors have not profited him as much as reason would seem to require. He goes for me, and with a great desire to do something which may redound to my advantage, if it is in his power. I know not here what instructions to give him that will benefit me, because I know not what is desired of him there. He goes determined to do for me all that is possible. See what can be done to advantage there, and labor for it, that he may know and

[60] Vanhagen, who has done more than any one man toward demonstrating the injustice which has been done Vespucci, and who has laboriously collected a vast amount of evidence and facts, writes: "Herrera, the chronicler of the West Indies, while borrowing nearly literally the Latin text of the 'Cosmographiæ Introductio' (Vespucci), with all the details, on this first voyage of Vespucci, and knowing that the Florentine navigator had accompanied Ojeda in 1499, thought this must have been the first voyage made by the former. In this belief he changed the date (1497) to 1499, and when he saw that the Florentine navigator's account began to disagree with the facts of which he had knowledge by other documents relating to Ojeda's first voyage in 1499, he raised the cry of imposture, and accused Vespucci of having confused everything on purpose, while it was he (Herrera) who was mistaken, and who by this mistake was later to lead into error Charlevoix, Robertson, Tiraboschi, and even Navarette and Humboldt."—"Analyse Critique de la Vie de Vespuce," p. 94.

speak of every thing and set things in motion. Let every thing be done secretly, that no suspicion may arise. I have said to him all that I can say touching this business, and I have informed him of the payments which have been made to me and which are yet to make. This letter is for the *adelantado* " (brother of Columbus); "also, that he may see wherein he can profit and advise him" (Vespucci) " of it, let his majesty believe that his ships were in the best and richest part of the Indies, and, if any thing further is required than what has been said, I will satisfy him by word of mouth, for it is impossible for me to tell by writing. May the Lord have you in his holy keeping!
"Done at Seville, February 5, 1505.
"Thy father, who loves thee better than himself,
"CHRISTOPHER COLUMBUS."

If the noble character of Vespucci needed vindication from the vile aspersions cast upon him by prejudiced or partial historians, the above letter of Columbus should silence further censure and complaint; it bears full testimony to the honorable conduct of the man, while the writer seems most desirous of profiting by his influence. With slight inconsistency, which will not surprise those who have perused the writings of Columbus, in the second sentence of his letter he says, "who is called to court on matters of navigation;" a little farther on we read, " He goes for me," which would lead us to suppose that Amerigo was called to court expressly to further the interests of Columbus. The first statement we know to have been the truth. Vespucci left Portugal at the instance of the crown of Spain, to take charge of an office which was subsequently erected into a department of the administration, pertaining to pilotage, navigation, and charts. He was to correct the errors carried into the latter by the teachings and maps of Columbus and others. Columbus had fallen into disgrace on account of his cruelty, the gross misstatements contained in his letters pertaining to his discoveries in the West, and the inaccuracy of his charts; the use of these, we have seen, was subsequently prohibited, and a penalty imposed upon the pilot who should sail by them." We do not

---

[61] Irving writes (book i., chapter iv.): " When the passion for maritime discovery was seeking aid to facilitate its enterprises, the knowledge and skill of an able cosmographer, like Columbus, would be properly appreciated, and the superior correct-

here propose to raise the veil of secrecy which Columbus in his letter seeks to cast upon a matter public in its character, of which it was his duty to speak and write frankly to the sovereign who had employed him; honesty does not thus shun the light. All this deceit is very different from the conduct of Amerigo, who in one of his letters thus excuses himself for not writing more in detail: "Much more have I diligently noted down in a pamphlet in which I have described this voyage, and which is now in the hands of his majesty, who I hope will return it to me shortly."

It is worthy of note that Vespucci was not summoned as a witness by the heirs of Columbus in their memorable lawsuit against the crown. Friend as he was, we have reason to believe he knew too much of the demerits of the claims set up, and of matters pertaining thereto, which Columbus desired to have kept *secret*. Those who write in the interest of Columbus, and against Vespucci, have represented the latter as soliciting the above letter for the purpose of introducing himself favorably at court, and thence affect to believe that Vespucci was a very obscure and unimportant individual. If we could for a moment believe that Amerigo either needed or desired the letter for such a purpose, we are frank to admit that his condition was low indeed; it was written at a period when Columbus had sunk to the greatest depth of degradation; five years before (and his condition had in all respects continued to grow more desperate to the day of his death), he writes: "I have now reached that point that there is no man so vile but thinks it his right to insult me. . . . If I were to build churches or hospitals, they would call them caves for robbers."

The time and place of Columbus's nativity remain undetermined, there is no genuine portrait of him; but about the country, family, and person of Amerigo, there is no dispute; his portrait and statues are placed among the household gods, even in the abodes of the humble in the Old World. As the children of the United States recognize the portrait of Washington, so do those of Italy that of the discoverer of America.

ness of his maps and charts would give him notoriety among men of science." From the facts which we have recorded above, it is evident that the government of Castile did not concur in the estimate of Mr. Irving touching the value of Columbus and his charts.

Vespucci injured none. He did not imagine or pretend to imagine himself in Asia when in America, as did Columbus; though many have sought to make him participate in the error of the latter, we have his own words to prove how just were his ideas upon the subject. In one of his letters he says: "These regions . . . *which it is legitimate to call the New World;*" and again, elsewhere: "Most of the ancients say that beyond the

PORTRAIT OF VESPUCCI.—(From an Original Painting from Life.)

equinoctial line toward the south there is no continent, but only sea, which they called Atlantic, and those who say that there is land say that it cannot be inhabited; this opinion is erroneous, as my last navigation has shown, for I have found in *this continent* people and animals as in our *Europe* or *Asia* or *Africa*." He thus makes distinct mention of the four quarters of the globe, as they are now recognized. Here, then, is another plea in favor of the name America."⁶² Columbus, to the last, whether through ignorance or willful deceit, persisted in declaring his discoveries to be India, Asia, the territories of the Grand-Khan. How could his name be given to countries already well known? or how could he be said to *discover* Asia, India, which had occupied so large a space in the world's history for unnumbered ages?

Amerigo's knowledge of astronomy and cosmography was much more profound than that of Columbus, who, indeed, at times appears ridiculously ignorant, and who, notwithstanding his novel theory that the world is *pear-shaped*, is represented in all works written upon the subject, from the child's picture-book to the graver history, as revealing to a hitherto ignorant civilization the "startling theory of the sphericity of the earth."

Vespucci does not seem to consider this doctrine of sphericity in the light of a strange or novel teaching; he draws the globe to illustrate his travels over a quarter of its circumference, and to show the relative position of the new lands with the old, but makes no such explanation as one naturally would when speaking of a new and "startling" theory.

History says that Columbus was the favorite of Isabella, though disliked by Ferdinand, while Amerigo was the latter's favorite mariner. This being an almost universal opinion, the same reasons which we have already cited as causing the comparative unpopularity of Ferdinand and popularity of Isabella may also be made to account for the ideas generally conceived of their supposed respective favorites. The Spanish authors, who so virulently attack Vespucci, wrote for the Church to which Isabella was professedly devoted. Pope Alexander VI., a Spaniard, deeded the Continent of America to Castile; the clergy ever sought to glorify Columbus; Isabella favored him until his faithlessness and cruelty made it impolitic if not impossible longer to protect him. Ferdinand, whose power as King of Aragon was not so great as that of Isabella of Castile, unwilling to trust the adventurer Columbus, but judging nevertheless that an expedition in search of these lands might be profitable, sought

⁶² Mr. Irving appends a note, relating to this matter, to his notice on Vespucci, in which he says: "The first suggestion of the name appears to have been in the Latin work already cited, published in St.-Diez, in Lorraine, in 1507, in which was inserted the letter of Vespucci to King René. The author, after speaking of the other three parts of the world, Asia, Africa, and Europe, recommends that the fourth shall be called Amerige or America, after Vespucci, whom he imagined its discoverer."

Amerigo, whose integrity inspired even the suspicious monarch with confidence. But it was necessary that the expeditions should be so quietly conducted as not to assume the aspect of rivaling those of Castile. It is probable, moreover, that the sagacity of Ferdinand, as well as the wisdom of Vespucci, prompted them to prosecute their discoveries in an unostentatious manner; they may have been strengthened in this wise resolve by having witnessed the sorry exhibition made up of a few naked savages bearing parrots on their shoulders, with which Columbus sought to challenge the admiration of the Spaniards, but which merely

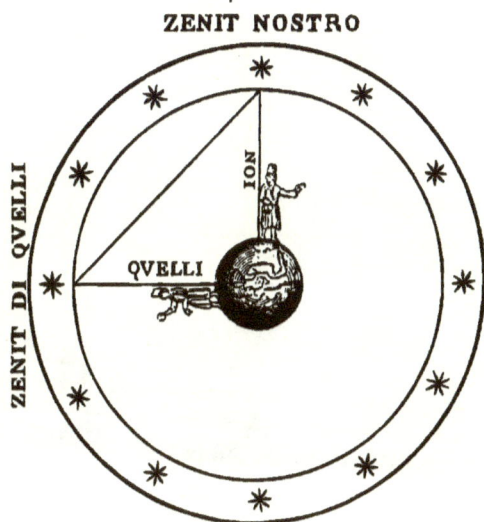

VESPUCCI'S ILLUSTRATION OF THE SPHERICITY OF THE EARTH.

succeeded in exciting derision, for at the time too many adventurers, who had listened to his golden falsehoods, had returned to their native land broken in health, ruined in fortune, sadder and wiser men, to tell a tale of deluded hopes, want, disaster, and despair.

We are constantly told that the weight of authority is on the side of Columbus; but how can the ardent seeker of truth, and truth only, fail to be discouraged when he finds how partial is the testimony in the case? Las Casas informs us that in all that relates to the discoveries in the New World the most worthy of credit is Peter Martyr of Anghieri; that whatever he relates respecting these discoveries was recorded in accordance with the accounts given by the admiral himself. Columbus thus becomes his own historian and eulogist, laying down the law by which the claims of all others are to be judged. He would naturally present his own side of the case, and, from what his writings lead us to suppose, would not scruple to slander those whose opinions or statements differed from his, or who had opposed any of his measures.

TRIUMPH OF AMERIGO.

Here, then, is an impartial testimony! To the glory of Columbus, a nation's history is prostituted, her great men ignored, her true benefactors assailed. Like the brazen image of Nebuchadnezzar, he is raised on high to be worshiped, and all who will not bow the knee must perish. Yet all the efforts of his enemies will not wrest the laurel from the brow of Amerigo. *America is the name given by the solemn verdict of a world to a continent. It is a goodly name;* like the laws of the Medes and Persians, it alters not; it shall not pass away until the heavens shall be wrapped together as a scroll, and the earth shall melt with fervent heat, and the angel who stood upon the sea and upon the earth shall proclaim that time shall be no longer!

CHAPTER VIII.

CONTEMPORARIES OF COLUMBUS—(CONTINUED).

PINZON—CABOT—CABRAL.

It would be impossible fairly to judge Columbus and his contemporaries without briefly noticing some of the most meritorious and notable of the latter, who, though less renowned than Vespucci, are well worthy a place beside him, and above Columbus.

Martin Alonzo and Vincent Yanez Pinzon were among the most deserving and worse maligned of these. It appears to have been the spirit of history to lessen the fame of the eminent navigators contemporaneous with Columbus, that he may appear preëminent. It seems sad to us that those who first visited the shores of our continent should occupy so small a space in history; that while many ignore even the names of Cabot and Cabral, and regard Vespucci as an impostor, Columbus should be styled by every school-boy the discoverer of America; it seems sad, we say, yet these wrongs appear as just when compared with the ingratitude of which the Pinzons have been the victims—the Pinzons, the life-blood of the first expedition of this very Columbus, who climbed to notoriety by means of their purse and good-will, and of one of whom he afterward speaks with the little-mindedness which characterized the man, as "one Pinzon," of whom he seems to preserve but a vague recollection.

When Columbus entered Spain, friendless, penniless, leaving behind him a history of piracy and crime which would cause all who knew, to distrust him, he first arrived at Palos, a little town, scarce more than a village, situated near the sea; he begged at the gates of the Convent de la Rabida for bread and lodging for himself and child. The prior ministered to his wants, and to this friar, Juan Perez by name, Columbus imparted the information he had received of there being certain lands to the west of the Canaries. Juan Perez introduced the wayfarer to the Pinzons, the first family of the place, men noted for their courage and nautical skill. Martin Alonzo, head of the family, listened with interest to the tale of Columbus, the more so as he also, during a visit to Rome, had heard rumors of the existence of these lands;" indeed, many seem to have suspected it, for among the Spanish state papers is a letter from Don Pedro de Ayala, dated 1498, in which he states that the merchants of Bristol had for seven years been sending out ships for the discovery of the island of Brazil, thus running back to a period more than a year anterior to the first voyage of Columbus.

During his conversation with Martin Alonzo, Columbus stated his desire to visit the court of Spain and solicit ships and the funds necessary for an expedition to reach and conquer these lands, but he was lacking wardrobe, money, and influence. Martin Alonzo provided him with the first two necessaries, and Juan Perez with the third, in the shape of a letter to Fernando de Talavera, confessor to the queen. After a lapse of several years, through these influences, Columbus returned to Palos with an order from Queen Isabella on the inhabitants of the town for two caravels equipped and manned, providing Columbus were to defray the expense of a third; this, of course, he would have been unable to do, had not the Pinzons come to his aid, Vincent Yanez laying down one million maravedis, which was the eighth part of the expense Columbus had boasted he would defray." The ships were made ready, but so great was the repugnance of the inhabitants of Palos to follow an unknown adventurer across the seas in search of distant lands, that the first caravels were scuttled and sunk. After they were replaced, Columbus found it impossible to persuade the mariners to accompany him. Martin Alonzo, who had been absent, now returned; he and his brother each took command of a vessel—Martin Alonzo of the Pinta, Vincent Yanez of the Niña. When the inhabitants of the town saw these brave and honest men, whom they loved and respected, putting their fortunes and their lives into the enterprise, they took courage and came forward with alacrity. Thus Columbus owed every thing, in this first expedition, to "the brave broth-

---

[63] See Navarette, "Colecc. Dip.," vol. iii., p. 559.
[64] See previous reference; also Irving, "Life of Columbus," book ii., chap. ix.

ers Pinzon" as they have been most justly termed. When we contrast the conduct of these men with that of Columbus, we are filled with admiration. While the latter for years refused to undertake the expedition unless receiving the greatest honors or emoluments, while sharing none of the expense, and while he succeeded in excluding all competitors by obtaining subsequently a revocation of the order allowing Spanish subjects to search for lands at their own expense for the benefit of the crown, thus narrowing the field of discovery, the Pinzons expend money and influence, leave their home and the town where their fathers had lived respected for generations, apparently without making any conditions for reward.[65] With such conduct before us, how can we for a moment entertain the idea that Columbus was actuated by a desire to promote science, to benefit mankind, or by any other motive than cupidity?

On the 3d of August, 1492, the three ships sailed, the one commanded by Columbus, the St. Mary, being the largest and finest; nevertheless, during the whole of the voyage, she was in the rear, the Pinta leading, as testified by Columbus's own journal. Here, also, explodes another popular error founded on the untruthfulness of Columbus, and those who have sung his praises. It is said that the men mutinied, that the rest of the expedition desired to return to Spain, but were led on and encouraged by the constancy of Columbus. Now, as we have stated above, the St. Mary was always in the rear, the others having frequently to lay by for her. It is scarcely probable that the Pinta and Niña would have continued thus in advance, had their commanders wished to turn back; besides, according to the testimony of several witnesses in the celebrated lawsuit of Don Diego Columbus against the crown, Columbus himself, after sailing some hundred leagues without finding land, wished to return, but was persuaded by the Pinzons to continue the voyage! Although we do not vouch for the truth of this testimony, it appears more probable than that the Pinzons, who were so greatly interested in the success of the expedition, should wish to abandon their projects.

[65] In the testimony in the lawsuit, already alluded to, it is stated that Martin Alonzo stipulated with Columbus for half the profits which should accrue to the latter. This may be true, but Columbus's habitual unfaithfulness caused him to ignore any such condition; and, the expedition not being a lucrative one, no claims were preferred at the time by the Pinzons, so that the matter remains uncertain.

Columbus, ignoring the ocean-current which drifted him northward, was sailing out of the track which had been laid down for him, when the Pinzons called his attention to this northward tendency, and urged him to adopt a more southerly course. He obstinately refused, alleging as a reason that it would shake the confidence of his men, and tend to lessen his importance, for him to appear uncertain as to where the land lay; nevertheless, as they did not find it, he finally consented to adopt a more southerly course, and thus arrived at the island of Hispaniola, which but for this change of route he would never have done. To whom, then, was the credit due, to Columbus or to Pinzon?

During the consultations with the Pinzons, as to a change of route, we read that from time to time maps and charts were consulted, by which Columbus was sailing. One of these was no doubt that of Alonzo Sanchez, the dead pilot, of whom we shall speak elsewhere, and from whom it is more than probable Columbus received nearly all his information regarding lands in the West.

After reaching the Caribi islands, by the route indicated by the Pinzons, Columbus declared he would have followed that course from the beginning had he not been *told that the land lay from north to south across his track;* he thus demonstrated himself that the voyage was based upon information received, and in no wise upon his own studies, conjectures, or knowledge. A reward of ten thousand maravedis annuity had been offered by the king and queen to the man who should first discover land. On board the Pinta, which, as we have said, was generally ahead of the two other vessels, there was an old mariner, Roderigo de Triana by name, who had long served under Martin Alonzo. The latter was evidently much attached to him, so much so that he wished him to obtain the above reward, and arranged in such sort that he should have every opportunity for doing so. In due time Roderigo declared land to be in sight, and the Pinta fired her gun as a signal. Columbus, when it was ascertained that the alarm was not a false one, stated that he had seen a light on the previous evening, and had *privately* spoken of it to Peter Gutierrez, groom of the chamber to the king. None of his crew were aware of the fact or had seen the light, and Columbus had made no demonstration; moreover, his ship being at that time far in the rear, it is less than probable that such was the case. Columbus, however, did not scruple to despoil the old mariner of his well-earned reward, and we read in Herrera: "But their majesties declared that the reward of ten thousand maravedis annuity belonged to the admiral, and it was always paid him at the shambles of Seville, because he saw a light amid darkness, meaning the spiritual light that was then coming into those barbarous people." "

Roderigo de Triana, after this warning that he should put no confidence in princes, disgusted at the injustice of the "admiral" and his sovereigns, left his country and turned Turk."

While at Hispaniola, Columbus lost his ship, and was taken on board the Niña, commanded by Vincent Yanez. Martin Alonzo sailed round the island, desiring to obtain a knowledge of the country. Columbus, when excusing himself to Ferdinand and Isabella for not bringing back as much gold as he had promised, ascribed his failure to this so-called desertion on the part of Pinzon, whom he declared to have been insubordinate. Martin Alonzo, who had so nobly befriended Columbus in adversity, was thus maligned by him, and through his unjust accusation forbidden to appear at court; his pride must have been deeply wounded, but it is probable that the ingratitude of Columbus touched him still more keenly. He died, it is said, broken-hearted at Palos, shortly after his return. He deserved a better fate.

Vincent Yanez soon after fitted out an expedition of four fine ships at his own expense," took with him two sons of Martin Alonzo, and sailed west till he discovered Brazil, three months before Cabral in May, 1500, accidentally reached its shores.

Charles V. raised the family of the Pinzons to nobility or *hidalguia*, and gave them an escutcheon, on which are seen four caravels and the motto arrogated to Columbus:

"A Castilla y a Leon,
Nuevo Mundo dio Pinzon."

---

[66] Herrera, "West Indies," vol. i., chapter xii., Stevens's translation.

[67] Navarette, "Colecc. Dip," vol. iii.

[68] When a private individual could do this, the absurdity of the statement contained in most works on the subject, that Isabella pawned her jewels to raise the necessary funds for equipping the three little caravels forming the first expedition,

This is substantially all that is recorded of the Pinzons: History passes lightly over their names, but Fate seems to have made all the reparation in her power; for, while the family of Columbus, which, so far as regards name or fame, began with him, has long since become extinct, the worthy Pinzons still flourish in their numerous descendants, who have perpetuated the virtues as well as the name of their illustrious ancestors, and on many of whose houses in the little towns of Palos and Moguer, to which they have remained faithful, the escutcheon (the only reward received by these noble and enterprising men from their sovereign) is still emblazoned.

JOHN CABOT was possibly the first modern discoverer of America; of his birthplace we have no certain information, but we know that he was by adoption, if not by birth, a citizen of Venice, for we find in the archives of that city an act dated March 29, 1496, by which the senate unanimously grants denization to Zuan Caboto, which act states that citizenship is granted him "as usual within and without for fifteen years;" we may, therefore, infer that he was of Venetian birth, as it was not usual to grant citizenship to foreigners residing in foreign countries, while it had been customary to grant it to citizens proposing to make a long sojourn abroad. Moreover, in the second license granted him by Henry VII., he is styled "Kabotto Venician." He had evidently, however, resided some time at Bristol in England, when the above act of citizenship was passed, and in 1497 Henry VII. granted him a license authorizing him and his heirs and assigns to make search for islands, provinces, or regions in the Eastern, Western, or Northern seas, and to occupy such territories as vassals of the English king, paying him one-fifth of the profits on merchandise. With this charter John Cabot, in 1497, embarked with one vessel, and sailed west seven hundred leagues. The particulars of this voyage and the impressions it created at the time are interestingly preserved to us in a letter by one Lorenzo Pasqualigo, Venetian merchant in London, to his brother in Venice, which is found in the archives of that city.

Lorenzo writes: "The Venetian, our countryman, who went with a ship from Bristol, in quest of new islands, is returned, and says that seven hundred leagues hence he discovered land, the

and which, as we have seen, were provided solely at the expense of the Pinzons and people of Palos, becomes apparent.

territory of the Grand-Khan" (*Gram Cam*). "He coasted for three hundred leagues, and landed; saw no human beings, but he has brought hither to the king certain snares which had been set to catch game, and a needle for making nets; he also found some felled trees, wherefore he supposed there were inhabitants, and returned to his ship in alarm.

"He was three months on the voyage, and on his return he saw two islands to starboard, but would not land, time being precious, as he was short of provisions. He says that the tides are slack, and do not flow as they do here. The King of England is much pleased with this intelligence.

"The king has promised that in spring our countryman shall have ten ships armed to his order, and at his request has conceded to him all prisoners, except such as are confined for high-treason, to man his fleet. The king has also given him money wherewith to amuse himself till then, and he is now at Bristol with his wife, who is also a Venetian, and with his sons. His name is Zuan Cabot, and he is styled the great admiral. Vast honor is paid him; he dresses in silk, and these English run after him like mad people, so that he can enlist as many of them as he pleases, and a number of our own rogues besides. The discoverer of these places planted on his new-found land a large cross, with one flag of England and another of St. Mark, by reason of his being a Venetian, so that our banner has floated very far afield.

"LONDON, *August* 23, 1497."

The promise of ten ships above alluded to is restricted in the second license granted by the king on February 3, 1498, to six English vessels, which Cabot has authority to impress, as also to enlist companies of volunteers. According to Lorenzo, he would not have much difficulty in doing this. Nevertheless it does not appear that John Cabot made any voyage under this license, nothing further of him being recorded; neither the date nor place of his death is known, and we are in equal ignorance as to his age. It is generally supposed that Newfoundland was that upon which he first touched in 1497, yet the description he gives of the country and of the animals therein leads us to suppose that Labrador must have been the main-land of which he speaks. We know, however, that he coasted three hundred leagues southward, and most probably visited Newfoundland also. Columbus, on his own showing, only visited the continent four months later.

Purchas says with some justice that these lands should rather have been called Cabotta. However that may be, the merit of priority seems to rest between Cabot and Amerigo Vespucci, as they both touched the continent in the same year; but, as the latter prosecuted his discoveries in a more scientific spirit and to a greater extent, the name which the land now bears may be regarded as a just tribute. Mr. Irving, who, like many extravagant admirers of Columbus, would at all cost annihilate the claims of Vespucci, admits, in his endeavors to do so, the justice of those of Cabot, and confounding the son Sebastian, who took part in the expedition with the father, John Cabot, writes: "In fact, the European who first reached the main-land of the New World was most probably Sebastian Cabot, a native of Venice, sailing in the employ of England. In 1497 he coasted its shores from Labrador to Florida."

SEBASTIAN CABOT was probably twenty years of age when he accompanied his father on the voyage of 1497. Much might be written of the character and achievements of this navigator. The wisdom and moderation which governed most of his undertakings stand out in relief against the barbarous deeds of many who attempted the discovery, conquest, and settlement of America.

The English authorities claim that Sebastian was born at Bristol, while the Venetians are equally anxious to prove him their compatriot by birth as well as parentage. The question, however, still remains undetermined. In 1498 he sailed with two ships, under the patent granted him jointly with his father, for the purpose of discovering the northwest passage. He sailed so far north that in the middle of July the daylight was almost continuous, and the numerous icebergs compelled him to change his course; in so doing, he touched upon the Continent of America, and perhaps upon Newfoundland. He sailed along the coast of the continent until he reached the latitude of Gibraltar, when he returned to England—disappointed that the object of his voyage had not been effected, and regarding his important discoveries as of so little moment that he allowed his patent to become void. Upon the death of Henry VII., he was summoned to Spain, to assist at the council for the New Indies; and in 1518 he was appointed Pilot-Major of Spain by Charles V., a circumstance which manifests in how great repute was his skill in navigation.

Having failed in his attempt to discover a northwest passage, he turned his thoughts upon the possibility of there existing a southwestern one, and went in search of the same in 1526. During this voyage he arrived at Brazil, sailed up the river La Plata, and discovered Paraguay. He remained about three years in this country, and then returned to Spain, where he continued to exercise his functions of pilot-major until 1548, when he was recalled to England; and a pension granted to him of two hundred and fifty marks (£166 13s. 4d). He was afterward requested to return to Spain, but declined.

He seems to have been much looked up to in England, and to have been consulted on the most important questions. Hakluyt writes: "Our merchants perceived the commodities and wares of England to be in small request about us and near unto us; and that those merchandises which strangers, in the time and memory of our ancestors, did earnestly seek and desire, were now neglected, and the price thereof abated, although they be carried to their own parts; and all foreign merchandises in great account, and their prices wonderfully raised. . . . And, whereas at the same time, Sebastian Cabota, a man in those days very renowned, happened to be in London, they began first of all to deal and consult diligently with him; and, after much search and conference together, it was at last concluded that three ships should be prepared and furnished out for search and discovery of the Northern part of the world, to open a way and passage for our men, and for travel to new and unknown lands." [69]

It was thus that through his influence was organized an expedition which, rounding the cape of Norway, was to discover a northeast passage to China. This expedition, though of course unsuccessful in its object, reached Archangel, and established trading operations with the Russians, which resulted afterward in the formation of the Russian Trading Company, one of England's greatest sources of wealth.

Charles V. wrote urgently in 1553, requesting that Cabot might return to Spain, where his services had been very valuable; but this he declined, and still continued in England. He

[69] Hakluyt, "Voyages," p. 280.

had made the deviations of the compass a study, and had sought to discover the point where they should cease. We find him demonstrating his opinions, and instructing the youthful King Edward on this point. He has, therefore, been styled by some the discoverer of the variations of the compass. It is more than probable, however, that neither he nor Columbus is entitled to this credit, but that the said variations have been noted and commented upon centuries before the birth of either.

In 1556 Sebastian organized another expedition of discovery, of which Stephen Burrough was the commander. In the latter's journal we find the following: "The 27th of April, being Monday, the Right Worshipful Sebastian Caboto came aboard our Pinnesse at Gravesende, accompanied with divers gentlemen and gentlewomen, who, after that they had viewed our pinnesse, and tasted of such cheere as we could make them aboard, they went on shore, giving to our mariners right liberal rewards; and *the Goode olde Gentleman,* Master Caboto, gave the poor most liberale almes; wishing them to pray for the good fortune and prosperous success of the Serchthrift, our pinnesse. And then, at the sign of the Christopher, he and his friends banketted, and made me and them that were in the company great cheere. And, for very joy that he had to see the towardness of our intended discovery, he entered into the dance himself among the rest of the young and lusty company; which, being ended, he and his friends departed most gently, commending us to the Governance of Almighty God."

On the death of Edward VI., he resigned his pension; and we find little more of this great man recorded in the history of the country which he had so greatly served. All that we learn of his character inspires us with respect. In Ramusio, he is described thus by one who had seen him: "I found him a most gentle and courteous person, who treated me with great kindness, and showed me a great many things; among the rest, a great map of the world, on which the several voyages of the Portuguese and Spaniards were laid down."

Much has been said in extenuation of the cruelty of Columbus, about the spirit of the times being one of bigotry and intolerance. We find no proof of any such spirit in the following items of the regulations written by Sebastian for the governance of Sir Hugh Willoughby's expedition in 1553. The good sense therein displayed materially increases our admiration for the man:

"22d item: Not to disclose to any nation the state of our religion, but to pass it over in silence, without any declaration of it; seeming to bear with such laws and rights as the place hath where you shall arrive.

"23d item: Forasmuch as our people and shippe may appear unto them strange and wondrous, and theirs, also, to ours—it is to be considered how they may be used—learning much of their natures and dispositions by some one such person as you may first either allure, or take to be brought aboard your ships; and there to learn, as you may without violence or force; and no woman to be tempted or intreated to incontinence or dishonestie.

"26th item: Every nation and region is to be considered advisedly; and not to provoke them by any disdaine, laughing contempt, or such like; but to use them with prudent circumspection, with all gentlenesse and curtesie. And not to tarry long in one place, until you shall have attained the most worthy place that may be found; in such sort as you may return with victuals sufficient prosperously." [70]

During the last part of his life, and after his death, Sebastian Cabot was the victim of great ingratitude on the part of the English; on which Mr. Biddle, his most able and exhaustive biographer, thus touchingly comments:

"The English language would probably be spoken in no part of America but for Sebastian Cabot. The commerce of England, and her navy, are admitted to have been deeply, incalculably, his debtors. Yet there is reason to fear that in his extreme age the allowance, which had been solemnly granted to him for life, was fraudulently broken in upon. His birthplace we have seen denied. His fame has been obscured by English writers, and every wild calumny against him adopted and circulated. All his own maps and discoveries, 'drawn and written by himself,' which it was hoped might come out in print, 'because so worthy monuments should not be buried in perpetual oblivion,' have been buried in perpetual oblivion. He gave a continent to England, yet no man can point to the few feet of earth she has allowed him in return."

[70] Hakluyt, "Voyages," p. 259.

This ingratitude is in great measure traceable to the partiality of which Columbus has ever been the object. Sebastian returned to England from his discoveries at the time when the famous negotiations were taking place for the marriage of Isabella's daughter to the Prince of Wales. Henry VII., crippled by internal dissensions, and desirous of obtaining an alliance with Spain, abandoned his plans of discovery at the suggestion of its sovereign, as the regions in which they were to be prosecuted were alleged to be within the limits of the grant of Pope Alexander to Spain."[71] And it was evidently the intention of that country to allow no rivals in the field ; policy, therefore, suggested to Henry that his wisest course was to desist, and the achievements of Sebastian were ignored.

History seems to have also resolved, with little reason and less justice, to allow no rival to Columbus. And it is evident that Sebastian Cabot is one of the many victims whose fame has been sacrificed to increase that of the former.

PEDRO ALVAREZ DE CABRAL, though little mentioned in most histories of the discovery of America, was probably one of the most intelligent and meritorious of the many adventurers who early reached that continent.

He was born in Portugal, toward the close of the fifteenth century. At that time the commerce of the East belonged, so far as regarded Europe, entirely to Venice. Portugal was thus excluded, and, desirous of securing to herself this great source of wealth, she sent out expeditions for the purpose of ascertaining whether, by coasting along the shores of Africa, a route from Portugal to India might not be discovered, by which to divert for the benefit of Portugal a part at least of the commerce of India. The feasibility of this plan had been demonstrated first by Bartholemew Diaz and afterward by Vasco de Gama, who in 1497 rounded the Cape of Good Hope. The King of Portugal, animated by this success, manned a fleet of thirteen ships with fit and experienced men, and placed them under the command

---

[71] On the 28th of March, 1496, Ferdinand and Isabella wrote to De Puebla, their ambassador in London, thus : "You write that a person like Columbus has come to England for the purpose of persuading the king to enter into an undertaking similar to that of the Indies. . . . Take care that the King of England be not deceived in this or in any other matter. . . . Besides, they " (voyages of discovery) " cannot be executed without prejudice to us, and to the King of Portugal."—*Spanish State Papers.*

of Cabral. This fleet was, perhaps, one of the finest sent out at that period. There were on board twelve hundred seamen and soldiers, besides numerous Franciscan friars, who were to act as missionaries in the new settlements to be founded. Cabral with justice regarded the coasting voyage effected by Vasco de Gama as a tedious and dangerous one, and conceived the idea of the present route by taking a southwesterly course till reaching the latitude of the cape, thus crossing the ocean twice. It was during this westerly digression that, sailing from the Cape Verde Islands, he came in sight of Brazil, latitude 10° south, on the 3d of May, 1500.

Coasting southward about seven degrees, he took possession of the continent in the name of King Emmanuel, of Portugal. Brazil remained thereafter a Portuguese possession, notwithstanding the Spaniard Vincent Yanez Pinzon had visited its shores in the month of January previous. Cabral had with him twenty men banished from Portugal, whom he had orders to leave in the different regions he discovered, as he thought fit. Two of these he left in Brazil; one of them we read of as having become expert in the language of the natives, and acting as interpreter.

Cabral now sent one of his ships back to Portugal with the news of this discovery, and with the remaining twelve sailed for India. While crossing the cape, he encountered severe storms, in one of which he lost four vessels. With the diminished remains of his once splendid fleet he reached India, touching at Mozambique and Calicut, at which latter he made some settlements and succeeded in establishing a factory; he then returned to Portugal, laden with the rich merchandise of the East. On his arrival in his native land he was received coolly by the king, owing to the losses he had sustained; nevertheless these losses were attributable to the dangers incurred during the voyage, and not to any want of skill or foresight on the part of Cabral, who from the evidence we have already cited had proved himself an able seaman, far abler than the much-lauded Columbus, who, let it be remembered, generally lost the vessel under his own immediate command, even when the others escaped. Cabral's own vessel weathered all storms. He also proved himself the more intelligent of the two on another point. When Columbus landed in Cuba, he imagined himself within three days' journey of China, and dispatched a messenger with a letter to the Grand-Khan, to return in six days! Cabral labored under no such delusion, but, after taking possession of the new country in his sovereign's name, immediately set sail for his original destination (India), in an opposite direction. We find no mention of Cabral after July, 1501, the date of his return to Portugal. He has been allowed to sink into semi-oblivion; nevertheless he was incontestably an able man, and deserved more gratitude from his sovereign, as well as more notice from posterity.

CHAPTER IX.

COLUMBUS—WHO AND WHAT WAS HE?

THE history of most famous men generally and most naturally begins with the date of their birth, and some particulars as to their parentage and birthplace; but the historian who attempts to discover these particulars with regard to Columbus, undertakes a long and fruitless task. Volumes might, indeed, be filled with an enumeration of the views entertained or professed by different authors on the subject, but so conflicting and various are they that, after reading them, the conscientious author must needs disregard them *all*.

Monferrat, Bogliasco, Chiavara, Oneglia, Quinto, Albisola, Nervi, Pradello, Cogoleto, Savona, Ferrara, Piacenza, and Genoa, have each in their turn been designated as the birthplace of Columbus.

The diverse opinions of contemporary authors are quoted by his son Fernando, who declares his inability to decide the question, and, after much apparent research, which amounts in reality to nothing, he dismisses the subject as a matter of no importance.

Herrera, after examining many authorities, among others the above, does not scruple to affirm that he was born at Genoa, " as all who write or treat of him do agree."

The reader may judge of the degree of credit to which the statements of Herrera are entitled after reading the evidence in this particular case, and observing the somewhat extraordinary conclusion at which he arrives.

Indeed, the partiality and prejudice evinced by extravagant eulogists of Columbus are very apparent in their attempts to determine the place of his nativity. One author (Salinero) declares that whoever should deny Genoa the honor of giving birth to this incomparable man ought to be regarded as a monster.

For our part, regarding Columbus as chiefly the creation of an after-thought, we believe that his birthplace has become the subject of invention, even as his exploits and learning have existed principally in the imagination of his biographers. A most accurate register of births was kept at Genoa, wherein very humble and obscure families can be traced back to a period anterior to Columbus, yet nowhere is his name to be found. We believe, therefore, that the honest wool-carder, Dominic Colon, who, it is asserted by one kind author, was the father of our hero, may be absolved from the charge; especially as he pursued the decidedly terrestrial vocation of wool-carding, while Fernando tells us, his father's ancestors always "traded by sea," a mild term for piracy.

If the birthplace of "the admiral" is yet unknown, all attempts to discover whence or from whom he derived his name have hitherto been still more fruitless. In vain have some, endeavoring to cast the glamour of noble descent over this created hero, sought his parentage among noble families bearing a name somewhat similar to that of Columbus. In vain others, wishing to make his individual greatness stand out in bolder relief, have made him the son of poor and even ignoble parents. There being no evidence, no real facts, each author has placed his hero in that rank of life which he himself considered most likely to give him prestige in the eyes of the world.

Perhaps, however, with the aid of an historian who certainly would not intentionally seek to bring disrepute upon Columbus (we speak of his son Fernando), we may be able to cast some light upon this hitherto vexed question.

In the fifth chapter of Fernando's history of his father, we find mentioned "a famous man of his name and family, called Colon, renowned upon the sea, . . . insomuch that they made use of his name to frighten children in the cradle. . . . This man was called Colon the Younger."

Here is the unqualified statement of Fernando, that Christopher was of the name and family of the individual known as Colon the Younger. He further states that in company of this Colon, a pirate, his father sailed "for a long time;" and describes an encounter between these pirates and some Flanders galleys, in which Christopher barely escaped to Lisbon with his life.

In the archives of Venice are the following particulars relative to the same affair, which throw a clearer light upon "the name and family" of the "great navigator" than his son is able or willing to do.

By reference to the above authority, we learn that six or seven ships, commanded by one called Columbus the Younger, and having on board the man now known as Christopher Columbus, lay off Cape St. Vincent, watching for the arrival of four Venetian merchant-ships, termed Flanders galleys; these they attacked on the 21st of August, 1485, and, after much slaughter, carried off an immense booty, stripping the officers and crew even of their clothing.

This affair is formally communicated by the Venetian senate to their various ambassadors abroad. The first mention is found in a dispatch, dated September 18, 1485, from the doge and senate to the ambassador at Milan:

"The capture of the Flanders galleys by ships commanded by a *son of Columbus* and Giovanni Griego."

Marin Sanuto, in his MS. "Lives of the Doges," preserved in St. Mark's Library, recounting the capture, says:

"Our galleys fell in with Colombo, *that is to say, Nicolo Griego.*"

In a decree of the Venetian senate, December 2, 1485, we find:

"Our Flanders galleys captured by Colombo's son and Zorzi Griego."

Again, in a document, dated April 9, 1486, treating of the capture of the galleys:

"Nicolo Griego, who is called Columbus junior (Colombo Zovene)."

One fact is hereby established beyond a doubt, namely, that the *Columbus junior, Colombo's son*, the Colon the Younger mentioned by Fernando, was in fact named Nicolo Griego. We, moreover, gather from the Venetian documents that three pirates Giovanni Griego, Nicolo Griego, and Zorzi Griego, occasionally assumed the name of Columbus. That the family name of the subject of this history was Griego, is therefore proved by the statement of his son, who says that Columbus the Younger "was of his name and family;" the said Columbus the Younger being always spoken of, in the Venetian state papers, as Nicolo Griego, sometimes called *Columbus the Younger.*

Of the two other Griegos mentioned as having taken part in the capture of the galleys, one was probably the father indicated in the allusion to Colombo's son, and the name Colon the Younger; the other was undoubtedly our Christopher, who, his son tells us, sailed a long time with Colon the Younger (Nicolo Griego), and assisted in the said capture of the galleys. He was then of the name and family of Griego, and sometimes adopted the *alias* of Columbus, as did his kinsmen; under this *alias,* thenceforth to become his name, he came to Spain. It was probably not till he had formed the pious project of obtaining the protection of the Church by representing himself as the CHRIST-BEARER, carrying the Gospel across the waters to heathen nations, that he changed his name of Giovanni or Zorzi, to that of Christopher, on the peculiar significance of which his son dwells at such length in his first chapter (from which we shall presently quote) naïvely avowing, however, that the particulars of his name and surname are not without some mystery; and elsewhere, speaking of the falseness of the statements made by Giustiniani, touching Columbus's parentage and early pursuits, he says: "If Giustiniani tells so many lies concerning things well known" (his discoveries, etc.), " it is not likely that he would tell the truth concerning the admiral's parents and profession, *all particulars concerning which are hidden.*"

Whether the mystery which hung as a cloud over the many years of Columbus's life previous to his relations with the Spanish court, was known to the son, who, well aware how charitably it covered a multitude of sins, was unwilling to remove it, or whether, which is far from probable, he was really ignorant of the facts which the Venetian state papers reveal,[72] we shall not here attempt to decide, nor can we be certain that Griego was

---

[72] Fernando, who in his preface, in which he declares all former histories of his father to be incorrect, promises unreserved frankness and sincerity, does not in his work fulfill this promise. He was, for years after the death of his father, in daily intercourse with his uncles Bartholomew and Diego. Why did he not ask them touching the name and family of this "incomparable" father, whom he modestly declares to be "worthy of eternal memory?" They were certainly competent to reveal the particulars which are "hidden." He evidently knew the history of which he professes ignorance, and knew also that mystery was the safest shroud.

the real name of any of the worthies who bore it. There is no mention of their being Italians; for aught we know they may have been Greek pirates, known in Italy, where the people are so apt to give significant titles by the name of their country only. Certain it is that Griego was the name most universally known, for we read "Nicolo Griego, sometimes called Columbus;" while, if the latter had been the name in most frequent use, it would be *Columbo, sometimes called Nicolo Griego.*"

As to the date of Columbus's birth, authors generally assert that it was *about* the year 1445 or 1446. We think, however, that, from motives easily discernible, they have abridged his career, and that fifteen or twenty years earlier would have been a more correct date.

The son, unable or unwilling to account for the period of his life which preceded 1485, was naturally desirous to make that period as short as possible, believing no doubt thirty years are more easily bridged over than fifty.

It is very safe to suppose that Columbus was fifty years of age, at least, at the time of the capture of the galleys, his illegitimate son Fernando (reported to be his younger son) professed to have witnessed the fitting out of the galleys, and to have been old enough to judge of their strength, etc." He moreover, tells us that his father was a light-haired man, and that at thirty his hair was quite white. This would be a physiological phenomenon, it being well known that light or sandy-haired people do not usually become gray until very late.

Ferdinand then tells us that his father was educated at Pavia, but the details already revealed as to his real name and antecedents render this improbable.

We are then told, on the same authority, that he early began a seafaring life, and made some voyages " to the East and West, of which, and many other things of those his first days, I " (Fernando) "have no perfect knowledge." " The delightful vagueness

---

[13] In addition to the above array of names, we find other authors declaring that he was known by, or confused with the names of, *Guillaume de Casseneuve*, surnamed *Conlomp, Conlon,* or *Colon,* whom history records as a pirate, while in English works it has been surmised that Christopher Columbus and *Christofre Colyns* were identical, not to mention the appellation of Christofer *Tauber* (dove) by which we find him designated in German works.

[14] *See* Fernando, "Historia del Amirante," chapter v.

[15] It is singular that, while giving the details of his father's youth and education,

of this allusion to voyages to the East and West is not much elucidated by the letter of Columbus to the Spanish sovereigns, in which he modestly extols his own knowledge in the following terms:

"MOST SERENE PRINCES: I went to sea very young, and have continued it to this day, . . . it is now forty years that I have been sailing to all those parts at present frequented, . . . and our Lord has been favorable to this my inclination, and I have received from Him the spirit of understanding. He has made me very skillful in navigation; knowing enough in astrology;

COLUMBUS DRAWS HIS MAP UNDER DIVINE INSPIRATION.—CUBA IN ASIA.

and so in geometry and arithmetic. God has given me genius, and hands apt to draw this globe; and on it the cities, rivers, islands, and all parts, in their proper places."

This modest panegyric of himself, in which the Almighty is represented as having exempted him from the usual laborious course of study by which the sciences he alludes to are ordinarily acquired by less favored mortals, does not contain the details or

he should be thus ignorant of the events of his adult life; but the good old adage is here illustrated: "Where ignorance is bliss, 'twere folly to be wise."

particulars of any one voyage, nor are such details to be found in any authority of the period. It is not probable that a navigator who had visited all the known parts of the world would have been so utterly ignored by his contemporaries.

That he led a seafaring life we are ready to believe. His son tells us his being addicted to sea-affairs was owing to the pirate of his name and family (Nicolo Griego), Colon the Younger. In the profession of piracy he most probably infested those seas where the richest booty was to be captured, the chief of which was the Mediterranean. We need not say that such a life is not particularly inducive to study, and that its votaries are not generally inclined to deep thought. For fifty years, almost the natural period of man's life, Columbus could scarce have entertained the slightest idea of making voyages of discovery, or of visiting the Indies; what accident subsequently induced him, in his latter years, to propose the project, we shall presently state.

He speaks of a voyage, made for the King of Naples, to capture a certain ship. This voyage is not improbable—sovereigns sometimes employed pirates in affairs of like nature—but the principal fact upon which he dwells in recounting it is, that he "changed the points of the compass" and deceived his men: "So at break of day we found ourselves near Cape Cartegna, all aboard thinking we had certainly been sailing for Marseilles."

This boast furnishes a clew to the whole character of the man; falsehood and deceit are ever, we shall find, its most prominent traits.

As to the voyage he professes to have made, "an hundred leagues beyond Thule" (Iceland); "whose southern part is seventy-three degrees distant from the equinoctial," we have but his own authority, while all the probabilities are against it. A pirate would find little to induce him to such an undertaking, the booty to be captured being much inferior to that abounding in the Mediterranean. He does not give any reasons for such a voyage, nor mention the ship he sailed in, or the port he sailed from; he gives nothing, in fact, but the most vague assertions. All contemporary writers, state papers, etc., are silent upon the subject, when less important matters are recorded.

For some years, it is unknown at what precise period, Columbus was engaged in the Guinea slave-trade—in which he subsequently showed himself such an adept with regard to the unfortunate Indians—as well to deserve the compliment paid him by Mr. Helps, who calls his proceedings and plans worthy "of a practised slave-dealer."[76]

That he was long addicted to piracy; that he was of the name and family of one Nicolo Griego; that he was past the

COLUMBUS.—(From a Picture in the Bibliothèque Impériale, Paris.)

prime of life in 1485, is, therefore, really all that can be gathered of the history of Christopher Columbus previous to that date. Those who propose to furnish this Griego with honest parents of the name of Columbus in Genoa, or any other place, undertake

[76] Helps, "History of Columbus," chap. x., p. 191.

a task as bootless as that of tracing back the lineage of the numerous family of doves, which flourish in the Place St. Mark in Venice, to the fugitive dove of Noah.

The reader has now seen how much the imagination of the various biographers of "the admiral" has been taxed to supply the circumstances of his birth and parentage. It is not, therefore, extraordinary to find that, in that other important task of describing the personal appearance of their hero, imagination has also played its part.

The several likenesses of Columbus engraved in this work, taken from his numerous histories and biographies, purport each

BUST OF COLUMBUS AT GENOA.

to be a copy "of *the only* original portrait of Columbus;" and from the resemblance they bear each other one would scarce suppose them to represent the same man. Indeed, it is admitted that, although living in an age when portrait-painting was universal, and when the features of most men of any note, and of many persons of humble rank, were thus handed down to posterity, Columbus appears to have been too insignificant for any country to have desired his likeness: those who have created the hero, have also invented the portraits. This subject received a thorough examination a few years ago, when a monument was about to be erected in Genoa to the memory of the navigator.

"It was wished," says Spotorno, "and very properly, that a likeness of the navigator should grace the monument. . . . There are several portraits of him, *but not one of them resembles another.* . . . *No one can flatter himself that Spain can produce a true portrait of Columbus.* . . . What, therefore, are we to conclude? We must adopt the conclusion of Prof. Marsand; after observing the difference between the various supposed portraits of Petrarch, not one resembling another, he says: 'Therefore they are all false; if they had been taken from life, they must have preserved more or less the original features, as in the case of Dante.' For these weighty reasons the sculptor, in executing the bust, was bound to copy none of the portraits hitherto published."

The pertinence of the above remarks, and the soundness of the conclusions to which they may have led, must be manifest to all who have studied these pretended portraits or their history. We have seen many; some published in Spain, some in Italy, others in England and America, in none of which is it possible to detect the least resemblance, except in those few that are copies of a fictitious original. These reproductions are rarely seen, save in England and America. The European publisher seems to have preferred the status of inventor to that of copyist; hence each *created* for himself a new and original portrait of the navigator, as unlike the other "originals" as could well be conceived.

Fernando, in symbolizing the person of his sire, makes no allusion to any painted or sculptored semblance of him; had there been any, he surely would have said that they did or did not resemble him.

In struggling on, without the aid of a painter, he says his visage was long, his eyes were white, he had a hawk nose; others say his hair was red, and that he had a pimpled face." That which has come down to us touching his person is not calculated to make a favorable impression upon the mind of the physiologist.

The supernatural far more than the real has ever been the mainstay of Columbus's eulogists. Fernando, one of the first, and

[17] Fernando, "Historia del Amirante," chapter iii.

M. De Lorgues, one of the last of his historians, may be said to be the two extremes which meet and rival each other in their mystic interpretations, and in ascribing miraculous and divine attributes to their hero.

Fernando thus admirably accounts for the *assumed* name of Christopher Columbus, and gives us an insight into the motives which induced its bearer to adopt it:

COLUMBUS REPRESENTED AS THE CHRIST-BEARER.

"We may mention many names which were given by secret impulse to denote the effect those persons were to produce, as in his are foretold and expressed the wonder he performed. For if we look upon the common surname of his ancestors, we may say he was true Columbus, or Columba, forasmuch as he conveyed the grace of the Holy Ghost into that New World, which he discovered, showing those people, who knew him not, which was God's Son, as the Holy Ghost did in the figure of a dove at St. John's baptism; and because he also carried the olive-branch and oil of baptism over the waters of the ocean, like Noah's dove, to denote the peace and union of those people with the Church, after they had been shut up in the ark of darkness and confusion. And the surname of Colon, which he revived, was proper to him, which in Greek signifies *a member*, that his proper name being Christopher, it might be known he was a member of Christ, by whom salvation was to be conveyed to those people.

METHODS OF CONVERTING THE INDIANS.—(From Las Casas's "Crudelitates Hispanorum in Indiis patratæ.")

"Moreover, if we would bring his name to the Latin pronunciation, that is, Christophorus Colonus, we may say that as St. Christopher is reported to have borne that name because he carried Christ over the deep waters with great danger to himself, whence came the denomination of Christopher, and, as he conveyed over the people whom no other could have been able to carry, so the Admiral Christophorus Colonus, imploring the assistance of Christ in that dangerous passage, went over safe himself and his company, that those Indian nations might become citizens and inhabitants of the Church triumphant in heaven; for it is to be believed that many souls which the devil expected to make a prey of, had they not passed through the water of baptism, were *by him* made inhabitants and dwellers in the eternal glory of heaven."

Whatever may be the deficiencies of Don Fernando as a logical writer, he has an unfailing resource in his piety. In every difficulty he can bring religion to his aid, and find a special Providence, "some secret impulse," in matters which to minds less favored have a somewhat ugly look. Columbus, he shows us, was entitled to all his names and to all his changes (he is wisely silent on the Griego question, as it would be difficult to find a holy meaning in that word). Throughout the history of this man, particularly as written by his son, fanaticism and hypocrisy are forever fathering the crimes of man upon the beneficence and justice of Heaven, converting into special providence and mysterious intention, deeds which, when related in plain language, are denominated as infamous by every honorable mind.

The peace which Columbus bore the hapless Indians was the peace of the grave; his olive-branch the scourge, the cruel tortures which drove them to that bourn; while the souls thus rescued from the hands of the devil were the descendants of countless generations of souls which, according to the miserable logic of Fernando, a beneficent God had left wholly in the power of the arch-enemy of man.

CHAPTER X.

SOURCE WHENCE COLUMBUS DERIVED THE INFORMATION WHICH INDUCED HIM TO UNDERTAKE HIS VOYAGES.

ALTHOUGH the history of Columbus after 1485 is not so perfectly veiled in obscurity as it is up to that period, yet we shall find it any thing but succinct or clear, owing chiefly to the systematic attempt to mislead as to dates and facts; which is most palpable in Fernando's history, and in all other histories which have been more or less influenced by it. An attempt is constantly made to carry *back*, as far as possible, the period at which Columbus first formed the project of a Western voyage.

Fernando tells us that his father's coming to Lisbon was the cause of his discovering the Indies; also, that he came to Lisbon after the piratical assault upon the Venetian merchant-ships; which is proved, on the unimpeachable authority of the Venetian state papers, to have taken place in 1485. Only seven years, therefore, elapsed between his arrival in Lisbon—"*which was the cause of his discovering the Indies*"—and his departure on his first voyage in 1492. Fernando is careful, however, to suppress the date of the engagement with the galleys, and writes his history in such wise as to make it appear that a long interval elapsed between the arrival of his father in Lisbon and his subsequent arrival in Spain; which, he tells us, took place in 1484. We see at a glance that this date is false, for the capture of the galleys took place in 1485, and Fernando recounts how his father, saving himself with the aid of an oar, swam ashore; came to Lisbon; married there; subsequently went to Madeira, where he resided some time; returned to Portugal; negotiated with the king of that country; and, finally, as his exorbitant conditions were not acceptable to the Portuguese monarch, came to Spain in 1484—a year previous to his first arrival in Lisbon! He also gives what purports to be the copy of a letter, written by Paul Toscanella, upon navigation and geography, to Ferdinand Martinez, a servant of King John of Portugal, dated Florence, June 25, 1474.

Toscanella was a renowned Italian astronomer of the period. He erected the famous solstitial gnomen at the cathedral in Florence. The presence of the above letter from him among the

Toscanella in his Study.

papers of Columbus, or his son and historian, as well as the manner in which the latter seeks to account for its possession, and the use he appears desirous to make of it, must create distrust in the minds of such as shall give the matter a careful examination.

Fernando tells us his father "got knowledge" of the above letter, "and soon by means of Laurence Gerardi, a Florentine residing at Lisbon, writ upon the subject to the said Mr. Paul." He does not, however, tell us at what time Girardi, acting as secret agent, opened correspondence with Toscanella or Columbus upon the subject. The copies of the letters of Columbus to his middle-man in Lisbon, or to Paul Toscanelli, which would be invaluable in this place, are nowhere forthcoming; but, in lieu thereof, Fernando gives what he would have his readers believe to be the copy of a letter from the learned Florentine to his father. This is shorn of its date and destination, and, moreover, contains expressions which stamp it as a forgery.

Fernando thus quotes, or professes to quote:

The Letter from Paul, a Physician of Florence, concerning the Discovery of the Indies.

"To Christopher Colon Paul, the physician, wishes health.

"I perceive your noble and earnest desire to sail to those parts where the spice is produced, and therefore, in answer to a letter of yours, I send you the copy of another letter, which some days since I writ to a friend of mine—and servant to the King of Portugal, before the wars of Castile—in answer to another he writ to me, by his highness's order, upon the same account. And I send you another sea-chart like that I sent him, which will satisfy your demands.

"The copy of that letter is this."

Then follows the letter from Toscanella to Martinez, with its date 1474.

Above is all that is given of the pretended letter from Paul, the physician, to Columbus; and it is also the authority upon which historians affirm that the latter had formed his project of discovery as early as 1474. A careful analysis of the letter we quote, and consideration of the facts regarding it, will, however, raise suspicion, which amounts to certainty the further we investigate the affair, that it was never written by Toscanella to Columbus :

1. Ferdinand tells us his father first arrived in Lisbon after the capture of the Flanders galleys (1485), and that his coming to Lisbon was the cause of his discoveries. It is abundantly proved that Columbus actually took part in this engagement; *he was not therefore in Lisbon, and had not been there when Toscanella wrote to Martinez.*

2. It was not in keeping with Italian courtesy, and the courtly character of Toscanella himself—had Columbus, in fact, ever made application to him for information and instruction touching the Western passage to India—to send the latter the copy of a letter, written to another person, retaining the date, destination, and sundry personal observations, that were un-

doubtedly pertinent as to Martinez, but certainly not in their application to Columbus.

3. The purported letter of Toscanella to Columbus was evidently written by one who endeavored to prove too much. In order that Columbus may appear to have entertained his ideas of discovery in 1474, and for fear lest the reader should suppose that the copy was sent some years after the original had been written, Toscanella is made to say:

"I send you the copy of a letter which I writ *some days since*, to a friend of mine, and servant of the King of Portugal, *before the wars of Castile.*"

Does it not appear peculiar that he should thus specify a letter as having been written before a great historic event, which was only written some days since ? Where was the necessity of such a declaration to Columbus, who upon receipt of the letter would have inferred from its date at what period it was written ? What have the wars of Castile to do with the letter ?—clearly nothing. The allusion to them can have no reference to the *status* of Martinez, as the fact that he was *then* in the service of the King of Portugal is not only proved in Toscanella's letter to him, dated June 25, 1474, but is corroborated in the pretended letter to Columbus. The latter's having been written long *after* the death of Toscanella, and *after* the wars of Castile, may account for its having occurred to the writer that it would help his case to insert such a clause.

Then, too, the words "in answer to a letter of yours" have the suspicious appearance of having been written by one who was eager to prove that Columbus had written to Toscanella, and feared that fact might be doubted. A correspondent might indeed write, "In answer to your letter of such a date," but "In answer to a letter of yours" would be somewhat superfluous information, as he to whom the letter was addressed would be fully advised in the premises.

Furthermore, Toscanella, in furnishing a stranger with the copy of a letter which had been written by request of the King of Portugal, and the original of which was preserved in the archives of that country, would have betrayed the confidence of the monarch and committed a gross indiscretion. Toscanella, the companion of princes, the friend of the glorious Medici, wise, learned, and experienced, would hardly provide a needy adventurer at the capital of Portugal with the means of driving an unscrupulous and exorbitant bargain with the sovereign with whom he corresponded upon the same subject.

Who and what Columbus was, we have already shown, a nameless pirate (if, indeed, one bearing so many *aliases* may be termed nameless). Had the learned Florentine known him, he would not, we believe, have corresponded with him, and, not having known him, it is still less probable that he did so. The testimony of Columbus is insufficient to remove suspicion, or rather to disprove the forgery which the circumstances we have cited render so apparent.

Many able writers, upon the sole authority of the words *some days since* in this pretended letter from Toscanella to Columbus, and of the letter to Martinez, dated 1474, affirm that Columbus was that year in Lisbon. Among these may be cited Mr. R. H. Major, of the British Museum, who, speaking of the encounter with the galleys, doubts the fact of Columbus's having been present thereat and declares Fernando's relation to be somewhat apocryphal, basing his doubts upon the letter from Toscanella, "for it is certain," he says, "that Columbus was in Lisbon previous to 1474 (for in that year he has a letter addressed to him in that city, in reply to one written by himself from the same place")."[78]

Now, as it is by no means certain that Columbus was in Lisbon, for there is nothing to prove it save the words "some days since" in the evidently forged letter without a date, and as the statement that Columbus was on board one of the pirate-ships that attacked the galleys is made in an unqualified manner by Fernando and confirmed by public documents, we think Mr. Major and other authors rashly discard a plain and evidently truthful statement for one that is merely hypothetical.

There could hardly have been any correspondence between Toscanella and Columbus *after* 1485, as the aged and worthy Florentine, unfortunately for the glory of our hero, died in 1482; we believe therefore that Columbus "got knowledge" of the letter to Martinez at least ten years after it was written, and by means unknown to us, but undoubtedly surreptitious, obtained a copy thereof, probably about the year 1486. Fernando at a subsequent period inserted it in his work, that he might lead his read-

---

[78] Major, "Introduction to Letters of Columbus," p. xxxix.

ers to believe that the project of his father was coeval with the said letter of 1474, thereby bridging over an awkward chasm. Whether the forged preface, purporting to have been addressed by Paul to Columbus, was the work of the latter or his son we know not; either was capable of such an act in such a cause. Fernando had ample opportunities; he was a priest, engaged in collecting a library, in recording and magnifying the glory of his family, regardless of propriety or truth; he was also a member of the same literary junta with Juan Vespucci, who succeeded to the department in navigation, created by or for Amerigo, where it is to be presumed the originals or copies of all important papers relative to navigation were kept, especially those bearing upon the long-sought-for passage to India by the West. It may be urged that his holy vocation would render him incapable of such a crime as forgery, but this clerical plea will scarce avail, when we consider the character of the clergy in his time. It was the age of Alexander VI., the notorious Borgia—of assassination, forgery, and perjury, far more than of sanctity and prayer; and when the archbishop forges the papal bull granting a dispensation to Ferdinand and Isabella from the penalties of an incestuous marriage,"[19] why might not Fernando indulge in the comparatively innocent occupation of manufacturing epistles and falsifying dates to brighten the escutcheon of the Christ-bearer?

We are safe, in the case of the piratical assault, to follow the narrative of Fernando, discarding and correcting as far as possible all dates that are flagrantly inaccurate. He tells us that the ships caught fire; that the crews, to save themselves, leaped into the water, where his father, being an expert swimmer, seized a floating oar, and with its aid reached the shore.

Behold, then, our hero struggling onward, clinging to an oar, behind him the burning galleys, before him the shores of Portugal! These he reaches, is succored, and proceeds to Lisbon, according to his son, "to begin a new state of life;" and as he did nothing wrong, behaved well, and "was comely," he married Doña Felipa Muniz de Perestrela. With respect to his beginning a new life, we know not precisely whether we are to infer that he proposed to betake himself to a seafaring life, or to abandon it. Was he about to give up a nefarious pursuit and lead

---

[19] Prescott, "Ferdinand and Isabella," chapter iii., p. 121.

the life of an honest man, or was he to continue piracy in a new field, upon a grander scale?

However this may be, his stay in Lisbon was short; his wife's father having left some possessions in Madeira, he and his wife took up their abode in that island.

A year could hardly have elapsed before the event took place which, it is evident, first attracted the attention of Columbus to Western lands, and was as it were the turning-point in his life. Modern authors affect to ignore or treat with contempt the story of Columbus's having received his first information from a shipwrecked pilot who died in his house; but their answers to a statement which is to be found in almost all early writers (except Fernando, who seems anxious to give any other reason for his father's undertaking, and evinces a desire to lead us as far as

COLUMBUS ESCAPES FROM THE BURNING GALLEYS.

possible from this one, though he makes a vague allusion to it in his eighth chapter, speaking of Oviedo's mention of it, which he endeavors in a manner to nullify by diverting attention to an opposite direction), are not what may be considered erudite or convincing.

Spotorno says: "As to the idle tale which was current in

Spain, that he had taken the idea of the New World from a pilot of whom a number of fables are told, I shall not stop to refute it."[80]

This summary dismissal of the subject is about the best and most satisfactory answer to the story that we have found. Mr. Irving naïvely shows us the reasons which have induced the eulogists of Columbus to discredit it. He frankly admits that "its veracity would destroy all his" (Columbus's) "merit as an original discoverer."[81] The idle tale, so current in Spain, rests, however, upon the very authorities the biographers of Columbus so often quote. It is related by Oviedo, who was a contemporary of Columbus, and had spent more than forty years in the royal service of Spain, beginning with Ferdinand and Isabella, and who had visited, and been appointed royal historiographer of, the Indies.

It is recounted, at length, in Gomara's "History of the Indies," which was published in the Spanish language, within the realm, and sanctioned by the license of the Archbishop of Saragossa. Gomara was himself a priest, and cannot therefore be supposed to have written any falsehood detrimental to Columbus, especially as he represents the latter as so saintly a character that he asserts "rude crosses erected by him healed the sick and performed miracles many years after his death."[82]

Garcilasso de la Vega also gives perfect credence to the history of the pilot; and Eden prefixes it to Locke's English translation of Peter Martyr, "for the better understanding of the whole work."

Alonzo de Ovalle, a Jesuit father, whose "Relation of the Kingdom of Chili" was printed in Rome in 1649, does not agree with Mr. Irving, that to give credence to the story of the pilot, which he evidently regards as truthful, is to detract from the glory of Columbus.[83] Indeed, most early authors considered the fact as established, and argued for the greatness of Columbus in spite of it. The deviation from truth has yearly widened as authors became more extravagant and bigoted in their adulation, so that it was finally discarded.

This is so important a matter that we cannot forbear giving

---

[80] Spotorno, "Historia Memoria," p. 29.
[81] Irving, "Appendix," No. xi.
[82] Gomara, "Historia de las Indias," cap. xxxiii.
[83] Churchill's "Voyages," vol. iii., p. 88.

here the various accounts to be found in early writers, with the still more convincing proof of the history having been incorporated in 1666, by Captain Galardi, in the introduction to a work which he dedicated to the legal representative of the family of Columbus.

An Extract from " The Royal Commentaries of Peru," written originally in Spanish by the Inca, Garcilasso de la Vega, and rendered into English by Sir Paul Rycaut, in the Year 1688:

"About the year 1484, a certain Pilot, Native of *Helva* in the County of *Niebla*, called *Alonso Sanchez*, usually Traded in a small Vessel from *Spain* to the *Canaries;* and there Lading the Commodities of that Countrey, sailed to the *Maderas*, and thence freighted with Sugar and Conserves, returned home into *Spain;* this was his constant course and traffick, when, in one of these Voyages meeting with a most violent Tempest, and not able to bear sail, he was forced to put before the Wind for the space of twenty-eight or twenty-nine days, not knowing where or whither he went, for in all that time he was not able to take an observation of the height of the Sun; and so grievous was the storm, that the Mariners could with no convenience either eat or sleep: At length, after so many long and tedious days, the Wind abating, they found themselves near an Island, which it was, is not certainly known, but it is believed to have been *San Domingo*, because that lyes just West from the *Canaries*, whence a storm at East had driven the Ship, which is the more strange, because the Easterly Winds seldom blow hard in those Seas, and rather make fair weather, than tempestuous. But God, who is all-sufficient, intending to bestow his mercies, can make causes produce effects contrary to their nature; as when he drew water from the Rock, and cured the blind with Clay; in like manner his immense goodness and compassion, designing to transmit the light of the true Gospel into the new World, made use of these unusual means to convert them from the Idolatry of Gentilism, and from their foolish and dark superstitions, as shall be related in the sequel of this History.

"The Master, landing on the shore, observed the height of the Sun, and so noted particularly in writing what he had seen, and what had happened in this Voyage out, and home; and, having supplied himself with fresh water and wood, he put to Sea again;

but having not well observed his course thither, his way to return was the more difficult, and made his Voyage so long, that he began to want both water and provisions, which being added to their former sufferings, the people fell sick, and died in that manner, that of seventeen persons which came out of *Spain*, there remained but five only alive, when they arrived at *Terceras*, of which the Master was one. These came all to lodge at the House of that famous *Genoese*, called *Christopher Colon*, because they knew him to be a great Seaman and Cosmographer, and one who made Sea-carts to sail by; and for this reason he received them with much kindness, and treated them with all things necessary, that so he might learn from them the particulars which occurred, and the discoveries they had made in this laborious Voyage: but in regard they brought a languishing distemper with them, caused by their Sufferings at Sea, and of which they could not be recovered by the kind usage of *Colon*, they all happened to dye in his house, leaving their labours for his inheritance; the which he improved with such readiness of mind, that he underwent more, and greater, than they, in regard that they lasted longer; and at length he so well succeeded in his enterprise, that he bestowed the New World, with all its riches, upon *Spain*, and therefore deservedly obtained this Motto to be inscribed on his Armes:

'To Castile, *and to* Leon,
The New World was given by Colon.'

" In this manner the New World was first discovered, for which greatness *Spain* is beholding to that little village of *Helva*, which produced such a Son, as gave *Colon* information of things not seen, or known before; the which secrets, like a prudent person, he concealed, till under assurances of silence he first disclosed them to such persons of authority about the Catholick Kings, as were to be assistant and usefull to him in his design, which could never have been laid, or chalked out by the art of Cosmography, or the imagination of man, had not *Alonso de Sanchez* given the first light and conjecture to this discovery; which *Colon* so readily improved, that in seventy-eight days he made his Voyage to the Isle of *Guanatiancio*, though he was detained some days at *Gomera* to take in Provisions."

Extract from "Eden's Preface to Peter Martyr's Decades:"

"*Certaine Preambles here followe, gathered by* R. EDEN *heretofore, for the better Understanding of the whole Worke.*

"*Of the First Discovering of the West Indies.*

"A Certayne Carauell sayling in the West Ocean, about the coaastes of Spayne, hadd a forcible and continuall winde from the East, whereby it was driuen to a land vnknowne, and not described in any Map or Carde of the Sea, and was driuen still along by the coaste of the same for the space of many daies, vntil it came to a hauen, where in a short time the most part of the mariners, being long before very weake and feble by reason of hunger and trauayle, dyed: so that only the Pilot, with three or foure other, remayned aliue. And not only they that dyed, did not enjoy the Indies whiche they first discoucred to their misfortune, but the residue also that liued had in maner as litle fruition of the same: not leauing, or at the least not openly publishing any memorie thereof, neyther of the place or what it was called, or in what yeere it was founde: Albeit, the fault was not theirs, but rather the malice of others, or the enuie of that, which we cal fortune. I do not therefore marueile, that the aunciente histories affirme, that great things procede and increase of small and obscure beginninges, sith we haue seene the same verified in this finding of the Indies, being so notable and newe a thing. We neede not be curious to seeke the name of the Pilot, sith death made a short ende of his doinges. Some will, that he came from *Andaluzia*, and traded to the Ilandes of *Canaria*, and Iland of *Madera*, when this large and mortall nauigation chaunced vnto him. Other say that hee was a *Byscanne* and traded into Englande and France. Other also, that hee was a Portugall, and that either he went or came from *Mina* or *India:* whiche agreeth well with the name of the newe landes, as I haue sayd before. Againe, some there be that say that he brought the *Carauell* to Portugall, or the Ilande of *Madera*, or to some other of the Ilandes called *De los Azores*. Yet doe none of them affirme anything, although they all affirme that the Pilot dyed in the house of *Christopher Colon*, with whom remayned all suche writinges and annotations as he had made of his voyage in the said Carauell, as well of such thinges as he observed both by land and sea, as also of the elouation of the pole in those lands which he had discouered."

"What manner of man Christopher Colon (otherwise called Columbus) was, and how he came first to the knowledge of the Indies.

"Christopher *Colon* was borne in *Cugureo,* or (as some say) in *Nerui,* a village in the territory of *Genua* in Italie. Hee descended as some thinke, of the house of the *Pelestreles* of *Placentia* in *Lombardie.* He beganne of a chylde to bee a maryner: of whose arte they haue great exercise on the ryuer of *Genua.* He traded many yeeres into *Suria,* and other parts of the East. After this he became a maister in making cardes for the sea, whereby he hadde great vantage. Hee came to *Portugall* to know the reason and description of the South coasts of Affrica, and the nauigations of the Portugalles, thereby to make his cardes more perfect to be solde. Hee maryed in Portugall, as some say: or as many say, in the Iland of *Madera,* where he dwelt at such time as the said Carauell arryued there, whose Pilot sojourned in his house, and dyed also there, bequathing to *Colon* his carde of the description of such newe landes as he had found, whereby *Colon* hadde the first knowledge of the Indies. Some haue thought that *Colon* was well learned in the Latine tongue and the science of Cosmographie: and that he was thereby first moued to seeke the lands of *Antipodes,* and the rich Iland of *Cipango,* whereof *Marchus Paulus* writeth. Also that he had reade what *Plato* in his dialogues of *Timeus* and *Cicias,* writeth of the great Ilande of *Atlantide,* and of a great lande in the west Ocean vndiscouered, being bigger than Asia and Affrica. Furthermore that he had knowledge what *Aristotle* and *Thephrastus* saye in their bookes of Maruayles, where they write that certayne marchauntes of Carthage, sayling from the strayghtes of *Gibralter* towarde the West and South, founde after many daies a great Ilande not inhabited, yet replenished with all thinges requisite, and hauing many nauigable riuers. In deede *Colon* was not greatly learned: yet of good understanding. And when he had knowledge of the sayde newe landes by the information of the deade Pilotte, made relation thereof to certayne learned menne, with whom he conferred as touching the lyke thinges mentioned of olde authors. Hee communicated this secrete and conferred chiefely with a Fryar named *John Parez* of *Marchena,* that dwelt in the *Monastery* of *Ribida.* So that I verily beleeve, that in manner all that he declared, and manie thinges more that hee left vnspoken, were written by the sayde Spanyish Pilotte that dyed in his house. For I am purswaded, that if *Colon* by science attained to the knowledge of the Indies, hee woulde long before haue communicated this secrete to his own countrey-menne the *Genuenses*, that trauayle all the worlde for gaynes, and not haue come into Spayne for this purpose. But doubtless hee neuer thought of any suche thing, beefore he chaunced to bee acquainted with the sayd Pylotte, who founde those landes by fortune, according to the sayinge of Plinie, *Quod ars docere non potuit, casus inuenit*. That is, That arte coulde not teache, chaunce founde. Albeit, the more Christian opinion is, to thinke that GOD of his singular prouidence and infinitte goodnesse, at the length with eyes of compassion as it were looking downe from heauen vpon the Sonnes of Adam, so long kept vnder Sathan's captiuitie, intended even then (for causes to him onelie knowne) to rayse those windes of mercy whereby that Carauell (herein most lyke vnto the shyppe of *Noe*, whereby the remnant of the whole worlde was saued, as by this Carauell this newe worlde receyued the first hope of their saluation) was driuen to these landes. But wee will nowe declare what great thinges followed of this small begynning, and howe *Colon* followed this matter, reuealed vnto him not without GODS prouidence."

"After the death of the Pilot and maryners of the Spanyishe Carauell that discouered the Indies, *Christopher Colon* purposed to seeke the same."

Extract from " *Purchas's Pilgrimage*," *edition of* 1625:

"This history is thus related by *Gomara* and Joannes Mariana : a certain caravel sailing in the ocean, by a strong east wind long continued was carried to a land unknown, which was not expressed in the maps and charts. It was much longer in returning than in going; and arriving, had none left alive but the Pilot, and three or four mariners, the rest being dead of famine and other extremities; of which also the remnant perished in few days, leaving to *Columbus* (then the pilot's host) their papers, and some grounds of this discovery. The time, place, country, and name of the man is uncertain. Some esteem this pilot an Andalusian, and that he traded at Madeira, when this befell him. Some, a Biscayan, and that his traffic was in England and France. And some, a Portuguese, that traded to Mina

(India). Some say he arrived in Portugal, others at Madeira, or at one of the Azores: all agree that he died in the house of *Christopher Columbus.* It is most likely at Madeira."

Were we to attempt to give extracts from all the old writers who corroborate the story of the dead pilot, we might fill a volume; the above will, however, suffice, and we will conclude with the following extract from a dedication to the Duke of Veraguas, the legal representative of the family of Columbus, dated 1666; written by Captain Galardi, the duke's secretary, on the personal history of Columbus; put forth as the authorized family version, founded on the documents of the house.[84] We believe it is time that over-zealous historians, and the world at large, should cease to be more jealous of the honor of Columbus than were his immediate descendants and heirs to his honors.

" *To the Right Honorable* LORD DON PEDRO NUÑO COLON (*Columbus*) *and Portugal;* GRAND ADMIRAL OF THE INDIES, *Grandee of Spain, Duke of Veraguas and de la Vega, Marquis of Jamaica, Count of Gelves, Marquis of Villa Mizar, Captain-General of the Naval Army, and Admiral of the Low Countries, Camp-Master-General in the Army, and Captain-General of the* ROYAL, *which is on the highseas.*

" MY LORD : . . . .

" If I am unfortunate enough to be suspected of adulation, I can bring in support of my apology the entire world, which owes to your ancestors the finest, noblest, most opulent and magnificent of its possessions. The annals of the foregoing century, as well as ours, will advance at my head, and it is thence that I borrow my just defense, and it is there that what I advance will be gloriously authorized. But it is too bad, my lord, to dwell upon the bark when it is time to enter into the essence and substance of the matter.

" I will here omit any detailed account of your remote ancestry. Suffice it to say that you drew your origin from Terraro Colon (Columbus), lord of the castle of Cucaro, who rendered very important services to his country, as had also done his illus-

[84] This extract forms part of a " Dedicatory Letter to a Summary of European Politics, specially of Spanish Affairs," during the century 1550-1650, published at Madrid, 1666.

trious progenitors Emery and Lanca. I go on to Dominic Colon (Columbus) who gave birth to Christofle (Christopher), that unique glory and the admiration of his age. But the wonderful grandeur of an event so glorious demands some amplification, and some pause in this relation of a family history which has filled the universe with its praise and applause. Christopher Columbus, whose courage was intrepid, and his industry equal to the greatness of his soul, obligingly entertained in his house in the island of Madeira, the pilot of a vessel which the violence of a storm had carried off very far into the ocean, *and in sight of unknown lands.* That man, who also had a nobly-constituted nature, touched with the kind interest with which his host generously endeavored to reëstablish his strength, left him at his death a striking testimony of his esteem and of gratitude proportioned to that ingenuous benevolence which Columbus had displayed to an unknown and unfortunate man. In fact, he left to Columbus the very important legacy of his instructions concerning that which had happened to him on a voyage so painful and difficult, and gave him such sketches of the lands, and directions as to its position and distance, as were possible.

"This was probably the essential cause and first impulse of his persuasion that the earth had other limits, and that the sun rose and set in another hemisphere. He opened his mind upon this idea to Don Alonzo V., King of Portugal, who decried it as wild and imaginary. Henry VII. of England added mockery to reproach, and told him that he did not feed upon deceptive notions, the ridiculous effect of a cracked and wounded brain. Columbus took no offense; he offered up this shame as a sacrifice to the utility to posterity of his great idea, satisfied that it would add to the praises of a just gratitude, the laudation of a patience which was proof against injuries, insults, and contempt. Ferdinand and Isabella were his last resource, to gain whom the credit of the Cardinal Mendoza contributed very largely, facilitating an audience which he had been demanding for seven consecutive years, with so much ardor, and it was then that his reasons made a breach in the opinion of those great kings, who promised to sustain this important undertaking. But as the conquest of Granada had exhausted their finances, Luis de St. Angel, secretary of Ferdinand, lent for the expedition the sum of sixteen thousand ducats.

"This small amount of money, three vessels, and one hundred and twenty men, were the entire fleet, the army and the treasure, to put an entire world under the glorious dominion of Castile, with more than a thousand millions of souls. Columbus left Palos and carried on full sail toward the goal to which his greatness of soul urged him. He had, however, less to encounter from the boisterous ocean than from the opposition and obstinacy of his crew, who clamored against his persisting in so apparently imaginary and hopeless an enterprise. Before so many evils, Columbus never faltered, and at length overcame in a conflict in which the four elements were in concert with his fellow-creatures to damp his energy and defeat his invincible constancy.

"Toward the coast of Florida he came upon the Lucayan Islands, and discovered at different times Hispaniola, Cuba, Jamaica, and the Island San Juan, with a great part of that immense continent which stretches from the Straits of Magellan to the promontory of Bogador, through a prodigious extent of seas and coasts, fully five thousand leagues counted from the antarctic to the arctic pole.

"On his return from his first voyage (he made four voyages altogether), Ferdinand and Isabella, as a mark of their peculiar esteem, heard him seated; and, besides the confirmation of the tenth part of their taxes in the Indies, declared him their hereditary grand-admiral. Yet, however, during his lifetime and after his death, his successful enterprise was applauded, it is quite certain that the reward never equaled the greatness of the service nor the utility which it unceasingly renders to the state. Indeed, Columbus might with much greater reason make that touching reproach with which Ferdinand Cortez subsequently moved the heart of Philip II., when, long unable to obtain an audience of the king, driven to despair and reckless of his life, he one day accosted that Solomon of his age, taking him by the arm and stopping him short, in these words:

"'V. M. escuche un hombre que le ha ganado mas Reynos que los que le dexaron su padre y sus aguelos.'

"'Sire! listen to a man who has gained for you more kingdoms than those which were left you by your father and ancestors.'

"Philip on this replied very obligingly:

"'Teneis razon, padre!'

"'Quite right, old friend!'

"And at the same time sent him away very well satisfied. In like manner Columbus might well have maintained before Ferdinand, without offending the majesty of that august monarch, that he had acquired and facilitated the conquest of more states than the king had received by hereditary succession from his ancestors. Don Diego Columbus, his son, succeeded Christopher as Marquis of Jamaica and first Duke of Veraguas, by a special grace of Charles V., who did it only at the instance of Don Ferdinand Henriquez, erecting into a duchy his land of Medina del Rio Seco. Ferdinand, brother of Diego, left at his death to the great Cathedral of Seville his library of thirteen thousand volumes, and among them his own work, the life of his incomparable father, which in a very elegant style he devoted to posterity.

"Don Luis was the universal heir of Don Diego, and Don Nuño Colon and Portugal received after him this grand inheritance as the second son of Don Alvaro de Portugal, Count of Gelves, and Doña Leonara de Cordova, his wife, granddaughter of Don George of Portugal, first Count of Gelves and Doña Isabel Colon (Columbus), third daughter of Don Diego Colon, Duke of Veraguas, Grand-Admiral of the Indies. Finally, Don Alvaro Colon and Portugal was the successor of Don Nuño, as you are of the former. . . .

"This, my lord, is a sketch of the glory of your illustrious progenitors. A bolder hand will one day make the sketch complete, with all its colors and details proportioned to the glory and finish of the subject.

"It is my own ambition, but for the present I must be content to subscribe myself for my whole existence, my lord, your very devoted and obedient servant,

  (Signed) "P. FERDINAND DE GALARDI,

"Captain of cavalry in the service of his Catholic Majesty, and secretary to the Duke of Veraguas," etc.

Upon what authority, we ask, do historians reject a statement made in such unqualified terms, by *quasi* contemporary authors who wrote in the praise of Columbus—who were licensed by the Church? Above all, how can they suppose that Galardi, while extolling in most fulsome terms the greatness of Columbus to the representative of his family, would introduce into his eulogy a falsehood detrimental to the glory of his hero? The very fact that he mentions the history of the dead pilot *in such a place, to such a person*, proves, it appears to us, that it was universally admitted.

It is but natural that Fernando should make no direct mention of it. He seems to have possessed certain distorted ideas of greatness which caused him to become exceedingly indignant with Justiniani for saying his father was a mechanic—a sentiment which comes with but bad grace from an ecclesiastic. When, therefore, he devotes several lengthy chapters to show how Columbus was led by a study of the ancients, his own reason, and the letter from Toscanella, to perform his voyage, he evidently seeks to lead us as far as possible from the true motive (the death of the pilot and the papers he left in Columbus's hands) which would greatly simplify the proceeding, and has not so learned an appearance as the reasons he gives; these seem rather to have been assigned to parry a fatal blow, for sailing by a chart already laid down by one who had performed the voyage, was no very extraordinary feat, as he no doubt felt. Yet, notwithstanding all his efforts, there is much in his history which supports the statement.

Had Columbus really, by deep study, arrived at the conclusion that land must exist to the westward, would he have been as positive of the exact situation of that land as he shows himself; and as his son shows him to have been throughout? He admits of no hypothesis, but asserts that, by sailing a given distance in a westerly direction, they shall reach certain lands which, he tells us, *he has been informed stretched from north to south across his track*. On one occasion he refuses to alter his course, "because," says Fernando, "he thought it was lessening the reputation of his undertaking to run from one place to another, seeking that which he always asserted he well knew where to find."

This conduct is precisely the reverse of that which a discoverer would pursue. The latter would run from place to place, seeking that which he was to discover, and could not well know where to find. Again, we are told by Fernando:

" He had always proposed to himself to find land according to the place they were then in, since, as they well knew, he had often told them he never expected to find land till he was seven hundred and fifty leagues to the westward of the Canaries, within which distance he had further said he should discover Hispaniola, which he then called Cipango; and there is no doubt but he had found it *had not he known it was reported* to lie in length from north to south, for which reason he had not inclined more to the south to run upon it."

Is this the language of a discoverer? Is it not rather that of one who had inherited the labors of Alonzo de Sanchez or some other navigator, who is robbed of his well-earned fame? Who reported the land to lie in length from north to south and at the distance west from the Canaries of seven hundred and fifty leagues? Surely no one who had not seen it. The information touching the distance and position of the land is too specific to have been derived from any but an eye-witness, and, having received this information from such a source, he could not believe that Hispaniola was Cipango (Japan). No intelligent man, above all, no navigator or traveler who had visited India, China, or Japan, or studied the geography of the period, could mistake the island of Hispaniola for any of these countries. Toscanella, in his chart, laid down a western passage to Asia, but was too learned a man to make a mistake of half the circumference of the globe, as he would have done had he placed India and the known portions of Asia seven hundred and fifty leagues west of the Canaries.

Again, Pinzon wished Columbus to change his course, believing (correctly) that land was near them to the southwest; but the admiral, writes Fernando, "knowing for certain it was no land, he would not lose time to discover it, as all his men would have had him; forasmuch as he was not yet come to the place where he expected, by his computation, to find land."

Columbus, on his own testimony, corroborates, in a great measure, the statement that he sailed by the log-book of the unfortunate mariner, "who happened to die in his house." In his journal, September 25, 1492, we read:

"Martin Alonzo Pinzon conferred with the admiral on the *chart in which lands were laid down*, as the ships were then in their neighborhood—and had been for three days—in which the admiral agreed; but, as the ships had not seen them, it was considered they had been drifted northward of them by the current.

... The admiral directed the course to be altered to the south-west."

"*October* 3, 1492.—The admiral considered the ships were to the westward of *the islands marked on the chart.*"

These statements, and the fact that he professed to know the exact point where they should find land, prove this to have been no voyage of discovery, and Columbus to have been erroneously termed a discoverer.

That it was no study or scientific knowledge which imbued him with the idea of his Western voyage, must be evident to all

THE SHIPWRECKED PILOT ENTERS THE HOUSE OF COLUMBUS.

who shall give the matter consideration, and shall read, with unbiassed judgment, the various histories which have been written upon the subject—from that of his son Fernando, which Washington Irving terms the "corner-stone of the history of the American Continent," down to the brilliant but unreliable work of Irving himself—and the enthusiastic and ecstatic history by M. de Lorgues, who will not rest content till Columbus be numbered among the saints.

Without a knowledge of the history of the dead pilot, we vainly endeavor to explain the many inconsistencies we have mentioned; with that knowledge, all becomes clear, simple, and probable.

Columbus, the needy adventurer, and but half-reformed pirate, receives into his house, on the lonely shores of Madeira, a pilot and three sailors, sole survivors of a crew whose ship had been driven westward by adverse winds, till it touched upon land unknown to European navigators at that time. The pilot had recorded exactly the latitude and longitude of these lands, the distance he sailed, and the course he pursued. He and his companions all *happen to die in the house of Columbus,* into whose hands fall the papers of the deceased. Seeing in these documents matter wherewith to make his fortune and acquire fame, at small risk or peril, Columbus determines to profit by them, and profit largely, too. His conditions are not those of a learned and honest navigator exposing his views, which might be carried out by any experienced seaman, but of one who, being possessed of certain secret information, proposes to sell it at a high price.

Where, then, is the extraordinary courage so much extolled by his biographers, as they represent him, guided only by his own intuitive knowledge, or scientific research, sailing across what was supposed to be a boundless ocean, and discovering a land which he alone had divined? Did it require such wonderful fortitude to undertake a voyage every league of which was laid down by one who had already performed it?

Columbus was as certain of his course, and of the distance between the Canaries and the lands in question, as he was that he was not sailing to Asia, but to certain islands where his ambition and vanity would be gratified by the sounding titles of viceroy and admiral. Viceroy, indeed, over naked savages!—Admiral of three fishing-smacks! But there is much in a name, or at least our hero thought so.

With these facts before us, Columbus—as he is, and as historians have made him—reminds us of the Arabian fable, in which we are told how a poor fisherman brought up in his net a small casket. Upon his opening it, a great smoke emerges, which assumes the proportions of a gigantic human form—a powerful genius —striking wonder, admiration, and terror, into the heart of the fisherman. But soon the great genius dissolves into smoke, his huge form subsides into the tiny casket which has hitherto contained him; and the fisherman, no longer fearing or admiring, may fling the casket back into the waves whence he drew it.

Columbus, in his own day, was but lightly esteemed, as he and his historians admit. Yet the latter have surrounded him with such a mist of fiction, with such incense of praise, that his real character, being veiled or but partially revealed, he has appeared to many great and wonderful. Let the test of reason and judgment, however, be applied; let the reader of these histories calmly scrutinize these statements, and pause to consider what were the actions which are the theme of so much laudation, and the mist is dispersed, the incense disappears, and the character of Columbus shrinks into its really diminutive proportions. Well would it be for him if his name could be cast into the sea of oblivion, where his crimes and petty arrogance might never more be the subject of horror and contempt!

CHAPTER XI.

PREPARATIONS FOR THE FIRST VOYAGE OF COLUMBUS.

THE pilot being dead, Columbus determined to trade upon the papers he had left, with the aid of which he hoped to attain rank and fortune.

According to Fernando, his father had obtained information which induced him to "believe for certain that there were such islands." Here is evidence that it was upon information *received* that the latter based his operations, which might appear somewhat inexplicable when we have been told, by Fernando, that study and thought were the incentives to the discovery, did we not bear in mind that it applies perfectly to the dead pilot. The information received, which caused such certainty in the mind of Columbus, was the waif of Alonzo de Sanchez; and the former, believing this knowledge and opinion to be "excellently well founded," he resolved to put it in practice, and to sail westward in search of these countries.

This he could not do without the protection of some monarch. It was also necessary that the nautical skill and pecuniary expense of the expedition should be provided by other parties. He therefore proceeded to Portugal, to lay his plans before the king of that country, "because he lived under him."

His terms, the same which he subsequently offers in Castile, are justly thought by the King of Portugal too exorbitant for him to accede to. "The admiral," says Fernando, "being of a noble and generous spirit, would capitulate to his great benefit and 'honor.'" We fail to perceive a noble and generous spirit in one who greedily exacts immense benefit and reward, while totally dependent on others for the means wherewith to carry out his scheme. It has required this assurance from Fernando, and the corroboration it has received from subsequent historians, to make the conduct of the admiral appear other than grasping, and unworthy of true greatness. This, at any rate, was the opinion which the King of Portugal evidently entertained. He refused to accept the conditions; but, according to Fernando, "resolved to send a caravel privately to attempt that which the admiral had proposed to him;" that, in the event of the countries having been found, he might not be called upon to give the immense rewards Columbus had claimed. This story rests upon the unreliable testimony of the Columbos, and should therefore be regarded with suspicion; yet, had the king so acted, it would have been but just.

If the name and history of the dead pilot are unknown to fame, it is the fault of Columbus, who culminates a long life of piracy by robbing, of the glory that belonged to him, a dead man, whom he had received in double trust, who had died beneath his roof! And, though he will be more wary in Spain, he had evidently revealed to the King of Portugal the source whence he derived his information. That monarch may not have thought it more dishonorable to revisit these lands on his own account, than for Columbus to drive an unscrupulous bargain over the spoils of a dead man; he may rather have thought it a meritorious act to

>   . . . "spoil the spoiler as we may,
>   And from the robber rend the prey."

It is this reported conduct on the part of the king that Fernando assigns as a reason for his father's becoming disgusted with, and leaving, Portugal; "stealing away privately, lest the king should stop him," and accept his conditions. There exists, however, a document which leads us to suppose that Columbus feared to be stopped by the *alguazil* rather than by the relenting monarch. A Portuguese document plainly shows that he had become liable to arrest for debt and crime.[65] This accounts for the extraordinary aversion he suddenly evinced for the kingdom of Portugal, as also for his flight into Spain, where we next find him begging, penniless, at the Convent de la Rabida, receiving from Pinzon the money, and from Juan Perez, prior of the convent, and former confessor of the queen, the letter wherewith to present himself at the Spanish court, whither he resolves to journey, and there make the offers which the King of Portugal had

[65] Navarrete, vol. ii., p. 10.

refused. "But," says Fernando, "for fear lest the King (Queen?) of Castile should not consent to his undertaking, and he might be forced to propose it to some other prince, which would take up much time, he sent a brother he had with him, called Bartholomew Colon, to England, to confer with the king of that country."

Bartholomew is said to have fallen into the hands of pirates, yet, nevertheless, reached England, and presented Henry VII. with a map or chart, at the same time telling him of the offer his brother Christopher made, to discover lands in the West, for the English kingdom. The king, we are told, readily accepted the offer, and ordered Columbus to be sent for. All this, according to Fernando, took place in the year 1480! "But," continues the latter, "God having reserved it for Castile, the admiral had, at that time, gone on his voyage, and returned with success."

It may not be amiss, in order to prove further the deplorable want of exactitude, with regard to dates, which pervades Fernando's history, to call attention to the year 1480, set down by him as that in which Bartholomew presented the king with the map and the conditions offered by Christopher. It is more than twelve years previous to his first voyage (1492). The action of the king appears to have been prompt: "Having seen the map" (he is represented as having seen it in 1480), "and what the admiral offered him, he readily accepted of it, and ordered him to be sent for." Yet we are told, on the same authority, that, by the time Bartholomew informed Columbus of a matter which was of such vital importance to him, he had performed his first voyage and returned; at a time, too, when intimate relations, both commercial and diplomatic, existed between England and Spain; and when, therefore, a period of twelve years was not necessary for the transmission of a communication from one country to the other. We merely mention this to show how inconsistent Fernando proves himself throughout, for it is not possible that Bartholomew could have gone to England on any such errand in 1480, as Columbus did not visit Lisbon till 1485. Fernando here, again, attempts to antedate the dead pilot.

Columbus did not, evidently, steal into Spain till 1487. We have already said that Pinzon provided him, on his first arrival, with money sufficient to carry him to court. The reader will be prepared to believe that his finances soon ran low; and we find that, on the 5th of May, 1487, a stranger, called Christopher Columbus, came to Seville, asked for and received, by order of the Bishop of Palencia, a sum of money equal to about thirty dollars.[56] This is said to be the earliest authentic date, proving his presence in Spain, which can be found. We may, therefore, safely conclude that the space of time between his first arrival in Lisbon, and his stealthy flight therefrom in March or April, 1487, was chiefly spent in Madeira, attending to the matter of the dead pilot, and arranging for the successful use of his charts; thence

CONFERENCE BETWEEN COLUMBUS AND JUAN PEREZ.

he returned to Lisbon, proffered his services, staid but a very short time, to arrive in Spain in 1487. This is the only manner in which the history of Columbus can be made consistent and clear throughout, because it is evidently the only true version of that history.

When Columbus arrived at the convent-gate at Palos, hungry and penniless, he was received and cared for by the charitable monks. To the prior, Juan Perez, he spoke of his plans. This worthy friar advised him to confer with the Pinzons, the most influential family of the town, and experienced navigators.

[56] Navarrete, "Colecc. Dip.," vol. ii., p. 11.

Martin Alonzo Pinzon, having, during a recent sojourn in Rome, heard rumors of Western lands, saw nothing improbable in the recital of Columbus, and advised him to lay his plans before the sovereigns. The latter informed him of his destitute circumstances, which would not allow him to perform such a journey, much less appear at court. Pinzon liberally advanced him the necessary funds, while Juan Perez offered to care for his little son, and furnished him with a letter of recommendation to his successor as confessor to the queen.[87]

All these circumstances, though far less shameful than many others of his career, Fernando ungenerously fails to mention, but accounts for Columbus having obtained audience with their Majesties by his being "affable and of pleasant conversation;" and would make it appear that he contracted friendships at court with such persons as were likely to favor his enterprise. The son seems unwilling to let us perceive the destitute condition of his father when he arrived in Spain; and, above all, he would conceal the fact that the Pinzons, whom Columbus so shamefully requited, were the first to encourage and assist him.

With the letter from Juan Perez, Columbus arrived at Cordova, where the court was then held, and laid his plans, or as much of them as he chose to reveal, before their Catholic Majesties, who commanded them to be submitted to the Prior of Prado, and other cosmographers, who were so ignorant, *we are told*, and so far behind this "unlettered admiral," in geographical knowledge, that they condemned the scheme, for reasons both various and absurd, and reported that what Columbus proposed was impracticable. For these reasons, according to Fernando and other historians, and because the conditions of Columbus were considered too exorbitant, their Majesties refused to accept his proposition. Here is a gross slander upon the learned men of that period. Let us bear in mind that the Arabs had for centuries enlightened Spain with their learning; that the schools of Cordova, of Salamanca, and other cities, possessed spheres, zodiacs, etc., which had long aided to instruct thousands, giving them just ideas of the heavens and the earth; yet Fernando, and even modern writers, would have us believe that the most learned of these schools scoffed at the idea of antipodes, and of the sphe-

---

[87] Navarrete, "Colecc. Dip.," vol. iii.; Probanzas del Fiscal; Irving, "Columbus," book ii., chapter i.

ricity of the globe, and were more ignorant than the unlettered seaman who tells us the world is pear-shaped!

The exorbitancy of Columbus's claims seems to have been the only reason for the refusal. The latter evidently exposed no theory, but merely spoke of certain lands of which he had mysterious knowledge, and which he proposes to conquer for their Majesties. When called upon to be more explicit, he refuses "so far to explain himself," as he had done in Portugal, lest he should be deprived of his reward—that is, he forbore mentioning the history of the dead pilot; and, as he would not show more plainly upon what he based his stupendous claims, the affair was allowed to drop.

Had Columbus based his project on theory, why need he have refused to explain that theory? A scientific discussion would have done little to convince men so obstinate in their error as historians represent the *savants* of Salamanca to have been; but the circumstance of the dead pilot would have carried conviction into the heart of the most unbelieving; and that is why Columbus refused to explain himself further, lest he should be deprived of his reward. He evidently had information as to a specific spot, not mere scientific data for argument. No doubt, in his attempt to account on scientific principles for this information, he showed himself as ignorant as he does in his writings, and may justly have incurred the ridicule of the assembled scholars.

The reader will not be surprised that the sovereigns hesitated in acceding to the claims of Columbus when he perceives how advantageous to him they were. The following were the terms agreed upon by their Catholic Majesties, on the 17th of April, 1492:

"First: Their highnesses, as sovereigns of the ocean, constitute Don Christopher Columbus their admiral in all those islands and continents, that, by his industry, shall be discovered *or conquered* in the said ocean, during his own life, and after his death to his heirs and successors, one by one forever, with all the preëminences and prerogatives to that office pertaining; and in the same manner as *Don Alonzo Henriquez*, their Great-Admiral of Castile and his predecessors in said office had enjoyed the same within their districts.

"Item: Their highnesses appoint the said Don Christopher

Columbus their viceroy and governor-general of all the islands and continents which (as has been said) he shall discover or conquer in the said ocean, and that he choose three persons for the government of each of them, for each office; and that their highnesses take and make choice of one of them, as shall be most for their service, and so the lands will be the better governed, which our Lord shall permit him to discover, or conquer, for the service of their highnesses.

"Item: That all and whatsoever commodities, whether pearls, precious stones, gold, silver, spice, or other things whatsoever; or merchandise of any kind, name, or manner whatever, they may be, that shall be bought, exchanged, found, won, or had, within the limits of the said admiralship, their highnesses, from this time, grant to the said Don Christopher; and it is their will, that he have and enjoy the tenth part of it for himself, deducting the charges that shall be made toward the same, so that, of what shall remain clear and free, he have and take the tenth part for himself, and dispose of it at his own will, the other nine parts remaining for their Majesties.

"Item: In case that on account of the said merchandise, which he shall bring from the said islands, or lands, which shall (as has been said) be discovered or conquered, or of those that shall be taken in exchange of them of other merchants, any lawsuit should happen to arise, in the place where the said commerce and trade shall be made and carried on, if by reason of his said office of admiral it shall belong to him to take cognizance of such controversy, it may please their highnesses, that he or his deputy, and no other judge, shall try the said cause, if it appertains to the said office of admiral as the same has been enjoyed by the Admiral Don Alonzo Henriquez, or his predecessors in their districts, and according to justice.

"Item: That all ships which shall be fitted out for the said trade and commerce, whensoever and as often as they shall be fitted, shall be liable to the said Don Christopher Columbus, if he shall think fit to lay out the eighth part of what shall be expended in fitting them out, and that he accordingly have and receive the eighth part of the profits of such ships."

Herrera, from whom the above terms are quoted, carefully omits, however, the important preliminary articles which were drawn up, and upon which these terms were based. His reason for this is obvious: In these preliminaries, preserved among the state papers of Spain, Columbus wisely makes a provision by which, in the event of its being discovered that he traded upon knowledge received from the dead pilot, *his claims might still be protected*. This preliminary document, written in April, 1492, commences with the following significant clause:

"The favors which Christopher Columbus has asked from the King and Queen of Spain, and which *they grant him, in recompense for the discoveries which he has made in the ocean seas*, and as recompense for the voyage which *he is about to undertake*, are the following." [88]

No author, not even Fernando, with his manifest exaggeration of his father's achievements and knowledge, pretends that Columbus had been on a voyage of discovery previous to 1492; to what, then, does the phrase "discoveries which he has made in the ocean seas" allude? It is distinctly stated that he has already made discoveries; this could not apply to scientific theory and speculation, which yet remained to be proved, but it applies perfectly to the very specific knowledge received from the pilot Sanchez, upon which Columbus bases his claim of having *already discovered*.

The phraseology of the contract, the excuse given by the sovereigns for their refusal at first to accept it—which was that, being engaged in fighting the Moors, they could not enter upon any *other* war just then—the large number of armed men crowded into the three small vessels which formed his first expedition (for, though Fernando says it was composed of ninety men, other authors assert that "he was sent with one hundred and twenty soldiers, besides seamen")—the cannon with which they were provided—Columbus's repeated after-allusions to his conquest, when insisting upon a share of the spoils and in the government of the people—all prove that he did not rest his claims entirely upon discovery, but more upon *conquest*.[89] Under the clause

---

[88] State papers, 1492; document 70.

[89] When complaining that a judge had been sent out by Isabella to investigate his conduct, he writes: "I ought to be judged as a captain, sent from Spain to the Indies, to conquer a nation numerous and warlike . . . where, by the Divine will, I have subdued another world to the dominion of the king and queen, our sovereigns. . . . I ought to be judged by cavaliers who had themselves won the meed of victory; by gentlemen, indeed, and not by lawyers." He seems here to have forgotten that, of this

"*or conquer*," his prerogatives are as completely protected as they could be by all the discoveries that it was possible for him to make or imagine; besides which, they could not be prejudiced, should the lands have been previously discovered by a hundred dead or living navigators; that is, if the contract were legal. He professed to the sovereigns of Spain that he was undertaking an embassy from them to the grand-khan, as he clearly states in his journal, which he pompously opens as follows:

"*In nomine D. N. Jesu Christi:*

"*Whereas*, most Christian, most high, most excellent, and most powerful princes, King and Queen of the Spains, and of the islands of the sea, our sovereigns, in the present year 1492, after your highnesses had put an end to the war with the Moors, who ruled in Europe, and had concluded that warfare in the great city of Granada, where, on the 2d of January of this present year, I saw the royal banners of your highnesses placed by force of arms upon the towers of Alhambra, which is the fortress of that city, and beheld the Moorish king sally forth from the gates of the city, and kiss the royal hands of your highnesses, and of my lord the prince; and immediately, in that same month, in consequence of the information which I had given your highnesses of the lands of India, and of a prince who is called the Grand-Khan—which is to say, in our language, King of kings—how that many times he and his predecessors had sent to Rome, to entreat for doctors of our holy faith to instruct him in the same, and that the Holy Father had never provided for them, and that so many people were lost believing in idolatries, and imbibing doctrines of perdition; therefore, your highnesses, as Catholic Christians and princes, lovers and promoters of the holy Christian faith, and enemies of the sect of Mohammed, and of all idolatries and heresies, determined to send me, Christopher Columbus, to the said parts of India, to see the said princes, and the people, and the lands, and discover the nature and disposition of them all, and the means to be taken for the conversion of them to our holy faith; and ordered that I should not go by land to the East, by which it is the custom to go, but by a voyage

---

numerous and warlike people, he once wrote: "So loving, so tractable, so peaceable, are these people that, I swear to your Majesties, there is not in the world a better nation," etc., etc.

to the West, by which course, unto the present time, we do not know for certain that any one hath passed.

"Your highnesses, therefore, after having expelled all the Jews from your kingdoms and territories, commanded me, in the same month of January, to proceed with a sufficient armament to the said parts of India; and, for this purpose, bestowed great favors upon me, ennobling me, that thenceforward I might style myself Don, appointing me high-admiral of the ocean sea, and perpetual viceroy and governor of all the islands and continents I should discover and acquire, and which henceforward may be discovered and gained in the ocean sea; and that my eldest son should succeed me, and so on, from generation to generation, forever.

"I departed, therefore, from the city of Granada, on Saturday, the 12th of May, of the same year, 1492, to Palos, a seaport, where I armed three ships well calculated for such service, and sailed from that port well furnished with provisions, and with many seamen, on Friday, 3d of August, of the same year, half an hour before sunrise; and took the route for the Canary Islands of your highnesses, to steer my course thence, and navigate until I should arrive at the Indies, *and deliver the embassy* of your highnesses to those princes, and accomplish that which you had commanded."

This short extract is a sample of the writings of Columbus, for it contains two manifest falsehoods. We know that it was not he who armed the vessels for the expedition, as he boasts to have done; nor are we to suppose that he believed the countries he was in search of to be the rich and well-known regions of India in Asia, which it had hitherto been customary to reach eastward by land. The dead pilot had well informed him of the nature of the lands and people, but by the pretense of sailing to Asia, the trade with which was the subject of so much rivalry, he, in the language of his son, "sought to tempt their Catholic Majesties," and induce them to grant the extraordinarily advantageous terms he craved.

When his solicitations had been refused at the Spanish court, he returned to Palos, that he might confer with those who had befriended him. Fernando tells us, he made up his mind to offer his services to France; but we believe this pretense of his having laid his plans before all the powers of Europe, is merely made to increase the importance of Columbus. We are confirmed in this belief by the incongruity of Fernando's narrative. In his eleventh and twelfth chapters, he tells us his father was not informed that Henry VII. had acceded to the proposals made by Bartholomew Columbus till after his return from his first voyage; that he stole away from Portugal because the king of that country did not accept his terms, and had deceived him. In his fourteenth chapter, we read that he was "very desirous that Spain should reap the benefit of his undertaking, . . . because he had long resided there, while following his project, and because he had got children there; which was the cause why he rejected the offers made him by other princes, as he declares in a letter he writ their highnesses, in these words: 'That I might serve your highnesses, I refused to take up with France, England, and Portugal.'"

It is possible, as Columbus was nowise scrupulously veracious, that he may have written in such terms to the Spanish sovereigns, thinking that, should they believe other sovereigns competed with them, they would be the more readily persuaded to grant his requests; but the fact that he did refuse to serve the nations above mentioned is by no means thereby established.

According to Fernando's own showing, his father only knew that the King of England would accept his offer after he had returned from his first voyage; he could scarcely, therefore, be said to refuse that which had not been tendered him. That he traded with France is a statement made and supported only by Columbus and his son.

He appears to have returned to Palos, where he urged his case upon his friends Juan Perez and the Pinzons, the former thinking he might possibly retain some of his old influence over the queen, whose confessor he had once been, borrowed a mule and departed at midnight for the royal camp of Santa Fé, before Granada, where it is probable his persuasions induced the queen to accede to Columbus's demands, giving an order on the town of Palos for two caravels, a third to be fitted out, at the expense of Columbus.

Fernando tells us it was one Luis de Santangel, who remonstrated with the queen upon her refusal, and that the latter, in her repentance, offered to pledge her jewels in order to defray the expense of the expedition. This story is as absurd as many others coined by Fernando to embellish the history of his father. The coffers of Spain were then well filled. The treasury of the queen had received an extraordinary increase from her perfidious conduct toward the Moors of Malaga, from whom she had obtained millions, holding out the hope of ransom, who, when they had given all the treasure they possessed, were sold

JUAN PEREZ ON HIS WAY TO COURT.

into slavery. The ostentatious luxury of Castile was the wonder of neighboring nations. Artisans could indulge their wives and daughters in a rivalry of display with nobles, at a cost far exceeding that of the contemplated expedition. It would seem extraordinary, therefore, that the expense of providing three small vessels, should have rested so heavily upon the royal coffers, that her Majesty should be obliged to resort to some Hebrew gentlemen to whom she might pawn her jewels. But had this been so, had the queen been as destitute as she is represented, it is evident that the expedition in question cost her little or nothing, and that she never had any necessity for pawning her property. The expense necessary for it was levied upon the little town of Palos, as a punishment for some offense against the crown, as appears from the following royal order, with which Columbus returned to that town:

"*Requisition upon the Municipality of Palos.*

"In consequence of the offense which we received at your hands, you were condemned by our council to render us the service of two caravels, armed at your own expense, for the space of twelve months, whenever and wherever it should be our pleasure to demand the service.
"April 30, 1492."

Many private individuals of moderate means would have been able, in any event, to furnish the outlay. The Pinzons provided Columbus, who possessed not a maravedi, with the eighth part of the expense which he had boasted he would defray; and thus, without outlay from the crown, a poor fishing-town, and two private gentlemen, equipped the fleet of three little vessels, which the Queen of Spain is represented as unable to do, unless she pawned her jewels.

Columbus, on arriving at Palos with his orders, did not meet with an enthusiastic reception from the inhabitants; they were unwilling to follow an unknown adventurer on a long voyage. Two of the ships, when provided, were secretly scuttled. The delay and difficulty increased, and threatened seriously to impede the undertaking, when the Pinzons, those brave brothers, seeing how matters stood, and having part of their fortune embarked in the enterprise, came forward and offered each to take command of a caravel. The men of Palos, by whom the Pinzons were held in great esteem and respect, now came forward willingly. Two small caravels, the Pinta and the Niña, were commanded respectively by Martin Alonzo and Vincent Yanez Pinzon; the St. Mary, the somewhat larger vessel equipped at the expense of the Pinzons, was under the command of the thenceforth "Admiral Don Christopher Columbus," his right to which title, like all new-born nobility, neither he nor his son will ever forget. As men are born poets and artists, so it would appear Columbus was born admiral. The opening chapter of Fernando's history makes the title ascend, on the Chinese principle beyond his birth, and thenceforth every incident of his life is referred to "*the admiral;*" when speaking of his early life, of his piracy, it is "*the admiral;*" when recounting his solicitations for the title at the Spanish court, it is "*the admiral*" who solicits.

This prospective enjoyment of a ponderous title is amusing in view of the ultimate grandeur of his command: three small vessels, ordinary fishing-smacks, of from thirty to sixty tons burden, two of them without decks, and for the best of these he is indebted to the man whom he will afterward gratefully term "one Pinzon."

CHAPTER XII.

THE FIRST VOYAGE OF COLUMBUS.

WITH this fleet Columbus set sail from the little port of Palos, on Friday, August 3, 1492, for the Canaries.

During the transit the rudder of the Pinta gave way, which

"Suddenly an immense sea-fish (some call it *balena*) was before them, and upon the body of this, holding itself immovable as a rock, the pilots moor their ships, and these most sacred men, celebrating the holy sacrifice of Mass, with previous confession, distribute the Paschal Lamb to all their companions, that is, the sacred communion. . . . What a sight do you imagine this to have been! What joy to these pious and simple men, seeking God with all their mind and strength; when in so immense a beast they saw the pledges offered to their divine Father."—(PHILOPONO, "Christophorus Colombus," 1621.) Such is the character of the histories which have given Columbus his fame, such the incidents they record!

accident Columbus attributed to the malice of those who fitted out the vessel. Fernando, still more unjust, ascribes the accident to the "malice of Pinzon," who commanded her, which is not only ungenerous, but absurd, when we bear in mind that Pinzon, more than Columbus or the sovereigns of Castile, had aided in fitting out the fleet for which "the admiral" had so long solicited in vain.

Columbus, although unable to afford Pinzon any assistance in repairing his damaged rudder, yet, flushed with his new-born honors, must needs come alongside, " as was the custom for commanders at sea." Martin Alonzo, however, stood in little need of assistance; his ingenuity enabled him promptly to repair the damage; but the imperfect rudder was unable to withstand the heavy sea they encountered, and again broke loose. It was therefore considered advisable to seek another vessel at the Canaries. Columbus for this purpose put in at the island of Gomera. Here he found no ship available, but was told that the Lady Beatrix Bobadilla was expected shortly with a vessel of *forty tons* burden; he, therefore, deeming such a vessel suitable for his undertaking, determined to wait for and impress it into his service, to replace the damaged Pinta.

The Lady Beatrix, sailing earlier than was expected, Columbus was balked in his design upon her ship; he therefore rejoined the Pinta at the Grand Canary, and ordered her repaired.

There is a trifling incident, during the transit from one island to another, which may prove how persistently facts are distorted by historians to magnify the glory of Columbus.

Fernando tells us that the Peak of Teneriffe in eruption was discerned by the seamen, and they *admired thereat*. This simple statement has been exaggerated by subsequent writers, till Mr. Irving, whose narrative is taken principally from that of Fernando, tells us that the men were terrified until reassured by Columbus.

There is certainly but little necessity for coloring Fernando's history of his father: that Mr. Irving did not think so is, however, rendered manifest by his converting the *" men admired"* into the men *" were terrified."* Putting this exaggeration of Fernando's statement aside, it is absurd to suppose that sailors who had navigated the Mediterranean, as did most Spanish seamen at that time, and who were therefore familiar with the volcanoes of Etna and Vesuvius, should have been so terrified at beholding a phenomenon of like nature.

The Pinta being repaired, the three little vessels once more put to sea, touching at Gomera for provisions, and finally losing sight of land on the 9th of September, 1492.

It is needless to follow them in the narrative of Fernando, or in Irving's still more highly colored one. The most prominent feature of both is the glorification of Columbus; for this purpose they twist and turn circumstances which are detrimental to their object till they make them redound to the glory of their hero. Yet what was his real object?

> "What sought he thus afar?
> Bright jewels of the mine,
> The wealth of seas, the spoils of war,
> The enslavement of his kind."

The sailors are represented as weeping at the slightest squall, trembling in abject terror during a calm, complaining of favorable winds, while Columbus reassures and encourages them.

We are told that the fleet's crew mutinied and was fain to turn back, till overawed by the determination and courage of "the admiral;" that they had even gone so far as to have resolved to throw Columbus overboard, and account for his disappearance by declaring that he fell into the sea while making observations.

We are not told how Columbus (upon whose authority the story was circulated) was informed of these sinister intentions. It would seem improbable that the conspirators should have made him their confidant, unless indeed they conspired and divulged the conspiracy from an amiable desire to contribute their mite to the aureole with which his biographers have encircled the head of Columbus. It needs but little reflection to perceive the improbability of this story. Sailors, even when really alarmed and in imminent danger, never act in the childish manner described, but are too absorbed, in their efforts to weather the storm, to weep or tremble; and human nature has not changed materially since the days of our hero.

The impossibility of a mutiny is evident, Columbus's own log-book showing that Martin Alonzo and Vincent Yanez kept their vessels ahead during the whole voyage (and were obliged constantly to "lie by for the admiral"); this they would scarce have done had they desired to turn back.

Martin Alonzo first observed that the current had drifted them northward of the islands laid down in the chart of the dead pilot. To this he drew the attention of Columbus; the latter, with characteristic false pride, refused to alter his course, lest he should appear more ignorant than Pinzon, and lessen his own importance.

At this, the men on board his ship may indeed have murmured. They knew, as did Columbus, that they were bound for a given point, and when they heard their commander refuse to sail toward that point, when borne too far north of it by the ocean-current, of which he was ignorant, for the paltry reason that his mistake had been discovered by another, it is but natural they should have felt indignant.

In his desire to appear the sole navigator of the expedition, Columbus gives himself undue credit for deceit: he alleges that he kept one log-book for himself, containing a true reckoning, another containing a false, for the purpose of deceiving his crew, in which he diminished the distances made each day, that they might not lose courage at the vast distance they had sailed. No doubt our hero would have relished this deception, but it is to be feared that in this case we must take the will for the deed, as there is too much contradictory evidence to any such proceeding. Both the Pinzons were skillful navigators, each of them commanded a caravel, and they were generally ahead. They naturally made frequent observations; the pilots also could not have been so easily deceived. Should we, therefore, give credence to this story, we must make the Pinzons, the pilots, and officers, parties to the fraud, an imputation for which there is no basis save the statement of Columbus. Besides, if the latter had thus deceived his crew, it would have rendered another of his statements futile. On leaving the Canaries he declared that, when they had sailed seven hundred and fifty leagues west, they should reach land. The false reckoning and its diminished distances, in leading the men to believe they were farther from their destination than they really were, and that the voyage would be prolonged beyond their expectations, would therefore have defeated his avowed object. For these reasons we believe this deception to have existed only in the imagination of Columbus, who in vanity would make it appear that he alone in that first expedition possessed the courage necessary for so arduous an undertaking, and sufficient knowledge to make correct calculations. He contradicts the latter inference, however, by his own statement, contained in his journal for September 17, 1492, in which he writes that he ordered the pilots to make an observation of the heavens. The idea that skillful pilots and captains could be deceived by false reckonings is too absurd for belief.

When Columbus finally consented to adopt the more southerly course recommended by the Pinzons, the signs of land multiplied, whereupon he declared that he had always proposed to find land *just there*. Fernando relates that he made the crew an impressive speech to this effect, when signs of land became so numerous as to be incontestable, calling upon all to remember how he had commanded, upon leaving the Canaries, that, after

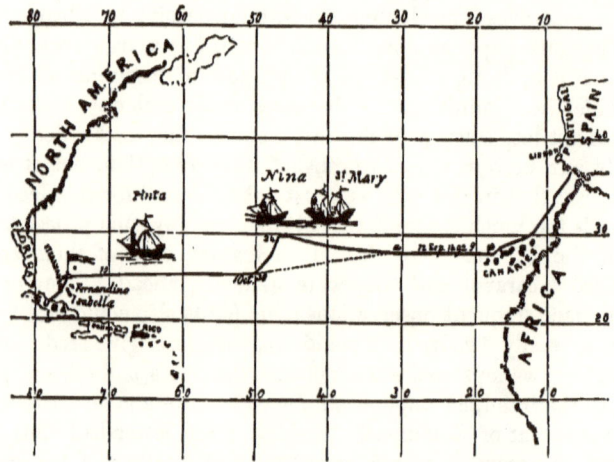

ROUTE PURSUED BY COLUMBUS ON HIS FIRST VOYAGE.

sailing seven hundred leagues westward, they should lie by from midnight till morning lest they should run upon land unawares. This harangue must have lost its intended effect of inspiring the hearers with an exalted idea of the speaker's infallibility, when they remembered that but for the Pinzons he would have drifted far north of the islands to which he professed to be sailing, and of the location of which he was so certain.

"He now desired the men to keep a lookout for land, promising him who should first descry it a doublet of velvet in addition to the thirty crowns a year to be awarded by the sovereigns to the first discoverer."

This promise he was very certain not to be called upon to fulfill, as he had evidently fully determined to defraud whomsoever should rightfully earn either reward.

At ten o'clock of that same night, which was that of October 11, 1492, "the admiral" thought he saw a light ashore, but said it was so blind he could not affirm it to be land; he therefore *privately* called Peter Gutierrez, groom of the chamber to the king, who saw it. He then called Roderigo Sanchez de Segovia, who, probably "through malice, and a desire to rob Columbus of his well-earned fame," could not see it.

Be this as it may, Columbus made no demonstration; his crew knew nothing of what he alleges to have transpired. At two o'clock the next morning, the Pinta, "being far ahead," fired a gun, in signal of land, which was first discovered by one Juan Rodrigues Bermejo, generally called Roderigo de Triana. This mariner, who so justly earned the reward, was, however, defrauded, and the pension granted to Columbus because he had seen a light in darkness, signifying the spiritual light he was to spread in these dark regions.

This spiritual light seen by Columbus at ten o'clock in the evening is evidently but an invention for the purpose of increasing his revenue at the expense of a poor sailor. The story rests solely upon the testimony of Columbus. Peter Gutierrez, who was so privately called, and who is said to have seen the light, was one of the unlucky crew left in the island of Hispaniola and massacred before the return of Columbus. It was, therefore, safe to make him a witness, as he could affirm or refute nothing. According to his own showing, Columbus was in the rear of the Pinta, we will suppose two leagues, which is a reasonable estimate, as it is stated that the Pinta was far ahead; add four hours' sailing before the wind, at the rate of, say, ten miles an hour, and the two leagues the Pinta was distant from land when she fired the gun, and we have a distance of over fifty miles from the point at which Columbus invented his spiritual light, and the low, flat shore of the island of San Salvador. The vessels of Columbus were small; the globular form of the earth would render a torch in the hands of a man upon shore invisible to those on board Columbus's craft even at half the distance they were from land on the evening of October 11th. Irving, who perceived the inconsistency, very justly observes: "Had Columbus seen a light ahead, four hours' swift sailing would have brought him high and dry upon the shore; while, on the other hand, had he seen a light in any other direction, it is scarcely probable he would have sailed *from* it." Besides which, he says nothing till *after* the signal from the Pinta, when he claims the reward which, in common justice, belonged to Roderigo de Triana, and which was paid Columbus yearly at the shambles of Seville; an indication, it would seem, of the ignominious means by which he obtained it. The whole fraud is too palpable to leave a doubt as to its perpetration. Indeed, his son seems to have had some misgivings as to the apparent probability of the story; so he once more brings in the superhuman, and causes his father to perceive a *spiritual* light from a point at which no real light could have been distinguished by mortal vision, as all who have carefully observed the swell of the ocean will bear witness.[90]

[90] Navarrete, in one of his observations (vol. iii., p. 612) on the testimony in the lawsuit between Diego Columbus and the crown, notes the impossibility of Columbus having seen a light. He writes: "The admiral says that '*this island*' (Guanahani, or San Salvador) '*is very flat, without any mountain.*' How then can he pretend to have seen, at ten o'clock at night, at a distance of fourteen leagues, a light which rose and fell on a flat shore destitute of elevations?" A note is here inserted by Navarrete, to the following effect: "Calculating by the table of tangents of the horizon according to the altitude of the point from which they advanced, and supposing the vision of the observer to be elevated twelve feet (Burgos) above the level of the sea (which is as much as can be supposed, when the smallness of the caravels is borne in mind), the result is, that the land must have had an elevation of twenty-two hundred and fifty-four feet above the level of the sea, for its summit or highest point to have been visible at fourteen leagues' distance." He continues: "How is it that the men of the Pinta, which was in advance, did not see it" (the light) "even as they discovered land at two in the morning? Why did he not shorten sail and lie-to when, at ten at night, *he was certain he was near land*—as was done when the Pinta sighted it—as prudence and reason would have required, when we consider the swift sailing of the ships? Why does he say that at first he saw the light so confusedly that he dared not affirm it to be land, as it would appear to few an indication thereof, and that he, nevertheless, afterward *held it for certain*, yet took none of the precautions which such certainty of opinion would have required? Might this not have been the binnacle or some other light of the Pinta which was ahead, or of the Niña, which would have been visible at another point of the compass (for he does not inform us in which direction he saw the light)?—and it might very well have been alternately visible and invisible according as the ship rose and fell. Those who think that the light seen by Columbus was Watling's Island, in the neighborhood of which he must have passed at ten o'clock at night, have not considered or traced his route, and seen that, according to this supposition, the rate of sailing and the situation of that island, he had, at the hour indicated, crossed its meridian, leaving it southeast when he was navigating west."

All this considered, Navarrete concludes that credence should be given to the many witnesses who testified that it was Juan Rodriguez Bermejo (Roderigo de Triana),

After the signal from the Pinta, the fleet lay by till daylight, when the whole expedition landed. After weeping abundantly and kissing the ground, with other demonstrations equally absurd, Columbus named the island San Salvador, taking possession for Castile. And then, bidding all swear allegiance to him as Viceroy of India, and the crew, we are generally told by historians, fawning and kissing the feet of Columbus, beg his forgiveness for all their misdeeds; which servile scene is as improbable as the story of the mutiny is evidently false.

The natives flocked to the shore, and Columbus, believing himself in India, named them Indians, which name the aborigines of America still bear, in commemoration of his ignorance or duplicity. They admire and wonder at the white men greatly. "The admiral especially," says Irving, "attracted the attention of the natives, his commanding height, his air of authority, his scarlet dress, together with the attention paid him by his companions, all pointed him out as *the* man." We presume that, with the naked savage of the forest, the scarlet dress was alone sufficient to excite admiration, the other imposing qualities are, we believe, gratuitous embellishments on the part of Irving.

The friendliness of the Indians is amply dwelt upon by Columbus and his son, as also their innocence and childlike harmlessness. Seven of them, however, Columbus captured and carried off *to act as interpreters;* and here we remark the extraordinary gift of language with which Columbus or the Indians (most probably the former, who may have added the gift of tongues to his other miraculous attainments) are favored.

Immediately on landing in the midst of a race totally different from any he had hitherto seen, speaking a language which bore not the slightest resemblance in formation to those of Europe, he nevertheless converses with them, is directed by them to lands where gold is found, hears from them of neighboring warlike people; in fact, obtains with ease all the information he requires. In other words, we are amazed at the falsehoods

---

a sailor on board the Pinta, who first sighted land, and whom the generous and noble-minded admiral was mean enough to deprive of his just reward; but refrains from one word of censure of Columbus, and merely says, he supposes that the granting of the pension to the latter was but "one of those favoritisms so frequent in courts, as *after the death of Pinzon* the influence of the admiral increased and spread." Such is the blind partiality with which historians record one of the basest acts of a base man.

of Columbus, who, finding the lands, though fertile, devoid of those Asiatic treasures which were the object of the voyage, and which Spain prized so highly, and fearing to lose the royal patronage, must needs represent them as rich in mines; pretending, that he may be the more readily believed, to have received information to that effect from the natives.

Bent, above all, upon the acquisition of treasure, he forbade all trade with the natives, save for gold, of which he could procure but small quantities, but hears or pretends to hear of abundance in other parts. It is probable the little gold found in the island was the particles in the rivers and sands, which the Indians converted into small ornaments. He confesses that San Salvador contained no riches, and proceeds to another island, which he named St. Mary of the Conception. Here one of the Indians who had been captured at San Salvador escaped to a canoe of natives, who paddled ashore and fled to the woods; the canoe was seized by the Spaniards and carried off as a prize. "Such," to quote Mr. Irving, "were the gentle and sage precautions continually taken by Columbus to give the natives a favorable impression of the Spaniards."

Next to St. Mary of the Conception, Columbus visits Fernandina, which he declares the most fertile of all the islands. Here he professes to inhale the odors of the rich spices of Asia, which he is, however, unable to find, but is told by the ever-accommodating natives that they abound to the southwest.

Here also the veracious admiral informs us nightingales are so numerous as in their flight to darken the sky!

The *hamacs* and cotton aprons of the natives, indications of the real wealth of the island, are disregarded or but lightly dwelt upon, Columbus being eager to find the gold he was in search of.

Fernandina they leave for Isabella, called by the natives Saometto; hence they proceed to Cuba, which Columbus named Juanna; this he explored, to what effect we may judge, when we read in his own letter to Santangel, which is preserved in the archives of Spain, that here are men with tails[91] (elsewhere he writes of men with dogs' heads); that the island is

---

[91] "One of the provinces is called Cavan. Men having tails are born there."—Columbus's letter to the Escribano de Racion of the islands of the Indies, February 15, 1493.

larger than England and Scotland, that it abounds in spices, mines, etc.

He declared that he had reached the Continent of Asia, and Irving relates an incident which here occurred, with so little apparent consciousness of its reflecting discredit upon Columbus that we will give it in his own words:

"He imagined that he must be on the borders of Cathay, and about one hundred leagues from the capital of the grand khan. Anxious to delay as little as possible in the territory of this inferior prince, he determined not to await the arrival of messengers, but to dispatch two envoys to seek the neighboring monarch at his residence.

"For this mission he chose two Spaniards, Roderigo de Jerez, and Luis de Torres; the latter a converted Jew, who knew Hebrew and Chaldaic, and even something of Arabic, one or the other of which languages Columbus supposed might be known to this Oriental prince.

"Two Indians were sent with them as guides, one a native of Guanahani, and the other an inhabitant of the hamlet on the bank of the river. The ambassadors were furnished with strings of beads and other trinkets for their traveling expenses. Instructions were given them to inform the king that Columbus had been sent by the Castilian sovereigns a bearer of letters and a present, which he was to deliver personally, for the purpose of establishing an amicable intercourse between these powers. They were likewise instructed to inform themselves accurately about the situation and distances of certain provinces, ports, and rivers, which the admiral specified by name from the descriptions which he had of the coast of Asia. . . .

"With these provisions and instructions the ambassadors departed, six days being allowed them to go and return. Many, at the present day, will smile at this embassy to a naked savage chieftain in the interior of Cuba, in mistake for an Asiatic monarch."

It is not probable that Columbus imagined himself in Cathay. His son denies that such was the case, declaring that he never mistook the New World for Asia," but that he had sailed, as *pro-*

---

[92] While censuring one Mr. Roderick, Archdeacon of Seville, who with his followers "blamed the admiral" for calling those parts Indies which are not Indies, Fernando tells us his father did not give them that name because he really thought them to be

fessed ambassador to the grand-khan we know from his own statement, already quoted, in which he declares this embassy to be the object of his voyage. The following is the missive which he had undertaken to deliver to the Asiatic prince:

"*Ferdinand and Isabella to King* ——

"Have heard that he and his subjects entertain great love for them and for Spain; are, moreover, informed that he and his subjects very much wish to hear from Spain; send, therefore, their admiral, Christopher Columbus, who will tell him that they are in good health and perfect prosperity.

"Granada, *April* 30, 1492."

Columbus, in Cuba, sends an Embassy to an Asiatic Prince.

He evidently made some pretense of carrying out this mission. When his messenger returned, instead of glowing ac-

the Indies, but " because he knew all men were sensible of the riches and wealth of India ; and therefore by that name he thought to tempt their Catholic Majesties, who were doubtful of his undertaking, telling them he went to discover the Indies by way of the West."—" Historia del. Amirante," chapter vi.

Herrera corroborates this statement thus: " There was no other ground for calling this New World by the name of Indies, than the design of the Admiral Christopher Columbus to excite the princes he was treating with the more."

counts of flourishing populous towns, and a civilized, luxurious people, they speak of towns composed of five huts, of naked though kindly savages, from whom they receive little gold trinkets, and three of whom accompany them on their return. All of which, if we are to believe his biographers, did not dissuade Columbus from the idea that he was in those opulent regions described by Marco Palo in gorgeous and glowing colors.

The vessels now left Cuba in search of the supposed Babeque, during which search Martin Alonzo became separated from the other caravels. At this, Columbus was greatly disconcerted; he seems to have been very dependent upon Pinzon, and, upon the departure of the latter, becomes pusillanimously discouraged, alleging for every failure in what he had promised or represented, that, had Pinzon remained with him, it would have been otherwise.

Many authors can hardly find sufficient vent for their indignation at what they term this desertion on the part of Pinzon; but the latter, who had been one of the chief promoters of the scheme, can hardly have been expected to take no other part in the exploration save that of following Columbus, to whom he certainly owed nothing, but who may be said to have owed him nearly every thing in the accomplishment of his enterprise.

It was on the 7th of December that Columbus first landed on the beautiful island of Hayti, which was thenceforward to be the chief scene of his inhumanity and crime.

Here were signs of greater civilization; the ground was cultivated. The people, however, who fled in affright, were naked, like the inhabitants of the other islands.

The Spaniards captured a young and handsome woman, whose sole apparel was a small gold ornament in the nose; this, small as it was, served to awaken the covetous greed of Columbus. He took possession of the island, planting, in sign thereof, a huge wooden cross; the same, perhaps, to which Gomara ascribes such miraculous healing powers in after-years.

Peter Martyr gives a touching and it is believed substantially truthful description of the inhabitants of this lovely island, showing that they had little need of missionaries; above all, such wolves in sheep's clothing as Columbus.

"It is certain," he writes, "that the land among these people is as common as the sun and water; and, that 'mine and thine,' the seeds of all misery, have no place with them. They are content with so little that, in so large a country, they have rather superfluity than scarceness; so that they seem to live in the golden world, without toil, living in open gardens, not intrenched with dikes, divided with hedges, or defended with walls.

"They deal truly one with another, without laws, without books, and without judges.

"They take him for an evil and mischievous man who taketh pleasure in doing hurt to another; and, albeit they delight not in superfluities, yet they make provision for the increase of such roots whereof they make bread, content with such simple diet, whereby health is preserved and disease avoided." [93]

When we read the above, and remember how all this happiness and virtue was converted into misery and crime upon the advent of the Christian, we might almost fancy the following a "leaf from the log-book" of Columbus, so admirably does it portray the case:

"A purple island on our lee .
 Of coral-growth to-day we made,
And down the simple natives ran,
 Half in surprise and half afraid.
'Poor heathen souls!' our chaplain cried,
 And all his mission zeal awoke;
A boat was lowered, he shot the reefs,
 And singled out a chief and spoke:

"'We come' he said, 'across the seas,
 From a great land, that soars sublime,
Rich in a faith direct from God
 And in the garnered spoils of time;
There man is great and woman fair,
 And all in life and death are free,
And wealth and culture make the earth
 What God designed his earth to be.'

"'Religion there has lost its taint,
 No superstition clouds the mind;
We either worship God or saint,
 Or both are in one creed combined.
All mysteries are narrowed down—
 We have no doubt of right or wrong—
Mere questions about bread and wine,
 And burning candles all day long!

[93] Peter Martyr, "Decade I.," book iii.

"'Science has made us wise as gods,
   Has made us strong and potent too,
Happy as well, I need not add,
   Since there is naught we cannot do.
Each word—our land is great in words—
   By courier through the empire flies,
We ride on horses and on mules,
   And that *must* make us good and wise.

"'Our rich are favorites of Heaven;
   Each seeks the other to outvie,
By trying to create a want,
   Or wants created, to supply.
Their virtues make them shining lights,
   Their vices public service aid;
Luxurious living scatters wealth,
   And wanton waste is good for trade.'

"'These men are blest!' the savage cried,
   'Favored of Fortune o'er and o'er;
But all your people are not rich?'
   'Well, no, of course, we have our poor:
Their toil is hard, their food is scant,
   But then they clearly understand
That God designed them to be thus,
   And not to perish from the land.

"'No doubt some hunger day by day,
   Some toil on toil incessant heap;
But they have *all one* day of rest,
   Besides the rest they get in sleep!
And they are taught that work exalts,
   That toil the lot of man will leaven,
And, failing happiness on earth,
   They can make sure of it in heaven.

"'And then'—'No more!' the savage cried,
   'Hence! to your favored nation go,
Leave us our skies, our shores, our sea,
   The simple freedom that we know,
Leave us long days of happy ease,
   Not toilsome weariness of breath;
Leave us a life that *is* a life,
   And not endurance filched from death.'" [94]

[94] This poem, entitled "A Leaf from a Log," appeared in an English periodical of recent date. We have slightly altered the fourth verse, in order to render it applicable to the epoch of Columbus.

When the natives had overcome their instinctive fear, their reception of the Spaniards was most kindly. A delegation of the latter was sent to explore the interior, and returned full of praises of the hospitality they had received; still, there were no signs of gold in abundance. Columbus, indeed, heard reports of banners of wrought gold, of pearls and precious stones, but, beyond a few trinkets from the natives, he can procure nothing. He understands, however, that, in *another* region, there is abundance. He receives some masks, with eyes and ears of gold, and some plates of gold, which are "very thin."

On the 24th of December, while lying off the coast of Hispaniola (which was the name he gave Hayti), "it pleased the Lord, seeing me gone to bed," writes Columbus, "and we being in a dead calm—and the sea as still as water in a dish—all the men went to bed, leaving the helm to a *grumete* (apprentice). Thus it came to pass that the current easily carried away the ship upon one of those shoals which, though it was night, made such a roaring noise that they might be heard and discovered a league off."

Here the vessel struck; several of the crew lowered a boat and fled to the other caravel. Columbus, perceiving imminent danger, as the tide was ebbing, ordered the masts to be cut down, but this tardy precaution was in vain. The St. Martha, the best and largest of the caravels, was completely wrecked. Vincent Yanez Pinzon refused to receive the fugitive crew on board the Niña. They therefore returned to the wreck, and Columbus bade them seek the king of that part of the country, and inform him of the disaster, telling him the vessel had been lost in an attempt to *visit and serve him,* and begging his assistance. This he did, that he might make the chief feel in a measure responsible, and secure his aid, with that of his followers, to transport the goods from the wreck ashore. There was no necessity for this lie, as the well-disposed, kindly natives would have probably tendered all the assistance in their power to the strangers they had so hospitably received without it, but Columbus could never persuade himself to adopt a straightforward course where a crooked one was possible.

To his appeal the good Guacanagari responded, not only by sending all the canoes and men he could muster to transport the freight ashore, but himself standing guard while this was being done, that all might be safely delivered to the Spaniards.

The sheer carelessness and incapacity of Columbus, in thus losing his vessel in a dead calm, are fully demonstrated. We do not wonder he had need of the skill and superior knowledge of Martin Alonzo Pinzon. In his relation of the accident, he again shows the inconsistency which characterizes him. We are first told that the current carried the ship to the shoal; then that the sea was ebbing from the shoal, so that the ship could not move. Thus did the elements combine and change at his will, that he might appear blameless in the disaster.

The hospitality and the gentle nature of the savages, who are the subjects of the many eulogiums pronounced by Columbus, Peter Martyr, and others, together with the loss of his vessel, which would render it almost impossible for the whole crew to return to Spain, determined him to form a colony at the spot where he had landed, which he called La Navidad. Here a fortress was built from the remains of the wreck, "strong enough," says Columbus, " to subjugate the whole island."

He also writes in his letter to Santangel, that La Navidad is conveniently situated for commerce with the grand-khan, and with the continent; and also offers great facilities for *the export of slaves*, showing thus early what were his designs upon the simple natives he so much extolled.[95]

His preparations being complete, and some forty men having been selected to remain in the island, in charge of the fortress, under Peter Gutierrez and Diego de Arana, orders were given them by Columbus to collect as much gold as possible against his return. He then determined no longer to delay his departure for Spain; he feared that Pinzon would arrive there before him, and complain of him or speak against the enterprise. Like all guilty consciences, he feared an informer; and, though Pinzon

---

[95] "Has taken possession of all the islands in the name of Ferdinand and Isabella who can dispose of them as absolutely as of the kingdom of Castile. Has taken possession of a place in the island of Hispaniola, which is very well situated for commerce with the continent and with the grand-khan. He baptized the town Navidad. Has fortified it. . . . Has made the king his best friend, so that he is very proud of the settlement. But even should the natives change their minds, they would be unable to do any harm to the garrison. . . . The garrison would suffice to destroy the whole island. . . . Slaves might be exported to any extent which might be wanted."— CHRISTOPHER COLUMBUS *to the Escribano de Racion, February 15, 1493.*

would not be likely to represent as a failure an enterprise in which he had so much involved, he may have had it in his power to expose many evil or absurd doings on the part of Columbus. This the latter resolved he should have no opportunity of doing. He therefore bade farewell to Guacanagari, and, to inspire the natives with awe for the war-implements of the Spaniards, Fernando tells us his father shot a bullet at the ship, which passed right through it and fell into the water. What ship was thus treated we are not told; the material of the wrecked St. Martha had been employed in building the fortress, and it is improbable that Columbus would have thus riddled a hole in the Niña, his only remaining ship. Fernando tells us also that his father showed the natives swords and rapiers, and other arms, out of which statement Mr. Irving's brilliant and vivid imagination conjures up a princely entertainment of tournaments and mock fights, which it is scarcely probable the crew of the little caravels would have been competent to enact.

Columbus now set sail on his return-voyage. Before leaving Hispaniola he was hailed by the Pinta, and, though excessively indignant with Pinzon, we are told that he restrained his wrath, knowing that, should an open quarrel take place, the greater portion of the crew would side with Pinzon. He pretended that Pinzon had traded for much gold, which he appropriated to himself and crew. How Columbus acquired this information remains a mystery; the crew of the Pinta would hardly have revealed a secret so profitable to themselves, still less would Pinzon himself have made the confession.

Although Columbus had himself seized more than a dozen natives to carry to Spain, he insisted that four which Pinzon had on board should be sent back to their native land. Petty spite and envy, together with that base ingratitude, common to all little minds, which causes them, when under deep obligations (as was Columbus to Pinzon), to seek some excuse for quarrel, that they may appear justified in forgetting past favors, seem to have actuated his conduct toward Martin Alonzo.

Several days were spent among the islands. Columbus saw three mermaids,[*] and two islands opposite each other, the one inhabited solely by women of a warlike nature, the other solely by men; the latter, he recounts, visit the former once a year to

[*] *See* Columbus's journal; "Herrera, West Indies," decade i., book ii., chapter i.

perpetuate the race: the male offspring is sent to the males, and the female portion is retained by the Amazonian natives of the first isle.

Irving, speaking of Columbus's repeated descriptions of these islands, and of many other falsehoods of which he was guilty— such as reporting encounters with mermaids, men with tails, dogs' heads, one eye, together with his assertions that the small

Things seen by Columbus on his First Voyage.—(Grouped from De Bry.)

island of San Salvador contained a harbor capable of holding all the ships in Christendom, besides other embellishments, such as hearing the song of the nightingale, unknown in the Western Hemisphere—indulgently states that he was constantly *deluding himself* into the belief that his best hopes were realized, that he was in Asia. It would certainly appear, however, from the testimony of his son, already quoted, Herrera, and others, that Columbus was *the deluder, not the deluded*, and that these fables were invented by him as seeming corroborations of his statement that he had been in those regions described by Marco Polo. We do not see how one who pretends to have seen what never existed, can be called *self-deluded*. By this mild expedient all extravagant tales of travel and adventure need no longer be regarded as false. Sindbad the sailor, Baron Munchhausen, Gulliver, might merely have been self-deluded men, who believed implicitly in the truth of their own stories; at any rate, the same credence should be vouchsafed to them as to the creator of fables of mermaids, tailed and one-eyed men, Amazons, men with dogs' heads, etc., etc.

While coasting round Hispaniola, the Spaniards encountered a warlike tribe of natives, differing wholly from the gentle creatures they had hitherto dealt with. The first skirmish here took place between the Indians and Christians. The former were routed. Their chief, after sending Columbus the wampum-belt of peace, visited him, and on returning to his home sent him a coronet of gold for a present. Columbus continued to sail west for some time, in search of the island of the Caribs, but finally resolved to return with all haste to Spain. A favorable wind arising, the prows of the two caravels were therefore turned eastward.

CHAPTER XIII.

HOMEWARD VOYAGE.

From the outset of this voyage, Columbus, according to most historians, encountered the most terrible storms that ever tossed helpless mariner upon the huge billows of the deep; other storms have raged, and will rage, but none so awful—they would have us believe—as those which assailed our hero on his homeward voyage.

Even after the vessels had emerged from the tract swept by the trade-winds, the storm continued, and Columbus sought to propitiate Heaven by holy vows. First, he and his crew cast lots, which of them should make a pilgrimage to our Lady of Guadaloupe. The lots consisted of as many beans as there were men—on one of the beans a cross had been marked—he who drew this one performed the pilgrimage. The admiral drew first, and the lot fell to him. Twice more were lots cast, and once again the lot falls to Columbus, but, the storm not abating, the whole crew made a vow that they would go barefoot in their shirts to a shrine dedicated to the Virgin, at the first land they should reach.

Columbus, during this voyage, "sought to confuse the pilots in their reckoning, so that he alone might possess a clear knowledge of the route," a proceeding which elicits any thing but censure from his biographers.

The Pinta, scudding before the strong south wind which prevailed, became separated from the other vessel, and was soon lost sight of altogether. The waves ran high, and the Niña, according to Fernando and others, was in imminent danger for want of ballast, so that Columbus ordered the empty water-casks to be filled with sea-water.

The various accounts of the terrible weather which prevailed are very apochryphal, inconsistency and contradiction being constantly apparent; thus, while the son and the majority of historians report that the ship was too light, and had to be ballasted as above, Columbus, in his letter to Santangel, speaking of this same storm, makes no mention of any such expedient, but says, on the contrary, that the ship had to be lightened by throwing the cargo overboard. It is difficult to decide which account is truthful, or whether either of them is to be believed.

We are next told of Columbus's expedient, when in imminent danger, for making the world acquainted with his discovery.

ARREST OF THE CREW ABOUT TO PERFORM THEIR PIOUS VOW IN THE ISLAND OF ST. MARY.

He wrote, according to his own statement, a detailed account of the voyage, describing the situation of the islands, their resources, etc., sealed and addressed it to the king, wrapped it in a waxed cloth, placed the whole in the centre of a cake of wax, and, passing the package through the bung-hole of an empty cask, which he stopped up, cast it into the sea. This story is, to say the least, improbable; and its improbability, together with the inconsistency of the reports as to the ballast, leads us to believe that this terrific storm was magnified and exaggerated, to make Columbus appear the greater in nautical skill, ingenuity, and pious endurance.

The Niña finally reached the island of St. Mary (one of the Azores), where a detachment of the crew was sent ashore, *minus* all clothing save their shirts, to accomplish the pious vow above recorded.

The governor of the island, Castañeda, had known Columbus in his former days of piracy, and, upon perceiving this motley crew parading the streets in such unseemly guise, and learning under whom they sailed, he may not improbably have imagined a piratical enterprise. He had the whole detachment arrested, and their boat seized. Upon Columbus indignantly remonstrating, and declaring that he was sailing in the service of the crown of Spain, the governor, at first incredulous, finally sent officers on board to examine the papers of the quondam pirate. Rather to his surprise, the assertions of Columbus were found to be correct, whereupon the men were released, the boat restored, the crew supplied with provisions, and Columbus himself treated with all courtesy and kindness. These are the bare facts in the case, which Fernando and his successors do not fail so to embellish as to make the proceeding rather magnify the glory of Columbus than otherwise.

The former relates that the King of Portugal had ordered the arrest of the "admiral," that Spain might be deprived of his services. We read, moreover, that, upon the governor's refusal to release his men and boat, "the admiral" made a solemn vow, which he called his whole crew to witness, that he would not depart thence "till he had taken one hundred Portuguese, to carry them into Castile, and destroyed all the island."

All this is related in such high-flown language as to inspire the reader with an exalted idea of the dignified defiance of "the admiral." But, when we remember that forty men of this small expedition had been left in Hispaniola; that the Pinta, the larger of the two remaining vessels, was on her way to Spain, separated from Columbus; and when we read, in the same chapter [97] which records his vow to take prisoners and devastate an island, that he had but *three* able seamen left on board, and that he was without a boat, his threat savors much of the Bombastes Furioso.

As to the pretended orders from the King of Portugal to arrest Columbus, had any such been issued, the commissions and

[97] Fernando, "Historia del Amirante," chapter xxxix.

papers of the admiral would have had little power to induce the governor to disobey them.

The arrest was made by Castañeda on his own authority, he having been acquainted with Columbus's piratical antecedents,[96] but, on learning that the latter was "leading a new life," he released his men without further ado.

We, moreover, learn from Fernando how "the admiral" informed the people of St. Mary that he was Viceroy of the Indies, which he had discovered, whereat they are reported to have been greatly elated.

That Columbus was absurdly boastful, we are ready to believe. Like all *parvenus*, he could not remain silent as to his rank and achievements, lest perchance they should be ignored; but we are less ready to believe that the Portuguese of St. Mary rejoiced so exceedingly because an adventurer in the employ of a rival power had visited certain lands, of what importance soever they might be.

Columbus, after a short sojourn at St. Mary, resumed his homeward voyage. Another storm arose, another vow was made, and lots are cast to determine who shall go barefooted, in his shirt (a costume which seems to have been a favorite with our hero), on a pilgrimage to the Virgin of Huelva, and spend the night upon his knees before the shrine; again the lot falls upon Columbus, "God showing thereby," says his son, "that his offering was more acceptable than those of the others."

Las Casas gives a somewhat different explanation; he says: "Thus again was expressed the disapproval of his proceedings by Providence; and that these repeated visitations were sent, in punishment, for his having torn from their home the unfortunate natives who were on board the Niña."

Did we believe in the miraculous, we should consider the latter explanation by far the more valid of the two; but it was evidently a trick of Columbus, whereby he might increase his pious reputation, and gain credit with the Church. It was not difficult, we presume, for him to draw out what he already held, and the frequent repetition of the farce makes it evident that he had the marked bean in his hand, and thus manœuvred, that he might appear miraculously to draw it every time, in testimony that his offering was the most acceptable.

[96] A. B. Becher, "Landfall of Columbus," p. 268.

BOASTFUL CONDUCT OF COLUMBUS. 215

The tempest was still at its height when the vessel sighted land, which proved to be the rock of Lisbon. Here Columbus was obliged to put in, because of the fury of the storm; and, not content with enlarging to the people upon the unheard-of wealth of the countries he had discovered, he spread, or caused to be spread, abroad a report that the Niña was loaded down with gold. And then he wrote to the King of Portugal, informing him of his discoveries, and demanding permission to go on to Lisbon, averring that he would be more safe, as the report concerning the gold might tempt the people, where he then was, to rob him.

COLUMBUS BEFORE THE SHRINE OF THE VIRGIN.

We are not surprised, knowing the boastful, false pride of the man, to find him contemptibly elated at being thus able to flaunt his discovery in the face of a prince who had refused to engage in it; but the arrogance and boastfulness of the pirate, become admiral, exceed all belief.

When an officer summoned him to give an account of himself, he replied, that the king's admirals were not obliged to obey such summons, and it was with difficulty he was persuaded to show his papers; but upon his doing so, if we believe his son, these very Portuguese, toward whom he is bearing himself thus haughtily, come in all humility with fifes and drums to receive him. The people of Portugal rejoice with exceeding great joy that their rival Spain has acquired new territory, and, according to this admiral, endless riches. They might indeed have envied, but it was not in human nature to rejoice. The whole of this enthusiasm was evidently invented by Columbus and his son, and but too greedily caught up and exaggerated by subsequent writers.

Irving, after the brilliant account he gives of the reception of Columbus in Portugal, and of the honors paid him there, somewhat inconsistently adds:

"His rational exultation was construed into an insulting triumph, and they accused him of assuming a boastful tone when talking with the king of his discoveries, as if he would revenge himself upon the monarch for having rejected his proposition. . . .

"The Portuguese historians, in general, charge Columbus with having conducted himself loftily with the king. . . . Faria .y Souza, in 'Europa Portuguesa,' goes so far as to say that Columbus entered into the port of Rastello merely to make Portugal sensible, by the sight of the trophies of his discovery, how much she had lost by not accepting his propositions."

Knowing what we do of the character of Columbus, far from considering this view of the case exaggerated, we should have been surprised had he not so conducted himself. What surprises us is, that historians should represent the King of Portugal as humbling himself to the utmost, notwithstanding all this flaunting arrogance. He invited (we read) Columbus to see him; the latter (always magnifying his own importance, and always a coward) feared that his assassination was intended, but finally condescended so far as to visit the monarch. The latter (according to the universally-repeated story) bade him sit in his presence, don his cap, and of course, that the importance of the affair may be complete, insinuated that this great conquest belonged by right to Portugal, etc., etc. The most prominent man of the kingdom was assigned as the host of Columbus; the queen earnestly entreats him not to pass her by without visiting her; in short, this *ci-devant* pirate (should we believe his son and other biographers) is, at the court of the monarch who had refused his services on account of his exorbitant claims, and from whose dominions he had ignominiously fled, a second Mordecai, the man "whom the king delighteth to honor!"

Allowing this extremely improbable relation to be true, and Columbus to have received these honors, it was wanting in good taste and delicacy for him to accept them; his reporting his discoveries to another and rival monarch, before doing so to the sovereigns who had employed him, was itself an act deserving the severest censure, and which no desire to excite the envy and regret of Portugal can justify or palliate.

RABO DE JUNCO.

CHAPTER XIV.

ARRIVAL IN SPAIN, AND RECEPTION AT BARCELONA.

COLUMBUS remained in Lisbon ten days; and finally, on Friday, the 15th of March, 1493, arrived at the port of Palos, seven months and eleven days having elapsed since his departure therefrom, August 3, 1492.

Here, on the same day, Martin Alonzo Pinzon anchored before his native town. He had sent the sovereigns word of his return, but they had already received a dispatch from Columbus, at Lisbon, in which he had basely enlarged upon what he termed the "insubordination of Pinzon." The latter, therefore, received a prohibition to appear at court, which so deeply wounded his pride, and so bitterly reminded him of the ingratitude of men, that he returned to his home, sick at heart and in body. He shortly after died, it is said, of a broken heart, caused by the manner in which the sovereigns rewarded him for having bravely embarked in the enterprise at its unpromising outset, and at the return Columbus gave him for having protected him in adversity, supplied him with the funds without which he was powerless to carry out his scheme, and finally accompanied him to encourage an unwilling crew. Thus died a man both good and brave, a victim to the ingratitude of one who possessed neither of these qualities.

Time and history will each year show the name of Pinzon in a fairer light, while, should justice and truth obtain, that of Columbus will each year lose more and more of its borrowed lustre.

Leaving his broken-hearted benefactor to die, "the admiral" started from Palos to present himself to the sovereigns at Barcelona. He was a month in reaching his destination; "being obliged," says his son, "to stay some little, by the way, though but never so little," to gratify the curiosity of the people in the cities through which he passed. We presume it required little persuasion to induce the admiral to make all the parade in his power.

Fernando, in his life of his father,[92] would have his readers believe that there was much joy in Barcelona upon the arrival of the latter. His statement is indorsed by Herrera, but Mr. Irving gives a still more glowing account of the transaction.

CHRISTOPHER COLUMBUS.—(From Herrera's "West Indies.")

For various reasons we believe, however, that no such demonstration took place as that described by Fernando. These reasons are obvious.

We will follow the gradual growth in the description of this pageant, as it passes from pen to pen, of the authors who vie with each other in covering Columbus with glory.

[92] "Historia del Amirante," chapter xlii.

The first account seems to have been written by Peter Martyr, a contemporary, who, in his correspondence with many distinguished persons of the day, noted most of the passing incidents and events of the Spanish court.

He thus relates the affair to Fernando de Talavera, Archbishop of Granada, under date of February 1, 1494:

"The king and queen, on the return of Columbus to Barcelona, from his honorable enterprise, appointed him admiral of the ocean sea, and caused him, on account of his illustrious deeds, to be seated in their presence; an honor and a favor, as you know, the highest with our sovereigns. They have dispatched him again to those regions, furnished with a fleet of eighteen ships. There is a prospect of great discoveries in the antarctic antipodes."

This is all that Peter Martyr, the distinguished letter-writer, says of a reception which Irving leads us to believe was the talk of every tongue, the admiration of a world.

The next writer in chronological order, who speaks of the arrival of Columbus in Barcelona, is his son Fernando. With him the account given by Peter Martyr grows somewhat; he says: "Thus holding on his way, he got to Barcelona about the middle of April, having before sent their Highnesses an account of the happy success of his voyage, which was extraordinary pleasing to them, and they ordered him a most solemn reception, as to a man who had done them such singular service. All the court and city went out to meet him; and their Catholic Majesties sat in public with great state, on rich chairs, under a canopy of cloth-of-gold, and, when he went to kiss their hands, they stood up to him as to a great lord, made a difficulty to give him their hands, and caused him to sit down."

Herrera copies substantially from the above, but enlarges in his turn; and, passing over numerous other authors, we come to Mr. Irving's admirably-written but delusive history of Columbus, and find the following:

"The fame of his discovery had resounded throughout the nation, and, as his route lay through several of the finest and most populous provinces of Spain, his journey appeared like the progress of a sovereign. Wherever he passed, the surrounding country poured forth its inhabitants, who lined the road and villages. In the large towns, the streets, windows, and balconies, were filled with eager spectators, who rent the air with acclamations. . . . It was about the middle of April that Columbus arrived at Barcelona, where every preparation had been made to give him a solemn and magnificent reception.

"The beauty and serenity of the weather in that genial season and favored climate contributed to give splendor to this memorable ceremony. As he drew near the place, many of the more youthful courtiers and *hidalgos* of gallant bearing, together with a vast concourse of the people, came forth to meet and welcome him. His entrance into this noble city has been compared to one of those triumphs which the Romans were accustomed to decree to conquerors. First, were paraded the Indians, painted according to their savage fashion, and decorated with their national ornaments of gold. After these were borne various kinds of live parrots, together with stuffed birds and animals of unknown species, and rare plants, supposed to be of precious qualities; while great care was taken to make a conspicuous display of Indian ornaments, bracelets, and other decorations of gold, which might give an idea of the wealth of the newly-discovered regions. After this followed Columbus on horseback, surrounded by a brilliant cavalcade of Spanish chivalry. The streets were almost impassable from the countless multitude; the windows and balconies were crowded with the fair; the very roofs were covered with spectators. It seemed as if the public eye could not be sated with gazing on the trophies of an unknown world, or on the remarkable man by whom it had been discovered. There was a solemnity in this event, that mingled a solemn feeling with the public joy. It was looked upon as a vast and signal dispensation of Providence, as a reward for the piety of the monarchs. . . . To receive him with suitable pomp and distinction, the sovereigns had ordered their throne to be placed in public, under a rich canopy of brocade of gold, in a vast and splendid saloon. Here the king and queen awaited his arrival, seated in state, with the Prince Juan beside them; and attended by the dignitaries of their court, and the principal nobility of Castile, Valencia, Catalonia, and Aragon, all impatient to behold the man who had conferred such incalculable benefit upon the nation. At length Columbus entered the hall, surrounded by a brilliant crowd of cavaliers. . . . As Columbus approached, the sovereigns arose, as if receiving a prince of the highest rank.

Bending his knees he requested to kiss their hands; but there was some hesitation on the part of their majesties to permit this act of vassalage. Raising him in the most gracious manner, they ordered him to seat himself in their presence: a rare honor in this proud and punctilious court. At the request of their majesties, Columbus now gave an account of the most striking events in his voyage, and a description of the islands which he had discovered. . . . The words of Columbus were listened to with the most profound emotion by the sovereigns. When he had finished, they sank on their knees, and, raising their clasped hands to heaven, their eyes filled with tears of joy and gratitude, they poured forth thanks and praises to God for so great a Providence: all present followed their example, a deep and solemn enthusiasm pervaded that splendid assembly, and prevented all common acclamations of triumph. The anthem of *Te Deum laudamus*, chanted by the choir of the royal chapel, with the melodious responses of the minstrels, rose up from the midst in a full body of sacred harmony, bearing up, as it were, the feelings and thoughts of the auditors to heaven. . . . . Such was the solemn and pious manner in which the brilliant court of Spain celebrated this sublime event; offering up a grateful tribute of melodious praise, and giving glory to God for the discovery of another world."

Such events, in which display and pomp play the greater part, are generally most graphically described by contemporaries and eye-witnesses, who have the scene yet present to their minds; and these descriptions rather dwindle and weaken as they pass from one historian to another.

How much more distinctly does Froissart bring before us tournaments, processions, and ceremonies of his time, than the subsequent historians who recount them; how many details we find in his chronicles which conjure up the scene with startling reality, and which we look for in vain elsewhere: and this is owing, not so much to his superior powers of description, as to the fact that he was himself a spectator or participant in what he described. But with this reception at Barcelona the reverse takes place; the description increases in detail and coloring as it comes down to us, because the imagination, and not the facts, play the greater part: imagination, from a simple, unadorned statement of a prosaic or unimportant fact, will create a wondrous scene.

For the writer of fiction and romance this is a glorious gift, but a most dangerous one for the historian, who, when possessed of it, will too often represent facts as he would have had them, rather than as they were. Thus it is that out of the words of Peter Martyr ("caused him to be seated in their presence") a scene is created which, were we to believe Mr. Irving, was the grandest pageant history records. "Behold how great a matter a little fire kindleth!"

Again, had all Spain gone forth to receive Columbus with acclamations, would Martyr, when writing, a year after the occurrence took place, to Fernando de Talavera, confessor to the queen, Archbishop of Granada, and member of the royal household, speak to him of the return of Columbus as of something of which he did not think it likely he would be informed? Would not the ready pen and fluent language of Peter Martyr have made the most of such a scene—particularly when we consider that he is represented as having been intimate with Columbus, and is declared by Las Casas to be the highest authority on matters relating to the discovery of the Indies, as he received his information from Columbus himself?

Nor are we without further evidence that the description of the reception prepared for Columbus at Barcelona is a gratuitous embellishment on the part of modern historians.

That eminent tourist, antiquarian, and scholar, the late Mr. George Sumner, gives the following curious item, which strongly corroborates our view of the case:

"From the brilliant description given by Irving and Prescott of the arrival of Columbus at Barcelona, and of his reception there by the Catholic sovereigns, it seemed to me as probable that some contemporary account of the arrival and reception, as well as of the sojourn of Columbus, might be found at Barcelona; and, while there, in the spring of 1844, I searched the admirably-arranged archives of Aragon, and also those of the city of Barcelona, for such notice, but without any success. I could not so much as find a mention of the name of Columbus. The 'Dietaria,' or day-book of Barcelona, notices the arrival of ambassadors, the movements of the king and queen, and even records incidents of as trifling note as those which in our day serve to fill the columns of a court journal; yet not a word appears in regard to Columbus. . . . In the 'Dietaria' of

Barcelona, under date of 15th of November 1492, is the following entry: 'The king, queen, and primogenito, entered to-day the city, and lodged in the palace of the Bishop of Urgil in the Calle Ancha.' This is followed by a description of the festivities which ensued: '1493, 4th February, king and queen went to Alserat. 14th, king and queen returned to Barcelona.'"

Thus is another popular error exploded upon which sensational historians have drawn so largely for their most striking chapters. Few of our readers will perhaps thank us for thus stripping Truth of the gay garments wherewith she has been decked for their greater delectation and amusement, but the truth, naked and prosaic, appears to have been that Columbus was received by the king and queen at the Calle Ancha, and allowed to sit in their presence while he gave the history of his voyage.

He assured their majesties that those whom he had left in the island could not fail to collect a ton of gold before his return. He dwelt upon the riches he professed to have heard of from the natives, and talked largely of being soon able to raise such an army as should release the Holy Sepulchre from the grasp of the infidel. Wealth, he declared, was to be gathered without cost and without labor. The riches of Asia were at the command of Spain. Upon these representations (how false we need not repeat) of the glowing success of his expedition, the title of admiral was confirmed to him by royal edict, as well as the privileges enumerated at length in the act granting him that rank.

An order, dated Barcelona, 30th of May, 1493, after the usual wordy preamble, reads as follows:

"To honor and promote you and your descendants and lineage in perpetuity, we have thought proper, and it is our desire, and we give you authority to bear on your shield of arms, a castle and a lion, which we give you for arms; that is to say, the castle *or*, on a field *vert*, in the *dexter* quarter; and in the *sinister* quarter, a lion *purpura, rampant*, on a field *argent;* and in the *dexter* base quarter, some islands *or*, in waves of the sea, and in the *sinister* base quarter the arms which you are accustomed to bear; which above said arms shall be acknowledged as yours, and those of your descendants in perpetuity hereafter."

ARMORIAL FICTIONS.

We have read much of the motto—
"A Castilla y a Leon
Nuevo mundo dio Colon "—
and of its being awarded to Columbus by the sovereigns, that he might bear it on his arms as some recompense for his mighty deeds; we find it, moreover, inscribed on the existing coat-of-arms of the family, by Captain Galardi, in the fulsome dedica-

tion from which we have already quoted, and from which we take the above engraving. It is therefore with some surprise that we find no mention of any such motto, not only in the above act granting the coat-of-arms, nor in any of the authentic documents in which the transactions between our hero and the crown are recorded. Nor is it once alluded to by Columbus; vanity would undoubtedly have prompted him to dwell largely, in the latter part of his life, when he had fallen into disgrace, and was vainly seeking to secure some prestige at court, upon so striking and public an acknowledgment on the part of the sovereigns.

One of the early historians speaks of the coat-of-arms, as above, and says: "To this he" (Columbus) "afterward added the motto—

> 'To Castile and to Leon
> A new world gave Colon.'"

Fernando does not even pretend that the device existed in the lifetime of his father, but speaks of it as having been placed on a magnificent tomb erected to his memory at Seville. No such inscription or tomb is there to be found, and as the reputation of Columbus has increased, or rather its glory been wholly created, since his death, we may safely presume, had such an inscription existed when Fernando wrote the history of his father, it would have been preserved to our time. Of this, however, we will speak more at length in due season (*see* Chapter XXVIII.).

That the motto in question was never granted Columbus as the legend of his coat-of-arms, is certain; whether it was the invention of Christopher, or Fernando Columbus, we cannot determine; but that it emanated from the fertile brain of one or the other is evident, for, had it been granted him officially, there would either be some mention of it in the act granting him a coat-of-arms, or, if it were afterward added, some formal statement to that effect would exist; but such a statement is not to be found.

With his too evident desire to mystify in all matters where the truth might belittle Columbus, Irving, speaking of the coat-of-arms, vaguely adds: "To this was afterward added the motto, 'A Castilla,'" etc.

He does not *say* it was granted by the sovereigns, but such would be the inference of every reader unacquainted with the truth.

The item of the grant which authorized Columbus to bear his *own* arms on the lower sinister quarter of the escutcheon was somewhat superfluous, though none of his biographers mention the fact. A coat-of-arms was an ensign of nobility, and Columbus's most zealous advocate, Spotorno, admits that he must have been of ignoble birth, very rationally adding that, had it been otherwise, "he" (Columbus) "would most certainly have boasted of the fact to the haughty Spanish nobles," who could never consider the pirate admiral their compeer.[100] It is evident that he possessed no arms, as the quarter allotted to them was filled with several anchors; this goes far to prove that the much-talked-of coat-of-arms was granted rather from necessity than as a reward. The Admiral of Spain could not be other than noble; none were noble who bore no escutcheon; when, therefore, the rank of admiral, which gave him a place among the high-born of Spain, was confirmed to Columbus, the insignia of nobility was of necessity added.

[100] Spotorno, "Int.," pp. xciii., xciv.

THE MANATI, AS REPRESENTED IN PHILOPONO.—*See* Appendix.

CHAPTER XV.

SECOND VOYAGE OF COLUMBUS.

THE golden falsehoods of Columbus fired the cupidity not only of the sovereigns, but of many of the Spanish *hidalgos;* with all haste a dispatch was sent to the Pope (Alexander VI.), requesting a grant of the lands discovered, which was immediately granted. The promptitude with which the sovereign pontiff deeded a continent of unknown limits to Spain, can only be accounted for by the fact that he was himself a Spaniard by birth, and that, in her zeal for the Church and vigorous prosecution of the Inquisition, Isabella might be termed the right arm of the Church.

No sooner was the papal grant received, than a fleet of seventeen, according to some—eighteen vessels, according to others—was forthwith equipped; and so many of high and low degree were anxious to form part of the expedition, that this time it was not a question of compelling an unwilling crew to undertake the voyage, but of inducing equally unwilling citizens to remain behind.

On the 25th of September the fleet, well freighted with all the necessaries for colonization, and with about fifteen hundred Spaniards of all ranks, eager for the wealth Columbus had promised, left the port of Cadiz. They proceeded to the Canary Islands, on leaving which, Columbus gave to the captain of each ship sealed instructions containing directions as to the route he was to pursue; these, however, were only to be opened in case the ships became separated from Columbus by adverse weather; "for," says Fernando, "he did not wish the route to be known, unless there was great need"—another evidence that he regarded the enterprise as a secret which had fortunately come into his possession for his own advancement, and not as the means of benefiting humanity or the kingdom of Spain.

Remembering the current which the unfortunate Pinzon had been the first to discover on the previous voyage, this time Columbus pursued a straight course, and, after twenty days' sailing, arrived, on the 3d of November, at an island which he named San Domingo, after the day of the week, which was Sunday. No inhabitants were seen. Another island was passed, and named Mari-galante, after the admiral's ship; the next, Guadalupe, after a monastery in Spain; this island was large, and on the shore they found a village, or settlement, the inhabitants of which had fled, leaving only children. Among various things which Columbus reports as having been found in this village, he speaks of an *iron pan*. Fernando, probably aware at the period in which he wrote his history that iron utensils were unknown among the natives, makes more explanation than the case would seem to require, unless he considered his father's reputation for veracity in peril. He conjectures that it might have been stone that resembled iron, that it might have come from the settlement at Hispaniola, or from the wrecked ships; he seems, in fact, most eager to prove his father truthful—a falsehood notwithstanding.

It is a matter of wonder to the reader of the history of Columbus, that he did not, upon arriving at the islands, at once proceed to the relief of the colony he had left at Navidad; but the reason soon becomes apparent when we read that at Guadalupe the admiral sent a boat ashore on the 5th of November, "to take somebody to inform him of his whereabouts, and which way Hispaniola lay." [101] A youth and six women were accordingly taken, and from them Columbus professes to learn that they are prisoners of a race of cannibals, who enslaved the women and devoured the men they captured in war.

This is the first time the grave charge of cannibalism is preferred against the natives of the New World, a charge which investigation and the laws of Nature alike show to be false. The Indians in those islands, on the showing of Columbus himself,[102]

[101] "Historia del Amirante," chapter xlvii.
[102] In the bull of Pope Alexander VI., deeding the lands to Spain, which is affirmed to have been granted *solely on the testimony of Columbus*, the inhabitants of the islands are described as "numerous, live peaceably, and, as it is affirmed, go naked, *and feed not upon flesh.*"

lived chiefly upon the nutritious roots which grow in their fertile homes, a diet which they varied with the fish which were found in such abundance in their rivers and along their shores. Nothing in the temperature of that region, or the temperament of the natives, would lead them to such a practice.

What, then, were the reasons which induced Columbus to prefer against them so monstrous a charge?

They are obvious. His enterprise, unless the means of enriching Spain, would avail him nothing in the eyes of that kingdom or its sovereigns; the gold he had promised so largely was only forthcoming in the smallest quantities; the spices of Asia were not to be found at all; he then turned his thoughts toward the gentle natives, who—the reminiscences of his experience in the Guinea-trade present in his mind—suggested themselves as a source of wealth. It was his intention to enslave them from the first, as is manifest in his letter to Santangel, written on his return from his first voyage, and in which he speaks of the facilities which the port of Navidad offers for the export of slaves. He may have spoken of this to Queen Isabella, who, to do her justice, was unwilling, at the outset, when she expected to acquire wealth of a different nature from these islands, to treat her new subjects thus outrageously.

Columbus, still bent upon the establishment of slavery, sought some excuse, therefore, and the most plausible was, to represent his victims as monsters, feeding upon human flesh, whom to enslave was to civilize. The story, moreover, would appear as a corroborative proof that he was in Asia, as many fables were then current reporting the existence of man-eaters in the extreme east of the continent; he would thus accomplish a double object.

Accordingly, on his return to the islands on his second voyage, he prefers the charge; and the document he dispatched to the sovereigns during his second sojourn in Hispaniola, with the comments they made on his propositions, show alike his motive and the objections he strove to subvert.

The first part of this document relates to the necessary provision for the colony, and contains excuses for not sending gold, together with a request for permission to build a fortress, and to all this the sovereigns affix approbatory remarks. In the seventh paragraph Columbus boldly launches into a proposal to enslave the Indians; he tells their highnesses he sends therewith some cannibals as slaves, to be converted, and taught the Spanish language, that they may act as interpreters. He omits no argument that might tend to hide the *venu* of his proposition; he affirms that the Indians of the other islands will greatly rejoice at the capture of their enemies. But the sovereigns are not thus to be blinded, and to this paragraph, adverting to the proposed conversion of the Indians to the Christian faith, they affix this comment: "This is well, and so it must be done, but let the admiral see whether it could not be managed there, that they should be brought to our holy Catholic faith, and the same with the Indians of the islands where he is."

In the next paragraph, Columbus systematizes his project. After enlarging on the benefits which will accrue to the souls of these monstrous devourers of human flesh, by their enslavement, he shows that the islands being in need of cattle and other domestic animals, a regular system of barter might be established, and ships coming to the colony laden with oxen, mules, etc., might return to Spain with a cargo of human live-stock, always from the cannibal portion of the population.

"These cattle," he writes, "might be sold at moderate prices, for the benefit of the bearers, and the latter might be paid with slaves taken from among the Caribs, who are a wild people, fit for any work; well proportioned, and very intelligent; and who, when they have got rid of the cruel habits to which they have become accustomed, will be better than any other slaves."

In his eagerness to show the value of this live-stock, he forgets, or is unaware that, in praising their intelligence, he furnishes a powerful argument against the truth of his imputation that they ate human flesh, for, wherever the disgusting practice has been found to exist, it has always been among human beings of the lowest order of intellect, scarce removed from brutes. "When they lose sight of their country," continues the admiral, "they will forget their cruel practices." This was evidently said in order that, when the gentle harmlessness of the poor slaves should surprise the Spaniards, they should believe they had only become thus gentle and harmless since they left their island-homes. He further adds, as a tempting suggestion to the sovereigns: "Their highnesses might fix duties on the slaves that might be taken over, upon their arrival in Spain."

Never was the establishment of slavery more deliberately planned and proposed. Ferdinand and Isabella at once perceived the enormity of the proposition, and to this paragraph they answer: "As regards this matter it is suspended for the present, until there come some other way of doing it" (converting the heathen there), "and let the admiral write what he thinks of this." A comment which disappointed but did not discourage Columbus. He knew the character of his royal mistress too well not to be assured that, when the natives should prove to be the only means of procuring wealth in the islands, she would herself consider their enslavement necessary for the salvation of their souls; and, in effect, though she will never consent to their exportation, yet by her order of 1503 she will compel them to work, as slaves only are compelled.

But to return to Columbus. From the six women and boy he captured, he asked information as to his whereabouts: not, according to his son, that he did not know the exact situation of Hispaniola, but merely because he wanted to hear what they had to say about it. He was now anxious to leave Guadalupe, but, nine of the men having gone ashore without his permission, he sent Alonzo de Ojeda and forty men to seek them. These returned, after a fruitless search, with marvelous accounts of the vegetable productions they had seen; and moreover affirmed, according to Columbus, that in traversing six leagues they crossed twenty rivers, an exaggeration which is so apparent to Fernando that he seeks to palliate his father's statement by suggesting that they might have crossed the same river several times. The truants found their way back to the ship, and so greatly was our humane admiral incensed at their having lost their way, that he ordered them put in irons, and their allowance of food retrenched!

They now set sail, and passed several islands, where they found coral and other curious productions. "Though the admiral," says his son, "was very desirous to know every thing, yet he resolved to hold on his course to Hispaniola; but, the weather being bad, he came to anchor on Thursday, the 13th of November, in an island, where *he ordered some Indians to be taken, to know whereabouts he was.*"

He did not finally arrive at Hispaniola till the 21st of November; thus, notwithstanding his anxiety to visit his colony, and his perfect knowledge of its situation, he was nearly a month from the time he arrived at San Domingo before he reached the same; he would not stop to examine the productions of the various islands, yet was continually stopping to capture Indians, of whom to inquire his latitude and longitude, of which, says the son, he was well aware. Such conduct would have been absurd. We will believe that Columbus was anxious to rejoin those he had left, but the means employed show him to have been totally ignorant of the location of the island.

With the assistance of the natives, he at length succeeded in reaching it. He found the fortress, which, he had assured the

INDIAN WIDOWS DECORATING THE GRAVES OF THEIR SLAUGHTERED HUSBANDS WITH THEIR HAIR.—(From De Bry's "America.")

sovereigns, was strong enough to keep the whole island in subjection, destroyed, and the entire colony massacred.

The good Guacanagari averred their destruction to be the work of a neighboring tribe, that of the powerful Cazique Caonabo; but he and all the Indians with one accord proclaimed the Spaniards to have made themselves objects of fear and hatred throughout the island by their insolence and licentiousness; they also reported them as having quarreled among themselves, and dispersed, plundering native villages in small bands, so that their destruction was regarded as an act of self-defense by the Indians.

Thus ominously did the first colony of Spaniards in the Western Hemisphere inaugurate their relations with the natives. Their fate was a terrible one, a violent death in a far-off land, where cries for assistance could reach no friendly ear, and would only bring around them their enemies in greater numbers; enemies so numerous that their little band dissolved before them like snow beneath a summer sun. But, terrible as was their death, they had brought it upon themselves; their enemies were the once friendly natives, whom they cruelly wronged, and who avenged the injuries heaped upon them by the stranger who invaded their homes, and made them desolate.

CHAPTER XVI.

SETTLEMENTS IN HISPANIOLA.

Columbus was apparently not so much concerned at the loss of his men as he was eager to find the gold which he hoped they had collected. He had left orders that, in case they were attacked,

Christopher Columbus.—(From De Bry's "America.")

they should throw all the treasure they might have amassed into a certain well. This was now carefully searched, but to no purpose—not a particle of gold was found. Columbus, being thoroughly disgusted, his opinion of the port of Navidad underwent a most radical change. Where before he saw a splendid harbor, whose situation afforded every advantage for the establishment of a flourishing colony and the building of an opulent city, he now perceives only flat, unhealthy ground, where to remain would be to perish. This fickleness is apparent throughout Columbus's transactions; he never attempted to represent matters as they were, but rather to make such statements as should secure favor for his projects. Hence, in the first place, he grossly exaggerates the advantages of Navidad as a seaport (particularly when he dwells upon its convenience for trade with Asia); and, in the next, he as grossly magnifies the disadvantages of the same place, that his abandonment of it might appear the more reasonable.

The site he next chose for a settlement was on the north side of the island. Here he resolved to build a town, as the situation, he declared, was unexceptionable. He therefore caused the ships to be unloaded, and proceeded to lay out a town, which he named Isabella.

Already the fatal effects of his falsehoods became manifest: here were hundreds of Spain's noblest sons, who had left civilized life and luxurious homes, allured by the tales of gold and Asiatic treasure to be gathered at will in a land as fair as Eden.

Upon landing at Isabella, provisions began to fail; the Spaniards were without a roof to protect them from the heavy and unwholesome night-mists which pervade those countries. Change of climate, scantiness of food, and exposure, brought sickness and death, while the gold was nowhere visible. The land was, indeed, fertile; and in a few years might be capable of sustaining thousands; but it was uncultivated, and the roots which served the simple natives as food were insufficient in quantity to sustain the large colony Columbus had brought out, even if the dainty palates of Castilian nobles could have accustomed themselves to such rude fare. Want and exposure spread sickness among all, particularly among the high-born. The first steps taken by Columbus toward building the new city were by no means calculated to alleviate the sufferings of his followers. He proceeded to build a church, a magazine, and a *house for himself*,[103] a triad which illustrates the ruling traits of his character

[103] Herrera, "Decade I.," chapter xl.

—hypocrisy, avarice, and selfishness. The latter is particularly apparent, in that he built shelter for himself before taking steps to secure greater comfort for hundreds higher born and gentler bred than he, who were dying from the effects of the hardships they endured, whom, sick and famishing, he compelled to labor in the erection of this very house. What wonder that, amid

House of Columbus in Ruins.

such a scene of disappointment, want, and sickness, murmurs became audible and discontent apparent? Historians are unanimous in their expressions of contempt for these Spaniards who expected to find in the New World the comforts of the regions they had left, and wealth beyond measure at their disposal besides. They represent Columbus as the much-injured victim of these visionaries, who reproached him with having allured them by inspiring false hopes; but these historians forget how rightly these reproaches were addressed to Columbus. He had not prepared his colonists for the hardships they were to endure. If they had indulged in golden visions, as delightful as illusive, Columbus was the magician who had conjured up such visions. He had declared the wealth of the islands to be so great that, in a short time, sufficient could be procured to raise an army and free the Holy Sepulchre. The few men he had left were to have collected at least a ton of gold before his return, and this without labor or expense save that of a few worthless bawbles which they gave the natives in exchange for the precious metal.

Nor did he represent the country as a new one. Asia, with its rich civilization, was within a few days' journey; the land was so beautiful, the natives so gentle, that paradise itself could scarce have been a more delightful sojourn. Such was the tale by which he secured the wealth of Spain—the flower of her nobility—for his enterprise. And what was the reality? They reach the western shore to find their countrymen massacred; the lands, though a valuable acquisition to the crown, could only be made such by labor; the farmer and the mechanic, rude sons of the soil, and the poor inured to hardships—not noble cavaliers—should have been the first to people them. So would it have been, but for the base manner in which Columbus deceived the sovereigns of Spain and their subjects. Had he represented the necessity of labor; had he not been eager to increase his importance and wealth by borrowing from the tales of Marco Polo, that he might appear to have visited the countries of Asia, which Spain and Portugal so longed to reach; had he not, we say, practised the grossest deception (we have shown how impossible it was that he could have been deceived), a very different crew would have emigrated with him—smaller in numbers, of the lower ranks, looking forward to a life of trial—and the sufferings of this unhappy multitude would never have existed.

When the building of the town was fairly under way, twelve ships were dispatched to Spain, and with them Antonio de Torres, the bearer of the dispatches before mentioned, in which Columbus develops his system of slave-trade. These ships set sail on the 2d of February, 1494. Many a sad eye watched them wistfully as they disappeared; many a sad heart sank into deeper gloom, as the last white sail vanished beneath the horizon.

As the unhappy Spaniards awakened from their dreams of splendor to the reality of a country in which was found neither food nor shelter, dissatisfaction daily increased; hatred for the pirate-admiral, who had so craftily allured them to destruction, became more and more apparent; nor were the harsh measures and tyrannical conduct of Columbus calculated to conciliate. At this early stage, bitter complaints are made against him; his disrespect of the Spanish gentlemen, his cruelty to the lower classes, the small pretenses upon which he reduced the rations of all ranks—all create ever-increasing indignation; and the disaffection, with which he now commenced to be regarded, will henceforth continue throughout his career.

This disaffection soon became more serious, and, at last, unable longer to restrain their indignation, many of the Spaniards organized a resistance against the tyranny of Columbus. Bernal Diaz de Pisa, who was controller of the expedition, and had occupied a position of some mark at court, headed the disaffected. The fact that a man of such standing protested against the conduct of Columbus, should cause unprejudiced writers to reflect whether such conduct could have been wholly blameless. This aspect of the case never seems, however, to present itself to the biographers of our hero. They record the falsehoods fabricated by him; they recount the disappointment and disaster which these falsehoods engendered; yet, when speaking of the just indignation of the deceived, they term it mutiny—rebellion, which could scarcely be punished too severely. Bernal Diaz wrote a detailed account of the misrepresentations perpetrated by Columbus; this was discovered, and we are called upon to admire the leniency of the latter, who merely confined Diaz on board a ship, to be sent to Spain for trial. The gentle narrators seem to think death itself would hardly have been too severe a penalty for so heinous an offense. It was, indeed, unheard-of audacity for any to presume so far as to assert that "the admiral" had exaggerated. Fernando writes: "Many had gone on that voyage upon the belief that, as soon as they landed, they might load themselves with gold, and so return, rich, home."

Such was indeed the case. But the falsehoods of Columbus had engendered that belief—a fact which seems to have escaped the notice of most writers upon this subject.

This rebellion being quelled, Alonzo de Ojeda, with a company of men, was sent to the district of Cibao to verify the report of there being gold-mines in that vicinity. He returned with such favorable accounts, that Columbus went thither and founded the fort of San Tomas, and established mining operations.

His progress through the country on this expedition was

characteristic: his band was sickly, weary, and disheartened; yet he must needs enter every Indian hamlet with trumpets sounding and banners flying, so irrepressible were his vanity and delight in exhibiting his newly-acquired rank.

During this journey, the Spaniards beheld, for the first time, that glorious plain which they named the Vega Real, and which was to become the theatre of so many tragic scenes. The expedition to Cibao, prompted by Columbus's impatience to acquire treasure, was premature, and a gross error on his part. The infant town of Isabella should have presented a somewhat more prosperous appearance before he attempted further settlement; the colony should have become somewhat acclimated, its health restored, before mining operations were commenced in the sterile mountains of Cibao. The consequence of this premature journey was, that but little advantage accrued to the Spaniards from mining which was commenced under such adverse circumstances.

The fort of San Tomas being built, it was garrisoned with fifty men, under Don Pedro Margarite, a gentleman who possessed the confidence of both the sovereigns, and whom Columbus himself professed greatly to esteem. The latter then set out on his return to Isabella; he found that colony languishing and perishing fast, for lack of provisions and the unhealthiness of the situation. He seems to have been singularly infelicitous in his selection of locations; for this same town of Isabella, though Columbus, in his letters to the sovereigns, had dwelt largely upon the advantages of its situation, was afterward abandoned, and, when deserted, became an object of dread and horror, not only on account of its extreme unhealthiness, but also of the terrible cruelties and crimes which had been perpetrated against the Spaniards within its walls. So great was the horror with which it was regarded, that cries and groans were reported to resound through its deserted streets, while visions of headless cavaliers appeared to the superstitious.

To quell the discontent which was daily increasing, and was wellnigh turned into desperation, Columbus sent four hundred of the least sickly of the colonists to the interior; Ojeda was to replace Margarite in the superintendence of the mines of Cibao and in the command of Fort San Tomas, while the latter was to lead the four hundred men on a raid through the country. We are told that Columbus enjoined justice toward the natives, and

RAID UPON THE NATIVES. 241

forbade violence; but, when we read that he instructed Margarite to conduct his expedition with the twofold object of overawing the natives and of feeding his men, without drawing on the colony for supplies, while they were to use every means in their power to take the cazique Caonabo prisoner, we are well assured Columbus never proposed the raid to be effected without violence.

SPANISH CRUELTIES.—(From De Bry's Las Casas.)

CHAPTER XVII.

FURTHER EXPLORATIONS.—CUBA DECLARED TO BE ASIA.

HAVING as he supposed insured the tranquillity of the colony, Columbus now intrusted its government to his brother Diego as president, with Bishop Boyle, who had been appointed by the Pope apostolic nuncio to those regions, and others as councilors, and sailed on a further voyage of discovery on the 24th of April, 1494.

During this voyage he discovered the island of Jamaica, and many smaller ones, but its most important feature was his coasting the island of Cuba under the impression that it was (or rather with a determination to represent it as) the Continent of Asia. Here his interpreter fails him, we are told; the Cuban dialects differing from those of the other islands.

Historians consider this as some excuse or palliation for the fables which our hero pretended to have heard from the natives, such as the existence of men with tails, who wore clothes to hide their deformity; and of a mighty monarch, entitled saint, who never spoke, but gave forth his commands in signs; and others equally absurd. It is said, so eager was Columbus to believe himself in Asia, that he readily misinterpreted signs, and regarded them as corroboration of his opinion that he was in the territory of the grand-khan. It is evident, however, that these stories were invented by him, that he might appear to be in those regions which Sir John Mandeville, Polo, and others, had described, and near the dominion of the fabled and saintly Prince Prester John.

That he knew he was not in Asia is evident from the extraordinary measures he took to convince the world he had reached that continent.

Had he been assured of that fact, he would have trusted to further investigation to establish its verity; on the other hand, if he knew he was practising a fraud, he would endeavor to procure as much testimony as possible to insure that fraud's gaining credence.

Which was the case, the reader may judge from the following passage in Irving's "History of Columbus," which scarcely needs comment:

"The admiral was determined, however, that the fact should not rest merely on his own assertion, having had recent proofs of a disposition to gainsay his statements and depreciate his discoveries. He sent round, therefore, a public notary, Fernand Perez de Luna, to each of the vessels, accompanied by four witnesses, who demanded formally of every person on board, from the captain to the ship-boy, whether he had any doubt that the land before him was a continent, the beginning and the end of the Indies, by which any one might return overland to Spain, and, by pursuing the coast of which, they could soon arrive among civilized people. If any one entertained a doubt, he was called upon to express it, that it might be removed.[104] On board the vessels were several experienced navigators, and men well versed in the geographical knowledge of the times. They examined their maps and charts, and the reckonings and journals of the voyage, and after deliberating maturely declared under oath that they had no doubt upon the subject. . . . Lest they should subsequently, out of malice or caprice, contradict the opinion thus solemnly avowed, it was proclaimed by the notary that whoever should offend in such a manner, if an officer, should pay a penalty of *ten thousand maravedis;* if a ship-boy or person of the like rank, he *should receive a hundred lashes and have his tongue cut out.* A formal statement was afterward drawn up by the notary, including the depositions and names of every individual."

Here Columbus, not content with speaking and writing a falsehood, *is guilty of subornation of perjury.* He manufactures perjury wholesale, which felony he would perpetuate by the barbarous means of scourging and cutting out the tongues of those who should speak the truth. Thus, by a system unknown

---

[104] Had there been any such hesitation, what followed renders it probable that any doubt expressed would have been very forcibly removed.

to Thales and Ptolemy, original if not scientific, did the much-lauded navigator and astronomer, the pious and humane "admiral," determine the latitude and longitude of the island of Cuba.[105]

We have given this incident in the language of Irving, that it may be seen how the extreme partiality of an author will so blind him to justice that he can record a deed as shameful as the above without pronouncing one word of censure upon its author.

COLUMBUS EXACTS AN OATH FROM HIS CREW THAT CUBA IS ASIA.

Having thus secured his reputation, Columbus turned once more toward Hispaniola. At the island of Saona, an eclipse took place, in observing which he made a mistake of more than eighteen degrees.[106]

Near the island of San Juan, whither he was going to capture some natives, he fell into a lethargy, which deprived him of sense and memory, an attack which Las Casas declares to have been sent as a "punishment to the admiral for the cruel manner in which he sought to propagate Christianity." We

---

[105] The documents containing the particulars of this forced perjury are to be found in Navarrete, "Colecc. Dip.," vol. i., p. 162.

[106] Irving, "Columbus," book vii., chapter vii.

should rather say, for the cruel manner in which he sought to enrich himself.

On arriving at Isabella, and recovering from his illness, he learned that his brother Bartholomew, whose voyage to England we have alluded to, had arrived.

On this brother, who afterward so ably seconded his measures of cruelty and oppression, he immediately conferred the rank of *adelantado*, or lieutenant-governor, a stretch of authority which the sovereigns resented, as they only had a right to confer titles.

SPANISH CRUELTIES.—(From De Bry's Las Casas.)

CHAPTER XVIII.

DISORDERS IN THE ISLAND.—MARGARITE AND BISHOP BOYLE RETURN TO SPAIN, BEARING COMPLAINTS AGAINST COLUMBUS.

THE island had grown more and more disorderly during Columbus's absence; all hope of peaceful relations between the Spaniards and natives had forever disappeared—as no doubt he intended should be the case—for, while the Indians remained peaceable and friendly, there was no excuse for enslaving them. The expedition of Margarite had roused them to hostility. As the Spaniards marched through the country, they seized all they could lay hands on. Their avarice, licentiousness, and brutality, exceeded all bounds; the principal caziques, with the exception of the faithful Guacanagari, joined in a league to expel the tyrants who thus violated the hospitality which had been so generously tendered them. Don Pedro Margarite, placed at the head of a hungry band, who were charged to march through the country and maintain themselves as best they could, found it impossible to enforce discipline. He saw with dismay the growing disorder throughout the colony, and felt that it should be remedied as speedily as possible, and the sovereigns made acquainted with the true state of things, that they might enforce measures for the proper government of the island.

This appears to have been the motive which induced Margarite, Bishop Boyle, and several Castilian nobles, to return to Spain in the ships which had brought out Bartholomew Columbus.

Bishop Boyle seems to have had peculiar reasons for hastening to Europe. He had been constituted, by the Pope, apostolic vicar and head of the Church in the Western lands. In this capacity he had remonstrated with Columbus on his cruel government, the latter paying no heed to ecclesiastical censure (by which it will be seen how sincere was his profession of love for the Church). Bishop Boyle excommunicated him; whereupon he refused to furnish the Pope's vicar and his attendants with any provisions, and they were literally starved out of the island, or, in the mild words of one author, Columbus's strong advocate, "Father Boyle was forced to take his departure the first opportunity, carrying with him heavy complaints against the justice of the admiral,"[107] with some reason, we should judge. His action, however, excites great indignation among historians, as also that of Margarite. Irving says the latter " and Boyle had hastened to Spain to make false representations of the miseries of the island."

Now, these miseries, according to Irving himself, could scarcely be exaggerated. Sickness and death still prevailed; nobles were compelled to work hard, and fare scantily. They rightly considered themselves deceived, and their indignation against the perpetrator of the deception was excusable—nay, justifiable.

We can readily imagine, however, the dismay with which Columbus heard of these departures. So long as his accounts of the islands were the only ones to reach the sovereigns, he could ever invent a plausible tale to win their approval. Margarite, however, with no inducements to misrepresent facts, would expose the falsehoods of which he had been guilty, and our hero was not unnaturally alarmed.

He turned his attention, however, to the unhappy Indians. Hearing that a body of the latter was advancing on Isabella, he attacked them, taking five hundred prisoners, to be sent as slaves to Spain. Henceforth he will no more speak of enslaving cannibals only, as he finds *prisoners of war* more available.

The capture of Caonabo was now his great object. To effect it, he employed the dauntless Alonzo de Ojeda. The expedition, no doubt, offered more peril than he himself was willing to encounter. He it was, however, who instructed Ojeda how to proceed; and the baseness and treachery of those instructions are well worthy of their author.

Ojeda appeared in the dominion of the cazique, declaring that he came on a friendly mission from Columbus. Caonabo,

---

[107] Spotorno, "Historia Memoria," p. 86.

who admired the bravery of Ojeda, received him courteously. The latter carried with him a set of fetters, highly wrought and polished. These, he told the chief, were ornaments, and induced him to don them as such, and to mount a horse, an animal of which the Indians stood greatly in awe. Alonzo persuaded Caonabo that all this was done to honor him. The latter was delighted to exhibit himself thus mounted and accoutred before his tribe, but Alonzo suddenly wheeled round with his little band of horsemen, and fled rapidly with the captured chief. The victim of this fraud ever, we are told, evinced the greatest contempt for Columbus, refusing to rise in his presence, while he did so deferentially whenever Ojeda appeared, thus evincing, he said, his respect for the one who had dared to execute what the other had only basely planned.

Soon after these events, Antonio de Torres returned from Spain, with four ships, bearing the provisions of which the famishing colony stood so much in need. He brought back with him Columbus's dispatches to the sovereigns, and the comments which the latter affixed thereto, in which they approved, as we have seen, all his proposals, except those relating to the enslavement of the Indians.

This approbation was very grateful to Columbus, but his delight must have been considerably embittered by the knowledge that they approved of his acts as he had represented them; and that, when Margarite and Boyle should have reached Spain, and informed them of the tyranny he practised, their praise would change to censure.

Thenceforth, indeed, the falsehoods of Columbus are discovered. He had shown how miserably incapable he was to govern, and the sovereigns lost confidence in him more and more; nor did his quarrels with every one with whom he had dealings serve to restore him to favor—a fact which cannot surprise us. A governor or other official of the present day, who should incur the enmity of all his colleagues, collectively and successively, would not be regarded with much confidence. The public would be apt to suppose that, where all were so unanimous in disapproving, there must have been some matter for disapproval.

Columbus commenced with his benefactor Pinzon, continued with Margarite, for whom he had first professed great esteem; with Bishop Boyle, the representative of the Church to which he professed such devotion; and thenceforth he disagreed with every one who took part with him in the affairs of the island.

The ships with which Torres had returned were immediately sent back to Spain with all the gold Columbus had been able to collect. This, however, was but a small quantity; and, as he feared Isabella's displeasure when she should receive no pecuniary profit from his enterprise, after his large promises, he sent over the five hundred Indians, to be sold as slaves, hoping that, when he declared them to be prisoners of war, her scruples would be allayed.

He must indeed have possessed great confidence that the sovereigns, when they found the Indians likely to be the only source of wealth to be derived from their new possessions, would consent to their enslavement; or else great hardihood, when he dared send back five hundred of the harmless natives of Hispaniola, in the very ships which had brought out the prohibition of king and queen against the enslavement even of those he declared to be cannibals.

When these ships had departed, hearing that the natives were collecting in large numbers in the Vega Real, Columbus sallied out to attack them. It is not said that they were either interfering with or molesting the Spaniards, but, as they did not answer his purpose, and procured him neither gold nor slaves, he suddenly divined hostile intentions on their part, and, the better to convert this heathen people to Christianity—such was his avowed object—he marched an army of Christians (?) with their horses and dogs into their midst. "He had with him," says Irving, "twenty bloodhounds, fearless and ferocious; when once they seized their prey, nothing could compel them to relinquish their hold." The horses, urged on by their cruel riders, bore down upon the unarmed and defenseless people, striking them to the earth, and trampling upon them; the horsemen dealt blows on all sides, with spear or lance, and the blows were not returned; none of these butchered and terrified Indians made the least resistance, while the bloodhounds, scarce more savage than their masters, sprang upon the naked bodies of the prostrate and the fleeing, dragging them to the earth and tearing out their bowels; those who escaped the slaughter were sold into slavery worse than death."[108]

[108] Irving, "Columbus," book viii., chapter vi.

250   LIFE OF COLUMBUS.

Leaving the hideous and ghastly scene of butchery, and assuming the air of a conqueror, Columbus now traversed the island, and proceeded to extort an immense revenue from the unoffending inhabitants. Ever greedy for gold, he required every person, above the age of fourteen years, to pay the amount of that metal which would fill a Flemish hawk-bell (about fifteen dollars) every three months; the chiefs paid a much larger quantity. In vain the poor islanders, crushed by this imposition, remonstrated; in vain the chiefs, in lieu thereof, offered to cultivate for him a breadth of land stretching across the island

SLAUGHTER IN THE VEGA REAL.

from sea to sea—enough, according to Las Casas, to furnish all Castile with bread for ten years: Columbus was inexorable; gold he must have, if it cost the life-blood of every Indian in the island to procure it! Herrera, in the following passage, furnishes an example of the tenderness with which the biographers of this man dealt with his worst crimes: "Columbus," he writes, "like a discreet man, being sensible that the wealth he sent must be his support, he pressed for gold, *though in other respects he was a good Christian and feared God*," which may be rightly interpreted thus: Columbus was cruel, avaricious, dishonest,

TERRIBLE OPPRESSION OF THE NATIVES.

but in other respects, and except where he failed, he was a good Christian!

The unfortunate Indians, reduced by Columbus and his brothers to the most abject slavery history has recorded, filled with despair, and seeing no prospect of relief from the oppression which had so suddenly and terribly fallen upon them, fled from their homes, which were homes no longer; from the haunts of the Christian to the mountains and caves; but Columbus relentlessly pursued them, and would have compelled them

ENSLAVEMENT OF THE INDIANS.

to return, but they sought refuge in the wildest, most inaccessible parts of the island; famished mothers, with starving children clinging around them or clasped in their arms, hid themselves in the mountain recesses, or, faint and broken-hearted, died by the wayside. The men dared neither hunt nor fish to appease the wants of their perishing families, lest Columbus and his bloodhounds should be upon them. Thousands perished; others, vanquished by hunger, delivered themselves up to their task-masters and returned to die in the mines and fields under the cruel lash of the Spaniard.

Not even the faithful Guacanagari was exempted from tribute; he found, indeed, that the day in which he had assisted the shipwrecked Columbus, he had taken a serpent into his bosom. He and his followers were as cruelly oppressed as those Indians who had been hostile to the Spaniards.

This method of exacting tribute and labor, inaugurated by Columbus, may be considered the origin of the cruel system of *repartimientos* which afterward prevailed in the West Indies.

Columbus had not been mistaken in his apprehensions of the effect the reports of Margarite and Boyle would have at the court of Spain. The story of the tyranny and cruelty practised by their admiral, alarmed the sovereigns, and they determined to investigate the matter; but, actuated no doubt by a desire to spare Columbus any unnecessary humiliation, they sent, as commissioner for this investigation, Juan Aguado, for whom the former professed the strongest friendship; they rightly supposed this friendliness between the two would prevent the latter from believing accusations blindly, but would cause him to be certain they were well founded before giving them credence. Upon his arrival, his investigations more than corroborated the statements of Margarite; on all sides, from noble and commoner, Spaniard and native, rose bitter complaints against the inhuman admiral and viceroy.

Historians, commenting upon this fact, say that an unfortunate man always finds accusers. They forget that, if ever Columbus was prosperous, these were the days of his prosperity. The last dispatches from the Spanish sovereigns had contained approval and praise, nevertheless all with one accord rose to denounce him; such unanimity would have been impossible, had he been faultless.

The result of Aguado's investigation was such, that in pure justice he strove to redress some of the existing wrongs; by this action he not only incurred the undying enmity of Columbus, but is vilified by historians, though the unfortunate man's only crime seems to have been that, when sent out to make investigations, he performed his mission conscientiously. The fact that his corroboration, as an impartial and disinterested party, of the accusations so universally made, is a strong evidence of Columbus's guilt, seems to escape notice. He does not appear to have abused his authority; he collected all the evidence and information required, and then proposed to return to Spain and make his report.

FLEET DESTROYED BY HURRICANE.

Columbus was now seriously alarmed, and resolved to return thither also, and make what defense he might. A tremendous hurricane, however, swept over the island and destroyed the entire fleet, which lay at anchor, with the exception of the Niña; the latter had to be repaired, and another vessel was built out of the wrecks; this retarded the departure alike of Columbus and Aguado.

During the delay, Columbus was informed of the discovery of other gold-mines, more productive than those of Cibao, in a beautiful region of the interior; they were discovered by a young Spaniard who had fled, having, as he supposed, murdered a comrade. On his reappearance with tidings of gold, Columbus, we are told, not only pardoned but looked upon him with great favor,[109] and proceeded to explore the new region, being desirous of abandoning Isabella, which he now considered as objectionable as Navidad.

[109] Irving, "Columbus," book viii., chapter x. The gold he declared potent to save from the pangs of purgatory, be thus proved to be equally potent in averting the gallows and the penitentiary.

CHAPTER XIX.

RETURN OF COLUMBUS TO SPAIN.—HIS THIRD VOYAGE.

HAVING sent his brother to examine the situation of the mines, who returned with favorable reports, and the vessels being now ready to sail, Columbus embarked in one and Aguado in the other; as many of the Spaniards as could, availed themselves of this opportunity of returning to their native land. The voyage was a long and disastrous one; the crew were half famished and in sorry plight when, on the 11th of June, 1496, they entered the bay of Cadiz, from which they had departed with such glowing hopes. "Never did a more miserable and disappointed crew return from a land of promise," says Irving. He forgets to add, whose misrepresentations were the cause of all this misery and disappointment.

A month elapsed before Columbus received a summons to appear at court, and his guilty conscience made him greatly fear for his reception there; his abject humility, as he proceeded to Burgos, contrasted as strikingly with his vaunting return from his first voyage, as did the splendid promises he had then made, with the miserable reality which had now become apparent.

Clad in the garb of a monk, with cringing humility apparent in mien and gesture, he appeared before the sovereigns. They received him more graciously than he had expected; some historians declare that no allusion whatever was made to the accusation of Margarite and Boyle; others go so far as to say that the sovereigns loaded him with benefits and praise; all agree, however, while making these assertions, that his fortunes are henceforth under a cloud, that the nation ridiculed him, and that the confidence of Ferdinand and Isabella was shaken. Bossi admits that it was intimated to him that he had best moderate the rigor of his rule in the islands; it is probable, therefore, that he received some censure.

In vain, to recover what prestige he ever possessed, did he announce that he had discovered that land of Ophir whence Solomon procured his gold; in vain did he dwell upon the advantages to be derived from his visit to Cuba, which, he averred, was the eastern extremity of Asia. His disheartened companions told a different tale. He met on all sides with derision, which the recollection of the pompous boasting he had indulged in on his return from his first voyage only served to increase; he became the butt of well-earned ridicule—an example of how falsehood and fraud will oftentimes turn to plague the inventor.

Though Isabella may have refrained from publicly disgracing the admiral, her actions show plainly what credit she gave his statements.

For a year and a half, he daily represented the necessity of sending out ships and provisions to Hispaniola. At the end of that time, two caravels were sent, under one *Coronal;* but he himself could not procure the squadron he solicited, with which to prosecute his discoveries—lack of funds was the excuse with which he was put off from day to day and month to month. Yet this excuse can hardly be considered valid, for, at that very period, a magnificent fleet of upward of a hundred vessels (we believe, a hundred and twenty), having on board twenty thousand persons, convoyed the Princess Juana to Flanders, for her marriage with the Archduke of Austria.

While Columbus was importuning for a fleet, Pedro Niño, who had left Cadiz for Hispaniola immediately after the arrival of the former in that port, returned to Spain, and circulated a report that he had on board much gold, in bars, the fainting hopes of Columbus revived. He was instructed by the crown to defray the expenses of his expedition out of this gold, and an appropriation of six million maravedis, which he had just with difficulty procured, was transferred to another channel. What, then, was his mortification, when he discovered that Niño had returned with a cargo of Indians to be sold as slaves —alluding to their sale for gold, and to their present imprisonment, he termed them *gold in bars*—satirically implying by this jest that they were likely to be the only gold derived from the islands.

If the boasting lies of Columbus had been derided before, how much greater did the derision now become! If he had been hitherto unable to procure vessels, how much less willing were the sovereigns now to make an outlay which, to all appearance, would profit them nothing!

A certain pride, however, forbade them wholly to abandon an enterprise in which they had embarked; and, to silence the importunities of Columbus, they ordered that such vessels as were necessary for the expedition should be *pressed* into the service, with their masters and pilots, and such remuneration to be offered the owners as the officers of the crown should think fit; their object being evidently to transfer the burden of the expenses from the crown to its subjects.

About this time, Columbus made his will, of which we shall require to speak more at length hereafter. He also succeeded in obtaining a revocation of a royal order which had been fulminated in 1495, by which subjects of Castile were allowed to make voyages of discovery at their own expense for the crown, a permission which he declared was in direct conflict with his interests, and *supplicated and begged as a favor* that it should be withdrawn."[110]

Six vessels were at length with difficulty procured. Columbus received permission to take out three hundred and thirty persons in royal pay, to colonize the islands; but so effectually had the Spaniards, who had already returned thence, succeeded in demonstrating the falseness of his representations, that it was found impossible to obtain the desired recruits. He then made a proposition, which proves alike his unprincipled character and the extremities to which he was reduced. He petitioned that malefactors might be released from their prisons, and expiate their offenses by a sojourn of two years or less in the new lands. To this proposition Isabella agreed, to her lasting dishonor; and, in so doing, effectually contradicts all who dwell upon her kindly disposition toward the unhappy Indians: such an element could hardly work for the good of their souls. The conversion intrusted to such hands must surely result in demoralizing, rather than elevating them. She and the pious admiral well knew that

[110] Navarrete, "Colecc. Dip.," vol. ii., p. 224.

lawless criminals, whom society had deemed unsafe in Spain, would be a hundred-fold worse when far removed from restraint, and turned loose upon the unhappy natives.[111]

Though he had thus procured ships and crew, Columbus still had great difficulty in obtaining supplies—difficulty which his quarrelsome disposition increased, if it did not create. Juan Rodriguez de Fonseca, Bishop of Badajoz, had been appointed head, or superintendent, of the affairs of the Indies. He is one of the multitude who have been vilified by historians because he conscientiously performed the duties of his office, instead of becoming the creature of Columbus. Indeed it is a fact, which the careful reader cannot fail to observe, that, in order to make a great and noble man of the latter, his biographers are obliged to vilify every one of his contemporaries with whom he had any dealings of importance.

Fonseca, fortunately for the crown, opposed the extravagant demands of the admiral. The quarrel between them originated in his somewhat reasonable remonstrance against the appointment of *twenty esquires* to wait solely on the latter on his second departure for the primitive regions of the West. Notwithstanding the railings of Columbus and his partisans, there is every evidence of Fonseca's having been an efficient officer and meritorious man. Had it been otherwise, he would not, as he did, have retained the confidence of the Spanish sovereigns, and remained at the head of Indian affairs for upward of thirty years, despite the accusations and complaints of the admiral. And here is another contradiction of that sensational fiction which so popularly represents Isabella as constantly sympathizing with and befriending Columbus, while thwarted by her hus-

[111] The act, or order, which authorizes this exportation of criminals, is thus worded: ". . . We will and ordain that all and every person, men and women, our subjects and natives, who may have committed, up to the day of the publication of this our letter, any murders and offenses, and other crimes, of whatever nature and quality they may be" (heresy and others are excepted), "who shall go and serve in person in the island of Hispaniola, and shall serve in it at their own expense, and in those things which the said admiral shall command and specify to them on our part; namely, those who have incurred the punishment of death, for two years, and those who have incurred any other punishment, although it may be the loss of a limb, for one year; shall receive a pardon for every crime and misdeed, of whatsoever nature, quality, or gravity it may be, which they may have done or committed up to the day of the publication of this our letter, excepting the cases above mentioned, . . . and we reëstablish the said delinquents in their former good fame, and in the state in which they were, before they had done and committed the aforesaid crimes."

band and officials. It requires but a moment's reflection for the absurdity of this view, which is so universally entertained, to become apparent. She was sovereign of Castile. Her husband's power in that kingdom was merely nominal. His influence, therefore, would have been ineffectual in injuring Columbus, had she desired to patronize him; and, though her authority was not absolute, yet it would have sufficed to remove Fonseca, who is said to have been the bitter enemy of her so-called *protégé*. Had she been as desirous of favoring the latter as is represented, she would therefore have replaced the bishop by some one more friendly to his interests.

It is most probable that the queen, now thoroughly understanding the grasping character of her admiral, was only too glad to intrust the superintendence of his expenditure to one on whom she could rely, to check his extravagance and expose his frauds. The ill repute of Fonseca, like the fame of Columbus, has been chiefly the work of modern times. Irving himself, who brands him as vile and despicable, confesses that contemporary historians do not speak unfavorably of the bishop; and, though he accounts for the fact by supposing that prudence restrained them from expressing their true opinion, this is a gratuitous supposition on his part.

The amiable manner in which our admiral comported himself toward those with whom he came in contact is illustrated by his treatment of one Ximeno de Breviesca, the treasurer of Fonseca. Ximeno had some business with him just before his departure on this third voyage, and, having occasion to protest, or possibly only to transmit Fonseca's protestation against some of his demands, Columbus knocked him down, kicked and buffeted him in a most brutal manner. As one more example of how his most inexcusable acts receive the sanction of his biographers, we will again quote Mr. Irving, who seems to regard such conduct as far from blamable. "He struck the despicable minion to the ground, and *spurned* him repeatedly with his foot," says Mr. Irving, relating the above event, "venting in this unguarded paroxysm the accumulated griefs which had long rankled in his mind."

De Lorgues thus records this somewhat equivocally saint-like act:

"The patriarch of the ocean made a step toward his insulter, and with his fist dealt a blow on his impudent face. The miserable wretch fell down stunned. The admiral *limited himself to giving a few kicks* to this vile snarler, who fled in the midst of hootings, concealing, under his humiliation and forced tears, his secret joy; for from that moment his fortune was made."

But De Lorgues denies that the above act was a "mark of ungovernable temper," and declares that, in perpetrating it, " Columbus did not yield to hastiness, or to the excitement of self-love," while it is evident that he desires us to admire the leniency of his hero, who *limited himself to giving a few kicks* to his prostrate victim."[119]

This outburst and insult to a public officer, which exposed the brutal vindictiveness of the man in all its violence, went far, as may be supposed, to confirm all the reports of his cruelties and insolence toward the Spaniards in Hispaniola. The sovereigns, when they heard of this outrage, committed within their own realm, must have readily conceived how the perpetrator would act when far removed from their supervision, and vested with supreme authority.

Leaving the remembrance of this last act, and the impression it must inevitably produce, to perform their work in Spain, Columbus set sail on the 30th of May, 1498, on his third voyage, in the name of the Holy Trinity.

At the Canary Islands he divided his fleet, and sent three vessels direct to Hispaniola, while he with the three others proceeded to the Cape Verde Islands, thence to sail due west under the equinoctial line, " it being his intention," says Fernando, " to discover the continent." Thus we perceive at once that, when in the island of Cuba he extorted the oath from his men that they were in Asia, he was perfectly aware of the perjury which he forced them to commit; for, had he then supposed he had discovered the continent, he would not now have declared that he was going to discover it.

His voyage lasted two months, part of which his vessels lay motionless in the scorching region of the calm latitudes; and, though he desired to pursue a southwesterly course, the condition of his ships forced him to make for Hispaniola.

On the 31st of July of this year, 1498, a sailor gave the cry

[119] De Lorgues, " Christophe Colomb," livre ii., chapter ix.

of land, and, shortly after, three mountains appeared, which, as the ships neared them, proved to be united at their bases. This circumstance Columbus interprets as a miracle, intending to show how acceptable were all his acts to the Almighty. He had sailed with his gang of thieves and murderers in the name of the Holy Trinity, and three mountains, symbolizing that Trinity, are the first land he descries. He gave the island (for such it was) the name of La Trinidad, which it bears to this day. He then rounded Cape Galera, which brought him to the southern side of the island; and it was while his vessels were taking in water at Point Alcatraz, the low lands of the Orinoco being visible from that point, that, according to all historians, he, on the 1st of August, 1498, beheld for the first time the Continent of America, which, in the preceding year, Amerigo Vespucci had visited, and coasted from the gulf of Honduras to Chesapeake Bay."[113] He was not, however, aware that the land before him was the continent, but imagined it to be another island.

The absurd story he tells of the sea rising like a high mountain, threatening to submerge the ships, is said by over-indulgent writers to have been the effect produced on his ardent imagination by the outpouring of the waters of the Orinoco into the ocean. To us it illustrates his character: the truth only would not, he feared, produce wonder enough. In his efforts to give supernatural semblance to all that occurred, he dealt largely in the marvelous. His age was one teeming with navigators, yet none of his contemporaries record such storms, such calms, such heat, such mutinous crews, such huge sea-monsters, as those which he imagined or invented.

Having escaped from this huge mountain of waters, he emerged from the northern strait which divides Trinidad from the continent, and which he named Boca del Drago, as he had already named the southern strait which formed the same division Boca del Sierpe.

Still in ignorance that the land before him was the continent, he coasted Paria in search of some outlet to the sea beyond. The natives received him kindly, and appeared more civilized than those he had found in the islands. Many of the women wore pearls, and he obtained a quantity of costly ones in ex-

[113] Cabot had also preceded Columbus, and reached North America on the 24th of June, 1497.

change for the merest trifles. At length, not finding the desired outlet, he concluded that this was the continent.

The description of this voyage, which he gives in a letter to the sovereigns, and the speculations in which he indulges to rouse their flagging interest, is certainly a valuable production as regards originality, and as a proof of the ignorance and absurdity of the man. Here he gives forth that truly novel theory that the earth is *pear-shaped*.

"I have always read," he writes, in a letter to their Catholic Majesties on his return from this voyage, "that the world, comprising the land and the water, was spherical, as is testified by the investigations of Ptolemy and others, who have proved it by the eclipses of the moon, and other observations made from east to west, as well as by the elevation of the pole from north to south."[114] But I have now seen so much irregularity, as I have already described, that I have come to another conclusion respecting the earth—namely, that it is not round, as they decribe, but of the form of a pear, which is very round, except where the stalk grows, at which part it is most prominent."

This opinion he bases upon the mildness of the climate in the Western Hemisphere near the equinoctial, as compared with the equatorial regions of Africa. This mildness he attributes to a gradual rise, or prominence, like a great mountain or upper portion of a pear. On the top of this mountain, or excrescence, *which is nearest the sky*, he declares the earthly paradise to be situated, which he proposes to add to the other possessions of their majesties."[115] There are not wanting men of intellect who,

---

[114] It is hereby rendered apparent that the theory of the earth's sphericity, which so many authors describe him as revealing to startled and incredulous contemporaries, was in his time, and had been for ages before it, generally accepted, and, in order to be novel, he is obliged to refute that theory.

[115] ". . . . I do not suppose that the earthly paradise is in the form of a rugged mountain, as the descriptions of it have made it appear, but, that it is on the summit of the spot which I have described as being in the form of the stalk of a pear, the approach to it from a distance must be by a constant and gradual ascent. . . . There are great indications of this being the terrestrial paradise, for its site coincides with the opinion of the holy and wise theologians whom I have mentioned; and, moreover, other evidences agree with the supposition. . . . But the more I reason on the subject, the more satisfied I become that the terrestrial paradise is situated in the spot I have described. . . . May it please the Lord to grant your highnesses a long life, and health and peace to follow out so noble an investigation!"—*Columbus's Letter to the Sovereigns, describing his Third Voyage*, 1498.

with more or less honesty, have defended this theory as plausible. We somewhat doubt that honesty, we confess, when we find that enthusiastic advocate for the canonization of Columbus, M. de Lorgues, asserting that in the above absurd speculation Columbus shows a knowledge of, if he did not discover, the inflation of the equator; we fail to see in it the faintest suspicion of equatorial inflation round the whole globe, which only diverges from a perfect sphere in so far as to become a slightly flattened one. He declares a prominence or excrescence to exist on *one* side of the globe, which is perfectly round on all other sides. He distinctly contrasts the region he speaks of with those of Africa, also situated on the equator. He also declares this excrescence to be *nearer the sky* than other parts of the globe. This totally defeats the idea of uniform inflation around its circumference, which evidently never for a moment entered the mind of Columbus.

In this letter, in which he describes in glowing colors the country, people, and productions of the continent, he forbears to speak of the pearls for which he had bartered with the natives, having, no doubt, a desire to keep them for himself as perquisites. This silence will hereafter bring him into trouble, as his men were well aware of the pearls being in his possession, and proclaimed the fact on their arrival in Hispaniola.

He now determined to return to that island. He had an infirmity of the eyes, which nearly deprived him of sight, and suffered from a disease which is reported to have been gout, though how that fatal consequence of ease and high living could attack one leading such a life as his requires explanation.

He made for Isabella, but arrived instead at San Domingo, the new colony on the south side, an inexactitude of calculation which is among the least perpetrated by "the admiral."

On his arrival he was met by the *adelantado*, Bartholomew Columbus, who gave him a woful account of the condition of the island. The lands were uncultivated, the people sick and dying, while the authority of his brothers, and even his own, was being questioned.

CHAPTER XX.

REBELLION OF ROLDAN.—CRUELTIES OF COLUMBUS.—MURDER OF MOXICA.

THE particulars of this rebellion form one of the most disgraceful pages in the history of Columbus; it illustrates alike his treachery, cowardice, and inability to rule, save by the grossest tyranny.

After his departure for Spain, his brother Bartholomew, whom he left in charge of the government, adopted forthwith the severest measures, constantly traveling from one part of the island to another, allowing the unfortunate Spaniards neither rest nor quiet, sternly exacting from the still more unfortunate natives enormous tribute; the latter revolted, but were speedily vanquished, their leaders put to cruel deaths, and a still heavier tribute imposed upon the masses.

Francisco Roldan had been appointed by Columbus *alcalde*, mayor or chief-justice of the island. It is difficult to form a just estimate of this man from the perusal of the histories of Columbus; nevertheless, as Fernando, who writes in his father's interest, says that he (Roldan) " acted from a pretense to further the public good," and, as through all his proceedings enough is apparent to prove that this was at least one of his motives, if not the principal, and as, moreover, he constituted himself the friend and protector of the Indians, we may infer that he was really far more meritorious than the generality of those who obtained office through the aid of Columbus. It soon became apparent, however, that he did not intend to become the blind partisan of the latter by disregarding the duties of his office. A manly frankness characterizes his dealings with Columbus and his brothers which commands respect. Incensed alike by the cruelties practised toward the Indians and the hardships imposed upon the Spaniards by the harsh and restless spirit of the *adelantado*, and discouraged at the deplorable condition of the island, he requested that a certain ship which the *adelantado* had built might be fitted out to convey him and some other cavaliers to Spain, there to lay their grievances before the sovereigns. His request was denied, upon the pretense that the ship was in want of tackle. This can hardly have been true, for it had but just returned with a heavy cargo of cotton, etc., from the district of Xaragua, ruled by Anacaona, widow of Caonabo, and Behechio, his brother, where it had been to collect tribute. Roldan was not deceived by the excuse; he represented to his friends that the tyrannical measures of the *adelantado* were unlawful, inasmuch as he had received his rank from the admiral, who had no right to confer titles, and declared that, in virtue of his office, he had determined to release the oppressed natives from the excessive tribute imposed upon them. His friends, who appear to have been the best men in the island,[116] agreed to sustain him in these measures. He received particularly ready assistance from Adrian de Moxica, a gentleman of wealth and standing, whose kinsman, Hernando de Guevara, had become enamored of and desired to wed a daughter of Queen Anacaona, and therefore ardently sought to further the interests of her people.

Roldan and his followers, determined no longer to recognize the authority of the *adelantado*, left Isabella. So great was the unpopularity or conscious guilt of the latter, that he dared not resent this proceeding, but sent a safe-conduct to Roldan, petitioning for an interview. Roldan reiterated his demand for a vessel, which was again refused upon the same grounds. He then not unnaturally inferred, what was probably the case, namely, that the *adelantado* was by no means desirous that an account of his proceedings should reach Spain. He strove to divest Roldan of his office; the latter very justly objected that their majesties alone—to whom the islands belonged—or their accredited representative could remove him; and declared, moreover,

---

[116] Fernando tells us that the few Spaniards who remained with the *adelantado*, were bribed to do so by the promise of two slaves apiece, to be given them if they did not go over to Roldan.—*Historia del Amirante*, chapter lxxv.

that the sovereigns did not wish the Indians to suffer as they did, nor the Spaniards to be so oppressed."[117]

He prepared to leave the city with his followers. The *adelantado* refused them provision. He therefore forced open the magazines in the king's name, took what he required, and proceeded to Xaragua, releasing the Indians on his way from tribute, and assuring them that all their Catholic Majesties required of them was that they should be good subjects.[118]

When Columbus returned to Hispaniola, and was made acquainted with these events, his first act was to proclaim Roldan and his followers rebels; but he seems to have hesitated in becoming openly hostile to him: he sent one Carvajal to offer him a safe-conduct and pardon for the past, if he would return to his allegiance.

Six hundred Indians, who had been made prisoners because their cazique had failed to pay tribute, were at that time confined on board five ships, to be sent to Spain as slaves, the ships only waiting till Columbus should be able to write that affairs in the island were quiet, before sailing. Roldan therefore made answer to Columbus's envoy that he desired and required no pardon, having committed no offense, but he merely requested that these Indians, whom he had taken under his protection, should be set at liberty; that he was acting legally, and that it was Columbus who, by enslaving them, disobeyed the royal commands. The latter refused to liberate the Indians, but sent them out immediately to Spain, dwelling, in his letter to the sovereigns, upon the advantages that would accrue to their treasury from the sale of four thousand yearly, at the same time reporting Roldan's insubordination.

Fear, however, or the conviction that his own cause was weak, induced him still to endeavor to come to an understanding with the latter, who, thus urged, drew up articles, and promised, on condition of Columbus signing them, to cease hostilities. This Columbus refused to do, saying that, were he to sign, he would bring himself, his brothers, and justice, into disrepute.[119] As Roldan, however, remained inexorable, Columbus, notwithstanding the above declaration, acceded to all his requests, which were, in substance, that two good ships should be fitted out, in

---

[117] "Historia del Amirante," chapters lxxv., lxxvi.
[118] Idem., chapter lxxvi. [119] Idem., chapter lxxx.

which he and such of his followers as wished to do so, might return to Spain, with an assurance that neither the admiral nor his friends should molest them. That those returning to Spain should receive certificates of good conduct, it was stipulated that the conditions precedent should be performed within ten days after the signing of the contract, or the agreement was to become void, Roldan, on his part, pledging himself to depart within fifty days after receiving the vessels.

Throughout all these proceedings, Columbus had been the suitor, Roldan the sued, which appears inconsistent with the reports of his bad behavior. Had he really been so blamable, Columbus would not have been so desirous to come to terms with him, but would have trusted to the royal power for bringing him to subjection. He knew that Roldan, in his protection of the Indians, and his remonstrances against the tyranny of himself and his brothers, was essentially in the right, and would be so regarded by the crown when the truth should be learned.

The agreement was signed November, 1498. It was not till the following April that two ships were furnished Roldan. He and his followers refused to embark, not so much because they had not arrived within the prescribed time, as because they were worm-eaten and insufficiently furnished with provisions, two somewhat awkward impediments to a long sea-voyage; he therefore declared his intention of seeking redress from the crown. This alarmed Columbus. He sent, in haste, another safe-conduct, and requested Roldan to come and treat with him. The latter accepted his invitation, and, fearlessly going on board the admiral's fleet, obtained the following terms:

All his followers who desired, should return to Spain by the first ships;

That those remaining behind should receive lands and houses;

That a proclamation should be made, that Roldan and his followers had been forced to act as they had by the fault of bad men;

That Roldan should be reappointed perpetual chief-justice, with power to appoint all subordinate justices.

Thus did the admiral reward the man whom he had accused of rebellion, attempted murder, treason, and robbery, by conferring upon him the highest office at his disposal.

If he were indeed guilty of the crimes imputed to him, nothing can excuse the dastardly conduct of Columbus in thus promoting him; if, on the other hand, he had only justly taken up arms against the tyranny and incompetency to rule of Columbus and his brothers, their cruelty and duplicity stand revealed. These transactions, therefore, whatever view we may take of them—whether we regard Roldan, as do the majority of historians, as a lawless rebel, or, what is more probable, as one who fearlessly and perseveringly stood up for the rights of his countrymen and the oppressed Indians—the part played by Columbus is alike despicable and revolting.

Not only did he give this so-called rebel office and justification, but conferred on him lands and other favors. When he, however, asked to visit these lands (a not unnatural request, it would seem), we are told that the admiral reluctantly consented.

On his way to Xaragua, Roldan appointed one of his friends *alcalde*, or justice. This appointment, though of no material importance, yet furnishes another proof of how modern authors have strayed still farther from the truth in their attempts to make Columbus immaculate, than contemporary writers. Mr. Irving says Columbus was justly indignant at this appointment, Roldan having no power to appoint associate justices. Fernando Columbus, who, as has been shown, does not always adhere strictly to the truth, and who may justly be supposed to represent his father in as favorable a light as possible, and not to palliate the faults of his father's enemies, allows that in the matter of this appointment Roldan was right. He says the latter "appointed Riquielme alcalde, *it being a part of his grant to appoint other alcaldes.*"[190]

How, then, can it be asserted that Columbus was *justly* indignant at an officer's properly exercising the functions of his office?

Two ships finally set sail for Spain in October, 1499, bearing thither many of Roldan's adherents, whom Columbus had presented with slaves and certificates of their good character and conduct on the island. These, however, he privately contradicted by secreting on board of one of the very ships, in the keeping of one of his confidants, a letter to the sovereigns, wherein he accused Roldan of the most heinous crimes, begged them not to give credence to the certificates of good character, as the men to whom he had furnished them were murderers, rebels, and

[190] "Historia del Amirante," chapter lxxxiii.

thieves, whom he advised their majesties to have seized immediately on their arrival, stripped of their possessions, and severely punished. It is difficult to imagine conduct at once more treacherous, despicable, and pusillanimous, than this.[121]

He also requested that a judge should be sent to administer justice in the island, said judge to be paid by him, and whose duties were to be so specified that they should not interfere with his prerogatives.[122] Such a justice, powerful to do the will of Columbus, but powerless against him, would have been a sorry acquisition for Hispaniola.

It was in this year, 1499, that Amerigo Vespucci, on his return from his second voyage, provisions falling short, put in at Hispaniola upon the suggestion of Alonza de Ojeda. Columbus immediately sent Roldan to express his indignation at their having landed without his permission. The latter found a party of the ship's crew busily engaged in making cassava-bread in an Indian village, thus demonstrating the innocence and necessity of their visit.

Alonzo de Ojeda was the nominal commander of the expedition, as the grant, allowing citizens to prosecute discoveries at their own expense for the crown, only extended to subjects of Castile. Vespucci was an Italian, in the service of the King of Aragon. It was Ojeda, therefore, who showed Roldan the papers authorizing the expedition, duly signed by Fonseca, head of the affairs of the Indies. This was unanswerable; but Ojeda, with more generosity than judgment, is said to have declared himself the patron of the many Spaniards, who, remembering his impulsive bravery, flocked around him, telling him their grievances—representing that they had received no pay since their arrival in the island, though the crown provided for their remuneration.

Ojeda promised to redress their wrongs, and to compel Columbus to pay them; at the same time bidding them put no faith in the promises of the latter, as he would only fulfill them so long as necessity compelled him to do so.[123]

He, moreover, informed them of what was soon to become apparent—namely, that the admiral was far from being in favor

---
[121] Irving, book xii., chapter v
[122] Letter of Columbus to Doña Juana de la Torres.—Irving, book xii., chapter v.
[123] "Historia del Amirante," chapter lxxxiv.

at the court of Spain, where only unfavorable reports of him had been received. He predicted, not without reason, as will be seen, the speedy and total downfall of the tyrant.

Roldan met the expedition, at the head of which Ojeda had placed himself. The latter remembering, perhaps, that he had been sent upon a voyage of discovery, and not to enforce justice, retired to his ship, and, after some further skirmishing and parleying, set sail for Spain.

We have mentioned the young Fernando de Guevara, who was desirous of wedding the daughter of Anacaona. That a young Spanish cavalier should become the lawful husband of an Indian maiden would be a dangerous blow to the policy of Columbus, which was to degrade and enslave the natives. He foresaw this would become impossible when these unfortunates should acquire allies among the Spaniards united to them by the strong ties of blood. Guevara was, therefore, forbidden to marry the young princess, and ordered to leave the island in Ojeda's ships. When we remember that Columbus had instructed Roldan to drive Ojeda from the island as a pirate, his presumption in sending a passenger for transport on board an enemy's ship, while a monstrous wrong to Guevara, was strictly in keeping with his general line of conduct. Finding that Ojeda had already departed, and feeling the injustice and cruelty with which he was treated, Guevara resolved to persevere, and to marry the Indian princess. He therefore secreted himself in the house of her mother, and sent for a priest to baptize his bride. He was discovered and driven out by the authorities, but with touching persistency returned once more, when he was made prisoner and conducted to the fortress of San Domingo, there to await the punishment of so heinous a crime as that of loving faithfully and honestly an Indian maiden. This persistent and lawful attachment, in the face of tyranny and persecution, is termed by Columbus a rebellion; and because Adrian de Moxica, kinsman to the unfortunate youth, remonstrated against his imprisonment, he was accused of "joining in the rebellion." After requesting the release of Guevara, and being refused, he set out with six or seven followers, to endeavor, it is said, to liberate him. Columbus, hearing of this, with his accustomed treachery came upon the little band unawares in the night, and made them prisoners.

270   LIFE OF COLUMBUS.

On all sides, we are told, murmurs of disaffection and hatred were heard against the admiral. He was aware of the utter detestation in which he was held, but hoped, by inspiring terror, to prevent an outburst against himself. Adrian de Moxica was in his power. He determined to put him to death, and thus intimidate all who should thereafter dare to oppose his wishes, or remonstrate against his tyranny. Without legal authority, and

COLUMBUS KICKS MOXICA FROM THE BATTLEMENTS.

with scarce the form of a trial, Moxica was condemned to instant death. He requested to be allowed to confess—a demand which was grudgingly granted by the saintlike Christopher. So great was his thirst for vengeance, that even this pious delay was more than he could brook. A priest being summoned, Moxica, in those last moments—we read in an old work—" confessing, delaying, and then beginning again, accused Columbus of having caused the troubles, whereupon he, indignant at his audacity, spurned him from the battlements." Some writers represent Moxica as delaying death as long as possible by prolonging his confession, at which Columbus, becoming indignant, ordered him to be thrown from the battlements. But from all we can gather, he met his fate fearlessly, and, in that last solemn moment, accused Columbus of the crimes which had brought misery upon the island. The latter, furious at being unable to conquer the spirit of his victim even in death, in an outburst of passion, similar to that he gave vent to in Cadiz toward Fonseca's treasurer, kicked the manacled prisoner from the high walls of the fortress into the fosse below.

Such is the atrocious act which historians record, yet seem blind to the horror it must inspire in all humane breasts; they expend their choicest pathos, and would move their readers to

SPANIARDS EXECUTED BY BARTHOLOMEW COLUMBUS.

tears, when relating the misfortunes (self-created) of Columbus, yet recount the awful murder of Moxica in terms seemingly unconscious that it should stir up any other feeling than that of admiration for the murderer.

Irving writes: "Columbus, losing all patience, in his mingled indignation and scorn, ordered the dastardly wretch to be flung headlong from the battlements."

Does it not surprise the reader that an author can use such language in describing such a scene, and thus make himself not merely the apologist, but the approver of brutal cruelty?

272   LIFE OF COLUMBUS.

De Lorgues, who seems not very unjustly to consider this act as militating somewhat against the canonization of Columbus, which he so strenuously advocates, denies his perpetration of it, and lays it to the charge of Roldan, a violation of truth too daring for any former historian to have attempted, as even the eulogists and most ardent admirers of Columbus admit his part in this atrocious crime. Muñoz circumstantially relates how Roldan left to the admiral the judgment of Moxica; how the admiral, in the dead of night, made the latter prisoner, conducted him to the fortress of Concepcion, and had him executed.[124]

The murder of Moxica was but a commencement of the summary proceedings of Columbus. He and his brother set out upon an expedition through the island, taking with them a priest. Wherever they came upon a disaffected Spaniard, he was seized, the priest confessed him, and he was hanged forthwith; this was done, we read, "that the Indians might be again brought to pay their tributes, to the end that their majesties might have wherewith to defray the expenses they were at, and the *admiral's enemies might give over railing.*"[125]

From PHILOPONO. (Nova Typis, etc.)

"The Indians were submissive, dreading the admiral, and so desirous to please him that they readily became Christians only to oblige him."—"Historia del Amirante," chapter lxxxiv.

[124] Muñoz, "Historia del Nuevo Mundo," libro vi., p. 338.
[125] Herrera, "West Indies," Decade I., book iv., chapter i.

CHAPTER XXI.

DISPLEASURE OF THE SOVEREIGNS AGAINST COLUMBUS.—THEY SEND OUT BOBADILLA TO INVESTIGATE HIS CONDUCT.—ACTION OF BOBADILLA.

WHILE Columbus thus outraged decency and humanity in the island of Hispaniola, his downfall was impending on the other side of the ocean. The king and queen, considering the many complaints made against him, as also the evident misrule prevailing in their Western possessions, the persistent export of slaves against their express command, and his repeated falsehoods and exaggerations, wisely resolved that his rule in Hispaniola, as in all the other newly-found lands, should cease. They appointed Francisco de Bobadilla to examine into the complaints made against him, also into the rebellion of which he accused Roldan. He was, in their name, to take possession of all fortresses, ships, and other property of the crown, to assume the rank and title of judge, and governor of the island.

As his biographers reach this period of Columbus's history, language, of whatever country, seems scarce to contain adequate terms in which to express their sympathizing pity for the martyr hero. The ingratitude of human nature in general, and princely nature in particular, is dwelt upon in strong, if not exactly original or novel terms.

He, however, who considers the facts calmly and dispassionately, will readily agree with us, that the sovereigns did not deal harshly with Columbus. They acted with all the consideration he could expect, and with far more leniency than he deserved. They had long doubted his efficiency as a ruler, and the disorders prevailing in Hispaniola, and his utter unpopularity, confirmed this doubt. They regretted the foolish haste with which they had intrusted him with many of their subjects. His enterprise, which he had promised should so largely enrich them, had cost much and paid nothing; ships returned to Spain from the distant islands far more heavily laden with complaints against Columbus than with the gold he had promised. His veracity and honesty appeared in a doubtful light, when no substantial corroboration was forthcoming of the wondrous tales he had circulated of a land so rich in gold that it could be no other than that of Ophir. Moreover, hundreds of unfortunates who had gone out under promises of royal pay, and whose salaries Columbus had withheld, congregated around the palace, loudly petitioning for pay, and exhibiting their poverty and misery wherever the king and queen showed themselves, exclaiming, when they saw the sons of Columbus (Fernando and Diego) in royal service, "Behold the sons of the Admiral of Mosquito-land, the discoverer of false and deceitful countries, to be the ruin and burial-place of Spanish *hidalgos!*"—"Which made us," observes Fernando, in his history, "cautious of appearing before them."

This accumulated evidence against Columbus determined the sovereigns to send out some one who should make them truthful reports as to the troubles prevailing in their new possessions. They chose, as we have stated, their commander, Francisco de Bobadilla, and on March 21, 1499, signed a commission, ordering him to "inquire what persons had risen against justice," and to proceed against them according to law. Two months later they seem to have fully resolved that Columbus should be superseded; and, on the 21st of May, two other commissions were furnished Bobadilla. The first gave the government of the Indies to the commander, Francisco de Bobadilla, and contains the following comprehensive and conclusive clause:

"It is our will that if the commander, Francisco de Bobadilla, should think it necessary for our service and the purpose of justice, that any cavalier or other persons, who are at present in those islands—or may arrive there—should leave them, and not return and reside in them, and that should come and present themselves before us, he may command, in our name, and oblige them to depart. And whomsoever he thus commands, we hereby order that immediately, without waiting to inquire or consult us, or to receive from us any other letter or command, and without interposing appeal or supplication, they obey whatever he shall say and order, under the penalties he shall impose on our part." [126]

All possibility of disobedience and resistance, or excuse therefor, seems to be here forestalled, but to little effect, as the conduct of Columbus will prove.

The second letter-patent, or commission, commanded Columbus and his brothers to deliver up to Bobadilla all fortresses, ships, arms, etc., "under penalty of incurring the punishment to which those are subject who refuse to surrender fortresses and other trusts when commanded by the sovereigns." [127]

Nor were these comprehensive commissions all. Foreseeing, no doubt, the reluctance with which Columbus would resign a position for which he was so unfit, the sovereigns addressed a letter to him, which they intrusted to Bobadilla. It ran thus:

"To CHRISTOPHER COLUMBUS, *our Admiral of the Ocean Sea:*

"We have ordered the commander, Francisco de Bobadilla, to acquaint you with some things from us; therefore we desire you to give him entire credit, and to obey him.

"GIVEN AT MADRID, *May* 21, 1499."

These commissions, we have seen, were signed in 1499, with ill-timed consideration. The sovereigns, however, still refrained from dispatching Bobadilla. Had they done so immediately, Moxica might have escaped his awful fate; and many others, who were put to death without trial, might have been spared.

It was not till the arrival of the ships containing Roldan's followers, and the slaves presented to them by Columbus, that the indignation of the queen was thoroughly aroused. "What right," she is said angrily to have exclaimed, "has my admiral to enslave my subjects?" She immediately ordered a proclamation to be made, that those slaves which had been given away by Columbus and brought to Spain, should be immediately delivered to Bobadilla (whom she determined to send out without further delay), and restored to liberty in their native land. According to Herrera and others, the penalty imposed upon those not delivering up the said slaves, was death.

Invested, then, with the remarkably full and unconditional

---

[126] Navarette, "Collec. Dip.," vol. ii., p. 266.
[127] Idem., p. 267.

authority as contained in the four letters-patent already mentioned, and provided, besides, with numerous blank letters, signed by the sovereigns, to be filled up as he thought proper, Bobadilla left Spain in July, 1500, to arrive in Hispaniola on the 23d of August of that year.

It becomes us carefully to examine this episode in the history of Columbus. Bobadilla has been energetically denounced. Fernando is foremost among those who accuse him of obstinacy, arrogance, and vindictiveness, and most historians have followed his example. But Fernando, we must remember, was the son of Columbus; and most of his biographers are his admirers and apologists, *quand même;* their opinions, therefore, should be received with extreme caution. There are, however, historians who give Bobadilla credit for ability and integrity, while those most bitter against him have never impugned his incontestable personal incorruptibility. He was intrusted with as high powers as a sovereign could confer upon a subject and agent, yet he did not abuse that power; and there is no evidence that the extraordinary trust reposed in him was ever used in a manner derogatory to his own honor, or detrimental to the interests of the crown. Regarded from a humane and moral point of view, his conduct was praiseworthy, while legally it was not only just and equitable, but the only course he could possibly have pursued in justice to the sovereigns, and in the discharge of his duties.

As the little fleet was sighted off the harbor of San Domingo, a canoe was sent out to inquire after a son of Columbus who was expected. This messenger was informed by Bobadilla that he had come out as *commissioner* to investigate charges touching the late rebellion. The master of the ships asked news of the island, and was told that seven of the Spaniards, into whose conduct Bobadilla came to inquire, were already hanged, and that five others, among them young Guevara, awaited a similar fate.

As soon as the report was spread that a commissioner had arrived to investigate the charges made against the so-called rebels, there was much commotion in the island, but of a different character from what might have been expected had Columbus been in the right. His brothers and adherents evinced manifest uneasiness, while the accused rejoiced that at length justice, and not despotism and personal spite, was to decide their fate.

Bobadilla remained on board his ship during the day succeeding his arrival; crowds of Spaniards visited him bearing but one tale, that of the oppressions and wrongs they had suffered at the hands of Columbus. These complaints, bitter and innumerable as they were, do not seem to have influenced Bobadilla, except in so far as to determine him to assume jurisdiction over the so-called rebels at once, and so retard or prevent, as justice might demand, the executions then pending. In this resolution he was strengthened by the sickening sight which met his eye as he entered the river; on either bank, the dead body of a Spaniard swung ghastly from a gibbet; these executions had apparently been recent—Columbus had anticipated his arrival and defeated the humane intentions of the sovereigns, in so far as these victims were concerned.

He landed the next morning, attended mass, and, after that ceremony (being informed that Columbus and his brother, the *adelantado*, were absent), in the presence of Don Diego, who was in command of the fortress, of Roderigo Perez, the servants of the admiral, and the large concourse assembled, ordered his commission (authorizing him to investigate the rebellion, and commanding Columbus, and *all* others in authority, to aid him in discharging his duties) to be read.

This, it will be remembered, was the simplest and least comprehensive of his letters-patent. He commenced, however, by reading it, thinking first to ascertain the causes of the trouble, and then, if necessary, investigate the conduct of Columbus and his brothers, and, if it proved blameworthy, to remove them. He therefore demanded that the persons of the prisoners should be surrendered to him, and the written accusations against them to be given into his keeping, requiring, at the same time, their accusers to appear before him.

The daily impending execution of the prisoners, by order of Columbus, rendered it necessary that their persons should be placed in safety, at least till they had been tried. The action of Bobadilla was, therefore, strictly lawful. Few, with any knowledge of law, or any feelings of justice, will fail to perceive that he could not have acted otherwise.

Don Diego, however, refused to deliver the prisoners, refused to recognize the authority of Bobadilla, and alleged that Columbus's power was superior to any the former could have been invested with.

Bobadilla regarded this as perhaps a natural and excusable caution under the circumstances; he imagined that, of course, when Diego should learn how full were his powers, he would no longer hesitate to obey the dictates of his sovereigns. He, therefore, the next morning, before the assembled multitude, read the second commission which created him governor of the island, and ordered that he should be implicitly obeyed, without demur or appeal. He then took the accustomed oath of office, and again demanded the surrender of the prisoners. But he soon learned that he was to encounter nothing but opposition and defiance from Columbus and his brothers. It would naturally be supposed that, when a judge arrived whose mission was to try, and to treat, according to their deserts, those whom he had accused of rebellion and heinous crimes, Columbus and his brothers would gladly have welcomed that judge, and assisted him to the utmost.

That they persisted from the first in regarding Bobadilla as an enemy may be thus explained: They knew that their conduct would not bear investigation; that, if it was once brought to light, their power was ended, and they themselves would perhaps suffer the penalty of their crimes, while the innocence of those they accused would be revealed. Columbus had indeed petitioned for a judge, but for one subservient to him—*in his pay*—whose justice should be what he willed. Bobadilla, coming with power superior to his own, received from the sovereigns, was not what he bargained for.

Diego Columbus would no more regard the second commission than he had done the first, and still refused to deliver the prisoners.

Bobadilla now perceived something more serious and offensive than caution in this obstinate resistance. He recognized how wisely he had been intrusted with a letter expressly ordering Columbus and his brothers to deliver up to him all fortresses, etc., and discovered that the sovereigns had foreseen the opposition he was to encounter. He therefore ordered this letter, a death-blow to the authority of Columbus, to be read; as well as another, dated May 30th, ordering him to pay the arrears due to those persons in royal service, whom Columbus had neglected or refused to remunerate. This proclamation was received with much applause. It is much to the credit of Bobadilla, and a proof of the moderation with which he proceeded, that he had not sooner read what was to render him and his mission popular.

Let us observe the wording of the first of these documents. It reads thus:

"Don Ferdinand and Doña Isabella, by the grace of God, etc. . . . to you Don Christopher Columbus, our admiral of the ocean, and to you the brothers of the said admiral, in whose power are fortresses, houses, ships, etc., we send for our governor of the islands, the commander Francisco de Bobadilla. . . . we order you to deliver the said fortresses, houses, etc., to the said commander, or the persons he shall appoint, and to give him complete power over the said fortresses, etc., all of which we command you to do under pain of incurring those penalties which those persons incur who refuse to deliver fortresses, or other things, when ordered to do so by their sovereigns."

This would appear explicit and peremptory enough. Don Diego, however, still refused to deliver either fortress or prisoners. Bobadilla then repaired to the fortress, and, when the *alcalde* who kept it appeared on the battlements, ordered the letter to be read to him, and the seals and signatures of the sovereigns to be held up to his view. The *alcalde*, however, having doubtless received his orders from Diego, refused to admit Bobadilla, who then appealed to the people and demanded their assistance, but urged that no violence should be employed save in case of resistance.

The fortress was easily taken, being no better constructed than most other public works erected by Columbus. The prisoners were discovered loaded with irons. Bobadilla delivered them to an *alguazil*.

Irving terms this conduct arrogant and precipitate, but the accusation is totally unfounded. Had the prisoners been delivered up to him, and his first commission been obeyed, Bobadilla would have proceeded first to the examination of the charges against them; then, if necessary, to that of the conduct of Columbus. The refusal to obey at the outset created the necessity of enforcing his authority by reading the other letters, which had been provided him to meet just such an emergency, and without the aid of which he was powerless, in view of Diego Columbus's insubordination, to perform the duties of his mission.

He might with justice have imprisoned Don Diego and the

alcalde who held the fortress, on the charge of treason, as they refused to obey the commands of their sovereigns. This he did not do, and if he afterward imprisons the three Columbos, it was not till still weightier evidence had convicted them of greater crimes, and rendered it necessary.

To relieve in a measure the extreme misery into which the Spaniards in Hispaniola had fallen, partly from the non-payment of their salaries, which had been withheld by Columbus, partly from the wretched state of the colony, Bobadilla now published a license allowing all to search for gold for twenty years, paying only one-eleventh instead of one-third, as they had done till now, to the government. This proceeding, though certainly humane and wise, excited the indignation of Columbus, whose tenth of the revenues would, he feared, be thus materially diminished; he, therefore, immediately on hearing of it, published a proclamation, in which he declared Bobadilla to have no power or authority, and forbade any to obey him.

The latter sent an *alcalde*, bearing a copy of the letters-patent, to acquaint him in due form with his appointment as governor, but forebore as yet sending the peremptory note addressed to Columbus only, bidding the latter obey him. But, in the face of all the letters of the sovereigns, which proclaimed that there was to be no appeal to them from any proceeding which Bobadilla might think fit, Columbus still resisted; published and proclaimed that Bobadilla's powers were not valid— that his own were greater. He declared, however, afterward, that he wrote to Bobadilla, assuring him that he would soon leave the island entirely to his government. This he only did, however, he confesses in his letter to the nurse of Prince John (Doña Juana de la Torres), which contains his own defense of his conduct in these proceedings, to gain time, that their highnesses might perhaps change their minds. This statement clearly proves his guilt. Had he, indeed, believed that Bobadilla was— as he had publicly proclaimed throughout the island—acting without due authority, he would not have desired delay in order that the sovereigns might change their minds; who, if they had no part in the proceedings of Bobadilla, and were unaware of his conduct, could not have *altered* a policy which they had never enjoined. The direct opposition to the royal commands (which directed that their agent was to be obeyed without appeal or delay), perpetrated by Columbus, rendered him clearly guilty of no less a crime than treason; and he and his brothers "incurred those penalties which those persons incur who refuse to deliver fortresses or other things, when ordered to do so by their sovereigns."[128]

It is absurd for historians to declare, as they constantly do, that Bobadilla overstepped his authority, and that Isabella never intended him to supersede Columbus, but merely to punish those who had rebelled against the latter. If this had been the case, why was he provided with those commissions in which Columbus and his brothers were expressly ordered to deliver to him all things pertaining to the crown?

Why should a letter have been written addressed solely to Columbus, commanding his obedience to and belief in Bobadilla?

The continued and insolent resistance he encountered convinced the new governor that consideration and delicacy were thrown away upon such a man as Columbus. He therefore sent to him Velasquez, deputy-treasurer, and a Franciscan friar, bearing the last-named letter. This document made Columbus fear the consequences of persisting in his insubordination; and, as it was accompanied by a summons from Bobadilla to appear before him, he, with a show of humility, set out for San Domingo. But rumors, which appear not without foundation, reached Bobadilla, that this humility was only feigned—that he was in reality attempting to rouse the native inhabitants of the Vega to aid him in opposing the new governor.[129]

Considering that the conduct of Columbus and his brother Diego had been, up to this time, in their refusal to obey the royal mandates, of so treasonable a nature as to render the reported attempt at rebellion probable, and justly holding that they deserved imprisonment for what was well proved against them, as well as for their resistance of the sovereign will as

[128] *See ante*, extract from royal mandate.

[129] "It is also said that the new governor sent letters to the king, written with the Admiralles hande, in strange and unknown sypherings, to his brother, the Lieutenant, being absent, willing him to be in a readiness, with a power of armed men to come and aid him, if the Governor shquld proffer him any violence. Whereof the Governor having knowledge (as he sayth), being also advertised that the Lieutenant was gone to his brother before the men, which he had prepared there in a readiness, apprehended them both unawares, before the multitude came together."—*Peter Martyr*, "Decade I.," book vii.

vested in him, Bobadilla had them both imprisoned and put in irons on board a caravel which was shortly to return to Spain.

With unpardonable unfairness, Irving, alluding to the imprisonment of Don Diego, says:

"The admiral's brother, Don Diego, was seized, thrown in irons, and confined on board a caravel, *without any reason being assigned for his imprisonment*," and does not hesitate to write thus after enumerating all the successive efforts of Bobadilla to obtain obedience to the orders of the sovereigns, whose letters he had publicly read and exhibited; after recording Diego's repeated refusal to recognize the royal authority; and after, in the very paragraph in which the above sentence occurs, recording the *rumor*, as he terms it, of Columbus seeking to excite the natives to rebellion.

There is certainly no more flagrant act of treason and disobedience to royal commands extant than the insubordination of Diego—indeed, of all the Columbos; yet, while he records these acts of insubordination and rebellion, Mr. Irving still has the courage to write that *Diego was imprisoned without any reason being assigned for his imprisonment.*

As for Christopher Columbus, the charges against him were manifold. It was alleged that he ill-treated and abused the natives, refusing to let them be baptized, that they might continue slaves;[120] that, acting as a kind of pawnbroker and money-lender, he had traded upon the necessities of the Spaniards—he had inveigled and impoverished, giving them barely wherewithal to keep them from starvation, then enforcing his collections through a royal *garnashee*.[121]

Nor was this all. The queen called him to account for dishonesty in office, thus:

"The said admiral having *farmed out the offices* of *alguazil* and notary in the island of Hispaniola, for a certain period, we command that the moneys and the revenues derived from the said offices be divided into ten parts, *nine* for us and *one* for the admiral, deducting first the expenses and indemnifications of the aforesaid offices."[122]

---

[120] Irving, "Columbus," book xiii., chapter iv.
[121] Navarette, vol. ii., p. 222.
[122] Navarette, "Collec. Dip." vol. ii., p. 308. Columbus complained of this order,

Peter Martyr thus sums up the accusations made against Columbus by the Spaniards in the island:

"They accuse the admiral and his brother to be unjust men, cruel enemies, and shedders of the Spanish blood, declaring that upon every light occasion they would rack them, hang them, and head them, and that they took pleasure therein; and that they departed from them as from cruel tyrants and wild beasts, rejoicing in blood, also the kings' enemies; affirming, likewise, that they well perceived their intent to be none other than to usurp the empire of the islands, which thing (they said) they suspected by a thousand conjectures, and especially in that they would permit none to resort to the gold-mines, but only such as were their familiars." [133]

All the above charges appear to have been substantiated; the proceedings were evidently had in all due form. Charlevoix relates that the suit against Columbus was conducted in writing—that written charges were sent to him, to which he replied in the same way. This was undoubtedly the case, as Bobadilla appears to have been an able judge and a discreet lawyer; and the allegation of many historians that he imprisoned Columbus without due cause or investigation, is contradicted in their own accounts of the proceedings; witness Irving and others.

The result of the investigation was, as we have seen, the imprisonment of Columbus. It was his own cook, we are told, who riveted the fetters, "with as much readiness and alacrity," quoth Las Casas, "as though he were serving him with the choicest viands."

This little incident is not without import. Columbus might perhaps have been unpopular with the multitude, and yet a good man; but when we find his own domestics, who owed place and living to him, and who would naturally be supposed to regret his downfall, rejoicing instead, we cannot but believe the man to have been thoroughly contemptible; the "graceless cook" riveting the fetters militates far more, we take it, against the personal character of Columbus, than of his culinary menial.

and urged his right to fill the offices with his servants, requiring them to perform the duties (poorly, we apprehend) while he pocketed the proceeds; yet we are continually called upon to admire the exalted and glorious opinions he entertained of his office.

[133] Peter Martyr, Decade I., book vii.

CHAPTER XXII.

COLUMBUS'S DEFENSE OF HIS CONDUCT REVIEWED.

It would be useless to attempt a further refutation of the tirades launched against the new governor by the numerous and partial biographers of Columbus, who at this period of his his-

COLUMBUS.—(From Muñoz, "Historia del Nuevo Mundo.")

tory, couple the name of Bobadilla with every opprobrious epithet propriety will allow; and the more modern the historian, and, therefore, the farther removed from the scene and time of action, the more virulent his attacks, as also his sympathy for his hero Christopher. We have stated what was the course pursued by Bobadilla; and even when the simple facts are related, without comment or explanation, it is plain to all that it was a just and equitable one. The true merits of the case can, however, be easily decided and established by leaving historians, whether partial or impartial, and proceeding at once to the fountain-head, viz., to what Columbus himself has to say. He certainly, more than any of his historians, was interested in proving his innocence, and we may reasonably suppose that he omitted no plea which could, in the slightest degree, exculpate him, and refrained from no charge against Bobadilla wherein there was the slightest semblance of truth.

Fortunately for us, this defense, written by Columbus to the nurse of Prince Juan, no doubt with the intention that it should be shown to the sovereigns, still exists; it was written during his voyage to Spain, or after his arrival there.

The lame and bungling explanation of his conduct, the ridiculous character of the charges he prefers against Bobadilla, and above all, the admissions he (no doubt unintentionally) makes in his letter, may furnish some facts which, though mixed with much falsehood, may enable the reader to judge of the relative merits of the accuser and the accused.

We quote the passages from this letter which relate especially to the question before us, and call the attention of the reader, now and then, to the absurdity, falsehood, or self-inculpation, they contain; for, though an unbiased, intelligent mind would at once perceive all this, historians have so persistently declared Bobadilla wrong, and Columbus right, that an unbiased judgment will not easily be formed.

Columbus writes: ". . . In the mean time Bobadilla arrived. . . . The day after his arrival he created himself governor."

Here is a specimen of our hero's veracity. Bobadilla did not *create himself governor,* but assumed that title and office in virtue of the full and comprehensive letters-patent from Isabella, who had clothed him with all the power in the premises the crown could devolve upon an agent, besides commanding Columbus in a special letter addressed to that worthy to obey him. We see, therefore, the insolence of the falsehood that Bobadilla *created* himself governor.

Columbus, too, would have it appear that his conduct was most precipitate. *The day after his arrival he created himself governor.* It will be remembered that Bobadilla did *not* assume the government until the brother of Columbus had repeatedly refused to deliver to him the prisoners he had been sent to try. This treasonable effrontery and disregard of royal orders created the *necessity* for Bobadilla to *act* as judge and governor, and act immediately, for those of the prisoners who were not already hanged were liable to execution at any moment, in violation alike of law, justice, and the royal command. There was certainly no undue haste on the part of Bobadilla. An oppression, worse than that visited upon the people of God in Egypt, pervaded the island—robbery, murder, and manslaughter, were practised by Columbus, who now raised himself in open rebellion against the crown as personated by Bobadilla.

The ghastly dead swung from the gibbets; the blood of Spaniards and of Indians, like that of Abel, cried to Heaven from the ground. Had he not moved promptly in the discharge of his duty, he would have deserved the odium of mankind, as well as the displeasure of his sovereigns; as it was, he resolved, even in San Domingo, to magnify the law and make it honorable; and, having used the mildest measures, and assumed the least of the authorities vested in him without success, he naturally produced his higher authority and proceeded to more vigorous measures, and seems thereby to deserve the commendation of all who prize humanity and justice.

The letter continues thus:

". . . . He" (Bobadilla) "published exemptions from the payment of the gold and of the tithes, and, in fine, announced a general franchise for the space of twenty years."

This action will be commended by the humane. Bobadilla did much to relieve both natives and colonists from the cruel tyranny and extortion practised by Columbus.

"Having brought with him a considerable number of blank letters, signed by their highnesses, he filled up some of them to the *alcalde* (Roldan) and his consorts full of favors and commendations; but he never sent either letter or message to me, nor has he done so to this day."

The possession of the blank letters signed by the sovereigns, constitutes most conclusive evidence of the confidence they reposed in Bobadilla. They seem to have furnished them that he might silence any unanticipated cavil on the part of Columbus, and be able to impress that lawless usurper with the necessity of respecting and obeying the man thus accredited by his masters. As to the charge made by Columbus that the new governor never sent him "either letter or message," its deliberate falsity is exposed by his own son Fernando, who says, in his history, that Bobadilla "required the admiral to repair to him without delay, because it was convenient for their majesties' service he should do so; *and, to back his summons*, on the 7th of September sent him the king's letter by Friar Juan de la Sera, which was to this effect."

Then follows the letter addressed to Columbus which we have already quoted. Yet, in the face of these facts, Columbus unblushingly asserts that Bobadilla sent him neither letter nor message. He then continues:

".... No sooner was I informed of his having granted these exemptions .... I made verbal and written declaration that his powers were incompetent to do so, as mine were the strongest."

When we reflect that these verbal and written declarations were made by Columbus, when fully advised of the ample powers vested in Bobadilla, and of the royal command that he and his brothers should obey him, and deliver up all fortresses to him, it will not be necessary to argue the question of veracity or treason as regards the action and assertion of Columbus. He certainly spoke as a liar, and acted as a traitor. The pretended motives which he declares to have prompted his misconduct are, therefore, but aggravations of his crime.

".... He ordered inquisition to be made respecting me, with reference to imputed misdeeds, such as were never invented in hell."

With this statement fresh from his pen, he will not hesitate to affirm, a little farther on: "Upon my oath I declare to you I have no idea why I am imprisoned." He was as well aware of the character of his crimes and the charges preferred against him, as was Guido Faux, or any other criminal that has suffered the penalty of the law.

". . . . In saying that the commander" (Bobadilla) "could not grant exemptions, I did what was proper."

He fails, however, to demonstrate how, when overtly disregarding and opposing the commands of his sovereigns, he was doing what was proper.

"If their highnesses were to give orders for a general inquiry here, I assure you it would discover such things as to make it wonderful the island is not swallowed up. I think you will remember, madam, that, when I was driven by a storm into Lisbon, I was falsely accused of going to the king, in order to deliver up the Indies to him."

When he enlarges upon the iniquities of the island, and wonders it was not swallowed up, he should have remembered that he had brought it into its present state of degradation and misery. His allusion to the charge of treason preferred after his visit to Portugal, is traveling from the case in hand, where his guilt is evident, to one where it appears more doubtful.

"However ignorant I may be, nobody can suppose me to be so ignorant as not to know that, if the Indies were mine, I should not be able to keep possession of them without the aid of a prince. Such being the case, where should I find greater support, and more certainty of not being entirely driven from them, than in the king and queen, our lords, who, from nothing, have raised me to such high honors?"

Notwithstanding his asseveration that he knows nothing of the charges made against him, he here seems to be defending himself against one of them, which was that he had made war upon the government, for the purpose of ultimately gaining possession of the new lands.

That Isabella had raised him from nothing to a position far above his deserts, all will agree; but it is not so easy to discover the pertinence of his allusion to the great support she was giving him in Hispaniola, and security against being ultimately driven from it, as she had, in a solemn and formal manner, after years of deliberation, removed him from office, and subsequently forbade his returning to Hispaniola.

". . . . What I have now unwillingly stated is to refute a malicious calumny which I would not willingly recall even in my dreams, as the behavior of Bobadilla would maliciously give another coloring to it; but I shall be able to prove that his ignorance, extreme cowardice, and inordinate cupidity, have been the cause of all that has happened."

This charge bears falsehood upon its face. Are we to believe that the advent of Bobadilla in the island, in 1500, caused all the avarice, cruelty, falsehood, and murder, perpetrated by Columbus during the seven years preceding that advent which had converted his "paradise" into a hell, complaints of which had caused Bobadilla to be sent out?

". . . . He neither spoke to me himself nor permitted any one else to speak to me, until now; and, upon my oath, I declare to you that I have no idea why I am imprisoned."

This, as we have shown, is a most barefaced falsehood. He first says Bobadilla caused investigation to be made touching crimes imputed to him, the like of which were never invented in hell. He attempts to defend himself against some of these charges, and then swears he knows not why he is imprisoned.

". . . . I have already mentioned that, with six hundred thousand maravedis, I should have paid everybody, without injury to any person, and that I possessed more than four millions of tithes, without touching the gold."

This allusion to his abundant resources does not come with a good grace when we remember the distress and suffering he had caused in the island (many dying of starvation) by withholding the pay of those who had labored for him, as well as for the crown. No wonder that Bobadilla, when he found this accumulation of gold and tithes, upon taking up his abode in the government-house, devoted a portion to the payment of what was so justly due the many unfortunate who had been defrauded.

". . . . Would to God that their highnesses had sent Bobadilla, or any other person, two years ago, because I should now be free from this scandal and infamy, nor should I have been deprived of my honor!"

He no doubt would have had fewer crimes to answer for, such as the murder of Moxica, the secretion of the pearls from the sovereigns, etc.

". . . . I aver that great numbers of men have been in the islands who did not deserve baptism in the eyes of God or man."

One would think Columbus, in very shame, would have refrained from such an assertion, when he remembered that he himself had requested the prisons to be thrown open and the convicts let loose upon the island.

". . . . When he" (Bobadilla) "heard of my approach, he caused Don Diego to be loaded with irons, and thrown into a caravel; he acted in the same manner toward myself and toward the *adelantado* when he arrived."

Bobadilla could not have done otherwise than imprison Columbus and his brothers, and it ill becomes them to complain of his severity. He neither executed them, as they had caused others to be executed for lesser crimes than those of which they stood convicted, neither did he kick them from the battlements of a fortress, but sent them to Spain, where their power for evil would be lessened.

". . . . I have been yet more concerned respecting the affair of the pearls—that I have not brought them to their highnesses; . . . . if I have not written respecting this" (the pearls) "to their highnesses, it is because I wished first to render an equally favorable account of the gold."

Here, again, we find him defending himself against one of the charges of which he professes to be ignorant. His excuse is a poor one: accused and convicted of having withheld the pearls, and the knowledge of their being in his possession, from the sovereigns, he replies that he was silent on this topic because he wished to have equally favorable accounts of the gold. It is evident he contemplated extorting further favors and honors from the sovereigns on the strength of these pearls. In this intention he was, however, frustrated by the arrival of Bobadilla, to whom this charge against him was brought with many others, and who, upon investigation, found it to be just, as indeed he here confesses it to be, and makes but a lame defense of his evident fraud.

". . . . I am judged in Spain as a governor who had been sent to a province or city, under regular government, where the laws could be executed without fear of endangering the public weal. In this I receive enormous wrong. . . . I ought to be judged as a captain sent from Spain to the Indies, to conquer a nation numerous and warlike."

Here we have proof, upon his own testimony, that he has uttered falsehoods from the commencement of his undertaking down to the period of which we write. In 1492, he would have the world believe that he had *discovered* an island, and that it was inhabited by a naked and inoffensive people, possessing neither arms, nor a knowledge of their use—a people so entirely powerless that a garrison of forty men would be sufficient to destroy the whole island."[134]

"But supposing," he says in a letter to Raphael Sanchez, on his return from his first voyage, speaking of the friendliness of the natives, "their feelings should become changed, and they should wish to injure those who have remained in the fortress, they could not do so, for they have no arms; they go naked, and are, moreover, too cowardly." Now, however, he would have the world believe he was sent to conquer a people already known to be *numerous* and *warlike;* he would be thought, not a discoverer, but a conqueror. He does not seem to perceive that when he admits the laws cannot be executed for fear of endangering the public weal, he speaks poorly for his own powers of governing, which had been inadequate, during seven years' despotic rule, to establish law and order among a people, according to his *first* description, innocent and defenseless; he loses sight of all self-inculpation this incongruity and contradiction may contain, in his desire to assume the new character of warrior, and *such* a warrior. He continues:

".... Where, by the divine will, I have subdued another world to the dominion of the king and queen, our lords, by which Spain, which was looked upon as poor, has become very rich."

We may here remark that, owing to his misconduct, the Western islands had been the cause of far more expense than profit to the Spanish realm.

"I ought to be judged as a captain who for so many years have borne arms without quitting them for an instant. I ought to be judged by cavaliers who have themselves won the meed of victory—by gentlemen, indeed, and not by lawyers."

It would be difficult to find a tribunal that would not condemn Columbus, even upon his own testimony. We do not, therefore, wonder that he would, by all means, avoid lawyers; no man of common-sense, certainly no lawyer, could be ignorant of his guilt; he had requested a judge to be sent out, learned in the law, to aid him in trying *others*, but in his *own* case he would be sole judge.

[134] *See* letter to Santangel.

"Under any other judgment I sustain great injury, because in the Indies there is neither civil right nor judgment-seat."

If there were no organized tribunals, why were Moxica and so many other Spaniards executed, without trial, in violation of law? Why were they not sent to Spain for trial, as Columbus petitioned for himself? In this confession of there existing neither civil right nor judgment-seat in Hispaniola, and in his declaration that he should receive enormous wrong if tried there, he plainly admits the enormous wrong perpetrated against those he had executed, or, more properly speaking, murdered, and he deserved no better fate than his victims.

He knew that, if those unfortunates had been sent to Spain, his downfall would have been speedy; they would have lived, and he no longer would have had human life at his disposal.

". . . . The tidings of the gold which I said I would give, are, that on Christmas-day, being greatly afflicted and tormented by wicked Christians and the Indians, at the moment of abandoning all, to save, if possible, my life, our Lord comforted me miraculously, saying to me, 'Take courage; do not abandon thyself to sadness and fear, I will provide for all. The seven years of the term of gold are not yet passed, and in this, as in the rest, I will redress thee.'"

These are the tidings for which Columbus waited before writing to the sovereigns about the pearls; they are eminently satisfactory. Imagine a steward or administrator, instead of giving an exact account of his stewardship, recounting a vision in which he is assured that all will be right, and that God will redress him! The blasphemy with which Columbus, whenever hard pushed for a defense, brings the Almighty to his aid, and invents a speech, which he puts in the mouth of the Deity, wherein his innocence is declared and his enemies threatened with punishment, is revolting in the extreme; and the enormity of the crimes he thus seeks to cover with divine sanction must render his hypocrisy still more odious in the eyes of the truly reverent.

". . . . See, now, what discernment was shown by Bobadilla, when he gave up every thing for nothing, and four millions of tithes without any reason, and even without being asked to do so, and without first giving notice to their highnesses."

This is an adroit attempt to turn royalty against Bobadilla, by appealing to the cupidity of the sovereigns, but it also demonstrates an insolent officiousness on the part of the writer, who would seem to ignore the absolute authority vested in Bobadilla by the crown.

".... If their highnesses shall give orders for me to be judged by others, which I fervently hope will not be the case, and impeach me respecting the affairs of the Indies, I humbly supplicate them to send out, at *my expense,* two conscientious and respectable persons, which will now be easily met with, since gold to the amount of five marks may be found in the space of four hours."

Columbus seems to have an idea of impeachment for treason, notwithstanding his oath of ignorance in the premises; therefore he wishes his judges to be in his pay; and, moreover, he would have them men whom the abundance of gold would tempt to the island. How unlikely it was that such men would be honest judges! It is needless to say, his proposition gives us a view of his notions concerning a court of justice, the purity and competency of a tribunal; "he too would have judges dependent upon his will alone for the tenure of their offices, and the amount and payment of their salaries." Such being the case, we cannot but wonder that historians, who would appear impartial, should have failed to condemn his corrupt views.

".... The governor" (Bobadilla), "on his arrival in San Domingo, took up his abode in my house; .... even a pirate does not behave in this manner toward the merchant that he plunders."

This accusation has at first a semblance of truth, as the reader may suppose it to have been the private residence of Columbus into which Bobadilla intruded; such was not the case—it was the "government-house" in which Columbus had resided at the capital of the island, and in which all succeeding governors were expected to take up their abode during their term of office. In time Bobadilla was succeeded by Ovando, yet we do not find the former complaining that the latter took up his abode "in his house;" such a complaint would have been as preposterous as for a retiring President of the United States to remonstrate against his successors inhabiting the White House.

".... That which grieved me most was the seizure of my papers, of which I have never been able to recover one; and those which would have been most useful to me in proving my innocence, are precisely those which he has kept most carefully concealed."

The seizure of papers is a usual proceeding in case of suspicion of most crimes, more especially of treason; but, though these papers might very well be used to prove his guilt, they could hardly have proved the innocence of Columbus. The very fact that in them he had foreseen accusation, and attempted to defend himself, would seem to furnish *prima-facie* evidence of his guilt, and would have gone far to prove him culpable before any legal tribunal. No wonder he feared lawyers. Let us remember, also, how Columbus declares, upon oath, that he is ignorant of the cause of his imprisonment; how, then, could he know the precise papers which would have proved his innocence, and the precise crime to which they related? In his despicable attempts to blacken Bobadilla, and in his efforts to establish his innocence, he entangles himself in contradictory statements, and furnishes conclusive evidence of his own guilt.

Such is the lame defense he makes. A perusal of this letter, with its absurdities, contradictions, and falsehoods, will alone be sufficient to convince the impartial that his word is not to be depended upon. It therefore goes far to weaken confidence in the histories which have hitherto been written of the man, for most authors, when making an assertion which they imagine liable to disbelief, either from the improbability or from the strong evidence against it, consider the statement that for this they have the word of Columbus himself, sufficient to remove all doubt.

With the above letter before him, the reader will be apt to think the fact of Columbus's making an assertion sufficient to render its veracity suspicious. We, therefore, without further attempt to prove the incorrectness (to use a mild term) with which authors have represented Columbus as a martyr, Bobadilla as a tyrant and usurper, have contented ourselves with placing Columbus's own account of the affair and defense of his conduct, as contained in this letter to Prince Juan's nurse, before him. It answers a twofold purpose, and not only proves the guilt of Columbus, regarding the charges brought against him, for which he was imprisoned by Bobadilla, but also the utter falsity of his word, and the caution with which a statement made by him, or upon his authority, should be received.

CHAPTER XXIII.

COLUMBUS SENT TO SPAIN IN DISGRACE. — BOBADILLA REPLACED BY OVANDO.

It is certain that the imprisonment of Columbus was regarded as a happy event by all the inhabitants of the island. Horns were blown in the vicinity of the ship on board which he was confined; lampoons and caricatures were posted in the streets, and the multitude gave way to heart-felt and almost wild rejoicing at being at last freed from the despotic rule of this insolent *parvenu*. Bobadilla had public opinion decidedly on his side, as he had law and equity. The testimony he had collected against the three brothers was carefully arranged and sent with them to Spain.

The ships which bore Columbus away from the scenes of his chief crimes, set sail in October, 1500, and, after a short voyage, landed him in Cadiz.

Historians unanimously declare that, on his arrival in Spain, the sovereigns ordered his immediate release, and professed the greatest indignation at the conduct of Bobadilla. It is evident, however, that, if they professed to be displeased, their displeasure was but feigned, and that they were in reality by no means ill pleased that the pirate whom they had so unwisely intrusted with power, and who had shown himself so utterly incapable and unworthy, should be deposed. There were, however, weighty reasons why Isabella should also be pleased at this deposition having been effected in such a manner as to admit of her denying entire participation in it. It was upon the testimony of Columbus, that Alexander VI. had deeded to Spain the islands, etc., he professed to have discovered. If it were not unkind, it would have been impolitic, therefore, publicly to denounce the man by whose perjury she hoped to have obtained a continent.

She appears to have been conscious that, to some extent, she was at the mercy of this man, whose power consisted in the very crimes and frauds of which she knew him to have been guilty, for he had shown her that there was no treachery too base, no perjury too great, for him to perpetrate and commit.

Isabella's policy, during her whole reign, may be chiefly if not solely expressed by the word "craft." No wonder, then, that she, her object accomplished—the rule of Columbus brought to a close in her new possessions, and he himself in Spain, with poor prospect of organizing a successful rebellion, whereby to usurp their government—should have dealt in fair promises, in delusive hopes, which she took care to put far in the prospective; no wonder, even, that she consented so far to sacrifice Bobadilla to the pride and malice of Columbus, as to promise his speedy removal, though even Fernando Columbus seems well to have divined what would have been the fate of that honest official, had he lived to reach Spain. Commenting upon the shipwreck and drowning of Bobadilla, Roldan, and others engaged in the so-called rebellion, he writes:

"I am satisfied it was the hand of God; for, had they arrived in Spain, they had never been punished as their crimes deserved, but rather have been favored and preferred."

Such being the case, it was easy and politic to dally with Columbus; and, while determined never to reinstate him in a power he had abused so shamefully, to make large promises. But, although Isabella refrained from punishing Columbus as his frauds and crimes deserved, and though she held out to him delusive hopes, which she never meant him to realize, it is evident that she did not altogether refrain from testifying to him her displeasure at his conduct. According to Charlevoix, she thus addressed him:

"Common report accuses you of acting with a degree of severity quite unsuitable for an infant colony, and likely to excite rebellion there; but the matter as to which I find it hardest to give you my pardon, is your conduct in reducing to slavery a number of Indians who had done nothing to deserve such a fate; this was contrary to my express orders. As your ill-fortune willed it, just at the time when I heard of this breach of my instructions, everybody was complaining of you, and no one spoke a word in your favor. And I felt obliged to send to the Indies a commissioner to investigate matters, and give me a true report; and, if necessary, to put limits to the authority which you were accused of overstepping. If you were found guilty of the charges, he was to relieve you of the government, and to send you to Spain, to give an account of your stewardship. . . . I cannot promise to reinstate you in your government; people are too much inflamed against you, and must have time to cool. As to your rank of admiral, I never intended to deprive you of it. But you must bide your time, and trust in me."

It was plain, therefore, that Columbus, though retaining his rank of admiral—which was somewhat of a sinecure, in which there might be some honor, but in which there was certainly little profit—was obliged to give up all present hope of returning in triumph to Hispaniola, and, vested with supreme power, there to wreak a terrible vengeance upon all who had opposed him.

And, although it may be alleged that the above is but an imaginary speech, which proves nothing, there is substantial and convincing testimony that it is a fair *résumé* of Isabella's policy toward Columbus. In a letter from the sovereigns to the latter, in answer to his solicitations for money, we read:

"Respecting the ten thousand pieces of money which you speak of, it is determined not to grant them this voyage, until we are better informed."

This letter is dated March 14, 1502.

When Columbus was eventually allowed to depart on his fourth voyage, he was forbidden to touch at Hispaniola, save on his return, and then only in case of extreme necessity.

The removal of Bobadilla was, however, to take place. Nicolas de Ovando, commander of Lares, was sent out to succeed him, in February, 1502, with the finest fleet which had as yet been sent to the new lands.

Ovando is said to have been "a wise and judicious man." Most contemporaries speak highly of his character and abilities. Nevertheless, his rule in the islands was characterized by many atrocious acts of cruelty, which can be laid to no one's charge but his. It is evident, therefore, that, though perhaps competent to govern his own race, he was incapable of judiciously governing the Indians.

On his arrival in Hispaniola, he was received with great respect by Bobadilla, toward whom he conducted himself with marked deference, more than he would have been likely to exhibit had the latter been in very deep disgrace with the sovereigns.

The short rule of Bobadilla had been attended with advantageous results to the crown, while the crushing tribute imposed by Columbus discouraged many from seeking gold. Immediately upon Bobadilla's reducing the royal tax, upon all precious metal found, from one-third to one-eleventh, it appears that the amount realized by the sovereigns was increased fourfuld;[135] and, though some authors allege that this was owing to cruel exactions and oppressions on his part, there appears to be no truth in this assertion, as the official acts of Bobadilla were with a view of alleviating and ameliorating the condition of both Spaniards and natives. Columbus's chief accusation against Bobadilla was that he was too lenient; that he "granted exemption from tithes," and "befriended all save the crown."

His success in amassing gold was due to his very leniency. Ovando pursued a totally different course; but of him, save where he is brought in contact with Columbus, we shall say very little, this being essentially a history of the latter.

[135] Helps, "History of Columbus," p. 209.

AN ALCATRAZ.

CHAPTER XXIV.

SOJOURN OF COLUMBUS IN SPAIN PREVIOUS TO HIS FOURTH VOYAGE.
—HIS WILL.—NEGOTIATIONS ATTEMPTED WITH GENOA.

For nearly two years Columbus remained in Spain. He had been liberated, indeed, from durance vile, by order of the sovereigns, but they exhibited none of that haste to reinstate him in power which would have been a natural consequence of their believing him guiltless. Nor was their failure so to do owing to the silence and reserve of Columbus; he was constantly importuning them, either in person or by letter, for a recognition of what he termed his rights; with so little success, however, that he is at one time fain to give up, and, fearing that all hope of power and wealth to be acquired from his so-called discoveries was at an end, he bethought himself of again assuming the cloak of extreme religious enthusiasm, which he had lately allowed to fall somewhat into disuse. He hoped thus to bring himself into the notice, perhaps obtain the support and assistance, of the Church —above all, of the papal chair.

He therefore now remembered that, on starting for the islands, in 1492, he had promised the sovereigns and the Church (made a solemn vow, in fact) that, at the expiration of seven years from that date, he would furnish fifty thousand foot-soldiers, and five thousand horse, for the purpose of making war on the infidel, and reclaiming the Holy Sepulchre. The seven years had more than expired, the islands he professed to have discovered had increased the expenditure instead of the revenue of the crown, while he himself was as penniless and powerless as when, on his arrival at Palos, he was indebted to the Pinzons for the very clothing in which he presented himself at court. Feeling the wretched contrast between his promise and performance, he clings to the hope that affected religious zeal will reinstate him somewhat in the good graces of his bigoted queen, and assure him the support of the Church. In this last he seems to have been successful. The priesthood have been the creators of his fame; and now, hoping that time will have obliterated the memory of his crimes, coolly propose to place him among the saints. He strongly urged that an expedition should be immediately set on foot to reclaim the Sepulchre; he assured the sovereigns that he had been divinely chosen, from his very birth, to perform two great missions: the first, to carry Christianity across the seas to the heathen of the Western lands; the second, to recover the Sepulchre of the Saviour. He writes upon this subject a letter in which hypocrisy, cant, and blasphemy, vie with each other for preëminence; but this pious proposition only absorbs him while all hope of his being again allowed to voyage westward is seemingly at an end. Soon, however, the excitement which prevailed, owing to the riches which were flowing into Portugal from the East Indies, by the route discovered by Vasco de Gama, emboldened our hero. He begged to be allowed to lay the wealth of those Indies at the feet of Spain, by giving her a safer and shorter passage to them than that enjoyed by Portugal. He boldly asserted, not hypothetically, but as an established certainty, that there existed a strait between the lands he had discovered, which would permit ships to sail into the Eastern Ocean, and reach China, Japan, and India. He appears for the moment to have dropped the pretense of having already reached those lands, and, moreover, failed to demonstrate wherefore, if such a strait existed, and he was aware of its existence, he had not, ere this, made the Spanish kingdom mistress of its advantages. This inconsistency is, however, one of the minor ones of which he is guilty.

This strait he placed between the southern shore of Cuba, which he still professes to regard as main-land, and the northern shores of the South American Continent, which shows either his utter insincerity, or that he had done very little toward exploring the latter.

The cupidity of the sovereigns was excited, as the wily admiral believed it would be; his departure, too, on a fourth voyage, would rid them of an importunate suppliant. Orders were therefore given, in 1501, for an expedition to be fitted out, though we perceive that but little faith was placed in him, for, notwithstanding the glorious promises he made, and the eagerness with which Spain would be supposed to embrace an opportunity of diverting a valuable commerce from her hated rival Portugal, several months elapsed before a fleet of four small vessels, the largest of seventy, the smallest of fifty, tons burden, were placed at his command. Their united crew comprised one hundred and fifty men.

The meanness of this outfit plainly shows that it was the man Columbus, more than his enterprise, who was held in abhorrence, for a fine fleet of thirty-six sail and a brilliant retinue had been accorded to Ovando.

Columbus, in obtaining this fleet, obtained what he professed solely to desire, namely, the means of discovering his strait and enriching Spain, especially the queen his mistress. But other thoughts are lurking in his brain; his conduct shows plainly that he fully understood the character of Isabella and her relations with him. Both of these crafty worthies, indeed, evidently understood each other—neither believed the statements nor respected the motives of the other. Isabella humored Columbus, to a certain extent, because she believed him capable of, and able to do her, some mischief, were his vindictiveness to be openly excited. Columbus, on the other hand, rightly judged that, though he was allowed to go unpunished, he had little to expect but promises from his "munificent patroness."

Therefore we find him, while professing the humblest allegiance to the queen, engaged, with his accustomed craft and dissimulation, in a scheme by which he hoped to interest other powers in securing to him what the crown of Spain had promised him in an unguarded moment, or from motives of policy, namely, the viceroyalty of the Western islands to him and his heirs forever, the tenth of the revenues arising therefrom, and the admiralty of the Western ocean.

We must remember, before taxing Spain with ingratitude, that, even at the period of which we write, when Europe was but just commencing a struggle against feudal and sovereign despotism, the people were more powerful, and the sovereign less so, in this kingdom than in any other. All have read of the famous oath of allegiance pronounced by the Cortes on the accession of a sovereign, whereby they promised to support the new monarch, on condition that he preserve the rights and respect the privileges (*fueros*) of the nation and people, ending with the emphatic *si no, no* (if not, not), which conveyed both a warning and a threat.

Such was the power already vested in the representatives of the people by the then potent Spanish nation. It was, therefore, without the range of the sovereign prerogative to grant in perpetuity the offices of admiral and viceroy to representatives and heirs of a foreigner, without regard to their possible merits or demerits. Isabella, who had not mounted the throne as a legitimate sovereign, but as a usurper who bargained for her place by the restriction of her rights, might, with the consent of the Cortes, confer on Columbus the title above named for life, but there her power ended.

This, as we have said, Columbus appears to have understood, and we therefore find him secretly engaged, or attempting to engage, in a correspondence with the powerful republic of Genoa, with a view to inducing the latter to aid him in ousting Spain from the Western islands, and in usurping their government for himself. His proceedings in this matter are carried on with such secrecy as to leave no doubt of their treasonable intent, nor does Mr. Irving venture to pass over this episode without mentioning that suspicions of this treason were prevalent in Spain. He admits that "the sovereigns *may have* entertained doubts *as to the innocence and* loyalty of Columbus." He further reports that "there was a rumor prevalent that Columbus, irritated at the suppression of his dignities by the court of Spain, intended to transfer his newly-discovered countries into the hands of his *native republic, Genoa,* or some other power;" and states that, during the time he passed in Spain previous to his fourth voyage, he took measures to "*secure his fame,* and *preserve the claims* of his family, by placing them under the *guardianship* of his native city," and by way of inducement, we suppose, to that city to undertake the guardianship, we shall find him writing a codicil, May 4, 1506, on the blank leaf of a breviary, "according to military usage," in which he declares the republic of Genoa his successor to the admiralty, should his male line become extinct!

The treason of such a bequest is so palpable as scarce to need comment. Columbus, the once pauper pirate, coolly makes over to a foreign power one of the offices of the Spanish crown; yet not one of his biographers appears to perceive the monstrous absurdity of such a proposition!

He had not, however, waited till his disgrace was incontestable, before commencing his treasonable practices. Previous to his third voyage, he had solicited and obtained permission from the crown to make his will, perpetuating his fortune and honors by entail (*mayorazgo*). This authorization, granted by the sovereigns, appears to restrict him to his "legitimate children," especially Diego, "notwithstanding your other children be aggrieved." It would seem, at any rate, that bequests to Genoa were not within its scope.

In virtue of this permit, he proceeded to make a will, by which he affects to dispose of millions of treasure, and of honors that should render him and his descendants famous throughout the land. If we cast a glance backward to the preparations for his third voyage, pending which this will was written, we shall perceive that Columbus was then, as always, poor; that his discoveries (if we give them that name) had become unpopular, himself odious—so unpopular, so odious, that none could be found voluntarily to follow him to his "earthly paradise." And in order to people it, and aid him in bearing Christianity to the benighted heathen, the dungeons were at his request thrown open, and the vilest criminals they contained might expiate their crimes by a short sojourn in those islands, whose civilization (?) they were to effect. The ships, crews, and cargoes, for his third expedition, were all impressed into the royal service. Thenceforth his condition became steadily more wretched and degraded, till we shall find him writing to Doña Juana de la Torres:

"I have now reached that point that there is no man so vile but thinks it his right to insult me."

And to the sovereigns:

"I am, indeed, in as ruined a condition as I have related. Hitherto I have wept for others: may Heaven now have mercy upon me, and may the earth weep for me! With regard to temporal things, I have not even a *blanca* for an offering. . . . All that was left to me, as well as to my brothers, has been taken away and sold, even to the frock I wore. . . . I did not come on this voyage" (his last) "to gain for myself honor or wealth; this is a certain fact, for *at that time all hope* of such a thing was dead."

The tone of his will was, however, very different from this cringing whine. We can merely make extracts, as it is an exceedingly lengthy document: like all his compositions, it contains many incongruities. Defining the order of inheritance in his family, he says:

"If God should dispose of him" (his brother Bartholomew) "*without heirs*, he is to be succeeded by *his sons*." Great care is to be taken "where the glory of God, or *my own*, or that of my family, is concerned. . . . For the *greater glory* of the Almighty, and that it may be the root and basis of my lineage, and a memento of the services I have rendered their highnesses, that, being born in Genoa, I came over to serve them in Castile. . . . I pray their highnesses that this, my privilege, be held valid. . . .

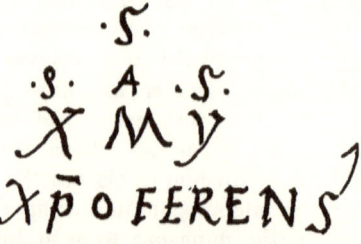

"Don Diego, my son, or any other who may inherit my name, in coming into possession of the inheritance, shall sign with the signature I *now* make use of, which is an *X*, with an *S.* over it, and an *M*, with a Roman *A* over it, and over that an *S.*, and then a Greek *Y*, with an *S.* over it, with its lines and points, as is my custom, as may be seen by my signature, of which there are many, and it will be seen by the present one."[136]

The authenticity of this will, or certain parts of it, has been

---

[136] This decidedly eccentric, if not affected, signature has been variously interpreted, the author having vouchsafed no explanation. Some suppose the ciphers above the signature (which all admit to be *Christ-bearer*, in Greek and Latin characters) to read " *Servidor Sus Altezas Sacras, Cristo, Maria, Ysabel*" (or possibly Joseph), 'Servant of their Sacred Highnesses, Christ, Mary, Isabel." M. Delorgues interprets them " *Servus Supplex Altissimi Salvatoris, Christus, Maria, Joseph*, the Suppliant Servant of the Most High Saviour, Christ, Mary, Joseph." Spotorno supposes the ciphers should be read from the bottom, upward, connecting the lower with the upper, and reading thus : " *Salva me, Christus, Maria, Josephus*." The matter is not of any material importance ; it only serves to show how religious affectation and a desire to mystify pervaded the most trivial acts of the self-styled Christ-bearer.

matter of much doubt; the above is one of the alleged forgeries. It is maintained that few men would enter thus elaborately into the description of a signature which they declare must be already well known. There seems to be some reason in this objection, yet, as there is no accounting for the vagaries and vanities of Columbus, the passage may, after all, be genuine.

"He" (the heir) "shall only write 'the Admiral,' whatever other titles the king may have conferred on him. This is understood as respects his signature, but not the enumeration of his titles, which he can make at full length, if agreeable; only the signature is to be 'the Admiral.'"

"Such," says Mr. Irving, "was the noble pride with which he valued this title of his real greatness." The same author writes: "His soul was elevated by the contemplation of his great and glorious office, when he considered himself under divine inspiration, imparting the will of Heaven, and fulfilling the high and holy purpose for which he had been predestined."

It is strange that, with this noble stimulus, Columbus should have fallen miserably short of what might be reasonably expected from an uninspired mortal. If he had been truly great, he would not have been so intoxicated by a few paltry titles. "He called me Don!" he exclaims with ecstatic delight; yet titles were cheap in Spain. A negro named Juan de Valladolid, called the negro count (*conde negro*), was, in 1474, appointed by Ferdinand and Isabella to the office of mayoral of the negroes. The appointment is made in the most flattering terms.[137]

"I also," continues Columbus in his will, "enjoin Don Diego, or any one that may inherit the estate, to have and maintain, in the city of Genoa, one person of our lineage to reside there

---

[137] "For the many good, loyal, and signal services which you have done us, and do each day, and because we know your sufficiency, ability, and good disposition, we constitute you mayoral and judge of all the negroes and mulattoes, free or slaves, which are in the very loyal and noble city of Seville and throughout the whole archbishopric thereof, and that the said negroes and mulattoes may not hold any festivals, nor pleadings among themselves, except before you, Juan de Valladolid, negro, our judge and mayoral of the said negroes and mulattoes; and we command that you, and you only, should take cognizance of the disputes, pleadings, marriages, and other things which may take place among them, forasmuch as you are a person sufficient for that office, and deserving of your power, and you know the laws and ordinances which ought to be kept, and we are informed that you are of noble lineage among the said negroes."—ORTEZ DE ZUÑIGA, "Annales Ecclesiasticos y Seculares de Sevilla," p. 374.

with his wife, and appoint him a sufficient revenue to enable him to live decently, as a person closely connected with the family, of which he is to be the root and basis in that city, from which great good may accrue to him, *inasmuch as I was born there and came from thence.*"

It is not surprising that those claiming other birthplaces for Columbus than Genoa, should regard the sentence we italicize as a forged interpolation: 1. He declares that the person to be supported in Genoa was to form the *root* and *basis* of his family there. This could scarcely be, were Columbus and his progenitors natives of the place. 2. It is somewhat strange, if Columbus in this will several times declared that he was a native of Genoa, that his son should not state the fact when treating of his birth and early years. He came into possession of his father's papers, and, had he found therein any such declaration of birthplace, it seems likely he would have inserted it in its proper place in his history of his father.

It is not improbable that these passages have been forged by the champions of Columbus to palliate, in a measure, the treason to Spain which is so apparent in his bequests and propositions to Genoa; but neither is it improbable that Columbus claimed to have been born there, in order that that city might consider he had some claim upon her, and be induced to aid him in his schemes for gaining possession of the islands with which he promised to enrich her.

Be this as it may, and whether the passages be forgeries, or whether Columbus really in his will professed to have been born in Genoa, it is certain that his most intimate friends, his family even, were kept ignorant of his having made such an assertion, and that he desired Spain to be utterly ignorant of all his transactions with Genoa.

"The said Diego," continues the will, "or whoever shall inherit the estate, must remit in bills, or in any other way, whatever he may be enabled to save out of the revenue of the estate, and direct purchase to be made in his name, or that of his heirs, in a stock in the Bank of St. George, which gives an interest of six per cent., and is secure money; and this shall be devoted to the purposes I am about to explain:

"Item: As it becomes every man of rank and property to serve God, either personally, or by means of his wealth, and as all moneys deposited with St. George are quite safe, and Genoa is a noble city, and powerful by sea, and as, at the time that I undertook to set out upon the discovery of the Indies, it was with the intention of supplicating the king and queen our lords that whatever money should be derived from the said Indies should be invested in the conquest of Jerusalem, and as I did so supplicate them, if they do this it will be well; if not, at all events, the said Diego, or such person as may succeed him in this trust, to collect together all the money he can, and accompany the king our lord, should he go to the conquest of Jerusalem, or else go there himself, with all the force he can command; and, in pursuing this intention, it will please the Lord to assist toward the accomplishment of the plan; and, should he not be able to effect the conquest of the whole, no doubt he will achieve it in part. Let him, therefore, collect and make a fund of all his wealth in St. George of Genoa, and let it multiply there till such time as it may appear to him that something of consequence may be effected as respects the project on Jerusalem, for I believe that, when their highnesses shall see that this is contemplated, they will wish to realize it themselves, or will afford him, as their servant and vassal, the means of doing it for them.

"Item: I charge my son Diego, and my descendants, especially whoever may inherit this estate, which consists, as aforesaid, of the tenth of whatsoever may be had or found in the Indies, and the eighth part of the lands and rents, all which, together with my rights and emoluments as admiral, viceroy, and governor, amount to more than twenty-five per cent., I say that I require of him to employ all this revenue, as well as his person and all the means in his power, in well and faithfully serving and supporting their highnesses, or their successors, even to the loss of life and property."

The extreme loyalty of this last injunction is entirely nullified and contradicted by the preceding one, in which the heir is directed to employ *all the revenue* he can save out of the estate in the purchase of stock in the Bank of St. George of Genoa, and by the following, in which he commands—

". . . . the said Diego, or whoever may possess the said estate, to labor and strive for the honor, welfare, and aggrandizement of the city of Genoa, and to make use of all his power and means in defending and enhancing the good and credit of that republic, in all things not contrary to the service of God, or the high dignity of the king and queen our lords and their successors."

The unlucky recipient of so many injunctions would have been puzzled to obey them all. He is enjoined to serve God and mammon—Spain and Genoa—to give to each of these powers all his energies, resources, and devotion, but it was in the nature of the author of this will to promise fidelity to all, while he would practise it toward none.

Besides the above public bequests, we find each of Columbus's family provided with a million or so. A church is to be built at Hispaniola, a theological seminary endowed, monuments erected, etc., etc. This ostentatious disposal of untold riches is plentifully interlarded with pious injunctions for the advancement of the interests of the Church, and of the Spanish sovereigns, but Genoa and the Bank of St. George figure principally.

This will was written, as we have said, previous to his departure on his third voyage, about the year 1497. In the year 1502, the period of his history at which we have now arrived, he made another will. This, however, was suppressed, for reasons to which Spotorno thus alludes:

"The motives of this we know not, but it would not be very rash to suppose that Columbus had poured out in it the bitterness of his heart against the court."

In other words, that, seeing he possessed nothing, present or prospective, he denounced his sovereign for not making him rich and honorable, in spite of his crimes.

Besides these wills he wrote two codicils. In the last of these he alludes to the testament of 1502, thereby working the invalidity of the document from which we have so largely quoted, and which was so full of promise to Genoa.

Having perused this and the codicil which creates Genoa admiral in Spain, we can entertain little doubt that the suspicion with which their author was regarded in the latter country was well founded. But there is still further evidence against him. He had himself assured the sovereigns that he knew it would be impossible for him to maintain himself in power in the Indies, even were he desirous of usurping it, without the aid of some prince. Spain manifestly forsaking him, he hoped to find in Genoa the protecting power which should render his design feasible.

He appears to have become acquainted, during his sojourn near the court, with Nicolas de Oderigo, ambassador from Genoa to that court. He may have induced Oderigo to believe that it was really in his power to enrich the republic, and that he (its ambassador) would receive honor and advancement for being the one to propose to his country the means of increasing her power and wealth.

This hypothesis is supported by letters written by Columbus to the Genoese ambassador. The first of these reads:

"*To the Ambassador,* SIGNOR NICOLO ODERIGO.

"SIR: It is impossible to describe the solitude which your departure has caused among us. I gave the book of my privileges to Signor Francisco di Rivarola, in order that he might forward it to you, along with a copy of the missive letters. I beg of you, as a particular favor, to write to Don Diego to acknowledge their receipt, and to mention where they are deposited. Another copy will be finished and sent to you in the same manner, and by the same Signor Francisco. You will find another letter in it, in which their highnesses promise to give me all that belongs to me, and to put Don Diego in possession of it. I am writing to Signor Gian Luigi, and to the Signora Caterina, and the letter will accompany this.

"I shall depart, in the name of the Holy Trinity, with the first favorable weather, with a considerable equipment. If Girolamo da Santa Stefano comes, he must wait for me, and not entangle himself with any one, for they will get from him whatever they can, and then leave him in the lurch. Let him come here, and he will be received by the king and queen until I arrive. May our Lord have you in his holy keeping!

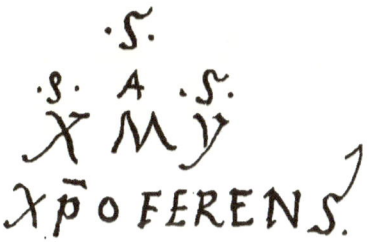

"*March* 21, 1502, IN SEVILLE, at your commands."

This letter, as we have seen, asserts that he sends to Genoa copies of all the grants which had been made him by the Spanish sovereigns. What was his object in sending these documents to a foreign land? It will be argued that it was to insure their preservation. This reason falls to the ground. We find every one of the said privileges, and documents relating thereto, preserved in the archives of Spain, where Columbus well knew they would be deposited in perfect security.

His real object was to dazzle Genoa with a representation of the immense advantage likely to accrue to her from an alliance with him. Genoa, however, was too wary to fall into the trap, however temptingly baited. She may have known how false Columbus had been to every one of his promises; how much disappointment and how little profit he had entailed upon Spain. She may have even been aware that the considerable equipment with which he informs Oderigo he was about to sail, consisted of four small vessels. At any rate, this powerful republic did not intend, by taking up the cudgels for this pauper pirate in disgrace, to draw upon herself the open enmity of Spain. Columbus's propositions, enticing though he endeavored to make them, seem to have fallen upon deaf ears; for, on his return from his fourth voyage, we find him writing as follows:

"*To the Most Learned Doctor*, NICOLO ODERIGO.

"LEARNED SIR: When I set off upon the voyage from which I have just returned, I spoke to you fully. I have no doubt you retained a complete recollection of every thing. I expected, upon my arrival, to have found here letters, and possibly a confidential person from you. At that time, I likewise gave to Francisco de Rivarola a book of copies of my letters, and another of my privileges, in a bag of colored Spanish leather with a silver lock, and two letters for the Bank of St. George, to which I assign the tenth of my revenues in diminution of the duties upon corn and other provisions. No acknowledgment of all this has reached me. Signor Francisco tells me that all arrived there in safety. If so, it was uncourteous in these gentlemen of St. George not to have favored me with an answer. Nor have they thereby improved their affairs, which gives one cause to say that whoever serves the public, serves nobody. I gave another book of my privileges, like the above, in Cadiz, to Franco Cataneo, the

ATTEMPTED NEGOTIATIONS WITH GENOA.

bearer of this, in order that he might likewise forward it to you, and that both of them might be securely deposited wherever you thought proper. Just before my departure, I received a letter from the king and queen, my lords, a copy of which you will find there. You will see that it came very opportunely. Nevertheless, Don Diego was not put in possession, as had been promised. While I was in the Indies, I wrote to their highnesses an account of my voyage by three or four opportunities. One of my letters having come back to my hands, I send it to you inclosed in this, with the supplement of my voyage in another letter, in order that you may give it to Signor Gian Luigi with the other advice, to whom I write that you will be the reader and interpreter of it. I would wish to have ostensible letters, speaking cautiously of the matter in which we are engaged. I arrived here very unwell, just before the queen, my mistress, died (who is now with God), without my seeing her. Till now, I cannot say how my affairs will finish. I believe her highness has provided well for them in her last will, and the king, my master, is very well disposed. Franco Cataneo will explain the rest more minutely to you.

"May our Lord preserve you in his care!

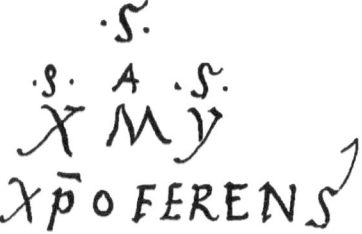

"*Admiral of the Ocean, Viceroy and*
    "*Governor-General of the Indies, etc.*
"SEVILLE, *December* 27, 1504."

It would be difficult to account for the extreme caution and secrecy here enjoined, if nothing treasonable were contemplated. Genoa well understood the matter; she knew that Columbus was unable to maintain himself, much less diminish duties on corn, etc. That he foresaw the light in which his proceedings would be regarded is evident from his desire to have it appear that his devotion to Genoa, and not his disgrace in Spain, caused his defection from the latter. He therefore writes that Isabella has remembered him in her will, and that Ferdinand is very well disposed toward him. It were needless to comment upon the inveracity of both these statements. This defection, which culminates in his proposals to Genoa, had evidently been contemplated from the commencement of his relations with Spain. Good Las Casas, who, throughout his work on the cruelties of the Spaniards in the Indies, prudently abstains from mentioning names, writes:

"The Spaniards first set sail to America, not for the honor of God, or as persons moved or incited thereunto by fervent zeal for the true faith, nor to promote the salvation of their neighbors, nor to serve the king, as they falsely boast and pretend to do, but, in truth, only stimulated and goaded on by insatiable avarice and ambition, that they might forever domineer, command, and tyrannize over the *West Indians*, whose kingdoms they hoped to divide and distribute among themselves; which, to deal candidly, is no more nor less than intentionally, by all these indirect ways, to disappoint and expel the Kings of Castile out of these dominions and territories, that they themselves, having usurped the supreme and regal empire, might first challenge it as their right, and then possess and enjoy it."

This usurpation Columbus first tried to accomplish himself, with the aid of his brothers. Finding this impossible, he seeks to make Genoa his ally, with what ultimate success we have shown.

But to return to his preparations for his fourth voyage. In February, 1502, he wrote a letter to the Pope Alexander VII., in which he apologized for not having repaired to Rome as he had intended, to give the Holy Father an account of his voyages. He dwells upon his pious intentions toward the Holy Sepulchre, and asserts that he has been prevented from raising his promised army, by the arts of the devil. He is, however, about to start on a fourth voyage, and on his return he will at once visit his holiness, and then present him with a copy of his accounts of his voyages, which is to be in the style of "Cæsar's Commentaries," and much more to the same purpose."[138] It is somewhat unjust for him to attribute the non-realization of his promises to the wiles of the devil, as he, and he alone, by his falsehood and crimes, had caused his enterprise to be despised, which, had

---

[138] Navarrete, "Colecc. Dip.," vol. ii., p. 311.

it been appreciated to its full extent, the riches emanating therefrom would have been insufficient to accomplish one tithe of what he had promised.

The modesty with which he informs his holiness that his narrative is written in the style of "Cæsar's Commentaries," is matter for admiration. The "unlettered admiral" would be considered as excelling even in the world of letters. It is to be regretted that his son Fernando, into whose hands this narrative no doubt eventually fell, with the rest of his father's papers (if, indeed, such a narrative ever existed), should have regarded its destruction as more advantageous to the glory of its author than its preservation.

It is not difficult to divine the purpose for which the above letter, full of pious professions and promises, was written. Columbus, by it, endeavored to predispose the Church, especially the papal chair, in his favor; such support would be very necessary should matters with Genoa shape to his liking.

Such were the crafty manœuvres by which he sought to secure the assistance of Genoa, and the sanction of the Church, for his projected rebellion against, or defection from, Spain; yet he did not allow them to interfere with his petitions to Isabella, whom he had not ceased to importune for reinstatement in power. She, while refusing his request, was nevertheless wearied with its repetition, together with that of his other numerous demands. Her letter to him, dated March 4, 1502, betrays something of this feeling. After refusing him money, she says:

"As to the other contents of your memorials and letters, respecting yourself and your sons and brothers, as you know that we are on the eve of a journey, and you on your departure, it cannot be attended to until we are permanently settled in some place, which if you were desirous to wait for, you would miss the voyage you are now going to undertake; wherefore it is better that, being provided with every thing necessary for your voyage, you should depart immediately, leaving to your son the care of soliciting whatever is contained in the aforesaid memorial."

That he "depart immediately" from Spain, and grant her weary ears a respite from the petitions which, while she does not peremptorily refuse, she nevertheless cannot and will not grant, this seems to have been the only present desire of the queen.

CHAPTER XXV.

FOURTH VOYAGE OF COLUMBUS.

Having, as he hoped, left his affairs in as promising condition as his disgrace at the Spanish court would allow, and secured Genoa and the Church as allies, Columbus at length set sail on the 9th of May, 1502, on his fourth and last voyage, with the considerable equipment already mentioned. He was accompanied by his natural son and subsequent historian Fernando, and by his brother Bartholomew. He sailed from Cadiz, by way of Morocco and the Canaries. At this stage of his history there occurs once more one of the many little inconsistencies to which we have already alluded as characterizing too many biographers of Columbus. According to the latter, the whole voyage from Cadiz to the Carib Islands only occupied twenty days—four days from Spain to the Canaries, and sixteen from the Canaries to the Western islands.

He writes to the sovereigns:

"My passage from Cadiz to the Canaries occupied four days, and thence to the Indies, from which I wrote, sixteen days. My intention was to expedite my voyage as much as possible while I had *good vessels*, good crews and stores. . . . *Up to the period* of my reaching these shores *I experienced most excellent weather.*"

Mr. Irving and others, however, would have it that it took him sixteen days (from the 9th of May to the 25th) to reach the Canaries, and twenty days (from the 25th of May to the 15th of June) to reach the Carib Islands, a total which more than doubles the time stated by Columbus himself. The reason for this we shall soon perceive. On reaching the islands, Columbus, after touching at one or two, made direct for San Domingo, and requested permission to enter the harbor.

We have already stated that the sovereigns had expressly forbidden him to touch at Hispaniola on his outward voyage, and only permitted him to do so on his return in case of necessity, and then merely for a short stay.[139] His excuse for now violating the royal command was, that one of his vessels sailed badly, could carry no canvas, thereby delaying the squadron. He therefore proposed to exchange it for one which Ovando had brought out.

The boldness of this pretext he has himself made evident in the passage we have quoted from his letter, and is manifest to his biographers, for, by admitting that he performed the whole voyage in twenty days (a remarkably quick trip), he shows that his squadron could not have been much delayed. Apparently for this reason, and to cover another of his falsehoods, and make his excuse appear more plausible, historians double the length of time consumed in his voyage.

Ovando, who had, no doubt, received his orders, refused to admit Columbus into the harbor of San Domingo, stating, as his reason for doing so, that it was against the desire of their highnesses. Nor could he consent to the proposed exchange of vessels; the fleet he had brought out was that day setting sail, laden with a richer cargo than had ever before left the Western islands, and bearing Bobadilla, Roldan, and many others, back to Spain. Admitting that Columbus really had a bad-sailing vessel, he could scarcely be expected to exchange one of the outgoing ships for this bad sailer, and thereby retard the progress of a fleet which was far more important than that of Columbus.

The sympathy and pathos expressed by Columbus's historians as they record the refusal he received at San Domingo, would be very touching if well founded. But even regarding Columbus, as they do, in the light of a noble and glorious martyr, few will be prepared to state that his landing in Hispaniola would have been judicious or safe. The island was swarming with his enemies, who might have taken it into their heads to execute upon him justice as summary as that which he had inflicted upon Moxica and scores of others; therefore his best friends would have advised him to stay away.

The refusal to exchange ships was, as we have already said,

[139] Navarrete "Colecc. Dip.," vol. i., p. 425.

an imperative duty. Ovando could not stay his fleet or endanger any of its cargo. It set sail the day of Columbus's arrival. The weather was at the time fair and still, but a sudden and violent storm arose, by which the greater part of the fleet was destroyed. Bobadilla, Roldan, and a host of others, perished; among them a captive Indian chief.

A story is to be found in most histories of Columbus, which represents him as foretelling this storm, and magnanimously urging Ovando to delay the departure of his vessels, but without being heeded. Tracing this assertion from one narrator to another, it appears that Fernando is its fountain-head, and the only authority for the prophecy. Columbus, in his relation of his fourth voyage, speaks of the storm, but makes no allusion to his having in any way predicted it; and he most assuredly would not have failed to hold forth this further proof of the divine aid and inspiration which he so constantly professed to receive, had there been the least possible ground for his doing so. The prophecy is, therefore, probably a gratuitous embellishment of Fernando's, who is peculiarly desirous that his readers should, at this period, perceive supreme intervention in his father's favor.

Thus we have seen that he regards the deaths of Bobadilla and Roldan as special acts of the Deity, who is thus made to take upon himself the punishment of the admiral's enemies; and by the same special providence, we are assured, the only ship of the great fleet which reached Spain in safety, was the poorest and weakest of all, but it had on board four thousand pieces of gold belonging to Columbus. The latter also safely weathered the storm which had been fatal to his enemies. Upon these miracles, as he terms them, M. de Lorgues builds a considerable portion of his claims for Columbus's canonization. Those who in their journey through life have observed the inscrutable ways of Divine Providence, and noted how often the wicked are allowed to prosper in worldly matters, while the good are as often buffeted by misfortune, will not perceive in the death of the unfortuate Spaniards, nor in the salvation of Columbus and his ill-gotten gains, any manifestation of the sanctity of the latter, or the baseness of the former.

His three vessels, separated by the storm, having rejoined him, and finding it impossible to obtain admittance to San

Domingo, Columbus, after a short sojourn in a sheltered part of the coast, set sail for Jamaica on the 14th of July, 1502. His crew felt bitterly their having been sent out under a man whose status was such that they were refused admittance into a port belonging to their own country, and to which even a foreign vessel would have been hospitably welcomed.

The stormy weather continued. During *sixty* days, only seventy leagues were made, owing to adverse winds and currents. At last the little island of Guanaja was reached. Columbus named it Isla de Pinos (Island of Pines), on account of the abundance of those trees.

A large canoe was seen approaching this island, laden with various products. It is described as being eight feet wide, very long. Part of it was covered with a rounded thatching of palm-leaves, after the manner of Venetian gondolas. It was most probably one of those partially-covered canoes which still navigate some of the inland rivers of South America, and are called *champanes*. The people it contained are described as far superior to any yet met with; the women wore long draperies of woven cotton; broad cinctures of the same material encircled the men about the loins. Their wares, too, indicated an approach to civilization. Woven cloth of cotton, earthen-ware utensils, almonds, cocoa (which the Spaniards then saw for the first time, and which has since furnished Spain with its national beverage), copper axes, crucibles in which this metal was melted—these constituted their chief cargo.

The accounts of Columbus's treatment of these natives are conflicting. Mr. Irving and most modern historians relate that the people exhibited no fear, and came willingly alongside the vessels, where they gladly exchanged their wares for hawk's bells and other baubles; that Columbus treated them with gentleness, and detained *only* one old man as a guide.

Fernando, who was on the spot, and who, great as is his desire to conceal his father's misdeeds, sometimes accidentally gives us an insight into the truth, makes it appear that Columbus did not deal so gently with these people as Irving and others would have it supposed. He says: "At that time they seemed to be, in a manner, beside themselves, being brought prisoners out of their canoe aboard the ship, among such strange and fierce people as we are to them."[140] These people are supposed to have come from Yucatan to trade among the islands. Had Columbus sailed in the direction whence they came, he would probably have reached the rich countries of Mexico, and thus have gained for Spain some material profit; but he was bent (or feigned to be so) upon finding his strait or passage to India, and proceeded in an opposite direction.

A southerly course brought him to the shores of the continent, which he coasted in an easterly direction. The storm, we read, still remained unabated; rain, wind, and current, com-

MASS CELEBRATED ON THE CONTINENT.

bined to baffle and perturb the now bedridden admiral. On the 14th of August, he, being unable to stir, ordered his brother

[140] "Historia del Amirante," chapter xci. The same authority also makes it evident that they were somewhat violently induced to come on board the Spanish ships, for, speaking of their superior modesty over the other tribes, he says: "It falling out that, on getting them aboard, some were taken by the clouts they had before their privities, they would immediately clap their hands to cover them; and the women would hide their faces, and wrap themselves up, as we said the Moorish women do at Granada." In fact, it is evident that the crew of the canoe were roughly seized, with their wares, Columbus keeping what part of these he saw fit, and giving in return a few worthless baubles. "And the admiral blessed God that it had pleased Him at once to give him samples of the commodities of that country, without exposing his men to any danger."

Bartholomew to go on shore and have mass celebrated by the Franciscan friar who accompanied the expedition. This was done.

On the 17th of the same month land was again sighted, and possession taken for Spain by the erection of a huge cross. Here a great number of natives were assembled, who offered the Spaniards cassava-bread, fowls, and vegetables, which they had with them in great abundance. Notwithstanding these evidences to the contrary, Columbus, having, no doubt, the ultimate enslavement of the poor wretches in view, declared them cannibals. "This was evident," he says, "from the brutality of their countenances." Anthropophagi would, we fear, be numerous even in civilized communities, were the above ear-marks infallible evidence of cannibalistic propensities.

One portion of the coast was named Costa de la Oreja, from the hideous manner in which the inhabitants of that country bored their ears.

Still opposed by wind and tide, Columbus now coasted Honduras. It is to be remarked that this continuous storm, severe as it no doubt was, is described by Columbus with much of that colored exaggeration which characterizes all his writings, after the manner of some story-tellers who never think the truth alone wonderful enough. He writes: "Eighty-eight days did this fearful tempest continue, during which I was at sea, and saw neither sun nor stars; my ships lay exposed, my sails torn, and anchors, rigging, cables, boats, and a great quantity of provisions, lost. My people were very weak and humble in spirit, many of them promising to lead a religious life, and all making vows and promising to perform pilgrimages, while some of them would frequently go to their messmates to make confession. Other tempests have been experienced, but never of so long duration, or so fearful as this."

At length, however, the vessels reached a prominent headland, whence the coast stretched south. The current, which had impeded their progress, divided upon this point and ran southward, assisting instead of opposing them. Columbus, therefore, named this Cape Gracias á Dios (Thanks to God), a name it still retains, though few of the places he baptized are now known by the appellations he gave them.

Thence he proceeded along the Mosquito coast. Arriving at a large river, the men put off to fill their casks with fresh water, when a wave overwhelmed one boat, which was lost with all its crew. The river was therefore named Rio del Desastro (of the Disaster).

The village of Cariari was the next point of any importance reached. Here the natives assumed the defensive upon the approach of the Spaniards, but, not being attacked, and the latter having made pacific demonstrations, they gained confidence.

An aged man appeared with two young girls. These, he intimated, were to be hostages for the Spaniards who might wish to land. The latter profited by this generous assurance, and went on shore to procure water.

We have various and conflicting accounts touching the character and conduct of these girls. Fernando and his father especially disagree in their description of them. The former writes:

"Those people showed more friendly than others had done, and in the girls appeared an undauntedness; for, though the Christians were such strangers to them, they expressed no manner of concern, but *always looked pleasant and modest,* which made the admiral treat them well, clothed, fed, and set them ashore again, where the fifty men were; and the old man that had delivered them received them again with much satisfaction." [141]

Columbus, however, thus describes the same scene:

"When I arrived, they sent me immediately two girls very showily dressed; the eldest could not be more than eleven years of age, and the other seven, and both *exhibited so much immodesty* that more could not be expected from public women. They carried concealed about them a magic powder. When they came, I gave them some articles to deck themselves out with, and directly sent them back to the shore." [142]

When Fernando wrote his statement, he was no doubt ignorant of his father's version, and, not considering that "the admiral's" character or veracity could be impugned by the truth, he made a correct statement.

It is matter for congratulation that several documents written by Columbus were never perused by Fernando; we are thus enabled to bring many falsehoods of each to light.

Friendly as were the people of Cariari, they, like all the tribes visited by Columbus, had more reason to mourn than rejoice at

---

[141] "Historia del Amirante," chapter xci.
[142] Letter of Columbus to the sovereigns, July 7, 1503.

CRUELTY OF COLUMBUS.   321

the visitation. Seven of them were seized and two retained, while the rest were allowed to return to their people; but the friends of the two prisoners took their capture greatly to heart. Heavily laden with products of their land (among other things, two small hogs), they offer all, and more, if the Spaniards will only restore their friends to liberty; but Columbus was inexorable; he wanted guides (did this scientific navigator and discoverer), having set down the poor old Indian of Guanaja at Cape Gracias á Dios. Thus he from time to time seized a hapless native, used him as guide till his knowledge of the country was exhausted, then set him down in a strange land, whence there was little probability of his reaching his far-away home. But the magnanimous, gentle, humane admiral, while refusing to deliver the Cariarians to their kinsmen, accepted the presents, notably the hogs, one of which afterward procured him sport cruel enough to gratify even his brutal tastes. Let us observe the gusto with which he recounts the torture inflicted upon two dumb brutes, merely for amusement, and we shall be assured, if any doubt lingers in our minds, that cruelty was with him a passion.

"I had, at that time," he writes, "two pigs and an Irish dog, who was always in great dread of them. An archer had wounded an animal like an ape, except that it was larger, and had a face like a man's; the arrow had pierced it from the neck to the tail, which made it so fierce that they were obliged to disable it by cutting off one of its arms and a leg. One of the pigs grew wild on seeing this, and fled; upon which *I ordered the begare* (as the inhabitants call him) *to be thrown to the pig*, and though the animal was nearly dead, and the arrow had passed quite through his body, yet he threw his tail round the snout of the pig, and then, holding him firmly, seized him by the nape of the neck with his remaining hand, as if he were engaged with an enemy. This action was so novel and extraordinary that I have thought it worth while to describe it here."

The cowardly superstition, which was one of the manly attributes of our hero, is also manifested during his stay at Cariari. A smoke which the natives created, and which the wind blew toward him, was, he declared, a necromantic spell they sought to cast upon him. It was probably the smoking of tobacco through pipes as he had already seen it smoked in the leaf.

322 LIFE OF COLUMBUS.

Details of this voyage are not wanting, as both Columbus and Fernando are very minute in their recitals. We shall not, however, be equally so, and follow him through all the mishaps and disasters of this his last expedition, but content ourselves with noting its more important features.

From time to time he procured gold from the natives, who were, as a rule, friendly. Here, he traded for large plates of gold which were worn suspended from the neck; there, he would increase the respect of the harmless natives by discharging a cannon among them.[143] Now, he comes upon five large settlements

INDIANS SMOKING.—(From Philopono, "Nova Typis," etc., 1621.)

or towns, as he called them, one of which, Veragua, subsequently gave its name to the adjacent country. Here he *was told* there existed extensive gold-mines, but would not stay, being still bent upon finding the strait. He was, Mr. Irving tells us, under one of his frequent delusions. That he should be deluded and honest was possible, but when we find him constantly professing to

[143] "Therefore, to abate their pride and make them not contemn the Christians, the admiral caused a shot to be made at a company of them that was got together upon a hillock, and the ball, falling in the midst of them, made them sensible there was a thunder-bolt as well as thunder, so that for the future they durst not appear even behind the mountains."—("Historia del Amirante," chapter xclii.)

hear from the natives that he is within a short distance (ten days' journey on foot) of Cathay—the dominions of the grand-khan—that he is in the land of Ophir—when he assures the sovereigns, upon the authority of these same savages, that a little beyond a place called Ciguare, which he visits, will be found the Ganges, his honesty is somewhat to be impugned.

It is diverting also to remark that he has been taught by sad experience that it will not do to lie too barefacedly. He therefore places himself under cover of the Indians, and indulges in a little taunt at the sovereigns, in which his ill-concealed malice and anger are momentarily exposed.

"When I discovered the Indies," he writes to their majesties, "I said that they composed the richest lordship in the world; I spoke of gold, and pearls, and precious stones, of spices, and the traffic that might be carried on in them; and, because all these things were not forthcoming at once, I was abused. This punishment causes me to refrain from relating any thing but what the natives tell me."

Owing to the bad weather, the crazed and worm-eaten condition of his ships, as also, no doubt, to the fact that, though he had made the search for the strait a pretense for returning to Hispaniola, he did not himself believe in its existence, he at last abandoned it as fruitless, and made for Veragua. Not willing, however, to own that he has proclaimed the existence of a strait where none existed, his crew were again made to mutiny, and it was, we are told, in compliance with their urgent entreaties that he consented to return.

He sailed for Veragua, but the wind, veering as he changed his course, still remained contrary; the elements conspired against him—a frightful storm prevailed. The ships were in imminent danger, when the awfulness of the situation culminated in a huge water-spout, which appeared to be making toward them. Columbus proceeded, in a somewhat novel manner, to avert this new peril, by which he excites the enthusiastic admiration of his would-be canonizer, M. de Lorgues, whose description of the scene and of the sailor-like bearing of the admiral, we cannot resist inserting:

"It was one of those water-spouts which seamen call *fronks*, which were then so little known, and which have since submerged so many vessels. . . . At the cries of distress which reached his heart, the great man became suddenly reanimated. In face of the impending ruin he rises with his wonted vigor, in order to survey and weigh the peril. *He* also perceives the formidable thing that is approaching. The sea appeared to be sucked up toward the heavens. For this unknown phenomenon he saw no remedy. Art was useless and navigation powerless; besides, there was no steering any longer.

"Immediately Columbus, the adorer of the Word, suspected, in this terrific display of the brute forces of Nature, some satanic manœuvre. He could not exorcise the powers of the air, according to the rites of the Church, fearing to usurp the authority of the priesthood; but he called to mind that he was the chief of a Christian expedition, and that his object was a holy one; and he desired, in his way, to compel the spirit of darkness to yield the passage to him. He had blessed wax-candles immediately lighted and put in the lanterns; then he girded himself with his sword over the cord of St. Francis, and, taking the book of the gospels, standing in the face of the water-spout, which was coming near, accosted it with the sublime declaration which commences the gospel of the well-beloved disciple of Jesus, St. John, the adoptive son of the blessed Virgin.

"Trying to raise his voice above the howling of the tempest, the messenger of salvation declared to Typhon that in the beginning was the Word; that the Word was with God, and that the Word was God; that all things have been made by him, and that without him was not any thing made that was made; that in him was life, and that the life was the light of men; that the light shineth in darkness, and that the darkness did not comprehend it; that the world was made by him, and that the world knew him not; that he came to his own and his own received him not; but that he has given to those who believe in his name, and who are not born of the flesh, or of blood, or of the will of man, the power to become the children of God; and that the WORD WAS MADE FLESH, and that he dwelt among us.

"Then, in the name of the divine Word, Jesus Christ, whose words calmed the winds and appeased the billows, Christopher Columbus commands the water-spout to spare those who, becoming children of God, go to carry the cross to the extremities of the earth, and navigate in the name of the thrice Holy Trinity. Then, drawing his sword with a full and ardent faith, he traces in the air, with the steel, the sign of the cross, and describes a circle around him with the sword, as if he had really severed or intercepted the water-spout. And, in fact—O prodigy!—the water-spout, which was coming straight toward the caravels, appearing to be pushed obliquely, passed between the half-submerged caravels, and went off, bellowing, to lose itself in the immensity of the Atlantic.

"This sudden retreat of a destructive phenomenon appeared to Columbus himself as a new favor from the Divine Majesty.

COLUMBUS VANQUISHES THE WATER-SPOUT.

The same piety which prompted him to have recourse to God to be preserved, prevented him from having any doubt that he was indebted to Him for his preservation in this extremity."[144]

Irving, who seeks throughout to give a wise and scholarly character to his hero, perceiving how fatal to such a reputation was the manner in which Columbus thought to influence a phenomenon of Nature, would lead us to suppose that it was the

[144] De Lorgues, "Christophe Colombe," vol. ii., liv. iv., chapter ii.

ignorant sailors (those convenient scape-goats who are forever made to fill the breaches in Columbus's biographies) who frantically repeated passages from St. John. M. de Lorgues is justly indignant at this new attempt to rob Columbus of his "well-earned fame." He says:

"It is vain for Mr. Irving to try to hide under the plural form the spontaneous initiative of Columbus, and to keep out of sight his individual action. The event itself intrinsically protests against such a disfigurement of history, and opposes to it both moral and physical impossibilities. How could the caravels, separated from each other by the terrible commotion of the elements, scarcely able to see each other across the watery vapors and the globules of foam filling the air, and still less hearing each other, how could they, we say, settle on a plan of combating the water-spout, agree about the choice of an evangelist, and fix on a passage deemed proper for warding off the peril? Not to mention other reasons, Irving does not seem to have considered that none of the pilots would, of themselves, have conceived an expedient so singularly foreign to nautical science,"[145] and, at the same time, so bold in a spiritual point of view."[146]

Whether owing to the admiral's impressive and appropriate exhortation, or in pursuance of its natural course, the water-spout passed without harming the little caravels. The storm had, however, separated one of them from the rest, and it was only after encountering great peril, and losing her boat, that she was enabled to rejoin the squadron, which was in sorry condition—provisions exhausted or rotten—when, on the 17th of December, it found welcome refuge in a port. Here, we are told, the natives lived in houses built in the tops of trees, like the nests of birds. Fernando, who seems to have entered fully into his father's spirit of invention, states that the practice was caused by the number of griffins which abound in that place. Mr. Irving, while drawing principally upon Fernando for his account of this voyage, wisely omits this absurdity, or travesties it into some appearance of truth by telling us the houses were thus built to escape from the wild beasts, etc., that abound in that region.

[145] In this we fully concur.
[146] De Lorgue, "Christophe Colombe," vol. ii., liv. iv., chapter ii.

WAR BETWEEN SPANIARDS AND NATIVES.

Leaving this port after much buffeting against adverse winds and waves, the caravels entered another, where the stock of wood, water, and provisions, was replenished, and whence they started on the 3d of January, 1503, and shortly reached a river near Veragua, which Columbus named Belen (Bethlehem).

Bartholomew, with the assistance of the friendly natives, especially of their chief Quibian, explored the country and found it rich in gold; it was, therefore, determined to form a settlement on the banks of the Belen, where Bartholomew should be left with eighty men to amass gold, while Columbus returned to Spain. The settlement was made, but the licentious and covetous conduct of the Spaniards, here as elsewhere, made enemies of the friendly-disposed Indians. Hostilities soon commenced, and the chief Quibian was, with all his family, treacherously captured by Bartholomew, while all the gold (his possessing which constituted his chief offense) found in his house was, of course, seized. The chief succeeded in effecting his escape by plunging, bound as he was, into the sea; his family, wives, and children were, however, taken on board Columbus's vessel, and confined in the hold. This capture aroused the indignation of Quibian, who, with his followers, now thirsted for vengeance. The colony was attacked. Columbus had already crossed the shallow bar at the entrance of the river, leaving one caravel for the use of the settlement, and was anchored at sea ready to sail at the first fair wind. He sent a boat up the river to procure supplies of wood and water. This boat was attacked when far inland, and destroyed by the outraged natives, and of the eight men composing its crew only one reached the settlement to tell the tale. Columbus, outside the river, remained alike ignorant of the loss of the boat and crew, and of the hostile disposition of the natives, who he hoped would have been frightened into submission by the fate of their chief's family. The latter, immured in the loathsome hold of the wretched caravel, now resolved upon one brave and desperate attempt to recover freedom. Piling up the stones which served as ballast to the ship, they climbed upon them, and succeeded in springing open the hatches, notwithstanding several sailors lay sleeping upon them, and a number, plunging into the sea, escaped. Some, however, were secured ere they could leap overboard; these unfortunates were all found dead the next day, having themselves ended their

328   LIFE OF COLUMBUS.

lives rather than submit to be the slaves of their cruel and ungrateful captors.

Columbus was seriously alarmed at the effect the reappearance of the prisoners would have upon their countrymen; he feared that the recital of what they had endured would rouse again the hatred and hostility of the tribes. He was, however, unable to reënter the river and learn the condition of the colony, or the fate of the men he had sent inland, on account of the heavy surge at the mouth of the Belen.

It was at this period, when, by his mismanagement, affairs

Pretended Interview of Columbus with the Deity.

had reached a most disagreeable crisis, that one of Columbus's visions and convenient conversations with the Deity took place, if we are to believe himself, who thus describes the scene:

"All hope of escape was gone. I toiled up to the highest part of the ship, and, with a quivering voice and fast-falling tears, I called upon your highnesses' war-captains from each point of the compass [147] to come to my succor, but there was no

---

[147] An appeal likely to be promptly responded to.

reply. At length, groaning with exhaustion, I fell asleep and heard a compassionate voice address me thus:

"'O fool, and slow to believe and to serve thy God, the God of all! What did He do more for Moses, or for David his servant, than He has done for thee? From thine infancy, He has kept thee under his constant and watchful care. When He saw thee arrived at an age which suited his designs respecting thee, He brought wonderful renown to thy name throughout all the land. He gave thee for thine own the Indies, which form so rich a portion of the world, and thou hast divided them as it pleased thee, for He gave thee power to do so. He gave thee, also, the keys of those barriers of the ocean sea which were closed with such mighty chains; and thou wast obeyed through many lands, and gained an honorable fame throughout Christendom. What more did the Most High do for the people of Israel when He brought them out of Egypt, or for David, who from a shepherd He made to be king in Judea? Turn to Him, and acknowledge thine error. His mercy is infinite; thine old age shall not prevent thee from accomplishing any great undertaking. He holds under his sway the greatest possessions. Abraham had exceeded a hundred years of age when he begat Isaac, nor was Sarah young. Thou criest out for uncertain help; answer who has afflicted thee so much, and so often—God or the World? The privileges promised by God, He never fails in bestowing, nor does He ever declare, after a service has been rendered Him, that such was not agreeable with his intention, or that He had regarded the matter in another light; nor does He inflict suffering, in order to give effect to the manifestations of his power. His acts answer to his words, and it is his custom to perform all his promises with interest. Thus I have told thee what the Creator has done for thee, and what He does for all men. Even now He partially shows thee the reward of so many toils and dangers incurred by thee in the service of others.'"

There is, we cannot too often repeat, something revolting in this maudlin defense of Columbus, put by him in the mouth of the Almighty, whom, in his blasphemous effrontery, he causes to threaten all who do not believe in and cherish him. He even, behind the screen of Divinity, hazards a thrust at Isabella, and reveals, for a moment, the sharp claws which he usually concealed beneath his smooth and cringing sycophancy. If this be madness, yet there is method in it.

Matters did not much improve in spite of Columbus's very sensible appeal to her majesty's war-captains. Doubt and apprehension every day increased, till a hardy pilot, Pedro Ledesma by name, volunteered to swim ashore and investigate. This he did, and discovered the colonists beleaguered by ever-increasing numbers of natives, and in despair at being left in that land at the mercy of the much-injured Indians. He also learned the fate of the boat and crew, and, upon reporting these facts to Columbus, the latter concluded to abandon the settlement. The caravel which had been left in the river had been allowed to become utterly unseaworthy, and was abandoned; all the men, therefore, embarked in the three remaining vessels.

It appears that Columbus regarded the gold-mines of Veragua as the only real benefit likely to accrue to Spain from his enterprises. He now took such precautions as to render it, he hoped, impossible for any but himself to return to them. He, therefore confiscated the charts of the pilots and mariners, and boastingly writes to the sovereigns: "Let them answer and say if they know where Veragua is situated. I assert that they can give no other account than that they went to lands where there was an abundance of gold, and this they can certify surely enough; but they do not know the way to return thither for such a purpose; they would be obliged to go on a voyage of discovery as much as if they had never been there before."[146]

He evidently hoped to get some hold on Isabella, and wished to make her believe that she was at his mercy, so far as regarded the possession of the gold-mines.

Adverse weather pertinaciously clings to Columbus, and, as he proceeded along the coast westward, he was obliged to abandon another of his vessels at Puerto Bello. The condition of the remaining two was not such as to warrant much trifling, yet Columbus sailed among the Mulata Islands, where once more he—apparently considering the territories of the grand-khan as

---

[146] One of the witnesses in the lawsuit between Diego Columbus and the crown, Pedro Mateos of Higuey, testified that he had accompanied Columbus on his fourth voyage, and that he "wrote a book in which he had laid down all the mountains and rivers of the said province (Veragua), and the admiral afterward took it away from him."—(Navarrete, "Colecc. Dip.," vol. iii., p. 584.)

somewhat ubiquitous—declared that he has reached one of the provinces belonging to that prince.

What led him to suppose, or pretend to suppose this, it is difficult to imagine, unless he hoped to inspire his disgusted crew with a little confidence in and respect for him.

These gyrations he seems to have performed with a view to confusing the pilots after taking away their charts; but regard for his own safety now made him adopt a northerly course and steer for Hispaniola direct.

The two caravels were about this time driven violently against each other; the bow of one and the stern of the other were shattered, and three anchors lost. The current bore the vessels westward, till they reached the island of Cuba, where cassava-bread was provided by the natives, and they again set sail for Hispaniola, but reached instead Jamaica, where, on the 23d of June, 1503, at a place which he called Santa Gloria, he ran the dilapidated remains of his "considerable equipment" hard aground, and he and his worn-out crew landed on the island, whence they could not again depart till, by some means, other vessels should be procured.

It may not be amiss here to call the attention of the reader to the fact that Columbus, notwithstanding all the nautical skill he might be supposed to have acquired during his long life, was singularly unfortunate with all the ships intrusted to him. We do not wonder that seamen objected to sail under him. Obstinate and arrogant, he would take no advice, yet was obviously incapable of directing a vessel. His carelessness cost him a vessel at Belen, another at Puerto Bello; the collision which shattered the other two seems an accident which some skill and caution might have prevented; but such details were apparently beneath the notice of this "extraordinary man."

Sheds were built on board the two stranded caravels, and a forced and permanent stay prepared for. Diego Mendez, who appears to have been the most able and energetic man of the expedition, made friendly treaties with the natives at different points, wherein it was agreed that they should every day bring, to certain specified places, provisions in exchange for European trinkets. This satisfactory arrangement effected, Columbus became desirous of communicating with Hispaniola. No means, however, of doing this existed, save native canoes; the distance was forty leagues; few would dare such an undertaking. Mendez, however, came again to the rescue. He possessed an excellent canoe, for which he had bartered with a chief who had shown him great friendship. This chief had also assigned him six Indians to manage the canoe. In this frail bark he now proposed to brave the wide sea and strong currents which divide Jamaica from Hispaniola. Taking with him one Spanish comrade and his six Indians, and having made his canoe as strong against wind and wave as was possible, besides providing it with sails, he pronounced himself ready to start on his perilous voyage. Columbus intrusted him with a letter to Ovando, soliciting a ship and provisions. He also sent by him a letter to the sovereigns, relating the events of this his fourth voyage, from which we have had occasion to make several quotations. This letter is a strange medley of arrogance and humility, boastfulness and begging. Here we find him declaring that he is in the land whence Solomon procured his gold.[149] There he implores their highnesses to pardon his bitter complaints, which are called forth by his ruined condition, and laments, with maudlin pathos, over his misfortunes, declaring that he had made this voyage without any hope of profit or emolument.

With this missive Diego Mendez departed. If ever man did his duty bravely and efficiently, Mendez so did his. It was owing to him that the Spaniards were rescued from starvation—owing to him that they now had some hope of departure from their island-prison. Unfortunately, however, he was captured, soon after his departure, by hostile Indians, from whom he with difficulty escaped. Regaining possession of his canoe, he returned to the harbor and stranded ships, and, nothing daunted, proposed again to attempt the undertaking, if a body of armed men could escort him as far as his boat should remain in sight.

Two canoes were manned for the voyage, each containing six Spaniards and ten natives. One was commanded by Mendez, the other by Fiesco. The latter received orders from Columbus to return to Jamaica and report as soon as the canoes

---

[149] "Josephus thinks that this gold was found in Aurea. If it were so, I contend that these mines of the Aurea are identical with those of Veragua, which, as I have said before, extends westward twenty days' journey, at an equal distance from the pole and the line. Solomon bought all of it—gold, precious stones, and silver—but your majesties need only send to seek them, to have them at your pleasure."

VOYAGE OF MENDEZ. 333

should reach Hispaniola. Mendez was first to interview Ovando and urge the immediate dispatch of a vessel to the relief of Columbus; then to proceed immediately to Spain and deliver to the sovereigns the important letter aforementioned.

Bartholomew, with a body of men, followed the canoes along the coast, watched them till they had entirely disappeared, and then returned to Santa Gloria.

INDIAN HAMMOCK.

CHAPTER XXVI.

SOJOURN OF COLUMBUS IN JAMAICA.—VOYAGE OF DIEGO MENDEZ.

ALTHOUGH the forced sojourn of the Spaniards in Jamaica commenced under as favorable auspices as could be expected, the common misfortune, into which all had alike fallen, does not

COLUMBUS USHERED TO HIS REPAST WHILE STRANDED AT JAMAICA.

appear to have abated the arrogance of Columbus, or the distrust and hatred with which he was regarded.

It is even said that, though in such miserable plight, he insisted upon the observance of all the etiquette which he considered due to the rank of viceroy, that he caused himself to be ushered into the thatch-sheds, to his frugal meals of Indian fare, by "gentlemen esquires," bearing *flabella*, while all rose at his approach.[160] The Franciscan garb, which, in mock humility, he had assumed, must have accorded well with this ridiculous vanity. Such absurdities are characteristic of Columbus, who was as tenacious of fictitious as he was incapable of inspiring real respect.

His conduct was such that, ere long, suppressed murmurs swelled into open rebellion, if indeed disaffection under such circumstances can be termed rebellion. It is impossible to judge rightly of the difficulties and disagreements occurring in Jamaica at this period, as the only account we have of them is from the pen of Fernando Columbus. From him all other authors have borrowed more or less. It is evident, however, that the majority of the men were hostile to Columbus; that only the sickly and feeble remained on his side. Fernando, who is not what may be termed an impartial historian, and who does not scruple to distort facts, or indeed invent them, when his father's reputation is at stake, nevertheless allows *quasi* admissions of the universal feeling of distrust entertained toward Columbus, to escape him. He writes thus:

"Francis de Porras came upon the quarter-deck of the admiral's ship, and said to him, 'My lord, what is the meaning that you will not go into Spain, and will keep us all here perishing?' The admiral, hearing these unusual, insolent words, and suspecting what the matter might be, very calmly answered he did not see which way they could go till those that were gone in the canoes sent a ship; that no man was more desirous to be gone than he, as well for his own private interests as for the good of them all, for whom he was accountable; but that, if he had any thing to propose, he would again call together the captains and principal men to consult, as had been done several times before. Porras replied that it was no time to talk, but that he should embark quickly or stay there by himself; and, so turning his back, added, in a loud voice, 'I am going to Spain with those that will follow me.' At which time, all his followers who were present began to cry out, 'We will go with you! We will go with you!' and, running about, possessed them-

---

[160] He was served at table as a grandee. "All hail!" was said to him on state occasions.—(HELPS, "Life of Columbus," p. 124.)

selves of the forecastle, poop, and round-tops, all in confusion, and crying, 'Let them die!' others, 'For Spain, for Spain!' and others, 'What shall we do, captain?' Though the admiral was then in bed, so lame of the gout that he could not stand, yet he could not forbear rising and stumbling out at this noise. But two or three worthy persons, his servants, laid hold of and with labor laid him in his bed, that the mutineers might not murder him. Then they ran to his brother, who was courageously come out with a half-pike in his hand, and, wresting it out of his hands, put him with his brother, desiring Captain Porras to go about his business, and not do some mischief they might all suffer for; that he might be satisfied they did not oppose his going, but if he should kill the admiral, he could not expect but to be severely punished, without hopes of any benefit. The tumult being somewhat appeased, the conspirators took ten canoes that were by the ship's side, and which the admiral had bought all about the island, and went aboard them as joyfully as if they had been in some port of Spain. Upon this, many more, who had no hand in the plot, in despair to see themselves, as they thought, forsaken, taking what they could along with them, went aboard the canoes with them, to the great sorrow and affliction of those few faithful servants who remained with the admiral, and of all the sick, who thought themselves lost forever, and without hopes of ever getting off. And it is certain that, had the people been well, not twenty men had remained with the admiral." [181]

As we have said, the above is the source whence subsequent authors have drawn for their versions of this episode, and the only contemporaneous one which has come down to us. As one author, the most impartial who has hitherto written upon Columbus, shrewdly observes, "It is possible Porras might have had something to say;" and, considering the numerous precedents existing, we deem it safe to believe that Columbus was here, as in his other misfortunes, more the victim of his own selfish and arrogant passions, than of the evil dispositions of other men.

The Spaniards, under Porras, were not successful in their attempt to reach Hispaniola. They returned to Jamaica, where they lived, for some time, as best they could.

[181] "Historia del Amirante," chapter cii.

AN ECLIPSE AND ITS EFFECT. 337

The Indians had, in the mean time, become wearied of the contributions under which they were laid, and provisions began to fail. It was then that Columbus had recourse to that wonderful stratagem which excites the admiration of his biographers, as being a proof of his great astronomical knowledge. Knowing that an eclipse of the moon was to take place on a certain night, he summoned the leading chiefs to a conference, at which he informed them that his God protected him in all things, as they might see, for Mendez and his followers, who had departed at his command, had arrived safely at their destination[152] (we need not comment upon this falsehood; the reader will have perceived its grossness, for, at the time, Columbus had received no news of Mendez), while Porras, who had attempted the same journey, in opposition to his wishes, had been unsuccessful. He told them his God was angry with them (the Indians) for not furnishing the white men with food, and, in testimony of this divine anger, the moon, of which he (Columbus) was the offspring,[153] would that night lose its brightness.

This prediction is not so wonderful as writers would lead us to suppose. Eclipses were predicted and the time of their appearance recorded then, as now, both in almanacs and in more comprehensive "tables of eclipses," which were predicted several years in advance. It was from this source that Columbus learned the approach of this particular eclipse. He, as we have seen, made a mistake of more than eighteen degrees when calculating one for himself. Such a miscalculation is too great a one for a good astronomer to be guilty of. Mr. Irving declares it to have been owing to the incorrectness of his tables of eclipse, thereby admitting the existence of the latter, but, when relating the stratagem with the Indians, he gives all the credit to Columbus's own skill and learning.

We think, at best, that this much-lauded device was but a sorry one, and for once agree with M. de Lorgues that such gross juggling was an unworthy way of working on the credulity of

[152] Irving, "Columbus," book xvi., chapter iii.

[153] Most historians content themselves with asserting that Columbus declared the eclipse to be a sign of the anger of God, and do not mention the relationship to the moon claimed by him. Ogilby records this additional absurdity, which appears to us so worthy of Columbus, and withal so probable to have emanated from him, that we consider it a fit adjunct to the whole farce it pertains to (*see* Ogilby's "America," chapter iii., section iii.).

the savages, and of bringing forward the sacred name of God. Gross and unworthy as it was, it is, however, evident that Columbus perpetrated it, and the plan seems to have worked well. The Indians professed penitence, and Columbus consented to intercede for them, and, when the shadow passed from the face of the planet, reappeared and informed them that its restored light was the result of his intercession. Thenceforth there was no scarcity of supplies.

It becomes us here to make some brief mention of the memorable voyage made by Diego Mendez to Hispaniola. This devoted man served Columbus faithfully and well, at the risk of his own life, but he later learned, by bitter experience, that selfish ingratitude was to be the only reward for these services.

Great must have been the hardships experienced by men sailing in open canoes across a wide track of ocean. Mendez appears to have organized an effective and safe routine. The Spaniards and Indian crew were divided into two bands, one of which watched and labored while the other slept.

The burning rays of the tropical sun poured down from a cloudless sky upon the uncovered canoes; the heat was intensified by the reflection from the water. Soon the Indian rowers became exhausted, water and provisions failed; the brave band endured unspeakable agonies. On the second night, one of the Indians, overcome by labor, heat, and agonizing thirst, died; the parched lips and powerless strokes of his companions premised a like fate for them. The last drop of water had been drunk, and despair had almost seized even the strong heart of Mendez, when the light of the rising moon revealed a small island. Thither they eagerly steered, the lagging oarsmen inspired with new vigor. The island (Navassa) proved to be a mass of rock, entirely destitute of vegetation; rain-water, however, abounded in the hollows and crevices. Several of the unfortunate Indians drank so eagerly and freely that they died on the spot. The more reasonable of the worn-out party, after assuaging their thirst, made a fire of drift-wood, and roasting the shell-fish, which they found in abundance, made a hearty meal, which restored them to their wonted vigor. The following day was spent on the island resting. In the evening the canoes again set sail, and, on the following morning, four days after their departure from Jamaica, landed at Cape Tiburn, in Hispaniola. "Here," says Diego Mendez, in his narrative, "I brought the canoe up to a very beautiful part of the coast, to which many of the natives soon came and brought with them many articles of food, so that I remained there two days to take rest."

These two days expired, he set out, taking with him six native Indians, for San Domingo, a coasting voyage of some thirty leagues. Fiesco would have returned to Jamaica, as had been agreed, but his companions and the exhausted Indians would not hear of a second time exposing themselves to the terrible hardships they had endured, so the sea-bound prisoners of Jamaica were kept in suspense.

On reaching San Domingo, Mendez was informed that Ovando was in Xaragua, a province fifty leagues distant. For this place he bravely set out on foot and alone, and reached his destination in safety, after achieving, as Mr. Irving justly says, "one of the most perilous expeditions ever undertaken by a devoted follower for the safety of his commander."

For seven months he remained in Xaragua, but no ship was sent to the relief of Columbus. Ovando has been virulently assailed for this culpable neglect. We may be permitted to doubt, however, whether he did not thereby act according to the wishes, if not in obedience to the direct orders, of the sovereigns. It is probable, indeed Irving hints as much, that Columbus's would-be negotiations with Genoa were better known than that worthy would have liked, and that, tidings of these having reached Ovando, he considered the fortuitous imprisonment at Jamaica an easy solution of the difficult problem, What to do with Columbus? He learned from Mendez that the Spaniards were not likely to lack food, and therefore considered that haste was unnecessary.

When eight months had elapsed since the departure of Mendez, a ship was sent to Jamaica, bearing a present from Ovando to the colony of a barrel of wine and two flitches of bacon, but there appears to have been no intention of permitting Columbus, as yet, to return into the world.

Escobar, who commanded the vessel, reached Jamaica in March, 1504. He came alongside the stranded caravels in a boat (his vessel remaining out at sea), and, having delivered the wine and bacon, rowed off to a short distance, whence he informed Columbus that there were no vessels then in Hispaniola of sufficient size to bring him away with all his followers; that, as soon as one arrived, the governor would send it to his relief.

Columbus, though feeling, as his son informs us, nothing but enmity at heart, dissimulated as usual, and wrote a most friendly letter to Ovando, declaring his satisfaction that he should have the management of affairs, and defending himself (as he generally did when feeling guilty) from a charge which had not been made against him, namely, that his designs in returning to Hispaniola were not of a loyal character.[154]

With this missive, Escobar departed, leaving the disappointed Spaniards again to lament, with some cause, let us admit, having joined their fortunes with those of a man so despised and distrusted by their sovereigns, as circumstances showed Columbus to be.

The disaffected rallied around the brothers Porras, and were loud in their complaints. Some, in distant parts, would not even believe that a ship had arrived and departed, but imagined this to be but another of the numerous falsehoods with which Columbus had cajoled and flattered them. It was in vain that the latter sent part of the bacon and wine as tangible proofs of his veracity. "The worthlessness of a man's word," says Irving, "may always be known by the extravagant means he uses to enforce it." Fully subscribing to this sentiment, we feel that the rebels were justified in disbelieving Columbus, maugre his bacon in an island where the commodity was scarce; at any rate, they resolved to separate themselves from one whose bad odor in Spain entailed upon his luckless followers such evil consequences, and who was, in himself, so little worthy of devotion or self-sacrifice.

A fight ensued, in which several of the disaffected were killed. Pedro de Ledesma, the pilot, who, by swimming ashore at Belen, had saved the lives of Bartholomew and his companions, was now covered with wounds, inflicted by that same Bartholomew, any one of which would have been sufficient to kill an ordinary man. Such, however, was the vigor of his constitution, that he recovered, to the astonishment of all. Porras was made prisoner, and Bartholomew returned to the ships, having had the

---

[154] Navarrete, "Colecc. Dip.," vol. ii., p. 486.

DEVOTION OF MENDEZ.

best of the fight. The rebels offered to capitulate, and were, we are told, generously pardoned by Columbus. It is probable that he, too, was of the opinion that Porras, if heard, might have something to say, and was therefore quite willing to come to terms. He, however, detained Porras prisoner, in order to have some hold on his followers.

At length two ships appeared, to the relief alike of Columbus and his enemies. One had been bought and fitted out by the faithful Mendez, the other was provided by Ovando.

Mendez had thus nobly and indefatigably labored for the accomplishment of his difficult mission. What reward, will be asked, was given by the noble, the great-hearted Columbus for such services? He *promised* him the office of *alguazil* of Hispaniola. This post was, nevertheless, given by Diego Columbus, who had joined in the promise made by his father, to Bartholomew, and all the solicitations of Mendez were powerless to procure any recognition of his devotion He died poor.

The king seems to have better appreciated the heroic deed than he for whom it was performed. He granted Mendez a coat-of-arms, upon which a canoe was engraved, in memory of his perilous voyage.

FLYING-FISH.

CHAPTER XXVII.

DELIVERY OF COLUMBUS AND HIS COMPANIONS. — HIS RETURN TO SPAIN. — HIS DEATH.

Just a year had elapsed since the two shattered caravels had stranded at Santa Gloria, when these two vessels reached Jamaica in June, 1504. On the 28th all embarked and joyfully bade farewell to the island which had so long been their prison. The transit to Hispaniola was a tempestuous one. The vessel was detained some days at the island Beata, whence Columbus wrote a letter, full of gratitude and professions of submission, to Ovando.[135] His conduct was soon to show the insincerity of these professions; even while he made them, he felt nothing but enmity at heart toward the governor.

Upon his landing, on the 13th of August, at San Domingo, Ovando received him with kindness and hospitality, installing him in the government-house, and, during the whole of his stay, treating him with urbanity and politeness. This is admitted by even the advocates of Columbus. They would have it believed, however, that Ovando's kindness was hypocritical, and cite as proof of this that he proceeded to inform himself as to the particulars of the late mutiny of Porras. This had taken place, be it remembered, within his jurisdiction, but, as he did not blindly accept, as convincing proof of the guilt of the mutineers, the testimony of Columbus, the latter waxed wroth, and, notwithstanding the letters he had written to Ovando, recognizing his authority and promising submission to it, he now openly and offensively declared that he was viceroy, and had, therefore, greater power than Ovando. He professed the utmost indignation that the latter should dare to question, or attempt to ascer-

[135] Navarrete, "Colecc. Dip.," vol. ii., p. 487.

tain, whether the six men who had been killed in Jamaica had deserved their fate. Six human lives, he held, were as nothing compared to his rank and dignity.

Ovando seems to have regarded this bluster with the amused indulgence accorded to a spoiled and petulant child. He still treated Columbus with polite consideration, but calmly proceeded to the duties of his office. Investigation was made, the result of which apparently went far to justify the mutiny; for Porras, though sent to Spain, was never punished.

Thoroughly disgusted with the state of affairs in San Domingo, and convinced that an attempt to reinstate himself in power must be futile, Columbus now determined to return, with all speed, to Spain. Two ships were placed at his disposal, and, after a month's sojourn in Hispaniola, he set sail. A storm, arising soon after his departure, carried away the mast of his ship. He sent it back to port, and embarked on the second, commanded by his brother Bartholomew. This homeward voyage was one continued storm,[156] and his ship was in sorry plight when, on the 7th of November, 1504, it landed him at San Lucar de la Barrameda. He was completely bedridden, and had himself transferred immediately to Seville.

Here he no doubt learned the fruitlessness of his attempt to excite the ambition of Genoa. She refrained from any espousal of his cause. The Genoese evidently tacitly, if not openly, refused to have any dealings with him. This refusal has been wrongly attributed, by some writers, to his low birth.[157]

There is a letter to be found in Navarrete, bearing the date

---

[156] The miraculous and extraordinary are made, as ever, to form a part of this voyage. Fernando, in his relation of it, will not content himself with reporting a terrific storm, such as might have been encountered by an ordinary mortal, but, in order that this "incomparable man" may be made to display his ingenuity, we read:

"The weather being fair, and *we very still, the mast flew into four pieces,* but the courage of the lieutenant (Bartholomew), and the admiral's ingenuity, though he could not rise out of his bed for the gout, found a remedy for this misfortune, making a jury-mast of a yard, and strengthening the middle of it with ropes, and some planks they took from the poop and stern."—("Historia del Amirante," chapter cviii.)

[157] Ogilby, who makes Genoa the birthplace of Columbus, says that Peter Bezarus, a countryman of Columbus, "gives unquestionable proofs of his mean extract, and, among other things, that the commonwealth of Genoa refused to receive the great legacy which Columbus left them in his will, because they fondly thought it a derogation to their honor, being so great a republic, to take any thing of bequest from a fisher's son."—(OGILBY, "America," chapter iii.)

of 1502, which purports to have been written by a "magistrate of St. George" to Columbus, complimenting the latter in high terms, but discussing none of the plans he had proposed. The authenticity of this document may, however, be doubted, as we find Columbus in 1504 complaining to Oderigo that no notice has been taken of his proposals.

This hope dashed to the ground, he became, once more, urgent in his appeals to the crown for a restitution of his dignities. We are told that he thought more of his titles and offices than of the pecuniary privileges which had been accorded to him. The reason for this is very evident: though his demands for money were constant and exorbitant, yet he was aware that the expenses of his enterprises had hitherto far exceeded his profits, and he, no doubt, appreciated the impossibility of becoming rich by claiming the fulfillment of his bond in that quarter.

The crown was now awakened to the fact that it had no power to grant the titles of viceroy and admiral in perpetuity; and the sovereigns, far from regretting this, or desiring to overstep their prerogative, were rejoiced at this loop-hole through which they were enabled to escape from the consequences of their foolish concessions.

For these titles, Columbus, with the tenacity of age and the puerility of childhood, solicited, but solicited in vain. The queen, who had been in a critical condition at the time of his arrival, expired a few days after, on the 26th of November, 1504. Henceforth it was to Ferdinand alone that Columbus addressed his demands; but Ferdinand met them, as Isabella had done, with tacit refusal.

He was, at this time, wretchedly poor—living by borrowing—and confesses that he "most times has not wherewithal to pay his bill" at the tavern where he lodges.

He wrote to Ferdinand, inveighing against Ovando, assuring that monarch that the latter was derelict in the performance of his duties, careless of the treasure, and, above all, *unpopular* in the island. It is strange that Columbus, who had been so exceedingly hateful to the people of that same island, should bring forward unpopularity as a proof of unworthiness, and still more strange that he did not perceive that, in admitting unpopularity to be a just cause for the removal of an officer, he fully justified the proceedings of Bobadilla toward himself.

His letters were not noticed; the Spanish court was weary of this "*nudo-nocchier promettitor di regni*" (pauper-pilot promiser of realms). He had failed in all he had promised, and, while tenacious that others should fulfill their promises, he had not fulfilled one of his. He had not visited the grand-khan; he had not brought tons of gold to Spain; he had not opened the commerce of the East to that kingdom; he had not even discovered the strait, of the existence of which he had been so confident that he had been allowed, though in disgrace, to make a fourth voyage in search of it. Yet these, by his own proposition, were the services for which the privileges he claimed were to be the guerdon; all this, which he had agreed to accomplish, and had not accomplished, was the basis of his contract. It is, therefore, unjust to accuse the sovereigns of ingratitude in not performing their part of it, when he had not performed his, even could they legally have accorded to him the titles in question, which we have shown they could not.

When written appeals failed, he proceeded in person to court, then held in Segovia. Once he attempted the journey, but infirmity compelled him to abandon it. At length, in the month of May, 1505, he reached his destination.

The king received him courteously, but we may imagine that, when the infirm, impecunious, and aged man before him sought to excite his interest and secure his favor by promising to undertake another voyage, wherein all former ones should be surpassed in services rendered, the sensible monarch must have with difficulty refrained from smiling.

If Columbus, twelve years previous, had been unable to perform what he had promised, how absurd would it have been to expect him now, when bedridden and fast failing of old age, to undertake voyages or render services! Ferdinand contented himself with recommending to Columbus that he should rest and nurse his infirmities.

He took no notice of his vindictive accusations against Ovando; he even offered him titles which might compensate him for those which the queen had, without authority, granted him. These Columbus refused. The king then proposed to leave the matter to arbitration, allowing Columbus to choose the arbiter. He selected Diego de Deza, formerly Bishop of Palencia, but since promoted to the archbishopric of Seville.

This prelate was, we are told, the old and tried friend of Columbus. Of him the latter thus writes: "He was the cause that their highnesses obtained possession of the Indies, who induced me to remain in Castile when I was on the road to leave it." And again:

"If the Bishop of Palencia has arrived, or should arrive, tell him how much I have been gratified by his prosperity; and that, if I come, I shall lodge with his Grace, even though he should not invite me; for we must return to our ancient fraternal affection."

Yet so evidently conscious was he of the illegality of his claims that, having chosen this friendly arbiter, he would only consent to submit to him the question of revenue, not that of titles and hereditary offices.

This, of course, defeated the whole plan of arbitration, for it was precisely the titles, and only the titles, which were matters for arbitrament; the question of revenue could be settled by any accountant. The matter, therefore, which might have now been arranged with some possible advantage to Columbus, was deferred. Unwilling to come to any but his own terms, and these being impossible to accede to, he was again an unheeded solicitor. It is about this time that we find him interesting Vespucci in his behalf, and eager to profit by the good standing of the latter at court (*see* chapter on Vespucci).

But the wretched old man was clinging to the vanities of the world when on the very verge of the tomb. His malady, aggravated by age, had increased rapidly, and his career was near its close. When conscious that his end was approaching, he sought to atone for the crimes of his life by strict religious discipline; he still wore the Franciscan garb—token of humility; he sought to propitiate Heaven by redoubling in prayer and fasting.

In the month of May, 1506, he made the codicils which we have mentioned, and, on the 20th of that month, breathed his last.

Well, perhaps, would it have been for him, had his name been allowed to sink into oblivion. Well, certainly, would it have been for justice, had not a fictitious glory been created for him at the expense of truly good and great men, out of the ruins of whose good names his renown had sprung up.

CHAPTER XXVIII.

BURIAL OF COLUMBUS.—HIS REPUTED TOMBS AND MONUMENTS.

THE falsehoods which have been promulgated concerning Columbus do not end at his death. We are told that, upon its occurrence, Ferdinand allowed his conscience to direct him, and, with tardy justice, ordered a magnificent tomb to be erected at Seville to his memory, bearing the following inscription:

> "A Castilla y a Leon
> Nuevo mundo dio Colon."

Such an act on the part of the king would have been a tacit admission that he had culpably neglected a great man who had thus benefited Spain. That he gave no such orders, that no monument was erected, is now an ascertained fact.

Mr. George Sumner, to whom we are indebted elsewhere, comes again to our assistance and that of truth. He quotes the inscription on the tomb of Fernando Columbus (the biographer, who died some thirty years after his father) in the cathedral at Seville, and reports the above inscription as forming a part of it. He continues:

"Throughout all Spain I know of no other inscription to the memory of Columbus. At Valladolid, where he died, and where his body lay for some years, there is none that I could discover, neither is there any trace of any at the *Cartuja*, near Seville, to which his body was afterward transferred, and in which his brother was buried."

Thus the inscription existed only on the grave of Fernando, illegitimate son of Columbus, who, having embraced an ecclesiastical career and devoted himself to letters, left his library to the Carthusian monks, on condition, we are told, of their placing over his grave, in the Cathedral of Seville, the above inscription. He died, as we have said, more than thirty years after Columbus.

It is a noticeable fact that the Government of Spain has ever abstained from any spontaneous recognition of Columbus and the claims set up for him by historians.

It is alleged that his remains were removed from the convent of the Franciscans, at Valladolid, to the Carthusian monastery near Seville, in 1513, and that, in 1536, they were transported to San Domingo, in Hispaniola. Be this as it may, we know that when Spain, in 1795, ceded the island of Hispaniola to France, she made no reservation of the ashes of Columbus, nor did she contemplate their removal, as she naturally would have done, had she regarded them in the light of national relics.

It was the officious zeal of the Admiral Aristozabal, who was sent to aid in surrendering the island to the French, which first imagined these remains to be of importance to Spain. So little, evidently, was thought of them, that this same Aristozabal was only "informed" that they were deposited in the island upon his arrival there. The information, however, stirs up his patriotism; he will not permit them to repose on French soil, and desires that their *re-retranslation* shall be of an *official* character, and accompanied with that kind of pomp and display which would have been so grateful to the living Columbus. The governor of the island entered into this project, though he confessed he had received no instructions from the Spanish Government concerning the matter; but "as he had not time, without great inconvenience," to consult the sovereign on the matter, he and Aristozabal, with the eagerly-proffered coöperation of the clergy, decided to act on their own responsibility, and transfer these sacred remains to Havana, in Cuba. This was done, we are told, with almost royal honors. But, however important the bones of Columbus had *become* to Spain in 1795, they evidently had not been much revered during the two hundred and fifty years previous, and, when all is told, and the pompous pageant which transported them to Havana described, it is by no means certain that the bones and mould scraped up with such care were the veritable ashes of Columbus.[158] If they were, why had they

---

[158] M. De Lorgues, speaking of the disappearance of the TRUE CROSS (set up by Columbus, which had worked so many miracles), says: "It is not strange that, in a country ruined and terrified, it was not known what had become of the TRUE CROSS,

been thus neglected? why had the slab or panel which closed the niche in the altar in which they are said to have lain, remained uninscribed? This attempt at honoring (when driven from the island) remains which had been allowed to repose unmarked for more than two hundred and fifty years of residence and possession, is too spasmodic and tardy to be regarded as the spontaneous admission, on the part of Spain, that she was under obligations to the man Columbus, or to his memory, and, though the above unauthorized acts of the governor and admiral are said to have afterward received the sanction of the crown, it is easy to perceive that this sanction was given, rather than, by disapproval, to give greater notoriety to an unpleasant matter.

Thus the last stone of the structure is overturned. It seemed to authors necessary, in order fitly to close their romances entitled histories of Columbus, and their record of the persecutions of which they represent him to have been the victim, to invent a sort of poetic justice, by which Ferdinand is made to order the erection of a superb monument with a pompous inscription, and, stung by remorse, in this act to confess his ingratitude and injustice. But, unfortunately for romance, though more fortunately for justice, this statement is a fiction; the fiction has been proved, and we are obliged to fear that the "cold and calculating Ferdinand" descended to his grave, complacently conscious of having treated Columbus as well as, if not better than, he deserved.

Fortunate would it have been for the honor of these United States, had their representatives, in this matter, acted as wisely as did Spain. Then the brazen doors at the national Capitol, so creditable, as works of art, to those who designed and cast them, would have illustrated some worthier theme; nor would the nation one day regret that Congress had felt it necessary to import brass from Bavaria, and to expend the public treasure in causing the bronze of Munich to symbolize *a fiction*. Here is wrought, with artistic skill, the *fabled* " triumphal entry into Barcelona," "full of the glory of success and waving banners.

. . . . when at San Domingo the exact burial-place of Columbus himself was forgotten."—(" Christophe Colombe," vol. ii., livre iv., chapter viii.)

It may be that these relic-hunters unconsciously gathered the remains of some victim of "the admiral," which, if conscious of the label upon the box which contained them, would indignantly start from their cerement.

All the halo of rose-color seems now to light the future of the great discoverer."[159] Yet this triumph is but a creation, as we have shown, of imaginative brains—the pageant never took place, and the arrival of Columbus at Barcelona was unnoticed by the chroniclers of that city, who recorded events of trivial importance.

Anon, we see Columbus aroused to "stern indignation at the capture of an Indian girl," which must cause those to smile who remember how often he "ordered some Indians to be taken," and who have marked his systematized efforts to establish a slave-trade.

Nor can we pass over the injustice with which such men as Vespucci and Pinzon are made to play the satellite to the pauper pirate.

A wiser lesson might have been learned from Venice. In the grand hall, in the palace of the doges, many successive panels are filled with the portraits of doges who had reflected honor upon the "mistress of the seas," and had aided in making Venice glorious. Over one, however, a dark veil is cast, and we read: "They did not place his portrait in the hall of the great council, but in the place where it should have been is the inscription: '*Hic est locus Marini Faliero decapitati pro criminibus*' (This is the place of Marino Faliero, decapitated for his crimes)."[160]

O Venice! O Washington! How diverse are your standards of legal and moral ethics! For the same crime, one mounts the scaffold, another is placed among the gods.

Nor does this brazen fiction "trammel up the consequences." The district in which the nation has reared its temple is humiliated by an effort to perpetuate the *alias* under which the piratical Griego disappeared from the gaze of an injured people, while states and municipalities will obscure the name of America by planting this *parasite* from sea to sea.

When Europe, and Asia, and Africa, shall ask America how long she will continue thus to honor the man, who after having basely robbed the dead, falsely styled himself a discoverer, and enslaved his fellow, *what answer shall she make?*

---

[159] *See* official description, also chapter xiv. of this volume.
[160] Marin Sanuto, "Cronica," vol. xxii., p. 639.

CHAPTER XXIX.

CHARACTER OF COLUMBUS.

THE character of Columbus, as portrayed by his actions, does not belie the impression given by his son's description of his personal appearance. Hypocrisy is largely predominant; to this revolting trait, to the shame of humanity be it said, he owes

SLAVE-AUCTION.

most of his fame, for the Church, charmed with the devotion he professed, has chanted his praises, and crushed any historian who would not join in them, as long as her power was sufficient. In our own day M. Roselly de Lorgues writes an enthusiastic and ecstatic panegyric, in which he relieves himself of his overburdening admiration by exclaiming, in huge capitals, "COLUMBUS WAS A SAINT!" And even American writers would warn off, as from sacred precincts, the profane who, creeping around the idol, would spy its feet of clay.

This blind partiality is, as we have said, in great measure due to Columbus's professions of religious zeal. This "great navigator," who had spent all his life at sea, cannot, on entering upon his self-styled "holy mission," even speak in the language of seamen; he discards all nautical parlance, substituting religious terms—"I sailed so many leagues between vespers and complines." He sailed in the name of the Blessed Virgin, the Holy Trinity, and Jesus Christ. He commanded his ship, appropriately (?) "clad in an humble garb, resembling in form and color the habit of a Franciscan monk, simply girded with a cord, and suffered his beard to grow like the brethren of that order." Three times out of four, when lots are cast to decide who shall perform certain penance, by the skillful manipulation of a marked bean he causes the lot to fall *miraculously* to him, "to show," his son modestly observes, "that his offerings were more acceptable to God than those of others."

All this religious affectation disgusts the truly reverent mind. Above all, when we find what atrocious acts were committed under its protection, and how widely the actions of Columbus differed from his professions when he had attained his end, and was far from all who could bring him to account.

On reaching the island of San Salvador, his first act was, we are told, to fall on his face and kiss the sand; his next, to take possession for Castile; his third, to make all swear allegiance to him as Viceroy of India. This done, he proceeded at leisure to capture the unoffending natives, and bear them into slavery. Years later, when his cruel government had driven Spaniards and natives alike to desperation, so that they sent across the ocean piteous appeals to be relieved from so merciless a tyrant, we find him accused of refusing to permit the baptism of these unfortunate Indians, for the welfare of whose souls he had professed such solicitude, because by embracing Christianity they exempted themselves from slavery, and could no longer minister to his love of gain.

His son tells us : "He was so strict in religious matters, that, for fasting and saying the divine offices, he might be thought professed in some religious order. So great was his aversion to swearing and cursing, that I protest I never heard him swear any other oath than by San Fernando, and when in the greatest passion with anybody he would vent his spleen by saying, 'God take you, for doing so and so.' When he was to write, his way of trying his pen was by writing the words '*Jesus cum Maria fit nobis in via*,'' and that in such a character as might very well serve to get his bread."

The praises here given are somewhat equivocal. He does not say his *father's life* and *acts* were such as to render him a

COLUMBUS TRIES HIS PEN.

bright example of goodness, but that, for *praying* and *fasting*, he might be thought to belong to some holy order. In matters pertaining to religion both father and son seem to have depended more upon the form than the substance; for reality and practical piety they substituted show and profession, and were far from conceiving the ideal of the poet who wrote:

"He prayeth best who loveth best
All creatures great and small,
For the good God who loveth us,
Hath made and loved them all."

FAC SIMILE OF THE HANDWRITING AND SIGNATURE OF COLUMBUS.—(From his MSS. deposited at Genoa.)[161]

[161] The above specimen of this exquisite handwriting would seem to suggest that copyists were at a premium.

To try one's pen with the words recorded by Fernando hardly suits the inspiration of genuine reverence, while the gentle oath, uttered with due vehemence, must have fully answered its purpose, and is vigorous enough to meet the requirements of the modern Anglo-Saxon.

From some such original as Columbus, Molière must have draw his inimitable "Tartufe," who is disturbed by the sin of having caught a flea while at prayers, and dispatched him with anger; who advertises his wearing a hair shirt, and, withal, would rob his dupe of home, fortune, and honor. Does not the following seem strangely applicable to our hero?

"The profession of hypocrite has marvelous advantages. How many thus redeem the scandal of youth, and, sagely making a buckler and cloak of religion, indulge their favorite sins with impunity! When found out, they are far from losing credit. A penitent air, a sigh of mortification, two turns of the eyes, and all goes on as before!"

No character in history has more truly, or, as regards posterity, more successfully made a cloak of religion wherewith to hide an ungodly life, than did Christopher Columbus. But hypocrisy availed him less in his own day. He himself, as we have shown, bears witness to the depth of ignominy into which he had fallen in the estimation of his fellow-men. Throughout his history, by whomsoever recounted, distrust and aversion are traceable in those of every rank and degree who had dealings with him, from the sovereigns to the "graceless cook."

Apparently no depravity could be attributed to him which was too gross for belief, and it was but natural and fitting that his ostentatious devotion and pious punctilio should augment the odium in which he was held, while the manner in which he represented himself as the chosen of God, THE CHRIST-BEARER, and the familiar terms in which he speaks of the Deity, are revolting in their blasphemy and hypocrisy.

But the feature of his life which chiefly troubles his would-be canonizers is his private moral character, in which are many ugly flaws which they are anxious to conceal or explain. Among these is his open and notorious illicit amour with Beatrix Enriquez of Cordova, which continued during a series of years. Of this there can be little doubt, notwithstanding the illogical and unsuccessful attempts of Messrs. De Lorgues and Cadoret to establish a marriage;[162] nor was it worth their while to attempt a refutation of a so universally-accepted statement, even had they been more fortunate in their mode of treating the subject. Columbus stands unanswerably convicted of many atrocious deeds beside which his illicit amours sink into insignificance. Why labor, then, to acquit him of an *offense*, while all the world is supposed to know that he was guilty of *crimes?* Nor is it less absurd to allege that his being guilty of such an offense would have called down upon him the indignation and censure of the Church, and the displeasure of Isabella. Was it for the Church, at whose head was the licentious and intriguing Borgia (Alexander VI.), to reprove one of its minor devotees for such peccadillos? Was it for Ferdinand, with his various mistresses and illegitimate children, or for his wife? Such an episode may rather have been supposed to his credit, and it is worse than futile to attempt to square his actions by any high moral standard.

One of the arguments brought forward by M. Cadoret to prove that Beatrix was the wife, not the mistress, of Columbus, and which he appears to consider convincing, is, that neither Bobadilla, Ovando, nor Fonseca, ever accused him of illicit connections, and that they, as his enemies, would surely have done so had there been foundation for such an accusation.

Not to repeat what we said above about the morals of the times, Bobadilla, Ovando, and Fonseca are reported, even by their enemies and detractors, to have been gentlemen by birth and breeding. The first two were sent to Hispaniola to examine into Columbus's conduct as governor, not into his private character. The third had the direction of financial matters concerning the islands, and his relations with Columbus did not extend beyond the functions of his office. The duties of all three only extended to his official career, and we may presume they neither troubled themselves about, nor would have had the indelicacy to force upon the public and crown, the details of his private life.

The fact that Columbus on his death-bed recommended Beatrix to the care of his son Diego, and his seeming remorse at hav-

---

[162] A Life of Columbus, by the Abbé Cadoret appeared in 1869, and is, we believe, the latest effort that has been made to prove a marriage between Beatrix and Columbus.

ing neglected her, is also dwelt upon by M. Cadoret as proof of his marriage to her.

"Neglect," he says, "when capable of stirring the conscience, must necessarily have been practised toward a legitimate wife."[163] Thus we are taught that the man who leads an unfortunate woman to shame and ruin, begets children by her, and then abandons her to poverty and disgrace, need feel neither remorse nor qualms of conscience. The brutality of such a sentiment need scarcely be dwelt upon, particularly as emanating from an avowed disciple of Him who said: "Neither do I condemn thee; go and sin no more."

The denial of Columbus's illicit connection with Beatrix is of recent date, and has been set on foot by that school of theologians who desire his canonization. Heretofore his most ardent admirers, even ministers of the Church, have admitted it. Spotorno, considering it futile to deny, seeks to make it redound to the advantage of his hero. "In yielding to his passions," he writes, "our navigator showed that he was but a man. In avowing his fault he exhibited the sincerity of his religious faith." Father Spotorno did not foresee, when he wrote the above, that a school should arise among his brethren, whose object should be to prove that "our navigator" was more than a man

Irving, that warmest and most eloquent advocate of Columbus, writes:

"Though Columbus had now relinquished all expectations of patronage from the Castilian sovereigns, he was unwilling to break off all connection with Spain. A tie of a tender nature still bound him to that country. During his first visit to Cordova, he had conceived a passion for a lady of that city, named Beatrix Enriquez. This attachment has been given as an additional cause of his lingering so long in Spain, and bearing with the delays he experienced. Like most of the particulars of this part of his life, his connection with this lady is wrapped in obscurity. It does not appear to have been sanctioned by marriage."[164]

Major, of the British Museum, asserts that, "but for an attachment which he (Columbus) had formed at Cordova, which

---

[163] Cadoret, "Vie de Christophe Colombe," appendice, p. 402.
[164] Irving, "Columbus," book ii., chapter vi.

made him reluctant to leave Spain, he would, in all probability, have repaired to France."[165]

A thorough knowledge of the character of Columbus, as portrayed in his acts, and an observance of the motives which actuated him after the commencement of his voyages, render some such explanation as that given by Irving and Major necessary to account for his remaining in Spain. It goes far to throw light on dark places. We have already seen how the difficulties said to have been raised in opposition to his schemes have been grossly exaggerated, if not invented. The pecuniary outlay necessary for the execution of his project was eventually supplied by private individuals and by the little town of Palos, without difficulty. The delay, then, was not caused by any of the reasons generally given. How much more probable that Columbus, the unprincipled pirate, should have preferred for a time a life of easy dalliance at Cordova with Beatrix, supported by his friends Juan Perez and Pinzon! When wearied of it he closed his negotiations and proceeded on his voyage.

There is much reason to believe that Columbus's private morals were impure. His sickness and distemper, so often mentioned, but so lightly dwelt upon by his biographers, were attended by such symptoms as to have led some to suppose that he was afflicted, not by the gout, but by that dreadful scourge which licentiousness has entailed upon man."[166]

---

[165] Major, "Select Letters of Columbus," introduction, p. 52.

[166] Voltaire may have spoken, and probably did speak, figuratively, when he said: "So man is not born wicked. How comes it, then, that so many are infected with the pestilence of wickedness? It is because they who bear rule over them, having caught the distemper, communicate it to others; as a woman, having the distemper which Christopher Columbus brought from America, has spread the venom all over Europe." But, however pertinent or impertinent to Columbus the above obscure allusion to him may have been, the great French philosopher was certainly mistaken in his assertion that the disease in question was of modern origin, or that it was brought to Europe from America. Mr. Prescott, in a foot-note, refers the curious on this subject to a work entitled "Lettere sulla Storia de' Mali Venerei, di Domenico Thiene, Venezia, 1823." "In this work," he says, "the author has assembled all the early notices of the disease of any authority, and discussed their import with great integrity and judgment. The following positions may be considered as established by his researches: 1. That neither Columbus nor his son, in their copious narratives and correspondence, allude, in any way, to the existence of such a disease in the New World. I must add," continues Mr. Prescott, "that an examination of the original document published by Navarrete since the date of Dr. Thiene's work, fully confirms this statement. 2. That among the frequent notices of the disease, during the

It is strange that historians should persist in representing Columbus to have been inspired by lofty and religious enthusiasm when undertaking his voyage of so-called discovery. In view of the facts, can it really be supposed that it was devotion

twenty-five years immediately following the discovery of America, there is not a single intimation of its having been brought from that country; but, on the contrary, a uniform derivation of it from some other source, generally France. 3. That the disorder was known and circumstantially described previous to the expedition of Charles VIII., and, of course, could not have been introduced by the Spaniards in that way, as vulgarly supposed. 4. That various contemporary authors trace its existence, in a variety of countries, as far back as 1493 and the beginning of 1494, showing a rapidity and extent of diffusion perfectly irreconcilable with its importation by Columbus in 1493. 5. Lastly, that it was not till after the close of Ferdinand and Isabella's reigns that the first work appeared, affecting to trace the origin of the disease to America."

If the conclusions at which Mr. Prescott and Dr. Thiene have arrived, be correct, it is not certain that the authorities cited by them sustain their verdict. Fernando Columbus, who is represented as silent upon this subject, says ("Historia del Amirante," chapter lxxiv.): "The admiral being come to San Domingo .... found that abundance of those he had left were dead, and, of those that remained, above one hundred and sixty were sick of the French pox."

In chapter lxi. he also states that "it had pleased His Divine Majesty .... to send such scarcity of provisions and such violent diseases among them" (the natives) "that they were reduced to one-third of what they had been at first, to make it appear more plain that such miraculous victories, and the subduing of nations, are his right, and not the effect of our power or conduct."

This loathsome visitation, in which Fernando professes to see the divine hand, appears to have formed a portion of the blessings borne by Columbus, *certainly from Spain to Hispaniola, or from Hispaniola to Spain*, probably both; and one of the results of his voyage was the conversion of Europe into a charnel-house, or vale of Hinnom, and the reduction of the population of the island to one-third of its former numbers.

Upon this subject it may be well to consult the history of the period. Peter Martyr, alluding to the case noticed by Fernando at San Domingo, says: "Such as desired to be cured of the troublesome disease of the pox," used a decoction of guaiacan-wood, which remedy, he informs us, was soon employed in the treatment of patients in Europe, "to draw the unhappy disease out of the bones and marrow." So efficacious did the wood and bark of this tree prove, that the pious Spaniards, after having tested its virtues, named it "*the holy tree.*" Herrera would have us regard this disease as of American origin. Alluding to the case mentioned by Fernando and Peter Martyr, he says: "Provisions now growing very scarce, many of the Spaniards fell sick; but, what was worse, by having to do with the Indian women, they contracted a distemper *common enough among the natives, but altogether unknown to them* (the Spaniards), which occasioned them to break out in blotches all over their bodies, of which many died, and others, thinking to be cured by change of air, returned to Spain, and spread the distemper there. However, it pleased God that the same place afforded the remedy as gave the evil, for, some time after, an Indian woman, wife to a Spaniard, showed the use of the wood called guaiacan, which relieved them. This is the disease now commonly known by the name of the French pox."—(Herrera, Decade I., book v., chapter v.)

to the Church, to Christianity, which made him haunt and importune the court of Spain for years? Was he, in truth, actuated by a noble desire to benefit a benighted portion of humanty, or does he not rather appear to have been stimulated by

In Ramusio's great work we find the following: "Your majesty may be assured that this sickness comes from the Indies, and is very common among the Indians; but it is not as virulent in those parts as among us, so that the Indians cure themselves easily in those islands with the wood (guaiacan), and in *terra firma* with herbs, or things they know of, for they are great herbalists. *The first time that this sickness was seen in Spain* was after Don Christopher Columbus had discovered the Indies and returned to these parts; and some Christians that came with him, who had accompanied him on his discovery, and those also who had gone with him on his second voyage, of whom there were many, brought over this sickness, and by them it was communicated to other persons. And in the year 1495, when the great captain, Don Gonsalvo Ferrando, of Cordoba, passed into Italy with troops to support the King of Naples, Don Ferdinand the Younger, against the King of France, by command of the Catholic sovereigns, Don Ferdinand and Doña Isabella of immortal memory, ancestors of your majesty, the sickness was brought over by some Spaniards, and that was the first time it was seen in Italy; and, as this was the time when the French, with the aforesaid King Charles, came into Italy, the Italians called the sickness French sickness, and the French called it Naples sickness, because they had never known it till this war, after which it was disseminated throughout Christendom, and passed into Africa."—(RAMUSIO, tome iii., p. 65.)

Army surgeons, and those familiar with the rapid spread of this disease, especially when aided by camp-followers, will not, we think, regard the time intervening between the return of Columbus and the developments above noted as too brief for compassing the wide-spread ruin generally recorded of this period.

Captain Jonathan Carver, in his account of travel in the Northwest, notices the successful manner in which the Indians residing in regions remote from civilization, treat this disease, displaying a skill evidently not acquired from contact with the white race.

The disease in question is undoubtedly of far earlier origin than the advent of Columbus in the Western islands. Its presence may be traced to the most ancient times, in writings both sacred and profane.

"His bones are full of the sin of his youth, which shall lie down with him in the dust," saith Job.

The Hindoo sacred writings, probably older than Job, contain evident allusions to this malady, among others the following: "Every man who has contracted disease from the use or abuse of women, shall be impure while it continues, and for ten days and ten nights after his restoration. . . . The mat of his bed is defiled, and must be burned. . . . The horse, the camel, the elephant, on which he may ride on pilgrimages, shall be impure, and shall be washed in water wherein is dissolved a sprig of cousa."

We read in Herodotus that, after the Scythians had overrun Asia, and were advancing upon Egypt, Psammetichus met them in Palestine, and, by presents and entreaties, prevailed upon them to return to their homes; that the Scythians, on their homeward march, came to Ascalon; that the greater part of their body passed through without molesting it, but that some remained behind and plundered the temple of the *Celestial* Venus; that "upon the Scythians who plundered this temple, avarice, petty ambition, and vanity? A perusal of the conditions he laid down suffices to convince us that the latter was the case. He affects love for Christ, for the Blessed Virgin. He would be the bearer of the Gospel to heathen nations, would

and, indeed, upon all their posterity, the deity entailed a fearful punishment—they were afflicted with the female disease. The Scythians themselves confess that their countrymen suffered this malady in consequence of the above crime." It seems probable that the Scythians in question, not only plundered the temple of the goddess, but received from her priestesses, whose lives were not the most chaste, the disease which thereafter afflicted them and their posterity. The fifteenth chapter of Leviticus contains instructions for cleanliness, evidently looking to this disease. The ordinance of circumcision is an ancient one, and was instituted to check its ravages. Herod of Judea died of it. Many references to ancient history might be made, tending to establish an antiquity much higher than that of the Spaniards in Hispaniola. In Europe its presence is traced as early at least as 1347. Jane I., Queen of the two Sicilies, ordered, in that year, that a public brothel be set up at Avignon, that the "wenches who played there" should be examined every Saturday by the abbess and a surgeon, "and if any of them had contracted any illness by their whoring, they should not be suffered to prostitute themselves, lest the youth who conversed with them should catch their distemper." Thus it appears that, more than a hundred years previous to the siege of Naples, in 1495, the date of the dissemination of the venereal disease, as fixed by many authors, we find regulations for preventing its spread. It seems probable that the inhabitants of Hispaniola may, like those of the Old World, have engendered this scourge, but it did not originate with them. It is true that, shortly after the return of Columbus from his first voyage, Europe became one vast lazar-house. But this was owing, not to the introduction of a *new* disease, but to the *increased virulence* of one already known, *consequent* upon sexual intercourse between persons of diverse races, *white* and *dark*. The disease, which before had been curable when contracted between members of the Caucasian family, when communicated by the Spaniards to the islanders of Hispaniola, and in a few days returned by the latter with interest, became, to the inhabitants of Europe, a new disease, which baffled the skill of the physician. Thus was inaugurated an "*irrepressible conflict*," or war of races, by which some of the Western islands were nearly depopulated. Many are the conjectures and explanations as to the origin of this virus. Some attempt to account for it by the use of water from poisoned wells; others, to lime mixed with the blood of diseased patients at the hospital of St. Lazarus. Phioravanti says that, in 1456, during the war between Alfonso V. of Arragon, and John, Duke of Anjou, provisions becoming scarce in both camps, the purveyors privately cut up the bodies of the slain, and dressed and sold them to the men for food; that, shortly, those who thus ate, broke out in ulcers, and, in a word, had the venereal disease. The French named this the Neapolitan disease, because they had contracted it in the kingdom of Naples. The Spanish and Italians called it the French disease, which name it bears to this day in Africa and the Turkish Empire. Some writers pronounce this scourge to be a special judgment from God, as the punishment of the wickedness of kings, priests, or people, as their peculiar notions suggest.

It is more reasonable, however, to suppose that, since the world began, the same disease has been a punishment for the transgression of the same laws (*see* Sanger on prostitution, and Ricord on venereal, for matter not here noticed).

reclaim the Holy Sepulchre, annihilate the infidel, *provided* the sovereigns will pay him well with offices, titles, riches, and honors—*without* all these he refuses to become the messenger of Christ to the New World. "He would not abate one tittle of his princely exactions." The heathen might die unconverted, and their souls be eternally damned, unless he obtain all he asked, and his demands were most exorbitant. We cannot wonder that, when the sovereigns heard this remarkably disinterested offer, it "caused them to smile" in mingled pity and contempt at the arrogance of the "pauper pilot," who proposed to raise a vast army at his own (or rather the sovereigns') expense, yet had not a maravedi wherewith to purchase a decent doublet to appear in their presence.

And if religion had little to do with his undertaking, science had still less. Notwithstanding his boasted learning in all that pertains to geography, astronomy, navigation, the form and size of our planet (and he and his biographers certainly set up high claims), he stands before the world as a deliberate falsifier of the learning of his age, in order that he may appear wise at the expense of the truth of history; and, nevertheless, succeeds in writing himself down most ignorant in the very sciences wherein he claims superhuman knowledge. We have seen his theory as to the earth's shape elsewhere. He writes:

"I affirm that the globe is not spherical."

And, to crown all his learned affirmations, he says:

"The world is but small. Out of seven divisions, the dry part occupies six, and the seventh is entirely covered by water. Experience has shown it, and I have written it with quotations from the Holy Scripture." [167]

His theories on the compass are unique:

"This morning," writes Fernando, "the Dutch compasses, varied, as they used to do, a point, and those of Genoa, that used to agree with them, varied but a very little; but afterward, sailing east, vary more, which is a sign we are one hundred leagues or more west of the Azores. . . .

"The Dutch needles varied a point, those of Genoa cutting the north-pole."

These variations Columbus attributes to the "several sorts of loadstone the needles are made by, for, till they come just to

[167] Letter to the sovereigns, July 7, 1503.

that longitude, they all varied a point, and there some held it; and those of Genoa cut the north star."

"I believe," continues this learned navigator, "the star (pole) has the quality of the four quarters, as has the needle, which, if *touched to the east side, points to the east, and so of the west and south;* and, therefore, he *that makes the compass covers the* loadstone with a cloth, all but the north part of it, viz., that which has the virtue to make steel point north."[168]

It would be difficult to imagine any thing more ambiguous and absurd than this affected science and real ignorance. This ignorance, which is so palpable to us, has not been so ignored by learned men as most biographers of Columbus would lead us to suppose. Las Casas calls him "an unlettered admiral." Humboldt says he was "a wholly unlettered seaman," and that "he was but little familiar with mathematics;" that he "made false observations in the neighborhood of the Azores," and regards him as "in absolute want of a knowledge of natural history." M. de Lorgues, a member of the Imperial Academy of Sciences, is "astonished at the ignorance of Columbus," and we have, on the same authority, that "several navigators of his time were regarded as his superiors in public opinion."

It is amusing to observe how ingeniously the admirers of Columbus pass over some circumstances, conceal or distort others, that all things may work together to prove the greatness of their hero. Witness the case of the two eclipses. The one he rightly predicts to the Indians is regarded as proof of his wonderful scientific knowledge; the miscalculation of eighteen degrees he makes in computing the other, is ascribed to his incorrect "tables of eclipse."

His biographers would have the world believe that his career of piracy was rendered reputable by reason of the alleged prevalence of that crime—that it was a fashion into which *Christian* nations had fallen—and lead us to infer that it was a popular if not a commendable vocation. The error of such a conclusion is apparent. Rienzi (the last of the tribunes) and the good people of his time were opposed to piracy, as Gibbon, in his "Decline and Fall of the Roman Empire," bears witness in the following relation:

"Martin Ursini had pillaged a shipwrecked vessel at the

[168] "Historia del Amirante," chapter lxiii.

mouth of the Tiber. His name, the purple of the two cardinals (his uncles), a recent marriage, and a mortal disease, were disregarded by the inexorable tribune who had chosen his victim. The public officers dragged him from his palace and nuptial bed. His trial was short and satisfactory. The bell of the Capitol convened the people. Stripped of his mantle, on his knees, and his hands bound behind his back, he heard the sentence of death, and, after a short confession, Ursini was led away to the gallows. After such an example, none, who were conscious of guilt, could hope for impunity, and the flight of the wicked, the licentious, and the idle, soon purified the city and territory of Rome. . . . At this time," the historian tells us, "*Rome was still the metropolis of the Christian world.*"

If such were the punishment incurred by one who had plundered an abandoned vessel, what should have been visited upon the plunderer of the Flanders galleys, the slaughterer of their crews, who had been guilty of many former piratical crimes?

How can we expect to read the truth regarding a man whose faults, ignorance, and crimes, are thus dealt with? After encountering many of these inconsistencies (and they abound in the various histories of the man) we naturally lose confidence in all the statements, particularly of a laudatory character, which these too partial historians have made.

What did Columbus originate, save fiction? Certainly not the idea of a western passage to India, for Fernando tells us that "the second motive that encouraged the admiral . . . . was the great authority of learned men who said that it was possible to sail from the western coast of Africa and Spain, westward, to the eastern bounds of India,"[199] and much more to the same purpose.

The form and size of the earth, the proportions of land and water of which it is composed, were earlier known and better understood by others than by himself; nor did he, we have shown, discover the variations of the magnetic needle. Most assuredly he did not discover America, or the islands adjacent thereto, as we have already made manifest by relating the circumstances which put him in possession of the fact that lands lay at such a distance to the west.

Gain was his great object, love of gold, not science or reli-

[199] " Historia del Amirante," chapter vii.

gion, his motive power. Gold was his god; to acquire riches he became a *pirate* and a *slave-dealer*, and the same desire prompted him to profess religion, attend mass, and repeat all the canonical hours—these were but baits wherewith he sought to catch the precious metal. He affects to believe that with gold he may purchase even the kingdom of heaven. He writes to the sovereigns:

"Gold is the most precious of all commodities; gold constitutes treasure, *and he who possesses it has all he needs in this world*, as also the means of rescuing souls from purgatory and restoring them to the enjoyments of paradise."

We do not wonder at the crimes of the man who propounds such a doctrine. Inordinate love of gold will surely steel the heart to all the noble impulses of humanity, but we must wonder that such a man should be admired and lauded; above all, that he should become a candidate for canonization.

His whole conduct relative to his "great and glorious undertaking" was deceit: he traded upon information received from one who could no longer assert his claims, and extorted the most extravagant rewards as the price of revealing such information.

The eulogists of Columbus, perceiving how obstinately he persisted in asserting that he had visited Asia, and desiring to prove him honest, even if ignorant, say that he died in the persuasion that he really had reached Asiatic India. His son, however, never supposed such to be the case, but that, "because he knew all men were sensible of the riches and wealth of India, therefore by that name he sought to tempt their Catholic majesties, by telling them he went to discover India by way of the West." This statement is apparently truthful. Columbus professed to be sailing to Asia to pour its wealth into the coffers of Spain; and what merchandise did he take with him to exchange for the precious wares of the richest lands of the earth? Glass beads! Hawk-bells! Trifles it would be an insult to offer any but the most primitive races. It must be evident to every reflective mind that such worthless baubles were never intended to be the medium of trade and barter with the enlightened merchants of the East. The idea is preposterous, and the fact that Columbus supplied himself with them shows plainly that he had not only been informed of the location of the islands he professed to discover, but also of the nature of their inhabitants. He availed himself of the protection and treasure of Spain and the Pinzons, avowedly that he might sail to India by a western passage, an idea which had been popular with the Portuguese for many years, but with the *real object* of reaching lands in the West, of the existence and situation of which he had perfect knowledge.

He would have been more than ordinarily ignorant not to have known that the latitude and longitude of the Canaries, or Fortunate Islands, as well as of the port in India to which he professed to be sailing, had been determined many centuries, and that, therefore, seven hundred and fifty leagues west of the former could not bring him to India beyond the Ganges. That he desired others to think this is, however, evident, from the shameful oath he required his men to take in the island of Cuba. Moreover, in his letter to his son Diego, in which he urges the latter to profit by the influence of Amerigo Vespucci at court, after enjoining secrecy, he says, "Let his majesty believe that his ships were in the richest and best parts of the Indies." This information, which appears to us fully to reveal the systematic deceit of Columbus, has been considerably softened by the English translators of his letter. They render "crea su majestad, *let* his majesty believe" (*crea* being the imperative of the verb), by the words "his majesty *believes*," which renders the phrase more ambiguous, and the fraud enjoined not so palpable.

The deceitful and treacherous acts of Columbus pervade his whole career. His contemporaries rarely gave credence to his statements, and he himself did not expect to be believed by those who knew him well, as is made manifest by the swinish evidence of his veracity which he thought necessary to send his men in Jamaica. Nor is this incredulity to be wondered at when we reflect upon the absurdity of many of his assertions. He laid claim to supernatural powers, and professed to believe in sorcery:

"In Cariari and the neighboring country there are great enchanters of a very fearful character."

His son tells us the Porrases persuaded their followers in Jamaica that "the coming of the caravel with news of Diego Mendez might make no impression on them. They intimated to them that it was no true caravel, but a phantom made by art-magic, the admiral being very skillful in that art."[170] We need not dwell upon the lack of dignity which Columbus's claim to such a knowledge makes evident.

The two prevailing traits of his character, hypocrisy and deceit, rarely, if ever, exist without their accompanying vices, cowardice and cruelty; and he is no exception to the rule, as the shocking cruelty with which he murdered Moxico and enslaved the Indians, the perfidy which he displayed in the capture of the chief Caonabo, with many other of his acts, will prove, while his quailing before Roldan—conferring upon him office,

CONVERSION OF THE HEATHEN.—(From De Bry's Las Casas.)

lands, slaves, and other property, giving him certificates of good character and conduct, while secretly traducing him to the sovereigns—leaves no doubt of his cowardice.

Humanity stands appalled at his frightful manifestations of cruelty, even as they are faintly portrayed by his too partial biographers. That delight in blood and thirst for gain which led him to embrace the life of a pirate and slave-catcher for the first fifty or sixty years of his life, did not abandon him when he assumed the mission of Christ-bearer.

[170] "Historia del Amirante," chapter cvi.

368 LIFE OF COLUMBUS.

If we need proof of this let us picture to ourselves, for a moment, those beautiful islands, their glowing vegetation and balmy climate, as first seen by Columbus. The peaceful and innocent inhabitants received him with childlike wonder and noble hospitality, imagining, alas! that those white-winged ships bore messengers from the skies. They eagerly tendered gifts, among which were the little ornaments of gold which were to be the cause of all their misery; for no sooner did the eyes of Columbus rest upon them, than he formed extravagant ideas of the riches he was to acquire without labor. Let us turn our eyes,

CONVERSION OF THE HEATHEN.—(From De Bry's Las Casas.)

then, upon these same beautiful islands when this blood-thirsty pirate, who blasphemously assumed the name of "Christ-bearer," had sown desolation among them; when the shrieks of the tortured, the groans of the captives who labor unceasingly, the cries of women and maidens whom husbands and fathers dare no longer protect, resound within their once peaceful shores; when he whom they had supposed a messenger from heaven, has brought among them the miseries of hell; and, as we mark the contrast, and remember how all this cruelty is wrought in the name of religion, the man Columbus inspires us with such horror and disgust that we are amazed there should exist historians who cry out with pity and indignation when he is sent from the scenes of his crimes in chains, yet find neither pity nor indignation for his thousand victims whose chains had been their least sufferings.

Let us remember, too, that, of the people whom he thus tortured and enslaved, Columbus had once written:

"So loving, so tractable, so peaceful are these people that I swear to your majesties there is not in the world a better na-

"Now (the captive cazique) being bound to the post, in order to his execution, a certain holy monk, of the Franciscan order, discoursed with him concerning God and the articles of our faith, . . . promising him eternal glory and repose if he truly believed them, or otherwise everlasting torments. After that Hathney had been silently pensive some time, he asked the monk whether the Spaniards also were admitted to heaven, and he answering that the gates of heaven were open to all that were good and godly, the cazique replied, without further consideration, that he would rather go to hell than heaven, for fear he should associate in the same mansion with so sanguinary a nation."—(LAS CASAS, "Crudelitates Hispanorum.")

tion. They love their neighbors as themselves, their discourse is ever sweet and gentle, and, though it is true they are naked, yet their manners are decorous and praiseworthy."

There are natures whose faults we admit, but whose noble qualities outbalance those faults—whose very failings seem to render them more attractive, as being rather noble excesses than defects. Truly great and noble men are often assailed by the public, and condemned by party-spirit; but we always find that those who were nearest them, seeing them daily in familiar intercourse, were devoted and admiring, alike through prosperity and adversity. Thus the weeping followers of the great Napoleon are proud to share his dreary exile on the lonely rock of St. Helena; but how different is the case with Columbus! Those who knew him the most intimately, despised him the most openly and cordially. We do not find that he stood nobly by one friend, or indeed that he ever entertained such a noble feeling as friendship. When he had obtained all that was possible from those who befriended him, they were requited by gross ingratitude or forgetfulness. Pinzon, who was the first to protect him, he repaid so cruelly as to cause that noble man to die broken-hearted. Diego Mendez, who saved his life in Jamaica, received, as reward, promises that were never fulfilled. The long list of those who associated with him in the islands is but a long list of quarrels. We look in vain through his life for any trait or action that would endear him to the hearts of men, for one deed that may be regarded as the impulse of a great and noble mind or generous heart; we find nothing but low cunning, arrogance, avarice, religious cant, deceit, and cruelty.

THE HEATHEN CONVERTED.—(From Philopono, "Nova Typis," etc., 1621.)

CHAPTER XXX.

LAWSUIT OF THE HEIRS OF COLUMBUS WITH THE CROWN.

As we have so repeatedly declared that not only did Columbus forfeit his right to the titles of viceroy, admiral, etc., by his own misconduct, but that the sovereigns were powerless to confer upon him such rank and titles in perpetuity, it may be well to note the events which took place touching his claim after his death.

CHRISTOPHER COLUMBUS.—(From an Italian Work.)

The importance of his negotiations and controversies with the sovereigns has been very much magnified; these controversies were the legitimate fruits of the ill-advised and illegal bargaining we have already recorded as taking place between Isabella and Columbus. The latter appears to have been as ignorant in law as in other matters; he had a wholesome dread of lawyers, and seems to have believed that, whatever he should succeed in inserting in his contract with the queen, would be valid. He was confident that the sovereigns had power, not only to put value upon base metal, but, as an old book hath it, "to give estimation to a mean person, by conferring upon him a mark of honor and dignity." [171]

Had his wisdom predominated over his avarice, he would have asked such reasonable compensation and reward as his services might merit, and the crown might legally promise. Such a contract could have been enforced by the courts of law, but such was not the character of the one in question. There can be little doubt that Columbus too late discovered the invalid character of his claim. We have seen how unwilling he was to have any but himself declare its import; he would not even submit the question to his tried friend, the Bishop of Palencia. The lameness of the subterfuge with which, after consenting to arbitration and selecting the arbiter, he finally declared that it was only the question of revenue [172] he was willing to submit to the decision of the latter, leaves little doubt as to the merits of the case, particularly when we find Ferdinand, though well aware of the friendship existing between the bishop and Columbus, cheerfully consenting to abide by his decision.

It is difficult to ascertain upon what basis Columbus expected the question of revenue to be decided. It depended upon the validity of the original contract; if that were void, no rents were due—but it is vain to seek logic, law, or reason, in his demands; no attention was paid to them during his lifetime, no deference shown to his opinions; new instructions were sent to Ovando, of which he was kept in ignorance. At one time, his claims were referred to the *council for the discharge of the queen's conscience*. This junta seems to have consulted, but no action was taken; it could hardly discharge the conscience of the de-

---

[171] Brydall, "Law of Nobility and Gentry," 1675, p. 58.

[172] Las Casas would excuse or explain the conduct of Columbus in this wise: "By which I understand that he did not think it necessary to put the latter point" (his titles) "in dispute, his right to it being clearly manifest." We fear that the logic of the Bishop of Chiapa is here somewhat on a par with that of Columbus, when we reflect that he comes to this conclusion well knowing that the latter had for years annoyed the court, by incessant application in person and by letter, for the recognition of his so-called rights, and that the crown had as constantly refused to reinstate him. In other words, we are called upon to believe that Columbus regarded a matter as beyond dispute which had been repeatedly decided against him, which decision he sought to reverse.

funct sovereign by reversing her judgment, and placing in power a man who had rebelled against her authority.

But, not only does it appear that Columbus's claims were unjustifiable—the contract on which they were based illegal—it is also evident that, admitting it to be just and valid, he had failed to perform what had been stipulated as its basis; had acted upon false pretenses; had traded upon knowledge received from the dead pilot; and had, moreover, so misconducted himself, that to intrust him with power or government would be a gross injustice to the people over whom he should be placed.

Notwithstanding these facts, after his death, his son Diego presented himself as heir-apparent to the honors from which his father had been deposed, and for two years preferred his claims without avail. In 1508, he resolved to enter upon a proceeding from which his father shrank, and declared to be "a controversy with the wind;" namely, to endeavor to establish his claim by law.

He therefore summoned King Ferdinand to appear before the Council of the Indies, and show cause why he, the said Diego, should not be inducted into the offices and honors from which his father had been ejected. We have not been able to learn that this body possessed judicial powers—we believe it did not; certainly it could not legally try the most important suit "the world has ever witnessed," as too partial historians are wont to term it. The crown, however, appears to have waived the question of jurisdiction, and to have consented to plead to the merits of the case, even before an inferior commission.

The royal plea appears to have been in itself sufficient to determine the case against Columbus in any court of law or equity. It was as follows:

1. That, if the contract of 1492 purported to grant to Columbus, or his heirs, the viceroyalty and admiralty in perpetuity, such grant was void, being hostile to the best interests of the state, and in violation of a solemn statute enacted and promulgated at Toledo in 1480, wherein it was ordained that no office involving the administration of justice should be granted in perpetuity; therefore, that these powers and privileges could only be granted to Columbus during his lifetime, and had been most justly taken from him during that period on account of his cruelty and disloyalty.

2. That such grants were contrary to, and in excess of, the inherent prerogative of the crown, and subversive of the rights of the Cortes and people, of which the latter could not be divested."[173]

This royal plea appears to strike at the root of the matter, and to have been unanswerable. In it the acts of the crown are subjected to the solemn test of the law, and Ferdinand declares the act of the late queen to be void in the eye of the law.

To this Diego made replication that "the contract was binding," but cited neither law nor precedent by which to sustain his replication, for the reason, we suppose, that none existed. "As to the allegation that his father had been deprived of his viceroyalty for his demerits, it was false, and his being sent from the islands by Bobadilla was audacious." Such is his extremely legal and forcible response, a somewhat "audacious" one, as it will be remembered that Bobadilla had performed no acts for which he had not royal authority, and that his conduct had been tacitly approved by Isabella, as she neither reinstated Columbus in power, nor consented that he should return to Hispaniola.

It needs no very expert lawyer to perceive that such a replication could not have the least weight in a legal decision, as it was not sustained by judicial authority; while the plea of the crown was unanswerable, because founded upon *the supreme law of the land*.

Another question, however, was agitating the public mind, and seemed to strike at the rights of Spain. It was very generally asserted that Columbus had not been the first to discover these lands: contemporary writers not only claimed this honor for living navigators, but actively *revived the memory of the dead pilot*.[174] These assertions, if proved correct, would have made manifest the fact that Spain had obtained the lands by fraud, and that Alexander VI. had granted the deed, and drawn the famous line of demarcation *on the false testimony of Columbus*.

The crown, perfectly secure against the claims of Diego, on the strength of the above plea, wisely considered it to her interests that the latter should make out a case, which, while securing to Spain all the advantages accruing from the falsehoods and

---

[173] Ferdinand had, moreover, been required to take the royal oath which forbade him to nominate *a foreigner* to office.

[174] Spotorno, "Historia Memoria," p. 29; Irving, Appendix No. 2.

treachery of Columbus, could not materially benefit his heirs. For this, Ferdinand considered the present a fit opportunity, and, while largely interested in Columbus's being proclaimed the original discoverer, he asserts that he was not, in order to enable Diego to prove that he was.

About one hundred witnesses were examined. The final decision was in favor of Columbus, the testimony being, according to most historians, "overwhelmingly in his favor." We may, however, be permitted to doubt the truth of this assertion, notwithstanding the ultimate decision, which was, as we have said, in accordance with the real wishes of Ferdinand.

We have not, like Mr. Irving, had the advantage of examining the original documents of this suit. It may, however, be presumed that Navarrete, whose "Coleccion Diplomatica" of all papers relating to the discoveries, was made with the avowed object of still further establishing the glory of Columbus, has given a tolerably complete *résumé* of the testimony, and that, if any hiatus exists, it is not the result of the omission of any thing favorable to the cause of the latter. This testimony we have carefully examined, and cannot agree with those historians who declare it to be "overwhelmingly in favor of Columbus." Notwithstanding their assertion, and the ultimate decision by the Council of the Indies in favor of his son, we rather regard it as proving how small a part of the glory or merits of the enterprise he was entitled to. No history written in the English language has heretofore considered it necessary to give this testimony to the public—the eulogists of Columbus wisely considered it could not but be detrimental to his cause in the eyes of an intelligent reader. They have, therefore, contented themselves with recording their perusal of it, and declaring it to be overwhelmingly in favor of their hero.

While the testimony taken by the *fiscal* (an officer who appears to have occupied a position combining the duties of an attorney-general and solicitor of the treasury) is pertinent, ample, and circumstantial, much of it tending to completely overturn the popular belief with regard to Columbus, the testimony on the part of Diego is as vague, irrelevant, and impertinent, as are his interrogatories. The witnesses examined for the crown are also men of some status, testifying to what they have seen and know; while those examined for Diego are, with one or two exceptions, ignorant men, who generally testify to what they have *heard* said. The important parts, indeed nearly the whole of this testimony, has been disregarded, either by accident or design, by the mass of historians, which leads us to suppose that their partiality is not altogether unwitting.

We have said the crown was most desirous (even at the sacrifice of being *apparently* defeated by a subject) to have the claims of Columbus, as prior discoverer, established. There is one circumstance connected with this lawsuit which strongly supports our statement. Vespucci, the learned cosmographer and navigator, the one man who could best have shattered Columbus's pretensions to having been the first to visit *terra firma*, *was not summoned* as a witness, when sailors before the mast, and ignorant men, were made to testify. The maligners of Vespucci seek to prove by this that he was little thought of; that the idea of his being the first to reach America was too preposterous to have been entertained; for, say they, had he been the discoverer, had the voyages he relates in his letters been really made, the crown, so largely interested in disproving Columbus's claims, would have called him as a witness. This reasoning is, however, erroneous; it assumes the crown to have been, in truth, interested in, and desirous of, annihilating the claims of Columbus. This was evidently not the case, for Amerigo was not examined, and the omission to do so was not owing to his being considered of too little importance, or to the knowledge or belief that he had not visited *terra firma* before Columbus; for he was, at that time, filling a most important office in recognition of the services he had rendered during his voyages: he had been appointed, not only surveyor-general of coasts in the new lands, but inspector and corrector of charts; all former charts had been *abolished* (Columbus's among the number), and a penalty imposed upon pilots sailing by any others than those made or authorized by Vespucci. This amply proves, not only the esteem in which his maritime knowledge and experience were held, but also that the counsel for the crown would not have overlooked him, had the latter been in truth anxious to overthrow the claims of Columbus; and that the forgetfulness was, therefore, intentional.

In view of these facts, and as a sample of the pertinence and validity of the testimony in favor of Columbus, we may cite that of Francisco Morales, styled by Irving "one of the best and most creditable of all the pilots," who, notwithstanding what we have already stated as to charts of the new lands, and Vespucci's supervision of them, testified that he had seen a sea-chart, made by Columbus, of the coast of Paria, and "*he believed all governed themselves by it.*"

The testimony taken by the *fiscal* is extremely interesting—it gives us an insight into the opinions entertained of Columbus and other voyagers by the people who sailed with them; it brings forward, in bold relief, the noble qualities of that generous victim of Columbus's ingratitude and avarice, Martin Alonzo Pinzon; it is from this source that we learn to what an extent Columbus was indebted to him; we find here a corroboration of the story of the *dead pilot*, and proof that *Columbus sailed by a chart* in which a certain route was laid down, *not on a voyage of discovery*, the results of which were vague and uncertain; we also learn how unjustly the mariner, Rodrigo de Triana, who first sighted land, was deprived of his reward.

All this is related in the most circumstantial manner by the various witnesses, who, as they relate minute occurrences, repeat portions of conversation, give a life-like and truthful coloring to their testimony, while the witnesses for Diego, with a few exceptions, merely affirm or deny in general terms, as his interests demand. As examples of interest, we may take the following:

Fourteenth interrogatory for the crown, which requires the witnesses to affirm or deny "whether they know that, after going to court, the admiral returned to Palos, where he found none who would give him ships, nor crews who would accompany him, and that the said Martin Alonzo, to serve their highnesses, gave him his two ships, and determined to go with him, with his relations and friends, because the said admiral promised him the half of all the privileges that their highnesses had promised if land were found, and had shown him the said privileges."

Eight witnesses testify to a knowledge of the above facts. A fair sample of all the testimony is that of Diego Penton, who testifies that "he knows the above, because he saw and was present; but whether Martin Alonzo gave his ships, because the admiral showed his privileges, this witness knows not, for he saw them go on the voyage, and knows that the said Martin Alonzo

Pinzon went with the said admiral, and this he knows, that, but for him, the said admiral had not gone then to discover."

The fifteenth interrogatory requires the witnesses to testify whether they know that on the voyage the admiral, not finding land where he had expected, asked Martin Alonzo what they should do.

Twelve witnesses testify more or less minutely to the points made in this interrogatory. Francisco Vallejo says that, "being two hundred leagues, more or less, distant from land, after leaving the Canaries, the Admiral Don Cristobal Colon spoke with all the captains, and with the said Martin Alonzo, and said to them, 'What shall we do?' This was on the 6th of October, of the year '92, and said: 'Captains, what shall we do, for my people complain bitterly? What do you advise?' And that then Vincent Yanez said: 'Let us go forward, sir, two thousand leagues, and, if then we find not what we are in search of, we may return.' Then said Martin Alonzo Pinzon, *who went as chief captain*: 'How, sir? We have but just left the town of Palos, and already you are discouraged! Forward, sir! God will give us victory! God forbid that we should return with such shame!' Then answered the said admiral, Don Christopher Columbus, 'May good fortune attend you!' And thus, through the said Martin Alonzo Pinzon, they went forward."

The seventeenth interrogatory requires the witness to testify "whether the said admiral asked Martin Alonzo whether they were pursuing a right course, and that the said Martin Alonzo said *no;* that he had many times told him that they were not going right, but that they should tack to the southwest, and would then find the land; and that the said admiral answered, 'Let us do so!' and that they then changed the course, by the advice of Martin Alonzo Pinzon, who was a man very learned in matters pertaining to the sea."

Of ten witnesses who testify to the above, the most succinct is Francis Garcia Vallejo, who says that "he was present and heard Martin Alonzo Pinzon say to the said admiral on this voyage, 'Sir, in my opinion, we should steer to the southwest; we shall then find land'—that the said Admiral Don Christopher Columbus answered: 'Let it be so, Martin Alonzo; let us do so'—and that then, by the advice of Martin Alonzo, they changed the course to the southwest; and he knows it was by the advice and industry of the said Martin Alonzo, because he was a man very learned in sea-matters; and all this he knows because he was present."

Again, it is proved by answers to the eighteenth interrogatory that, three or four days after the said change of course directed by Martin Alonzo, the island of Guanahani was reached. To this fifteen witnesses testify.

Nor do we fail to find, in the testimony of this lawsuit, evidence of the petty spite to which Columbus could descend. It is therein asserted that, Martin Alonzo having given his name to a river in Hispaniola, "the admiral changed the name of the said river and port, because the said Martin Alonzo had discovered it, and that there might remain no remembrance of him; nor would he allow any of his crew to call the port Martin Alonzo, but Puerto de Gracio, that there might be no memorial of Martin Alonzo, discoverer of the island of Hispaniola."

The extracts we have given are samples of the general character of the testimony, as the reader may ascertain by a perusal of the whole, as contained in Navarrete.

The Council of the Indies, however, decided the case in favor of Diego; but were the results such as would have accrued had the decision been given by a court of law powerful against, as well as for, the crown? In other words, were they such as to lead us to suppose the decision had been given, in spite of the prestige and power of the sovereign, by a court able to enforce the execution of its decrees? They were not. The Council of the Indies decided that Columbus was the first discoverer. This legalized and set at rest the claim of Spain to the lands said to have been discovered, but the plaintiff was in no wise benefited by the decision in his favor—he still continued penniless, still importuned humbly and in vain; he was neither recognized viceroy, nor did he touch any of the revenue, nor enter into any of the offices which would have been his, maugre any resistance on the part of Ferdinand, had his lawsuit been a valid one.

It was to a totally different cause that he owed the final recognition of his claims—he married into the family of Alva. The members of this proud house were powerful as proud, and, through their influence, the much-coveted titles of viceroy and admiral were accorded to the husband of their kinswoman; but these titles were shorn of any thing approaching the power they would seem to imply.

Ovando was recalled, and Diego and his wife, his half-brother Fernando, and his uncles Bartholomew and Diego, set sail for the new lands in 1509. The prestige of the lady's high birth and influential friends surrounded them with a numerous retinue, composed largely of young damsels, who, possessed of more rank than fortune, were about to seek rich husbands in the Western islands.

Diego appears to have inherited his father's quarrelsome and tyrannous disposition. His administration, restricted as was his power, soon became oppressive and odious, so that, within a few months of his arrival, a tribunal (entitled the Royal Audience) was established, to which appeals from the government might be taken.

Diego, autocratic and unreasonable, resented this as an infringement upon his rights. He became involved in lawsuit after lawsuit with the *fiscal*, so that Herrera declares "he might truly say he was heir to the troubles of his father," to which may be added that he was no less an heir to those vices of his father of which the troubles were a natural consequence.

At length the difficulties became so serious that Diego asked leave to appear at court and defend himself. His request was granted, and in 1515 he returned to Spain, where he remained five years, at the end of which time he was again allowed to return to the islands; but he had not been long at the head of affairs when he was charged with a design to usurp the government and throw off allegiance to Spain—a charge which appears to have been sufficiently well founded for the Council of the Indies to consider it necessary, not only severely to reprimand him, but also to command him, under penalty of forfeiting all his privileges, to place matters of government as they were under Ovando. This order was to be proclaimed and enforced by officers of the crown, in the island, even though Diego should refuse to regard it. The latter was ordered home to give an account of his stewardship. Regarding the recall as peremptory, he obeyed, and remained in Spain, where, till his death, in 1526, he wearied the court with requests similar to those of his father, and for like reasons as fruitless.

His infant son Luis, aged six years, was declared Admiral of the Indies. This lad, on reaching the age of reason, appears to have had more good sense and a truer perception of the state of affairs, and the legitimate extent of his claims, than his progenitors. He wisely gave up all pretensions to viceroyalty and revenue, and remained in Spain, receiving in lieu of these the title of Duke of Veragua and Marquis of Jamaica, with a pension of a thousand doubloons of gold. He died leaving no legitimate issue, and henceforth the Columbos are engaged in litigation among themselves, till, in 1608, the Council of the Indies declared the male line to be extinct, and Nuño or Nugno Gelves de Portogallo, grandson of Isabella, third daughter of Diego, son of Christopher Columbus, was invested with the titles and pension aforesaid.

Thus, Time, which is, in the main, just, settled at last the question which had so vexed the pirate admiral during his brief day, in a manner somewhat compatible with its merits. Had Columbus, in the inception, stipulated for possibilities, the validity of his contract would probably never have been questioned; he would not have sunk to the depth of misery and degradation in which death overtook him, nor would an enthusiastic throng of eulogists have been called upon to place him among the noble army of martyrs. Yet, as he deceitfully took advantage of the information received or purloined from the unfortunate pilot who died in his house at Madeira; as he took to himself all the merit and honors of the enterprise, recognizing and acknowledging neither the source of his knowledge nor the assistance he received from contemporaries, he was, we think, as deserving of his fate as he is undeserving of the plaudits of posterity.

For three hundred years his fame has steadily increased. It has reached its culmination; and already, from more than one quarter, reaction in favor of truth has made itself felt.

Though the writer was, perhaps, the first in the field, and may have more thoroughly and exhaustively than another examined into the case of Columbus *versus* his contemporaries, with a view of seeing some justice done to the latter, yet he has not been quite alone—other and powerful blows have been struck at the idol which the imagination and superstition of generations, with the assistance of ecclesiastical power, have erected. The field is a fresh and fruitful one. Coming research will every year, the author is convinced, confirm the statements and justify the reasoning contained in this work, which is the imperfect fruit of several years' study and research devoted to the subject.

PORTRAIT OF COLUMBUS.—(From a German Work.)

APPENDIX.

A RECAPITULATION of the works consulted by the author in the preparation of this volume would unnecessarily swell its proportions; it may suffice to say that he has, during a period of more than seven years, had access to many of the best libraries of Western Europe, especially the Bibliothèque Impériale, Paris; the British Museum, London; Bibliothèque Royale, Brussels; together with the valuable collections at Venice, Naples, Milan, Turin, Florence, etc., etc.

In the preparation of that portion of Chapter II. which treats of the mariner's compass, the author was aided by an Oriental scholar of great erudition, whose name he has not authority to mention, but whose learning and valuable assistance are held in grateful remembrance.

THE ILLUSTRATIONS.

It was the intention of the author, at one time, to have published this work in London. To this end the illustrations (with the exception of those on pages 250 and 270) were made in Belgium (some designed, others copied, and all engraved) by the late Wm. Brown, of Brussels. Some of those copied would seem, from the peculiarity of their subjects, or of the works from which they have been taken, to deserve some slight mention or explanation.

The cuts upon pages 69, 76, 83–89, are chiefly copies from earlier works upon the Northmen.

On page 96 is illustrated the account given by Fernando Columbus (in his "Historia del Amirante," chapter ii.) of the destruction of a polyglot edition of the Psalter, published at Genoa in 1516. Among other reasons alleged for the destruction of the writings of Giustiniani, besides that of calling Columbus a mechanic, Fernando charges him with telling "thirteen lies;" though, in a majority of the cases cited by him, the truth appears to have been on the side of the author of the Psalter. For instance, says Fernando: "He" (Giustiniani) "charges that the admiral took, by force of arms, on his first voyage, a canoe or Indian boat he saw, *whereas it appears that he had no war the first voyage with any Indians, and continued in peace and amity with them till the day of his departure from Hispaniola.*"

After the above statement, made avowedly in the vindication of sacred truth, it is refreshing to turn to the self-constituted vindicator's thirty-sixth chapter, the heading of which reads: "*Of the first skirmish between the Christians and Indians, which happened about the gulf of Samana, in Hispianola,*" and which forms a part of his account of the first voyage. The skirmish in question took place on *Sunday*, and appears to have been one of the Sabbath-day diversions of the pious admiral.

Fernando writes: "On Sunday, the 13th of January, being near the cape called *Enamorado*, the admiral sent the boat ashore, where our men found some Indians, with fierce countenances, on the shore, with bows and arrows, who seemed to be ready to engage, but, at the same time, were in a consternation. However, having some conference with them, they bought two of their bows and arrows, and with much difficulty prevailed to have one of them go aboard the Admiral." A party of men were sent on shore. "When our men landed, the Indian that had been aboard made the others lay down their bows and arrows, and a great cudgel they carry instead of a sword; for, as has been said, they have no iron at all. When they came to the boat, the Christians stepped ashore, and, having begun to trade for bows and arrows by order of the admiral, the Indians, who had already sold two, not only refused to sell any more, but, with scorn, made as if they would seize the Christians, and ran to their bows and arrows where they had left them, taking up with them ropes to bind our men. They, being upon their guard, seeing them come in that fury, though they were but seven, fell courageously upon them, and cut one with a sword on the buttock, and shot another with an arrow in the breast. The Indians, astonished at the resolution of our men, and the wounds our weapons made, fled most of them, leaving their bows and arrows; and many of them had been killed, had not the pilot of the caravel, who commanded the boat, protected them. The admiral was not at all displeased at this skirmish, imagining these were the Caribs all the other Indians so much dreaded, or that at least they bordered on them, they being a bold and resolute people, as appeared by their aspect, arms, and actions; and he hoped that the islanders, hearing how seven Christians had behaved themselves against fifty-five fierce Indians of that country, would the more respect and honor our men that were left behind at Nativity."

Thus it is evident that it was *he*, Fernando, and not Giustiniani, who in this case spoke falsely.

The seventh lie charged by Fernando is, that he stated that the admiral "returned by way of the Canary Islands, which is not the proper way for those vessels to return;" *yet he did so return*, as appears by the following extract:

"God gives victory to all those who walk in his paths, as is clear in this case. I have now found and seen the islands of which so many fables have been told. Next to God, I am most indebted to the King and Queen of Spain. The discovery is so great that the whole of Christendom ought to keep festivals and praise the Holy Trinity. An immense number of people will be converted to the Christian faith. Moreover, great material gains will be obtained. On the 2d they had frost and hail-storms in the Canary Islands.—Calavera, on the Canary Islands, 15th February (1493)."

"P. S.—Encountered such a storm on the Spanish seas, that I was obliged to lighten the ships by throwing the cargo overboard. Have been fortunate enough to gain the port of Lisbon. Will write to the King and Queen of Castile.—March 14 (1493)."—(*Christopher Columbus to the Escribano de Racion of the Islands of the Indies.*)

The eighth lie is made chiefly to grow out of the statement of Giustiniani that the admiral sent a messenger to the Spanish sovereigns, informing them of his discoveries and return, while "he himself was the messenger," says Fernando ("Historia del Amirante," chapter ii.). But, in chapter xl. of the same work, we read: "He" (the admiral) "came to an anchor in the river of Lisbon upon Monday, the 4th of March, *and presently sent away an express to their Catholic Majesties with the news of his arrival.*"

The tenth lie charged by Fernando is, that Giustiniani stated that the admiral "arrived in Hispaniola in twenty days, which is a very short time to reach the nearest island, and he performed it not in two months," etc., etc.

Columbus, in a letter to the sovereigns, writes as follows: "My passage from Cadiz to the Canaries occupied four days, and thence to the Indies, from which I wrote, sixteen days."

Fernando continues:

"So that, by his negligence and heedlessness in being well informed, and writing the truth of these particulars, which are so plain, we may easily discern what inquiry he made into that which was so obscure, wherein he contradicts himself, as has been made to appear. But, laying aside this controversy, wherewith, I believe, I have by this time tired the reader, we will only add that, considering the many mistakes and falsehoods found in the said Giustiniani's history and Psalter, the Senate of Genoa has laid a penalty upon any person that shall read or keep it; and has caused it to be carefully sought out in all places it has been sent to, that it may, by public decree, be destroyed and utterly extinguished. I will return to our main design, concluding with this assertion, that the admiral was a man of learning and great experience; that he did not employ his time in handicraft or mechanic exercises, but in such as became the grandeur and renown of his wonderful exploits; and will conclude this chapter with some words taken out of a letter he wrote himself to Prince John of Castile's nurse, which are these: 'I am not the first admiral of my family; let them give me what name they please; for, when all is done, David, that most prudent king, was first a shepherd, and afterward chosen King of Jerusalem, and I am servant of that same Lord who raised him to such dignity.'"

As the reader may wish to know more of the obnoxious writings of Giustiniani, we make the following extracts from his note in the Psalter to the fourth verse of the nineteenth psalm, referred to on pages 94 and 95 of this work:

"Now, as Columbus often declared himself to be chosen of God, that through him should be fulfilled this prophecy, I have thought it not inappropriate to insert here some account of his life. Christopher, surnamed Columbus, of the state of Genoa, born of low parentage, it was who, in our time, by his industry, explored, in a few months, more of land and ocean than almost all the rest of mortals in all by-gone ages. This wonderful fact rests not on the testimony of some vessels, but has been investigated and proved by the passing and repassing of whole fleets and armies. Columbus, in his boyish years having been taught just the lowest rudiments of learning, as he grew up, devoted himself to navigation (i. e., *piracy*). Afterward, his brother having gone to Portugal, and set up at Lisbon in the business of drawing maps for the use of mariners, representing the seas, coasts, and harbors, Columbus in this way learned from him the configuration of the coasts and the position of the islands, which his brother had probably ascertained from many persons who were in the habit of going every year from Portugal, by royal authority, to explore the unknown lands of Ethiopia, and the remote shores of the ocean between the south and west, he being often in conversation with them. . . . As soon as Columbus was sufficiently exactly made aware of these things" (*here we have a glimpse of the history of the dead pilot*), "he at length made known to certain grandees of the court of Spain what he had in contemplation, stipulating, however, that suitable provision should be made by the king, and to be prompt in doing it, *before the Portuguese should make their preparations to go among these new peoples*, and penetrate fresh regions hitherto unknown. The intelligence of this scheme was promptly communicated to the king, who, both from jealousy of the Portuguese and from ambition of this sort of honor of new discoveries, and of the glories which would accrue to him and his successors from this enterprise, was *allured* into the negotiation with Columbus; and, after it had lasted a long time, he commanded two vessels to be equipped. With these Columbus, setting out, steered to the Fortunate Islands; thence he took his departure, navigating a very little off the west line to the left, between southwest and west; when farther out, however, farther from southwest, and almost due west. When the voyage had continued a great many days, and, by their reckoning, they had already made four thousand miles (say twenty-five hundred English) in a direct line, the rest of the company lost hope, and desired to turn back; but he persisted in the enterprise, and, as far as he could judge, he undertook to promise that they were not more than one day's navigation from some continental lands or islands. His words did not fail to be realized. . . ." Here follows a more or less correct account of the islands discovered and their inhabitants, of Columbus's return to Spain and departure on his second voyage, when, continues Giustiniani, "Spain now sent out into a hitherto innocent world the poison of its vices, pride, and debauchery; not content with their triumph in this our continent, sailed away in quest of hitherto pure and harmless nations, and the woods which could barely satisfy our greed, being, as it were, exhausted by incessant hunting; sent forth into the most remote regions that wild-boar, among those whose appetites had till now been without excitement. But there also sailed those who could heal, by the art of Æsculapius, the people of the diseases that were to come upon them—the prey of lust and avarice (*see* note 166). They also carried out seeds and shoots of trees; but wheat, as was afterward ascertained, wherever sown, grew first to a great height immediately, and shortly afterward withered and vanished away, as if Nature condemned

APPENDIX. 387

the use of new kinds of food, and commanded them to be content with their roots."

These extracts may serve to give an idea of some of the earlier written histories of Columbus.

To return to the illustration on page 96, it may be well to add that the scenes represented on either side of the burning Psalter are copied from curious carved representations of tortures of the period of Columbus, which are preserved at the Musée of the Porte de Halle, at Brussels, Belgium.

AMERIGO VESPUCCI.

The portrait of Amerigo Vespucci on page 125 is, beyond question, a correct one; the fact that *all* the efforts, bearing a master's touch, whether sculptured, cast, painted, or engraved, purporting to represent him, are critically identical, would seem to vouch for its truthfulness, on the same principle as the non-similarity of all purported likenesses of Columbus would seem to prove their falsity. The late Mr. Brown, as well as the school to which he belonged, regarded it as authentic. It is believed that there is now in the United States an original portrait of this great man, painted from life by an Italian artist; that this portrait was until recently carefully preserved and much prized by the descendants of Vespucci, of which there is an *unwritten history*.

PORTRAIT IN THE BIBLIOTHÈQUE IMPÉRIALE.

On page 150 is one of the many *pretended* portraits of the so-called Christopher Columbus; it is from an engraving in the Bibliothèque Impériale, Paris, and is declared by many to be genuine.

From such study of his character as we have been able to make, we incline to the belief that this *creation* is more just to the subject than any we have consulted. Here "the great navigator" is clad and adorned, so far as we may judge, in an *appropriate* manner; beneath is appended a fac-simile of that remarkable signature by which he wrote himself down "THE CHRIST-BEARER." Though a hundred would not exaggerate the list of these *pretended* portraits, we have in this work reproduced but eight, believing that as these, though dissimilar in appearance, are all declared to be genuine, the reader may as rightly judge from them as from the hundred we do not reproduce. We shall only notice, in their order, such of those comprised in this work as have been the subject of special mention or controversy.

THE CHRIST-BEARER.

The apparently somewhat irreverent illustration on page 153 is a portrait of Columbus in his self-styled character of "Christ-bearer," copied from an old religious work wherein Columbus is greatly glorified. In this scene the pious artist seems to have symbolized, as clearly as possible, the *name, person, pretended character, attributes*, and *mission*, of our hero. A statue similar in design adorns one of the streets of Brussels.

The DOVE, typifying the HOLY GHOST, as it appeared at the baptism of

Stt John, is especially significant in connection with the subject of the engraving, who, when changing his name on abandoning his piratical career, appears to have thought that he might as well assume one which should in every way typify his pretended mission; and from the sacred symbol of the *dove*, called in Latin COLUMBA, and undergoing but slight variation in different languages, our hero not only *took his name*, but would lay claim to Divine ordination. "*He also carried the olive-branch and oil of baptism over the waters of the ocean*, LIKE NOAH'S DOVE."—(*See* FERNANDO, " Ilistoria del Amirante," chapter i.)

BUST OF COLUMBUS AT GENOA (PAGE 151).

Thinking it might be of interest to the reader to know how the *portraits*, as well as the *character*, of Columbus are invented, we copy the following satisfactory and dogmatical mode of treating the subject by Spotorno; the italics are ours:

"Girolamo Benzone, *who, although he never saw Columbus*, speaks of him with such minuteness, that it is evident he either copied some authentic account, or derived his information from the *viva-voce* details of Spaniards who had sailed with Columbus, gives the following account: 'He was a man of reasonably good stature, of strong and active body, sound judgment, lofty understanding, and agreeable aspect; he had sparkling eyes, red hair, aquiline nose, and rather large mouth; above all, he was a friend to justice, but passionate when provoked.'

"These particulars, which I communicated to the sculptor, *directed his hand and mind;* and his production has succeeded in obtaining distinguished praise from the connoisseurs of the fine arts. *Every one possessed of a grain of understanding, after seeing this head, which expresses the living and true lineaments of the hero, will throw aside every other portrait;* and especially that engraved on wood given in the 'Eulogies' of Giovio, in which the discoverer of America is represented with a hood and prelate's gown, as if he had been a conventual friar, or a hermit of St. Augustin." (SPOTORNO, "Introduction," pages cli., clii.)

MEN WITH DOGS' HEADS, ETC.

The illustration on page 210 represents the men with dogs' heads, tails, the lions, tigers, and griffins, which Columbus professed to have seen in the Western Hemisphere.

COLUMBUS AND HIS EGG (PAGE 225).

The curious contend that the story of the egg, illustrations of which have adorned so many works of art and letters, is symbolized on the shield or arms of the Columbos, as represented on page 225. Ridiculous as this affair certainly is, it has been made to appear, perhaps with some propriety, as one of the crowning efforts of the genius of the "great navigator;" it certainly is not more absurd than many of his well-authenticated exploits, and may, on the whole, tend to elevate and adorn the character of this great man; the fact that it was, like the log-book of Alonzo Sanchez, purloined from the dead, would seem to vindicate its fitness as an embellishment to the character of Columbus, while its *antiquity* at his birth will admirably accord with the studied confusion of dates found in most works which treat of him. His would-be canonizers, however, reject this story as trivial and absurd, and M. De Lorgues thus relegates the anecdote to its true source:

"It was with this solemn banquet (*supposed to have been given by Cardinal Mendoza*) that some have connected the anecdote of the egg, that insipid story to which the memory of Columbus probably owes its greatest popularity in Europe.

"One of the party, it is said, having asked him whether, if he had not discovered the Indies, some other person would not have done so, as his only response the admiral ordered an egg to be brought him, and proposed that it should be made to stand on one end on the table. One after the other of the guests tried in vain; then he took it, and, breaking it a little on one extremity, made it stand on the flattened one. Such, in substance, is the story as it is told. Washington Irving hesitates not to give it credit. To surpass him, no doubt, M. de Lamartine has this farce acted at the very table of King Ferdinand.

"We will not waste our time in demonstrating the absurdity of this tale, by its utter improbability. In the first place, it is without sense or wit; it proves nothing, it explains nothing. No consequence to the point can be inferred from it. It is no more an answer than it is an allusion; and presents, on the whole, but a gross piece of trickery. It was not by breaking an egg at the end, when the question was how to maintain it by its own equilibrium, that the admiral showed the cause of the discovery. It was not by this low artifice, this want of delicacy, that he would show his superiority of genius and of perseverance. Would Columbus have explained the favors with which Providence had loaded him, and justified the truth of his theory, by a juggler's trick? and, still more, by a clumsy trick, not to say an unfair one? The circumstances of time and place tend no less to contradict this silly story. Who would have dared, whether at the table of the sovereigns or at that of the grand-cardinal, to propose so impertinent a question to the Viceroy of the Indies? Who would have ventured a question that would be as disobliging as it would be disrespectful? And how could the admiral have forgotten the rules of etiquette (*supposing the 'unlettered seaman' could forget what he never knew*) to the point of giving orders to his august host, and ask that an egg be brought him? Was this sport compatible with the number and the dignity of the guests? None of the Spanish historians have mentioned such a circumstance. The Milanese Girolamo Benzoni, the only old historian who relates this miserable story, was, no doubt, unable to distinguish his former recollections from each other. At any rate, the anecdote of the egg is most positively of Italian origin; we recognize it as such, and we have every reason to believe that Columbus must have heard it from the lips of his own mother. With some probability it has been attributed to the celebrated architect Brunelleschi, by whom the church of Santa Maria del Fiore raises its cupola into the sky of Florence. Here the fact does not seem improbable, however trifling it may appear. Around a joyous table at a tavern, Florentine artists may come to these bantering questions, to these jugglings, where jesting holds the place of reason, and where one can avail himself of 'pill and poll,' rather than of logic. At such a table we can easily conceive such a trivial trick to be played, but not elsewhere. Before us Voltaire has said that the story of the egg was related of Brunelleschi ('Essai sur les Mœurs,' chapter cxlix.). Upon this point we are entirely of his opinion."—(DE LONGUES, vol. i., book i., chapter xi.)

It is curious to discover, however, that this trick, or mode of argument, did not originate even with Brunelleschi. The story of the egg is infinitely less witty, and seems to lose all point by the side of the following anecdote, which refers to a knight of the time of the Crusades: It was at Cardiff Castle, in Wales, according to an old Welsh chronicle, that Sir Foulk Fitzwarren was speaking of toils encountered and hardships endured in warring with the Saracens, and his knights murmured, and each one said he could have done as much as their chief had done. "But," said Sir Foulk, "these were nothing to one feat I accomplished." "What was that?" quoth they all. "I jumped," answered the knight, "from the ground to the top of yonder tower of my castle, which you know to be the tallest tower in these parts." So they laughed scornfully, and gainsayed his words. "If," said the knight, "you will dine with me at noonday to-morrow, I will do it once again." So every one of the knights came to the feast; and, when they had well eaten and drunken, "Now come," said Sir Foulk, "with me, and you shall see me jump from the ground to the top of the castle-tower." They proceeded to the foot of the stairs, and Sir Foulk jumped to the top of the first step, then on to another, and so on until upon the topmost step. "Oh!" said the knights, "we could do that ourselves." "So you could," said Sir Foulk, "now I have taught you the way to do it."

Thus it is that not only history, but gossip and trivial anecdote repeat themselves; verily, *there is no new thing under the sun!* As usual, in such cases as the one we speak of, the imitation falls far short of the original in pith and point.

THE MANATI.

The fish or animal in the illustration, taken from Philopono, which appears on page 227 of this work, is less apocryphal than this curious representation of it would lead us to suppose. The latter furnishes an instance of how difficult it is to delineate correctly from mere written description, or rather, perhaps, a proof of how largely the imagination was drawn upon in writing the history of the period and lands of which we treat. As the following quaint and interesting passage, however, from Peter Martyr, has apparently furnished the matter for a description of the manati (a specimen of which is now to be seen in Central Park, New York) in a late magazine for the instruction of youth, and, as the modern author, with the creature before him, has not found it necessary to deviate materially from the description given by the Italian scholar, we have thought the original might interest the curious:

"The king of this region, named Caramatexius, taketh great pleasure in fishing. Into his nets chanced a young fish, of the kind of those monsters of the sea which the inhabitors called manati. . . . This fish is four-footed, and in shape like unto a tortoise, although she be not covered with a shell, but with scales, and those of such hardness that no arrow can hurt her. Her scales are beset and defended with a thousand knobs, her back is plain, and her head utterly like the head of an ox. She liveth both in the water and on the land, is slow of moving, of condition meek, gentle, loving to mankind, and of marvelous sense of memory, as are the elephant and the dolphin. The king nourished this fish certain days at home with the bread of the country, made of yucca and panycke, and with such other roots as men are accustomed to eat, for, when she was yet young, he cast her into a pool or lake near unto his palace, there to be fed with the hand. This lake also receiveth waters and casteth not the same forth again; it was in time past called Guarabo, but is now called the Lake of Manati, after the name of this fish, which wandered safely in the same for the space of twenty-five years, and grew exceeding big. Whatsoever is written of the dolphins of Baian or Arion are much inferior to the doings of this fish, which, for her gentle nature, they named Matum, that is, gentle or noble; therefore, whensoever any of the king's familiars, especially such as are known to her, resort to the banks of the lake and call 'Matum! Matum!' then she (as mindful of such benefits as she hath received of men) lifteth up her head and cometh to the place whither she is called, and there receiveth meat at the hands of such as feed her. If any desire to pass over the lake, and make signs and tokens of their intent, she boweth herself to them, thereby, as it were, gently inviting them to mount upon her, and conveyeth them safely over. It hath been seen that this monstrous fish hath at one time safely carried over ten men, singing and playing. But if, by chance, when she lifted up her head, she espied any of the Christian men, she would immediately plunge down again into the water, and refuse to obey, because she had once received injury at the hands of a certain wanton young man among the Christians, who had cast a sharp dart at her, although she were not hurt by reason of the hardness of her skin—being rough, and full of scales and knobs, as we have said; yet did she bear in memory the injury she sustained, with so gentle a revenge, requiting the ingratitude of him which had dealt with her so ungently. From that day, whensoever she was called by any of her familiars, she first looked circumspectly about her, lest any were present appareled after the manner of the Christians; she would oftentimes play and wrestle upon the bank with the king's chamberlains, and especially with a young man whom the king favored well, being also accustomed to feed her. She would be sometimes as pleasant and full of play as it had been a monkey or marmoset, and was of long time a great comfort and solace to the whole island, for no small confluence, as well of the Christians as of the inhabitants, had daily concourse to behold so strange a miracle of Nature, the contemplation of which was no less pleasant than wonderful. They say that the meat of this kind of fish is of good taste, and that many are engendered in the seas thereabout. But, at length, this pleasant playfellow was lost, and carried into the sea by the great river Attibunicus, one of the four which divide the island, for at that time there chanced so terrible a tempest of wind and rain, with such floods ensuing, that the like hath not been heard of. By reason of this tempest, the river Attibunicus so overflowed the banks that it filled the whole vale, and mixed itself with all the other lakes, at which time, also, this gentle Matum and pleasant companion, following the vehement course and fall of the floods, was thereby restored to his old mother and native waters, and, since that time, never seen again."—(PETER MARTYR, decade iii., chapter viii.)

PORTRAIT OF COLUMBUS (PAGE 235).

The portrait of Columbus which appears on page 235 is a faithful copy of De Bry's. While we believe, with Spotorno, that this portrait and its history are forgeries, yet it appears to possess as high claims to authenticity as any of the myriad of these creations with which the curious are familiar. Spotorno comments justly upon the false claims of this portrait, though the conclusions at which he ultimately arrives are somewhat original, if not quite logical (*see* this Appendix, notice of cut on page 151). Of De Bry he writes:

"We have no wish to conceal the fact that Theodore De Bry pretended that he possessed a portrait of the hero, the same that was to be seen in an apartment of the Council of the Indies, from which place, having been stolen, and carried to the Netherlands for sale, it came finally into the hands of De Bry, who gave an engraving of it in his 'America.' This print has been copied in the 'Eulogium of Columbus,' by the Marquis Durazzo, printed by Bodini, and in the 'Life of Bossi,' published at Milan. There are numerous reasons for impugning the authenticity of De Bry's portrait. A man who feels no remorse at stealing, and is not even ashamed to avow himself a thief, will be ready enough to tell a lie for the purpose of extorting a few ducats from a credulous amateur. The history of the Spanish painters gives no countenance to this thief's story. But what is more, on comparing De Bry's engraving with Fernando's description, it will be seen that they entirely disagree. And Baron Vernazza, having compared that of De Bry with the one published by Bullart, and that given by Muñoz, as well as the Cuccaro portrait, finds an essential discrepancy in the whole of them."—(SPOTORNO, "Introduction," pages cxlv., cxlviii.)

Of the many ridiculous stories told of these portraits, there is none less worthy of belief than that portion of De Bry's which represents *his* to be a copy of one for which Columbus sat *at the instance* of Ferdinand and Isabella. Had this been so, the vanity of Fernando Columbus would have caused him to enlarge upon it in his history, while Christopher would have added, no doubt, to his recapitulation of the royal honors conferred upon him, when exclaiming, "He called me Don," by continuing, "and asked me to sit for my portrait that he might possess a memorial of his dear friend." At any rate, his silence and that of his son on the subject may be regarded as proof positive that the story of De Bry is an invention; to enhance the value of this invention he tells us that Columbus was an extraordinary genius, and most excellent man—upright, "pure, and noble-minded, and an earnest friend of peace and. justice." This last assertion will enable those who are competent to judge of the character of Columbus, to determine the value of the statements touching his portrait.

SPANISH CRUELTIES.

The numerous illustrations of the cruelties perpetrated on the natives of the Western Hemisphere would seem to explain themselves; they are taken chiefly from the work on Spanish cruelties in the New World, by Las Casas, illustrated by De Bry.

We may quote one or two descriptions of the scenes represented; the following, on the cut on page 245, is from the work of the venerable prelate:

"They erected certain gibbets, large, but low made, so that their feet almost reached the ground, every one of which was so arranged as to bear thirteen persons, in honor and reverence (as they blasphemously and derisively said) of our Redeemer and his twelve apostles, under which they made a fire to burn them to ashes while hanging on them; but those they intended to preserve alive they dismissed, having cut their hands half off, leaving them still hanging by the skin to carry these as letters missive to those that fly from them and lie skulking in the mountains, as a warning of their fate.

"The lords, and persons of noble extraction, were usually exposed to this kind of death: they ordered gridirons to be placed and supported with wooden forks, and, putting a small fire under them, these miserable wretches by degrees, with loud shrieks and exquisite torments, at last expired. I once saw four or five of these chiefs laid on these gridirons, but the shrill clamors which were heard there being offensive to the captain, by hindering his repose, he commanded them to be strangled with a halter. The executioner (whose name and parents at Seville are not unknown to me) prohibited the doing of it, but stuffed gags into their mouths to prevent the hearing of the noise (he himself making the fire) till they died, when they had been roasted as long as he thought convenient. I was an eye-witness of these and an innumerable number of other cruelties."

The following passage in Herrera is illustrated on page 253 : The Indians are carrying bread to the Spaniards, the latter "always using to carry their dogs along with them, while the Indians were busy carrying the bread to the caravel's boat; the cazique went about with a wand in his hand, hastening his people, and a Spaniard standing by, who held a dog in a chain; the dog, observing the cazique in motion, and the wand in his hand, offered several times to fly at him, so that the Spaniard could scarce hold him, and said to another, 'What if we should let him on?' No sooner had he spoke, than the other, in jest, said, 'At him!' thinking he could have held him; the dog, hearing the word, flew out with all his force, and breaking loose from the Spaniard, seized the cazique by the belly, tore out his bowels, and left him dead, the Spaniards going away to their caravel."—(HERRERA, decade i., book v., chapter ii.)

Thus did the Spaniards amuse themselves!

LAWS, SACRED AND PROFANE.

Las Casas tells us of the more lawful (?) and decorous manner of murdering the Indians for the sake of their supposed wealth. He says:

"These wicked Spaniards, like thieves, came to any place by stealth, half a mile off of any city, town, or village, and there in the night published and proclaimed the edict among themselves, after this manner: 'You caziques and Indians of this continent, the inhabitants of such a place' (which they named), 'we declare (or be it known to you all) that there is but one God, one pope, and one King of Castile, who is lord of these countries. Appear forth without delay, and take the oath of allegiance to the Spanish king, as his vassals.' So about the fourth watch of the night, or three in the morning, while these poor innocents were overwhelmed with heavy sleep, they ran violently on that place they named, set fire to the hovels, which were all thatched, and so, without notice, burned men, women, and children, and killed whom they pleased upon the spot; but those they reserved as captives were compelled, through torments, to confess where they had hid the gold, when they found little or none at their houses, and when the fire was extinguished, they came hastily in quest of the gold."

Later in the course of Spanish villainies, pious divines elaborated and rendered this proceeding more formal, as will appear from the subjoined copy. This paper was read to the Indians by the chaplains of the army, in order to justify, if not to sanctify, the slaughter about to be enacted, of persons who understood not a word of this remarkable production:

"MANIFESTO.

"I, servant of the high and mighty Kings of Castile and Leon, civilizers of barbarous nations, their messenger and captain, notify and make known to you, in the best way I can, that God our Lord, one and eternal, created the heavens and earth, and one man and one woman, from whom you, and we, and all the people of the earth, were and are descendants, procreated, and all those who shall come after us; but the vast number of generations which have proceeded from them in the course of more than five thousand years that have elapsed since the creation of the world, made it necessary that some of the human race should disperse in one direction, and some in another, and that they should divide themselves into many kingdoms and provinces, as they could not sustain and preserve themselves in one alone. All these people were given in charge, by God our Lord, to one person, named Saint Peter, who was thus made lord and superior of all the people of the earth, and head of the whole human lineage; whom all should obey, wherever they might live, and whatever might be their law, sect, or belief: he gave him also the whole world for his service and jurisdiction; and though he desired that he should establish his chair in Rome, as a place most convenient for governing the world, yet he permitted that he might establish his chair in any other part of the world, and judge and govern all the nations, Christians, Moors, Jews, Gentiles, and whatever other sect or belief might be. This person was denominated Pope, that is to say, Admirable, Supreme, Father, and Guardian, because he is father and governor of all mankind. This holy father was obeyed and honored as lord, king, and superior of the universe, by those who lived in his time, and, in like manner, have been obeyed and honored all those who have been elected to the pontificate; and thus it has continued until the present day, and will continue until the end of the world.

"One of these pontiffs, of whom I have spoken as lord of the world, made a donation of these islands and continents of the ocean sea, and all that they contain, to the Catholic Kings of Castile, who, at that time, were Ferdinand and Isabella, of glorious memory, and to their successors, our sovereigns, according to the tenor of certain papers, drawn up for the purpose (which you may see if you desire). Thus his Majesty is king and sovereign of these islands and continents by virtue of the said donation, and as king and sovereign, certain islands, and almost all, to whom this has been notified, have received his Majesty, and have obeyed and served, and do actually serve him. And, moreover, like good subjects, and with good-will, and without any resistance or delay, the moment they were informed of the foregoing, they obeyed all the religious men sent among them to preach and teach our holy faith; and these of their free and cheerful will, without any condition or reward, became Christians and continue so to be. And his Majesty received them kindly and benignantly, and ordered that they should be treated like his other subjects and vassals. You also are required and obliged to do the same. Therefore, in the best manner I can, I pray and entreat you, that you consider well what I have said, and that you take whatever time is reasonable to understand and deliberate upon it, and that you recognize the Church for sovereign and superior of the universal world, and the supreme pontiff, called Pope, in her name, and his Majesty, in his place, as superior and sovereign king of the islands and *terra firma* by virtue of the said donation; and that you consent that these religious fathers declare and preach to you the foregoing; and if you shall so do, you will do well, and will do that to which you are bounden and obliged; and his Majesty, and I, in his name, will receive you with all due love and charity, and will leave you your wives and children free from servitude, that you may freely do with them and with yourselves whatever you please and think proper, as have done the inhabitants of the other islands. And, besides this, his Majesty will give you many privileges and exemptions, and grant you many favors. If you do not do this, or wickedly and intentionally delay to do so, I certify to you that by the aid of God I will forcibly invade and make war upon you in all parts and modes that I can, and will subdue you to the yoke and obedience of the Church and of his Majesty; and I will take your wives and children, and make slaves of them, and sell them as such, and dispose of them as his Majesty may command: and I will take your effects, and will do you all the harm and injury in my power, as vassals who will not obey or receive their sovereign, and who resist and oppose him. And I protest that the deaths and disasters, which may in this manner be occasioned, will be the fault of yourselves, and not of his Majesty, nor of me, nor of those cavaliers who accompany me. And of what I here tell you and require of you, I call upon the notary here present to give me his signed testimonial."

It would be scarce possible more appropriately to close this brief mention of the inhumanity practised toward the wretched inhabitants of the New World by the Spaniards, than by quoting the following heart-rending description:

"The vast numbers employed in these mines are bound in fetters, and compelled to work day and night without intermission, and without the least hope of escape, for they set over them soldiers who speak a foreign language, so that there is no possibility of conciliating them by persuasion, or the kind feelings which result from familiar converse. . . . No attention is paid to their persons; they have not even a piece of rag to cover themselves; and so wretched is their condition that every one who witnesses it deplores the excessive misery they endure.

"No rest, no intermission from toil, are given either to the sick or maimed: neither the weakness of age nor women's infirmities are regarded; all are driven to their work with the lash, till at last, overcome with the intolerable weight of their afflictions, they die in the midst of their toil. So that these unhappy creatures always expect worse to come than what they endure at the present, and long for death as far preferable to life."

TOBACCO, SMOKING, CHEWING, SNUFF.—(*See* illustration, page 322.)

Roderigo de Jerez, and Luis de Torres, as agents or ambassadors of Columbus to the grand-khan (*see* pages 201, 202), on their return from that ridiculous mission, among other things reported that they saw the natives going about with brands of fire in their hands, together with a dried herb, which they rolled up in a leaf. Setting one end on fire, putting the other in their mouths, they drew in and puffed out the smoke; these rolls the natives called "tabaco," substantially the name by which the plant or weed is now known. The smoke was conveyed to the mouth through what they believed to be a charred stick. Las Casas tells us that the Indians, on being questioned as to this habit, informed him that it took away fatigue, and caused them to forget their troubles, and that he had known Spaniards in Hispaniola addicted to the same habit, who, when reproved, replied that it was not in their power to abandon it. He continues: "I do not know what savor or profit they found in them" (tabacos).

Fernando says: "The cazique and chief men never ceased putting a dry herb into their mouths and chewing it, and sometimes they took a sort of powder they carried with that herb, which looks very odd."—("Historia del Amirante," chapter xcvi.)

Navarette says: "Thus was the first lesson given to Europeans of this extraordinary habit, which has become universal; hence the origin of the much-prized and far-famed Havanas."

We copy the following from "The Landfall of Columbus," by Captain A. B. Becher, R. N., F. R. A. S., etc., etc., etc., London, 1856:

"Here," says Becher, alluding to the first time Spaniards witnessed the practice, "as Las Casas observes, is the origin of smoking tobacco, a practice which, however extensive it may be in other countries (and common enough it no doubt is there), has become so general in this, that, to the discredit of parents, it is even followed by children! The eternal cigar is seen in the mouth of old and young, even in that of the ragged urchin who swaggers along, not only astonishing those who see him at his early hardihood, but leaving them to wonder how he came by it, considering the price which must have been paid for it. As already observed, it is profitable to the state, if it is indulged in at the cost of the pocket, the health, and the personal comfort of society.

"The following, from an official source, is a statement of the amount of duty derived from tobacco in the United Kingdom for the last three years:

1853......................................£4,560,827
1854...................................... 4,751,776
1855...................................... 4,704,663."

Between September 1, 1862, and June 30, 1872, the United States collected the sum of $200,213,837 from tobacco, and for the year ending June, 1873, $34,386,303.09.

It is therefore apparent that, if this discovery has not profited the individual, it has swelled the revenue of states. To Spain it was of far greater value than all the gold derived from the mines of which Columbus gave such extravagant accounts.

It would seem that this plant might furnish a theme for those who write upon the wealth of nations.

The illustrations on pages 148 and 328 of this work might appear to some irreverent, yet it has not been the desire of the author to perpetrate any irreverence; he has considered that the disgusting and blasphemous manner in which Columbus shielded himself behind the Deity, and declared himself divinely justified in the commission of his most revolting crimes, cannot be too forcibly or palpably presented to the eye of the reader; and, if these engravings should shock the latter, how much more will he abhor the inventor of their subjects! We feel confident that he will exonerate us from any imputation of irreverence when he shall carefully examine the statements of Columbus which these engravings were intended to illustrate. *We have not "carried the war up to the manifesto."*

INDEX.

Abraham, 28.
Age of the human race, 3.
Alexander, his fleet, etc., 30, 47.
Alexander VI., Pope, 94, 126, 228, 356.
Alexandria, 29.
Alexandrian Library, 14.
Amalfi, a pilot of, 31.
America, ruins of Central, 16; similarity of latter to Egyptian, 18; metal used by the ancients of, 18; known to the ancients, 26; described by the Northmen, 71; discovered by the Northmen, 73, 87; called Vineland by Northmen, 76; probably discovered by Madoc, 89; also by the Zeni brothers, 91; the name bestowed by royal decree, 121.
Ancients, the, their architectural knowledge, 1; their advancement in science, 2, 5, 13, 21; their knowledge of geography, 25; their knowledge of the New World, 26; their extensive commerce, 28, 29; their ship-building, 30; their use of the chain-cable, compass, etc., 31, 52; their knowledge of printing, 60; their remarkable literature, 62; injustice done their attainments, 67.
Arabia Felix, 29.
Arabs, their learning, 66, 182.
Archimedes, 30.
Architecture of the ancients, 1, 2.
Aristotle, quoted, 45, 47, 167.
Arthur, Prince of Wales, 103.
Asia, its ruined cities, 2.
Astrolabe used by the ancients, 60.
Astronomy among the ancients, 2, 21.
Atlantis, island of, 27.
Aztecs, their ancient civilization, 15, 17, 19.

Baal, worship of, 3.
Baalbec, ruins of, 1.
Babel, Tower of, 2, 4.
Babylon, ruins of, 2, 4; study of astronomy in, 3.
Bacon, Roger, 35, 37, 38.

Barcelona, 218, 219.
Beamish, quoted, 71.
Beatrix Enriquez, Columbus's mistress, 355, 356.
Biarn, a Norse navigator, 72, 84, 86.
Bobadilla, Francisco, 273, 275, 277, 284, 287, 297, 316.
Borgia, Roderigo, Pope, 94, 126, 228, 356.
Boturini, quoted, 93.
Boyle, Bishop, pope's nuncio, 242, 246, 252.
Brahman religion, 63.
Brazil, 117, 118.
Bronze doors of United States Capitol, 349.
Brunetto, 35.

Cabot, John, account of, 134; his expedition to America, 134; much honor paid him, 135.
Cabot, Sebastian, said to have discovered variations of the magnetic needle, 51, 138; accompanies his father, etc., 136; appointed pilot-major of Spain, 137; discovers Paraguay, 137; his subsequent life, 138; the value of his discoveries, 139.
Cable-chain (see chain-cable).
Cabral, Pedro Alvarez de, 140, 141.
Cadmus, 14.
Cæsar, Julius, quoted, 31, 66.
Cannibalism, Indians of North America accused of, 319.
Canonization of Columbus proposed, 94, 316.
Cape-Cod, landing-place of Northmen, 73.
Capitol of the United States, bronze doors of, 349, 350.
Carthage, 29.
Central America, ruins of, 18.
Chain-cable known to the ancients, 31.
Charlevoix, quoted, 283, 296.
Charts, standard, made by Vespucius, 119; of Columbus very inaccurate, 123; of Alonzo Sanchez, 132, 165, 168, 174; Columbus draws by inspiration, 148.

INDEX. 399

China, Columbus takes Cuba to be, 201.
Chinese, ancient, understood the magnet, 46, 52, 54, 56, 58.
—— magnetic car, 53.
—— destroyed all their historical relics, 55.
Chrishna, quoted, 64.
Christ-bearer, a title assumed by Columbus, 146, 153.
Church, the, condemning books, 95; falsifying history, 95, 99, 120, 272.
Civilization of the New World, very ancient, 19.
Claudian, the poet, describes the compass, 40.
Coat-of-arms of Columbus, 225.
Colon, Columbus's family name, 144.
Colon (or Cólumbus), Bartholomew, 180, 245, 263, 304, 314, 327, 333, 340, 341, 343, 380.
Colon (or Columbus), Diego, 304, 305, 311, 341, 373, 380.
Columbus, Fernando, quoted, 86, 94, 144, 146, 153, 178, 220, 267, 287, 320; forged letters and documents to glorify his father, 161; indignant at Justiniani for mentioning his father's early life, 173; inscription on his tomb, 347.
Columbus, Christopher, his reputed discovery of the magnetic needle, 51; his egotism and selfishness, 86, 131, 334; the false histories regarding him, 92, 95, 143, 177, 192, 194; his pretended championship of the Christian religion, 94, 146, 153; an allusion to his early life considered an insult, 95, 173; regarded by King Ferdinand as an impostor, 99, 126; his nautical experience gained by piracy, 115; he is ignored by a contemporary historian, 121; aware of Amerigo Vespucci's claims of discovering the continent, 121; letter of Columbus to his son Diego, 122; falls into disgrace through his cruelty, etc., 123; and reaches a low stage of degradation, 124, 303; the time and place of his nativity unknown, 124, 143, 147, 167, 306, 343; his ridiculous ideas regarding the shape of the earth, 126, 183; his own historian and eulogist, 128; enters Spain penniless and with a bad reputation, 129, 179, 182; persuades the Pinzons to join him, 130; sailing of his expedition, 131, 187, 192; departs from the correct course, and is set right by the Pinzons, 132, 174, 195; basely robs an old sailor of a promised reward, 132, 197; accuses his patron Pinzon of desertion, 133; 203, 218; his name and ancestry, as stated by his son, 144; his family name is Griego, 145; engaged in a piratical adventure, 145, 161; the mystery that hangs over his early life, 146, 167; speculations as to his age, 147; boasts of receiving knowledge by inspiration, 148, 328; he confesses to falsehood and fraud, 149; his piracy and connection with the slave-trade, 149; his pretended portraits, 151, 219, 235, 284, 371, 382; his adoption of the name Christopher Columbus, 153; further items of his history as related by his son, 156; pretended letter of Tuscanella, the astronomer, to him, 158; his escape from the burning galleys on an oar, 161; his marriage, 161; removes to Madeira, 162; his idea of a New World gained from a dead pilot's papers, 162, 165, 168, 170, 173, 176, 179; Sanchez dies in his house, 165, 166; declared hereditary grand-admiral by Ferdinand and Isabella, 171, 183; his son receives titles of nobility, 172; proceeds to Portugal to offer terms to the king, 178; he flees from Portugal to avoid arrest for debt and crime, 179; attempts to sell his purported discovery to the King of England, 180; is entertained and aided by the prior, Juan Perez, 129, 167, 179, 181; the terms proposed by their majesties to Columbus, 183; returns to Palos, and secures the aid of Perez and the Pinzons, 188; his first expedition sails, 192; miracle of the great fish, 192; minor incidents of his trip, 193-195; further evidences of his vanity, deceit, and fraud, 195; Columbus pretended to have discovered land, 197; landing of the expedition, 199; his fruitless search for gold, 200; visits other islands, 200; imagines himself in China, 201; sends a message to the grand-khan, 202; poetical leaf from a log, 204; loses one of his ships by carelessness and incapacity, 206, 331; establishes a garrison at La Navidad, 207; sets sail on his return, 208, 210; his lying accounts of wonders seen on his voyage, 209; vows to make a pilgrimage to the shrine of the Virgin, 211; makes a record of his discoveries, in a storm, 212; his crew arrested while paying their vows, 213; Columbus pays vows to the Virgin, 215; his pretended reception in

Portugal, 216; arrives in Spain, 218; amusingly fanciful account of his reception, 221; his arrival and reception not recorded in the state archives, 223; receives title of admiral, and a coat-of-arms, 224; starts on his second voyage, 228; arrives at San Domingo, 229; his intention to establish slavery in the West Indies, 230; finds his colony at Hispaniola massacred, 233; attempts to lay out a town, 236; the deceptions he practised on the colonists, 238; they mutiny against Columbus, 239; he builds Fort San Tomas, 240; sends an expedition against the natives, 240; discovers Jamaica, 242; guilty of subornation of perjury, 243; appoints his brother Bartholomew to office, 245; Bishop Boyle remonstrates against his cruel government, 246; excommunicates him from the Church, 247; and goes to Spain with complaints against him, 247; captures the cazique Caonabo, by a mere stratagem, 248; sends five hundred Indians slaves to Spain, etc., 249; exacts a tribute of gold from the natives, 250; the sovereigns send a commissioner to investigate him, 252; he returns to Spain, 254; his deception and mendacity exposed, 255; again takes out an expedition, 256; assaults the treasurer of Bishop Fonseca, 258; sets sail on his third voyage, 259; first sees the Continent of America, 260; proceeds to Hispaniola, 262; the rebellion of Roldan, 264; Columbus endeavors to conciliate him, 265; Roldan forces from him terms, 266; more proofs of Columbus's duplicity, 267; his treatment of Guevara, 269; the murder of Moxica, 270; executes vengeance on the disaffected, 272; Bobadilla sent to Hispaniola, 273; supersedes Columbus, 275, 277; the latter obstructs him, 279, 280; Bobadilla arrests him and Diego, 281; his defense of his own conduct, 285; he leaves for Spain, a prisoner, 295; he is practically deposed from power, 297; remains in Spain two years, 299; pretends to plan a discovery of straits, 300, 318; his will, 303, 308; his desperate situation, 303; his signature, 304; sends his papers to Oderigo, 309, 310, 343; endeavors to wheedle the pope, 312; his fourth voyage, 314; is refused permission to land at San Domingo, 315; meets very stormy weather, 319; a specimen of his brutal tastes, 321; subdues a water-spout by incantations, 324; founds another settlement, 327; but again has trouble with the Indians, 327; the Deity appears to him in a vision, 328; gets up a "corner" on gold-mines, 330; mutiny is raised against him, 335; he predicts an eclipse of the moon, 337, 363; remains waiting at Jamaica eight months, 339; bloodshed between his followers, 340; arrives at San Domingo, 342; returns to Spain, 343; requests a restitution of his titles, 344; Ferdinand refuses his request, 345; his death, 346; his reputed monument and inscription, 347; his remains, 348; his character generally described, 351; his manuscript, 354; his licentiousness, 355; his "distempers," 358; his ignorance of geography and navigation, 362; his cruelty and cowardice, 367; his son Diego enters suit against the crown, 373; Columbus's heirs gain the suit, 375; his descendants, 381.

Commerce among the ancients, 28.
Compass, the mariner's, known to the ancients, 31, 56; described by Brunetto, 39; origin of the name, 49; supposed to be allied with sorcery, 51.
Confucius, 55; quoted, 64.
Cortez, Ferdinand, 171.
Cuba discovered, 200.

Danish language, 70.
Dante, 35, 37.
De Costa, B. F., quoted, 71, 76.
De Puebla, Dr., agent of Isabella, 101, 102, 140.

Earth, the sphericity of the, known to the ancients, 24; the Indian fable regarding, 92; the shape of, as imagined by Columbus, 126.
Egg, story of Columbus and the (*see* Appendix), 368.
Egypt, its ruins, 14.
Egyptians, their pyramids, 7; their science and learning, 13, 22; knew the use of the magnet, 44; poultry-raising by artificial means, 60.
Electricity understood by the ancients, 45.
Eric the Red, 72, 77.

Falsifying of history by the Church, 95, 99, 120, 122, 272.
Ferdinand of Aragon, his character, 97, 109, 112; restrictions on his conduct, 98, 99; his libertinism, 111;

Irving's estimate of him, 112; regards Columbus as an impostor, 99, 114, 126; aided Vespucci to make discoveries, 114; reëngages him to his service, 118; bestows Amerigo Vespucci's name on the new-found continent, 121; Columbus addresses him as surviving sovereign, 344.
Florence, inscription at Vespucci's birthplace, 114; rejoicings at Vespucci's success, 118.
Fonseca, Bishop, 257, 268.

Galen, quoted, 47.
Galileo, his knowledge of astronomy, 24, 25.
Genoa, claimed as Columbus's birthplace, 143, 306.
Geography, knowledge of, by ancients, 25.
Gira, or Giri, alleged inventor of the compass, 32.
Gish, plains of, 11.
Golden rule, taught by Confucius, 64.
Greece, 15, 23.
Greenland, 70, 77.
Griego, Nicolo, probable name of Columbus, 145.
Guistiniani, quoted, 94.
Gunpowder, discovery of, 38, 56; known to ancients, 56.

Hakluyt, quoted, 88, 137, 139.
Hanno, his voyage, 29.
Hayti discovered, 203.
Henry VII., 101, 134, 136, 140, 170, 180, 188.
Herculaneum, 27.
Hercules, the magnet named for him, 44, 47.
Heretics, the tortures inflicted on them, 96.
Herodotus, 4, 65.
Herrera, quoted, 95, 121, 122, 133, 184, 202, 208, 250, 275.
Hindoos, their knowledge of astronomy, 21; do. of the magnet, 42; their religion, literature, etc., 63.
Hipparchus, the Egyptian astronomer, 60.
History, knowledge of, among the ancients, 65; its true purposes and objects, 93, 96.
Homer, grandeur of, 62.
Horace, quoted, 36.
Human race, older than biblical accounts, 3.
——— sacrifices, not practised by the Aztecs, 19.
Humboldt, quoted, 88.

Iceland, 90.
Icelandic language, 70.
India, the cradle of astronomy, 22.
Indians, of America, their first trading with white men, 83; they attack the Northmen, 84; Amerigo Vespucci's description of them, 115; method used to convert them to Christ, 154. 367-370; their character described by Columbus, 186, 320; their conduct at his landing, 199; Peter Martyr's account of their happy condition, 203; they kindly receive Columbus, 206, 320; a warlike tribe attacks him, 210; a number are taken to Spain by Columbus, 221; he professes to find cannibals among them, 229, 319; he proposes to enslave them, 231; they murder the colony at La Navidad, 233; Spanish cruelties against them, 241-245; shocking cruelties by Columbus, 249, 272; their sufferings, 251; enslavement of Indians, 255, 265, 351; a party meets Columbus in a canoe, 317; he wheedles them by an eclipse of the moon, 338.
Indian trade, first, 83.
Inquisition, the and Galileo, 25; it grants license for books, 93; tortures inflicted on heretical authors by, 96; aided by Isabella, 99; its terrible cruelties in Spain, 100.
Ireland, 72, 82.
Irish said to have visited America, 86.
Irving, Washington, quoted, 92, 95, 98, 112, 123, 130, 136, 163, 175, 193, 197, 199, 216, 220, 243, 247, 258, 279, 282, 302, 305, 317, 357.
Isabella, Queen of Spain, her character, 97, 101, 111; her marriage to Ferdinand, 97; false eulogies on her "virtues," 99; aids the Inquisition in its cruel work, 99; confiscates the estates of condemned heretics, 100; retains De Puebla, a knave, as her agent, 103; bargains for the sale of her daughter, 103; haggles about passage-money of the latter to England, 105; her shameless mendacity, 106-109; an unnatural mother, 108; deception regarding the cost of her attire, 109; her portrait, 110; her double dealing and hypocrisy, 111; her decree against voyages of discovery, 117; makes Columbus her favorite, 126; declares him hereditary grand-admiral, 171, 224; the terms proposed by her to Columbus, 183; Isabella is induced by Perez and others to fit out Columbus, 188; the falsehood about pawning her jewels, 189; the sovereigns receive Columbus on his return, 220, 221; they reject his proposal to en-

slave Indians, 232; determine to investigate Columbus's government, 252; Isabella sends out a colony of convicts with him, 256; the sovereigns revoke Columbus's power, 273; she orders the enslaved Indians to be freed, 275; her policy encouraging Columbus, 296; gives him a significant hint, 313; her death, 344.
Italy, her ancient architecture, 15.

Jamaica discovered, 242.
Job, mentions printing, 60.
Josephus, his account of the ancients, 2, 66.
Justiniani's "Psalter" condemned to be burned, 94–96.

Karlsefne, a Northman, 79, 84.
Katherine, Princess, complains of her poverty, 108.
Kingsborough, Lord, quoted, 93.

Las Casas, quoted, 121, 154, 214, 223, 244, 283, 312.
Leif, son of Eric the Red, 74, 77, 79, 86.
Libraries among the Arabs, 66.
Literature among the ancients, 62.
Lithography mentioned by Job, 60.
Loadstone (*see* Magnet).
Lot, 28.
Love, symbolized by the magnet, 42.

Madoc, Prince, 88.
Magnetic needle, known to the ancients, 31; known to Friar Bacon, 39; described by Claudian, 40; how termed in different tongues, 42, 43; its use in the year 640, 49; known to the Chinese 2700 B. C., 52–54.
Magnifying lens known to ancients, 5; one constructed by Friar Bacon, 38.
Manou, quoted, 63.
Marco Polo, quoted, 203.
Marriage of Ferdinand and Isabella, 98.
—— huckstering between royal families, 104.
Martyr, Peter, quoted, 128, 203, 220, 223, 281, 283.
Measurement, ancient standard of, 9, 11.
Medici, house of, 114.
Mendez, Diego, 331, 338, 341.
Mexico, 16.
Moses, 14, 63.
Mount Hope, a Norske name, 83.
Moxica, a Spaniard, murdered by Columbus, 270, 271.

Navigation, decree concerning, in Spain, 119.
—— practised by the ancients, 25, 30.

Nebuchadnezzar's palace, 4.
Newfoundland, 73, 78, 135.
Nineveh, ruins of, 2, 14.
Noah's ark, 30.
Northmen, not the first to discover America, 19, 69; their early use of the compass, 33, 40; they land in America, 69, 73; their motives in coming to America, 70; their geographical knowledge, 71; name America Vineland, 76; introduce Christianity into Greenland, 77; other expeditions, 78–80; their character and acts, 86, 87.
Norway, 70.
Nova Scotia, landing-place of the Northmen, 73–80.

Oderigo, Nicolo de, 309, 310.
Odometer, used by ancient Chinese, 54.
Ojeda, Alonzo de, 238, 247, 268.
Ovando, Nicolas de, 297–301, 315, 339, 341, 342, 380.
Oxford, England, 35, 36.

Palmyra (Tadmor), ruins of, 5.
Palos, Spanish seaport, 187, 188, 190, 218.
Papal infallibility, 94.
Paschal chronicle, 4.
Perez, Juan, 129, 130, 167, 179, 181, 188.
Persians, their religion, 3.
Petrarch, 37.
Pharaoh Necho, 25–29.
Philip II., 171.
Phœnicians, the, extent of their commerce, 19–28; they used the compass, 44.
Pinzon, Martin Alonzo, and Vincent Yanez, 117, 129; Columbus engages their attention, 130; they aid him in his expedition, 130, 182–190; are entitled to the credit of its success, 131; accused of desertion by Columbus, 133, 203, 218; are raised to the rank of nobility, 133.
Piracy practised by Columbus, 145, 149.
Plato, refers to the New World, 26; his teachings, 65.
Polar Star, four thousand years ago, 13.
Pompeii, 27.
Pope, places full faith in Columbus, 94.
Pope Alexander VI., 94.
Porras, Francis de, 335, 341, 342.
Pork, eating of, forbidden, 63.
Portugal, King of, 118, 140, 178.
Prescott's "Spanish Conquest," 15, 99.
Printing, mentioned by Job, 60.
Ptolemy, Claudius, 23, 25, 46.
Public-school system, known five hundred years B. C., 66.
Publishing books in Spain, 93, 95.

INDEX. 403

Purchas, quoted, 89, 90, 168.
Pyramids, ruins of, 6, their object, 7; explored by Caliph al Mamoun, 9, 10.
Pythagoras, understood the solar system, 23.

Rafn, Professor, 71.
Religion, crimes committed in its name, 155.
Roldan, Francisco, his rebellion, 263, 316.
Romance tongue, 37.
Rome, ruins of, 15.
Ruins of ancient cities, 2, 4, 5, 15.
—— in Central America, 16.
—— in Mexico, similar to Egyptian, 19.

Saint Ambrose, quoted, 48.
Saint Paul, 30.
Saint Peter, 4.
San Domingo, discovered, 229.
San Salvador, discovered, 199.
Sanchez, Alonzo, a pilot, 132, 162, 164, 166, 168, 176, 179, 185.
Sesostris, 30.
Slave-trade, Columbus engaged in, 149.
—— seeks to restore it in the West Indies, 230.
Smith, J. Toulmin, quoted, 71.
Smyth, Professor C. Piazzi, royal astronomer, etc., 7, 8, and note, 9.
Socrates, 65.
Solis, Juan, 117.
Solomon, his song, 62.
Southey, quoted, 89.
Spain, court of, loose morals, 99; royal decree concerning navigators, 119; objects to English explorations, 140; Arabs aided its learning and science, 182.
Spaniards, etc., did not discover America, 19; their ancient libraries, 67; their laws concerning histories, 93.
Sphinx, the, 6.
Strabo, 15.
Strada, quoted, 61.
Suit, by Diego Columbus, against the crown, 373.
Sweden, 70.
Syphilis, its origin, etc., 358.

Tacitus, quoted, 72.
Tadmor (Palmyra), ruins of, 2.
Talmud, quoted, 63.
Telegraphing known to the ancients, 62.
Telescope, invented by Roger Bacon, 38.
Thebes, ruins of, 5.
Thorhall, a Northman, 80–82.

Thorwald, a Northman, 77–86.
Time, measurement of, in the Pyramids, 12.
Torquemada, grand-inquisitor, 99.
Tortures inflicted on heretical authors, 96.
Toscanella, the astronomer, 157, 174.
Trading with Indians, by Northmen, 83.
Trichina spiralis, known to the ancients, 63.
Truth the great object of history, 93.
Tyre, 28.

Vedas, quoted, 63.
Venereal (see Syphilis).
Venezuela, discovered by Vespucci, 115.
Venice, Zeni brothers' expedition from, 90; merchants of, arrested, etc.
Vespucci, Amerigo, 113; his nativity, etc., 114; enters a commercial life, 114; King Ferdinand confides in his ability, 114, 126; his first voyage, 115; Venezuela and its natives described by him, 115; a man of intellect and science, 117, 126; his second voyage in 1499, 117; his crew maltreated by Columbus's crew, 117; enters the service of the King of Portugal, 118; his subsequent voyages and explorations, 118, 268; reënters the service of Spain, 118, 123; office of pilot-major conferred on him, 119; commanded to make a standard chart, 119; his death, 120; his modesty regarding his own claims, 120; America named after him, 121; his discoveries belittled after his death, 122; Columbus's opinion regarding him, 122; the honor done to his memory in Italy, 124; his portrait, 125; not called as a witness in the suit of Columbus's heirs vs. the crown, 376.
Vineland, America so named by Northmen, 76.
Virginity of a princess, correspondence touching the, 103.
Volney, his "Ruins" quoted, 6.

Weights and measures, ancient, 11.
Welsh exploration of America, 88.
Western Hemisphere known to the ancients, 26.

Xenophon, 66.

Yucatan, mines in, 17.

Zeni brothers, Nicolo and Antonio, explorers, etc., 88–90.

THE END.

www.ingramcontent.com/pod-product-compliance
Lightning Source LLC
Chambersburg PA
CBHW050850300426
44111CB00010B/1202